ORTHO'S COMPLETE GUIDE TO

Successful
Gardening

ORTHO'S COMPLETE GUIDE TO
Successful

Project Editor **Barbara Ferguson**

Project Writer **Deni W. Stein**

Art Director **James Stockton**

Gardening

Ortho Books

Publisher
Robert L. Iacopi

Editorial Director
Min S. Yee

Managing Editors
Anne Coolman
Michael D. Smith

Senior Editor
Sally W. Smith

Production Manager
Laurie Sheldon

Horticulturists
Michael D. McKinley
Deni W. Stein

Associate Editors
Jim Beley
Diane Snow

Photo Editor
Pam Peirce

Production Editor
Alice Mace

Production Assistant
Darcie S. Furlan

Editorial Assistants
Laurie A. Black
Anne Dickson-Pederson
William F. Yusavage

National Sales Manager
Garry P. Wellman

Operations/Distribution
William T. Pletcher

Operations Assistant
Donna M. White

Administrative Assistant
Georgiann Wright

Address all inquiries to:
Ortho Books
Chevron Chemical Company
Consumer Products Division
575 Market Street
San Francisco, CA 94105

First Printing in August, 1983

3 4 5 6 7 8 9
84 85 86 87 88

ISBN 0-89721-018-2

Library of Congress Catalog Card
Number 83-61313

ORTHO
Chevron Chemical Company
Consumer Products Division

Contributing Editors:
Ken Burke
Will Kirkman
Scott R. Millard

Contributing Writers:
Walter L. Doty
Susan M. Lammers
Michael MacCaskey
James McNair
A. Cort Sinnes

Encyclopedia Database Editors:
W. Paul Osborne
William F. Yusavage

Illustration and Quotation Research:
Jean O'Korn

Illustrations:
Bouquet #4 by Pierre-Joseph Redouté, page 1
Embroidery design by Giovanni Ostaus (1567), page 265
Gerard's Herbal (1633), page 274
The Bettmann Archive, Inc., pages 36, 45, 66, 83, 135, 204, 230,
252, 346, and 377
Other illustrations from old French and English botanical and
herbal books, pages 109, 163, 307, and 328

Photographers:
(Names of photographers in alphabetical order are followed by
page numbers on which their work appears. R = right, C =
center, L = left, T = top, and B = bottom.) Ralph J. Adkins:
372BL, 374B; William A. Aplin: 56, 85, 107T, 191B, 213, 236,
238, 240B, 241T,B, 245, 277, 294, 302; Max E. Badgley: 369TL;
M. Baker: 139, 140, 141, 144, 146L,R, 147, 148, 150, 151B, 152,
153; Ray R. Bingham: 366B; Laurie Black: 55T, 112, 160–161L,
172R–173, 175, 190, 203L; John Blaustein: 35, 37, 68, 70, 71, 73,
98T,B, 212B, 347; Allen Boger: 372 LC; Bartow H. Bridges:
370B; Ralph Byther: 368BR, 372TC, 374T, 375TL; Kristie
Callan: 365T, 368TR, 372TL, 375C; Clyde Childress: 129, 195,
199B, 210–211, 215TL,TR, 217T,B, 275; Jack K. Clark: 365B;
Josephine Coatsworth: 18, 49, 76, 79B, 84, 94B–95, 101, 105B;
Sharon J. Collman: 367BR; Colour Library International (USA)
LTD.: 27, 39; J. A. Crozier: 369TR,BL; Maynard W. Cummings:
366C; James F. Dill: 367T; David Fischer: 28, 30, 32, 33;
Pamela Harper: 2–3; The Image Bank/Len DeMunde: 296;
A. L. Jones: 373T; F. Laemmlen: 373B; Michael Lamotte: 287;
Michael Landis: 8, 46–47, 64, 74, 77, 114–115, 116, 128,
164–165, 167, 181B, 185, 192, 208, 212A, 216T, 219, 221, 223T,B,
224T,B, 225, 226, 227T,B, 231T, 232, 233, 235, 237, 240T, 265,
266, 267L,TR,BR, 279, 281, 285, 290, 306, 308T, 310T, 344,
350B–351, 355, 359T,B, 362; Fred Lyon: 270, 319, 320A,
320B–321, 323, 324–325, 326, 327, 329, 330, 332, 333, 334, 335,
337, 339, 340, 341L; Phil Mayer: 370T; Charles A. McClurg:
368TL; Michael McKinley: 13, 14, 18, 19, 21, 24, 25, 36, 44–45,
50, 51, 52–53, 54, 55B, 57, 60–61, 60B, 62, 63, 65T, 79T, 80T,B,
81T,B, 87, 88, 89, 90, 93, 94A, 97, 102, 103, 105T, 106T,B, 107BR,
111, 122, 123, 136L, 137, 138, 142, 143, 149, 151T, 155, 159, 166,
169, 172L, 180, 182–183, 188, 189, 198, 203R, 205, 207, 215B,
216C,B, 244, 338T,B, 341R, 343, 356; James K. McNair: 16–17,
118, 119T, 120–121, 125, 131, 181T, 186–187; Ortho Books
Photo Collection: 15, 23, 41T,B, 59, 65B, 75, 78, 91, 107BL, 108,
110T,B, 113, 117, 119B, 126, 127, 133, 134, 157, 161R, 170, 176,
191T, 193, 196, 197T,B, 200, 206, 214, 222, 228–229, 231B, 239,
264, 269, 272, 273, 278T,B, 280, 282, 288, 291, 292, 293T,B, 295,
297, 299, 300–301, 303, 304, 305, 309, 345, 349, 350T, 353,
360–361, 363; J. Parker: 367BL; Dick Ray: 271; William
Reasons: 201, 283, 289T,B, 308B, 310B–311; Ann Reilly: 136R;
D. F. Schoeneweiss: 375BR; Martin Schweitzer: 179; A. F. Sherf:
366T; Michael D. Smith: 371T; Sherman V. Thompson: 371B;
Tom Tracy: 40, 48T,B, 67, 243, 246, 247L,R, 248, 250, 251, 252,
253, 255, 256, 257, 259, 260, 261, 263; Larry Weber: 11; Wolf
von dem Bussche: 162, 199T, 220, 234

Cover:
A flower bed of shasta daisies, yellow lilies, red gerberas, and
white dianthus.

Page 2 and 3:
Pink azaleas and white Cherokee roses add accent to a serene landscape.

Contents

Introduction

Plants touch our lives in many ways; they are part of the framework that shapes our thoughts, our emotions, and our physical well-being. Consciously, we weave them into our traditions and rituals. What would Christmas be without the spice-scented tree sparkling with ornaments. Valentine's day is synonymous with red roses, and Easter is traditionally celebrated with regal white lilies. June's orange blossoms often bear witness to wedding vows.

Less a part of our conscious intent, but just as important are the plants of everyday life: the sweet-smelling lawns where we stroll, the trees under which we picnic and dream, the shrubs, trees, and flowers that beckon to us as we hurry past.

Plants are the mainstay of life on this planet. They replenish the atmosphere with oxygen and provide us with all of our food, either directly or indirectly, through the food chain. We build many of our shelters and furnishings with wood and other plant products. And plants enrich our lives with beauty.

We enjoy plants with all of our senses. The sight of a sunny field of daffodils will uplift anyone's spirits. Imagine the sweet smell of lilacs, the tangy scent of fresh-cut lemons. No perfume can match the clean purity of these and many other plant fragrances.

Leaves rustling in the breeze, twigs snapping underfoot—plants comfort us with their sounds. Soft, mounded moss; rough, flaking bark; sharp, prickly spines; plants can be inviting or forbidding to our sense of touch.

As much or more than the other senses, plants appeal to our sense of taste. What can compare to the succulence of a freshly picked peach or the tart-sweet crispness of a cold apple?

Daffodils, yellow and purple violas, and white candytuft make an attractive mixed border.

Plants in the Garden

The earliest records of plant cultivation date back to 8000 B.C. The first agricultural efforts of early civilizations were of a functional nature only; plants were grown exclusively for food or utilitarian purposes.

Gardening as the art of plant cultivation developed much later. Gardens designed with decorative plantings first appear in 1500 B.C. in ancient Egypt, where the civilization had developed beyond the subsistence level. The leisure available to the royalty and privileged members of that society gave them the time to enjoy and admire beautiful plants.

Throughout history, each culture and civilization developed its own unique gardening style. Today, we can draw from this wealth of techniques and styles, many of which can be adapted in some way to our own gardens, no matter how large or small.

Indeed, the enthusiastic and creative gardener can derive as much pleasure and fulfillment from a tiny urban rooftop garden as from an extensive garden of several acres. Planning, planting, and caring for a garden can provide as keen a sense of connection with nature to the gardener who is tending a five-acre orchard as to the gardener who is growing vegetables in containers on the patio.

In fact, any size garden can be planned to suit your needs. If you have the time and interest, you can design and plant a stunning garden filled with ever-changing flowers, fruits, and vegetables. If you lead a busy lifestyle without much time for garden maintenance, you can choose plants that require a minimal amount of care. In this, as well as many other aspects, gardening is a versatile art. With garden plots becoming increasingly smaller in many parts of the country, imaginative gardeners are choosing plants that play more than one role; potted lemon trees can serve as patio specimens as well as producing fruit. Grape vines can be trained along an arbor to provide shade— and yield delicious bunches of grapes.

With a little background in basic garden design, plant care and maintenance, and plant pests and diseases, everyone can successfully create and enjoy a garden tailored to their individual lifestyle.

This bulb garden includes daffodils, tulips, and hyacinths. For information about bulb gardening, see pages 109–133.

Color & Design

Design and color are two distinct yet inseparable elements of a beautiful and functional garden. Design determines the shape of the garden: the arrangement of vertical and horizontal lines, the volume of plantings and structures—in short, the interrelationship of physical proportions in the garden space.

Color can complement garden design, or detract from it. Identical designs planted with flowers, trees, and shrubs of different colors can appear to be different gardens altogether.

An understanding of how design and color function separately and together will help you plan a garden that both you and others will admire and enjoy.

Designing the Garden

Two gardens can have exactly the same number and types of plants, yet one will be more attractive than the other. In almost every case, the difference is that the more beautiful garden has a strong underlying design or structure. The resulting sense of order provides a framework that will benefit any type of garden; it is especially important in a garden with many different flowering plants. The variations in size, shape, color, and texture of flowering plants can easily become a disordered-looking jumble if they are placed with no regard to design. But if the basic framework is strong, many combinations of plants and flowers will work well in the garden.

Unfortunately, the planning stage is too often ignored by beginning gardeners. Their gardens tend to expand at random, by bits and pieces; if some order does emerge, it is due more to luck than to conscious effort. In the long run, however, your garden will be much more attractive if you take the time to draw up some type of overall plan. By the time your garden matures, this underlying design may not be as obvious as in the beginning, but the organization the plan provides will still be strongly felt.

Planning the Design

The beginning of all truly successful gardens is a thoughtful plan. Such factors as lawn size and shape, paths and walkways, shrub borders, hedges, trees, statues, and background fences and walls are all considered, both individually and as contributors to the total scene.

There are basically five steps to designing a garden: (1) determine the point or points from which the garden most often will be viewed, and assess what aspects and areas you want to

Above: Garden planning benefits both small and large plantings. This small bed of perennials combines contrasting colors and varying heights in a simple design. Left: "The Persian Cyclamen" from *The Temple of Flora* by Robert Thornton.

highlight or obscure; (2) consider the shape and topography of your yard and decide which plants or other objects you cannot or do not want to move; (3) decide whether you want a formal or an informal design and what style should predominate; (4) test your ideas by mapping out your different design plans on paper; and finally, (5) choose your plants.

Determining Your Viewpoints

The first step in planning your garden is to determine from what angle or location it will most often be viewed. If you plan to view it primarily from inside the house, make sure to locate the garden, and specifically the flower beds, so that you can see them comfortably through a favorite window. If you plan to spend a lot of time on a deck or patio, lay out the garden with that spot in mind.

Considering Shape and Topography

At this point, you should start to get an idea of where you want to place major landscape elements in your garden. Although you will not yet have determined the specific design, you'll know generally where you want to plant a lawn or place a large shade tree. The next step is to consider the shape and topography of your yard. This will in turn help you to decide on the style of the garden. If your yard is irregular, with slopes, hills, or rock outcroppings, or if there are mature trees or specimen plants that you wish to leave standing, you'll find it difficult to carry out a formal design. Such a site lends itself naturally to an informal plan, and most gardeners with those conditions will take this course. On the other hand, if your yard is flat, with no outstanding natural features, you'll be free to choose whichever style you wish.

Formal versus Informal Design

In the informal garden, curved, flowing lines and a seeming disregard for symmetry dominate. The curves of lawn areas, patios, walkways, beds, and borders are usually gentle, wide arcs that frequently follow the natural terrain. One curve should lead into another, creating a feeling of natural harmony.

Formal gardens are composed primarily of straight lines and classical symmetry; that is, what appears on the right side of the garden is matched, sometimes nearly perfectly, on the left. The outermost dimension of the formal garden is frequently rectangular, and this shape is repeated in other parts of the plan—in pools, patios, and in flower beds and borders. Often a single object—such as a statue, pool, or sundial—serves as

The restored colonial garden below is very informal. The flower borders and beds have curving lines. The entire garden is designed asymmetrically and has no straight lines.

This sunken garden at Hampton Court, England, is classically formal in its design. The plantings are symmetrical, and the walkways and flower beds are layed out with straight lines. A carefully pruned shrub enclosing a statue creates the focal point.

the center of interest, usually placed for optimum effect toward the rear of the garden, directly in the line of vision from the gardener's favorite viewing spot.

A formal design is the easiest type of garden to lay out and, because of its visual simplicity, is usually the best choice for a small lot.

Once you have decided on the location of the garden and on a formal or informal plan, you are ready to draw up your plan.

Mapping the Garden

Graph paper will give you the most realistic picture of your space and its proportions. Paper with four squares to the inch is easy to work with; let each square represent one square foot of garden space.

Outline on the paper where you want your lawn, patio, and walkway; trees and shrub plantings; and flower beds and borders. Represent trees, shrubs, and permanent plants such as perennials with circles that delineate the mature spread of the plant. You might find it helpful to include more information about each plant in shorthand. For example, "DF" might indicate "deciduous, flowering," or "BE" might indicate "broad-leafed, evergreen." "T," "M," and "S" (for tall, medium, and short) might be used for height. Some gardeners find it helpful to use colored pencils to designate color.

When working out your design, don't forget to tie in background colors with your plantings. In most cases, you'll have to

The gardens at Versailles epitomize formal landscaping. They were designed to include magnificent views and vistas. Although the intricately patterned boxwood hedges shown here are composed of curving lines, overall, patterns are symmetrically arranged and repeated throughout the various parterres.

Graph paper, a compass, a ruler, triangles, circular templates, and a few other basic tools will help you design a neat, accurate garden plan.

settle for whatever wall or fence is currently on the property. You can liven up a dull fence by planting a vine that will eventually cover it. Or you can create a new background with a grouping of shrubs or a hedge.

Be sure to incorporate in your design specific plants that you know you want in your garden. Your plan can be as simple or as complex as you like, and you can draw as many as you like. When you come up with a scheme that really works, you'll know it.

Choosing Plants

Once you have gone through the previous steps in designing your garden, you're ready for that part of gardening that most people find the most fun of all—choosing your own plants. As you begin to make those choices, you may find it helpful to ask yourself these important questions:

Are there any favorite plants that you *must* have, or any colors that you should not include because they would clash with or be overwhelmed by the color of the house or of a background wall, fence, or planting?

Do you want one color scheme blooming all at once, or do you want a changing garden, with one wave of flowers giving way to the next?

Do you want a diversity of plant and flower forms, or would you prefer plants that are more or less similar in appearance?

Does your space limit you to dwarf trees and smaller plants, or can you accommodate some large shade trees and rangy plants?

In designing a garden, you need to take into account several specific characteristics of the plants you are considering to make the best choices. Obviously, the cultural requirements of the plants must match the soil, light, and climatic conditions in your garden. In addition, you need to note each plant's height, spread, form, texture, and color.

Height   The most important consideration regarding plant height is to avoid extreme changes. Try stair-step plantings, placing the tallest in the rear and the shortest in front. Of course, make sure you don't inadvertently screen off a desired view by accidentally choosing plants that will grow too tall.

Spread   The spread of a plant at maturity is extremely important in garden planning; unfortunately this characteristic is commonly overlooked by gardeners. Newly landscaped gardens, if planted with the correct spacings between plants, naturally look spare, with more soil showing than plant. In the eagerness

for a lush, full garden, the temptation is to fudge a little (or a lot) and space the young plants closer together than recommended. Although it may seem a nuisance to look up the spread of each plant and allow for it in your plan, if you fail to do this, you will eventually discover new meaning to the word "nuisance." Dealing with overcrowded plants most likely suffering from competition for light, water, and nutrients is no fun. Allow enough room for the plants you choose to grow to their full size, and they will reward you with healthy, lush growth.

The colorful shrubs lining this walkway have been carefully selected with their mature height and spread in mind. They have grown enough both in height and width to create a tall hedge that provides privacy.

Using a variety of flower and foliage textures and forms creates a more interesting and exciting garden. Spikey leaves, large, deeply lobed leaves, and different flower shapes have all been incorporated in the flower bed shown here.

Form Plants have their own forms, and these too are important design considerations. Most plants fall into five basic categories: rounded, vertical, open, upright and spreading, and prostrate. Some gardens are composed of only one form; others alternate and repeat certain forms. Many outstanding gardens are made up of complementary forms, mixing the rounded with the vertical. If you have some difficulty in considering form in your design, it may help to imagine the garden in silhouette.

Texture When we speak of the texture of a plant, we mean its appearance, not the way it feels to the touch. Plants may be said to be coarse, medium, or fine in texture. Texture is determined by such factors as the density of the foliage, the form of the plant, and the proximity of the flowers.

Texture can be used to create spatial illusions in the garden. Coarse-textured plants will appear closer to the viewer, and fine-textured plants will recede into the distance. This characteristic is useful, for example, if you wish to make the far end of the garden seem closer. You can do so by planting coarse-textured plants at the far end of the garden. Plants with a fine texture can make a shallow garden appear deeper.

Color Individual plants vary considerably in their color. The foliage and flower colors of plant varieties and cultivars should be considered before they are incorporated into your garden design. Make sure you've chosen the color you want, and remember that many plants change color seasonally.

Because color is such an important factor in the appearance of the garden as a whole, it's worthwhile to look at some of the basics of designing with color. This plant characteristic can turn a drab yard into a striking, cheerful landscape.

Color in the Garden

When you walk for the first time into a garden filled with
flowering plants and lush foliage, your most enduring memory
will likely be of the colors, rather than of the plant and flower
forms, the design, or some other feature of that garden. It's
true that the success of a garden is based on more than just
color, but color is the most impressive and memorable of all
garden qualities.

In the next few pages we'll discuss some of the time-honored
principles of color in the garden, principles that designers and
artists have employed for centuries. Although the value of these
principles has been proven over time, color is a highly personal
subject, and the garden is a forgiving place, where even "mistakes" can have merit. All gardeners should have the opportu-
nity to discover on their own what rules apply to their gardens
and fit their tastes.

Gardening with color is an activity as exciting as any other
creative endeavor, with the added joy that comes from working
with living, changing materials. Ideas for color schemes can
come from anywhere: a neighbor's garden, the colors found in a
single blossom, or from something as practical as new exterior
paint on the house.

This colorful flower border
gives the above garden a vibrant
appearance. Almost all the
colors of the rainbow are represented in the plant kingdom,
and gardeners have always
taken advantage of the infinite
color variations of flower,
foliage, fruit, and bark to create
beautiful and exciting gardens.

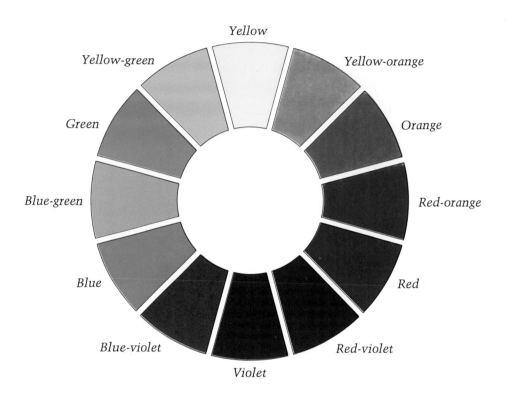

Yellow

Yellow-green

Yellow-orange

Green

Orange

Blue-green

Red-orange

Blue

Red

Blue-violet

Red-violet

Violet

The Color Wheel

The color wheel shows basic color interrelationships. Colors next to each other on the wheel are considered analogous —for example, red, red-violet, and violet. Colors opposite one another on the wheel are complementary—for example, red and green, yellow and violet, and orange and blue. Polychromatic color schemes incorporate any or all of the colors in the color wheel.

Nature's palette of colors is well represented in the plant kingdom; in fact, the range of colors is so varied that choosing plants for the color of their flowers, fruit, foliage, stems, or bark can be very confusing. Selecting trees and shrubs for the color of their leaves or berries can even be a bit intimidating because they are permanent, long-lived plants that are not likely to be removed if the color of their foliage clashes with the rest of the garden. Understanding the simple principles of color can help greatly in selecting plants and blending them in the garden.

The color wheel shown on this page may remind you of an art class, but don't be put off by its formal appearance: A color wheel is simply the easiest way to explain the basic interrelationships among colors.

The wheel is often used to identify the three primary colors— red, yellow, and blue—and to show how the other colors on the wheel are made from blending various quantities of these three. Because one can't blend or mix flowers of two different colors to produce a third color, this information is more important to artists than to gardeners. What is important to gardeners, however, is how colors clash with or complement one another, and the distinction between "warm" and "cool" colors.

Warm and Cool Colors

The colors in the wheel can be divided into warm and cool colors. Colors, of course, are neither physically warm nor cool, but they can make the viewer feel either way. The colors on the left-hand side of the wheel, from yellow to red, are considered warm colors. Those colors on the right-hand side, from green to violet, are cool colors. Red-violet and yellow-green have both warm and cool properties, one more than the other, depending on what other colors they are combined with.

To the eye, warm colors tend to advance and cool colors tend to recede: If planted side by side at a distance, the warm colors would appear closer; the cool colors, farther away. You can use these effects to create spatial illusions. A planting of predominately cool-colored flowers at the rear of your garden will make the yard seem larger; warm colors will make it seem smaller. Spot plantings can have a similar effect, seeming to deepen a part of the yard or to bring it closer.

Generally, cool colors are good for close-up viewing and warm colors are better for dramatic displays. Plantings of blue bellflower, violet meadow sage, and purple phlox may have quite an impact next to the patio or walkway, but planted in the background of the garden they would all but lose their effect. To emphasize cool colors, it's best to plant them closest to the point from which they'll be most often viewed. Warm-colored plants such as red hibiscus, yellow varieties of juniper, and orange cosmos can be used to bring a distant part of the yard into sharp focus. When combining warm and cool colors, remember that the cooler colors can be easily overwhelmed by the warm.

In this interplanting, the tulips' warm, bright red color jumps out at the viewer. The cool lavender-blue forget-me-nots are less noticeable.

Color Schemes

In certain combinations, colors have a harmonious effect. These harmonies are frequently discussed in four categories, easily identified on the color wheel.

Monochromatic Colors   Various tints and shades of one, and one only, of the pure colors (which are often called hues) is a monochromatic color scheme. A tint is lighter than the pure color and a shade is darker. Many of the most impressive gardens are planted in a monochromatic color scheme. An example would be red, various tints of pink, and a deep shade of red or maroon. Visualize a combination of maroon snapdragons, red- and rose-colored nicotiana, and pale pink dianthus, and you can begin to see the possibilities of such a color scheme. In reality, there are no totally monochromatic gardens: The various shades of "leaf green" will always be part of the combination, but their presence is a pleasant one that does not detract from the more dominant flower colors.

Many people take the monochromatic color scheme a step further, and plan a display of flowers or shrubs to complement the color of the house. This "total color concept" can be particularly effective and is worth experimenting with.

Analogous Colors   An analogous color scheme makes use of "neighbors" on the color wheel; any three colors found in sequence on the color wheel are said to comprise an analogous relationship. An example would be red-violet, violet, and blue-violet.

To expand the possibilities of such a color scheme, you can include tints and shades of each of the three colors. Because you have more flowers and colors to choose from, an analogous color scheme is easier to work with than a strictly monochromatic one, and the results can be truly memorable.

Gertrude Jekyll (1843–1932), an English writer and gardener whose influence helped produce some of the world's greatest gardens, developed what she called a tonal garden, based on rules similar to those for an analogous color scheme.

In the best of the gardens planned by Jekyll all of the colors, including leaf color, are tonally related. One garden (Folly Farm in Berkshire, England) planted at the turn of the century made use of silver-leafed plants and white, pale lavender, and ivory flowers. The colors of the foliage and flowers in turn complemented the colors of the stone walks and walls.

If this type of tonally related garden appeals to you, the following are suggestions for gray- or silver-foliaged plants: dusty

These pots of pelargoniums and petunias create an analogous color scheme of pink, violet, red-violet, and purple flowers.

miller 'Silver Queen', gray santolina, 'Tricolor' sage, snow-in-summer, artemisia 'Silver Queen', 'White Christmas' caladiums, lavender, and many species of dianthus. Some of the best white-flowering annuals include: floss flowers, asters, petunias, morning glory, verbena, and lobelia.

Complementary Colors   Colors that are opposite one another on the wheel—for example, red and green, yellow and violet, and orange and blue—are called complementary colors. These are powerful combinations, clashing to some, vibrant and vital to others. This scheme is best when executed with pure hues, rather than shades or tints, of the complementary colors. If you want to try to "blend" strong complementary colors, arrange plants so that they intermingle where the colors meet, rather than clearly defining the junctures. To tone these colors down, you can include silvery-leafed or white-flowered plants. If you want to plant intensely colored flowers like scarlet-red Oriental poppies, clear yellow rudbeckias, or hot pink Michaelmas daisies, you can always work up to the bright spots with plants of similar but less intense colors. Beds and borders designed along this principle are pleasantly cohesive.

This combination of blue forget-me-nots and orange tulips shows how vibrant a complementary color scheme can be. Complementary colors intensify each other. But such a color scheme is best used in sections of a garden; it is often too intense when used throughout.

Polychromatic Colors   For a carnival-like effect in the garden, try a polychromatic color scheme. Although the random combinations of any—and every—color around the wheel are often the result of gardening inexperience, there is nothing wrong with this type of color scheme. Indeed, there are many who go so far as to claim that because there are no "mistakes" in nature's own color scheme, it's also impossible for the gardener to produce any. One benefit of random plantings is the possibility of "happy accidents"—color combinations that may become the mainstay of the garden for seasons to come.

Experimenting with Color

If you are reluctant to combine certain flower colors, one good way to experiment on a small scale is to plant combinations in pots or other containers. Or plant one color in each pot and move the pots about until you find combinations that please you. This approach requires little time and effort, and the results can be surprisingly good. The plantings can then be carried out on a larger scale in the garden.

The great English gardener Vita Sackville-West used to carry a branch of a flowering plant or shrub around the garden until she found a place where it was most pleasing. It was then, and only then, that she decided either to leave the plant where it was or to move it to a new, more desirable location.

You can do the same thing with several pots of experimental color combinations, trying them in front of the house or in back, next to the steps, or wherever, until you find a spot where they look best with the plants already growing there.

A Color Sampler

On the following pages we present a sampling of flowers, grouped according to color.

Three of the photographs show an assortment of flowers loosely grouped around one of the three primary colors: red, yellow, and blue. Because of their popularity and importance in the garden, we have also included a collection of white and cream-colored flowers in a fourth photograph. For lists of flowers by color, see the chapters on annuals and perennials.

Remember that flowers are not the only source of color in the garden. Foliage, especially in autumn, is often marvelously hued and tinted, and bark, berries, and fruit all contribute their share of color to the garden. You'll find lists of plants noted for their colorful leaves, bark, and fruit in the trees, shrubs, herbs, and vegetables chapters.

Red

Red is quite a color. It is a little like the distant relative who always seems to shake things up at annual family gatherings—the color red has that same power. True reds are compelling. They invite closer inspection. They tempt. They are big colors and can be overwhelming to people with less adventurous tastes.

There was a time when attitudes toward color were arbitrary and strictly dictated. We found the following advice in the 1946 edition of *The New Garden Encyclopedia* and, as amusing as it now sounds, we wonder whether it may not contain an element of truth:

Red flowers are favorable for the weak and ailing to sit among, for rapid growing children below the physical norm to play in the midst of, for the aged and feeble to dwell with. We gather that it is an unfavorable color for general use, however, because of the tendency of workers under red light to irritability and quarrelsomeness; not until they were removed from it or allowed to spend part of their time in the blue room did they become normal.

With those admonitions aside, several garden designers believe that a garden really isn't complete without at least some red in it. And it's undeniable that a little red here and there really does bring other colors to life. Treat red with respect and it will add excitement to your garden.

In mixing pigments, when the pure color red is softened with white, it becomes another creature altogether. If red stands for force and vigor, pink stands for quite the opposite. The color is usually associated with diminutive flowers that require close-up inspection. And because of the number of fragrant pink flowers, like *Dianthus* (pinks), petunias, sweet peas, and stock, most people think of pink as a sweet-smelling color.

A classic but seldom-used combination is pink and red—especially effective in the garden, where the green foliage adds a moderating touch. Planted against a white wall or fence, the combination looks particularly fresh. Red petunias and pink verbena, red and pink geraniums together in the same container, or all-pink snapdragons and red salvia are just a few possibilities.

These pink to red flowers include dianthus, zinnias, cosmos, nicotiana, asters, salpiglossis, scabiosa, celosia, and snapdragons.

Blue

For some gardeners, blue flowers are an addiction. As sought
after as they are, there are few truly blue flowers, and the process
of collecting them and planting them in one place can become
a lifelong passion. An all-blue garden demands the viewer's
full attention, not only to fully enjoy the rarity of the colors, but
also to appreciate the jewellike quality of many of the flowers.

When you expand the color spectrum a bit to include the
shades and tints of purple and violet, you can create combinations with the rich intensity of a stained-glass window. Consider,
however, that the deep shades of these colors are often difficult
to distinguish from foliage, especially if the plants are in a shady
location. Plant purple and violet flowers in a bright location
close to the house, where they can be easily admired. Addition
of white or pink flowers will add vibrancy.

The family of blue includes many richly colored flowers.
Some of the more intense colors can be achieved with the
following varieties: 'Amethyst' and 'Sparkle' verbena; 'Violet
Flame' salvia; 'Sapphire' lobelia; 'Sugar Daddy', 'Blue Mariner',
and 'Malibu' petunias; azure blue asters; and 'Blue Boy'
cornflowers.

The out-of-print *New Garden Encyclopedia,* which we quoted
on the subject of the color red, has an equally unreserved
opinion of the blues. The editor suggests:

*. . . a blue garden for the nervous and highly-strung, for the
tired business man, for the child given to violent outbursts.
Being the antithesis of red, blue is not a stimulating color
and should be kept out of a garden if sluggish temperaments
are in need of stirring and awakening. But it may prove of
great help to the student or any desirous of contemplative
retreat.*

If the deeper shades of blue, violet, and purple tend to recede
into the overall garden, their best qualities are highlighted when
combined for an indoor bouquet. For this reason alone, flowers
in this color range are worth planting. If they don't fit into
your regular garden color scheme, consider planting them in a
separate cutting garden.

Many gardeners give these colors the sharper focus they need
by planting them in pots and placing them in conspicuous areas.

These flowers display many shades of blue, violet, and purple. They
include bachelor's buttons, nigella, lobelia, campanula, cosmos, statice,
scabiosa, foxglove, asters, and celosias.

Shades of yellow and orange are found in these marigolds, nasturtiums, strawflowers, calendulas, cosmos, gaillardias, celosias, zinnias, sunflowers, and snapdragons.

These cream and white flowers
include nigella, mignonette,
phlox, baby's breath, cosmos,
petunias, bells of Ireland,
zinnias, and stock.

Yellow

Perhaps it is because yellow is the color of the sun—the color associated with light and happiness—that it so frequently appears in gardens. Masses of yellow flowers bring an exuberant, cheerful quality to any garden. The very presence of this color seems to reaffirm the positive nature of gardening.

There is nothing quite so vibrant as a border of golden yellow nasturtiums next to a spring green lawn, as warm as a full marigold blossom in the peak of summer, or as faintly nostalgic as a planting of yellow and mahogany-colored snapdragons beside a rain-soaked garden path. Yellow is a powerful color, capable of evoking many moods.

To enhance the lively effects of yellow, try combining it with white; the effect practically sparkles. A yellow and white annual combination for a sunny spot is white petunias and lemon-yellow marigolds.

Yellow infused with red or brown produces the gold, orange, and red-orange spectrum. There are many flowers in these shades, most often appearing in the height of summer or in early fall. Planted together, they can mirror the colorful change of the seasons from summer to fall. They don't command attention as pure red or yellow does, but this is all to the better for many people's tastes.

White

White flowers are special to many gardeners. In fact, many famous gardens have been given over to white flowering plants alone. The color white suggests purity—a quality most people admire in gardens.

White reflects the most light of any color. Even at night, when other colors in the garden are subdued by darkness, white flowers shimmer in whatever light is available; the effect in moonlight can be spellbinding. White flowers are a powerful element in the garden and should be used wherever you want sparkle and light.

White flowers are also the favorites of many designers, who find special appeal in the graphic contrast of masses of white against lush, dark green foliage. Add a few white garden chairs, a small brick patio, and a black-and-white striped awning, and you've got a million-dollar look.

Cream- and ivory-colored flowers lack the brightness of pure white but possess a rich quality all their own. Cream-colored flowers are not remarkable for their ability to combine well with other colors (except yellow), but by themselves—particularly in cut flower arrangements—they are extremely attractive.

A daily or weekly diary of events in the garden makes an invaluable guide for next year's garden. Reviewing it will help you reproduce your successes and avoid repeating earlier mistakes.

A Garden Calendar

Without some kind of aid, it's virtually impossible to remember the exact blooming times of different plants from one season to the next. With a garden calendar, however, it's a simple matter to note the date on which you plant certain plants, when they bloom or fruit, and for how long. These notes alone will tell you in succeeding years almost exactly when to start seeds and transplant seedlings and bedding plants, and what to expect from the flowers, vegetables, trees, and shrubs that grow in your soil.

A garden calendar has many uses; in fact, they are countless. You can record not only planting dates and times of bloom and harvest, but notes on the performance of various plants; on colors, forms, and varieties you especially like and those you find less satisfactory; on fertilizers and soil amendments; on watering and feeding schedules; or on your own experiments with plants and different methods of culture. If you like, you can add notes on nursery and catalog seed sources, cuttings and seeds exchanged with your neighbors, gardening news and events—in short, on anything about gardening that excites your interest.

A garden calendar can be as simple as a piece of paper on which you jot down planting dates, or it can take the form of a "journal" recording the day-to-day progress of your garden and your skills.

Beyond providing information on your climate and your garden, a garden calendar can help you better organize gardening tasks. It can give you a good picture of the time and energy you spend in gardening and how you can best invest them, so that you can adjust your schedule and your expectations accordingly.

All of this will prove invaluable as your garden continues to grow from year to year. An additional benefit of the garden calendar is that it makes good reading and stimulates fond memories during the long winter months—encouraging you to look ahead with confidence to each new gardening season.

This cutting garden has been set up in a side yard not visible from the rest of the garden.

The Cutting Garden

If you're a person who enjoys bringing the colorful beauty of cut flowers indoors, you may want to consider setting aside a small bed primarily for an old-fashioned cutting garden.

Because the cutting garden is basically utilitarian, it should be laid out in a simple, practical manner. The plants can be planted in rows like a vegetable garden, with the tallest set so that they won't shade the lower-growing varieties. A seldom-used side yard is an ideal place for a cutting garden as long as it receives at least half a day of sun. The soil should, of course, be properly prepared.

Just about any garden plant can supply interesting material for bouquets and arrangements. Certainly, the many bright and colorful annuals, such as marigolds, zinnias, snapdragons, and sweet peas, make charming cut flower bouquets. Perennials such as delphiniums and peonies, and of course daffodils, tulips, and other bulbs, are perfect for cutting. And what is more classic than a dozen freshly picked red roses in a crystal vase?

Combine these traditional favorites with ornamental grasses, interestingly twisted branches, colorful leaves, and berries for a more creative arrangement. Or fill an urn with pussy willows, fall foliage, even bare twigs and branches for a striking effect.

Cutting the Flowers

The longevity of cut flowers can be increased by following a few simple rules.

Generally speaking, flowers should be cut in the morning or evening when they are plump with water; flowers cut in the middle of the day are often somewhat wilted and, once cut, have difficulty absorbing enough water.

Always use a sharp knife or pair of scissors to make the cleanest cut possible.

Take a bucket or pail of water into the garden and plunge the stems into the water immediately after cutting.

When you are ready to arrange the flowers, remove any foliage from the bases of the stems because these foul the water in the vase very quickly. Professional flower arrangers often cut the stems a second time before putting them into the vase. For the longest life, cut the flower stems underwater, and make the cut at an angle.

Place the arrangement in a cool room, away from direct sunlight. Cut flower "foods" available at some garden centers and florists can be added to the water to prolong the blossoms, but one of the best treatments is simply changing the water daily and recutting the stems after several days.

In addition to brightening your home, fresh flowers from your own garden make special gifts for friends and neighbors. And because the cutting garden is essentially a utilitarian one, it's a perfect spot to try new and unusual plants that you might hesitate to place in more visible or more formal areas.

If your cutting garden produces an abundance of flowers, you might also consider selling the surplus: Some specialty florists often want unusual flowers from home gardens.

In gardening as well as in architecture simplicity ought to be the governing taste.

Lord Kames, *Garden Ideas*

This basket of freshly cut flowers contains gerberas, statice, and snapdragons. If you intend to cut only a few flowers, carry a basket; but use a bucket of water for cutting large numbers of flowers so they won't wilt.

Climate, Microclimate, & Shade

If you've ever moved from one part of the country to another—particularly from north to south or vice versa—you may have been surprised at how different gardening is between the two regions. Regional differences play an important role in the location of plants in the garden. For instance, the azalea that can take almost full sun in Oyster Bay, Long Island, needs plenty of protection from the elements in Louisville, Kentucky.

The reason for such differences is that the intensity of the sun increases the closer you are to the equator. Add to that basic fact the multitude of climatic influences—fog, clouds, rain, wind, and others—and you quickly realize that blanket statements concerning the type of exposure to give a plant are difficult to make.

Climate Zones

A slightly modified version of the USDA Plant Hardiness Zone Map is illustrated on pages 42–43. Locate your zone on it and use it as a reference when you consult this book. Be aware that the map is meant to be a general guide and that the zones are approximate, based on average data. Climate often varies within zones; your local climate can be warmer or colder than the average for the zone, especially in mountain regions.

Microclimates

The many climatic variations that occur within an area even as small as a tiny garden are called microclimates. Differences in microclimates affect many aspects of gardening. For instance, you may find that your daffodils and tulips bloom several weeks earlier than those in a neighboring garden, and your maples may not change color as quickly in the fall. Once you become familiar with the microclimates that surround your house, the process of providing the right conditions for each plant becomes much easier. Some of the factors that create microclimates include slope and other topographical variations, exposure to the sun, proximity to bodies of water, prevailing winds, structures, and plants.

An understanding of the microclimates in your garden will not only allow you to select plants intelligently, but will also provide you with the option of altering some of those microclimates. For example, by protecting parts of the garden, you can provide the few degrees of temperature difference that can mean survival to a tender plant on a frosty night. Bear in mind that microclimatic modifications have limits—you won't be able to provide a safe location for a subtropical plant in a New England garden in winter.

Left: "The Snowdrop" from *The Temple of Flora* by Robert Thornton. Above: A rain-drenched fuchsia blossom.

Exposure and Microclimate

The sun's angle varies considerably throughout the year, but whatever the season, the sun's rays are always most intense and direct at noon or in the early afternoon. As a result, south- and west-facing slopes are always warmer than north and east slopes because the former absorb more of the sun's radiant energy.

Thermal belts are warm microclimates that occur midway on sloping land above valleys and other lowlands. These bands of mild temperature are localized; both above and below them, winters are distinctly colder. Therefore, if your garden is in a warm thermal belt, you probably will be able to grow a number of plants considered too tender for the general area.

South- and west-facing walls, buildings, and other surfaces also tend to be warmer and drier than north- or east-facing surfaces. A north-facing wall or building is never exposed to direct sunlight in our northern hemisphere, and is much cooler and moister as a result.

Many people are not aware that during midsummer, because of the earth's southern tilt, the sun rises in the northeast and sets in the northwest. Even though they do not receive direct sunlight during the cooler months, delicate, shade-loving plants growing in a location with a northeast or northwest exposure may suffer from sunburn during this time of year.

This fence, having a northeastern exposure, receives direct sun only during mid-summer. For the remainder of the year, the shade and moisture-loving plants growing here receive indirect light. Plants growing in such a location are unaccustomed to direct sun and will burn easily if not watered frequently during mid-summer.

Moisture and Microclimate

Areas alongside a lake or coastline usually experience more moderate temperatures than inland areas; many areas that are subject to humid weather also have moderate temperatures. Water absorbs heat slowly, but absorbs a great quantity of heat compared with many other substances. Because of this capacity to slowly absorb and give off a large amount of heat energy, temperatures do not fluctuate as quickly in moist climates as they do in dry.

Even within a garden, humidity and moisture levels can vary dramatically. Humidity levels can be quite high in a deeply shaded, north-facing, enclosed section of the garden where the air remains still. Plant diseases that thrive in wet conditions will be more of a problem in such moist spots. On the opposite side of the house, the microclimate may be the complete reverse—plants might be exposed to intense afternoon sun and drying breezes, and temperatures may fluctuate drastically from day to night.

Winds and Microclimate

Winds are another aspect of weather that affect the microclimate in your garden. Winter winds can add a substantial chill factor to your microclimate; drying hot summer winds are just as unpleasant. Certain geographical areas are especially subject to winds; homes located in a canyon, at the base of a bluff, or along a shoreline may be buffeted almost constantly by winds.

If you live in a windy area, be aware of the spots in your garden that are particularly exposed, and plant trees and shrubs that can tolerate cold or hot winds, or provide protection with a windbreak.

Stormy weather is almost always accompanied by strong winds. Certain geographical areas are especially subject to winds and the temperature extremes they often bring. Gardeners living in such areas must protect tender plants from freezing winds or hot, drying winds. Choosing plants that tolerate windy conditions is the ideal solution for gardeners in these areas.

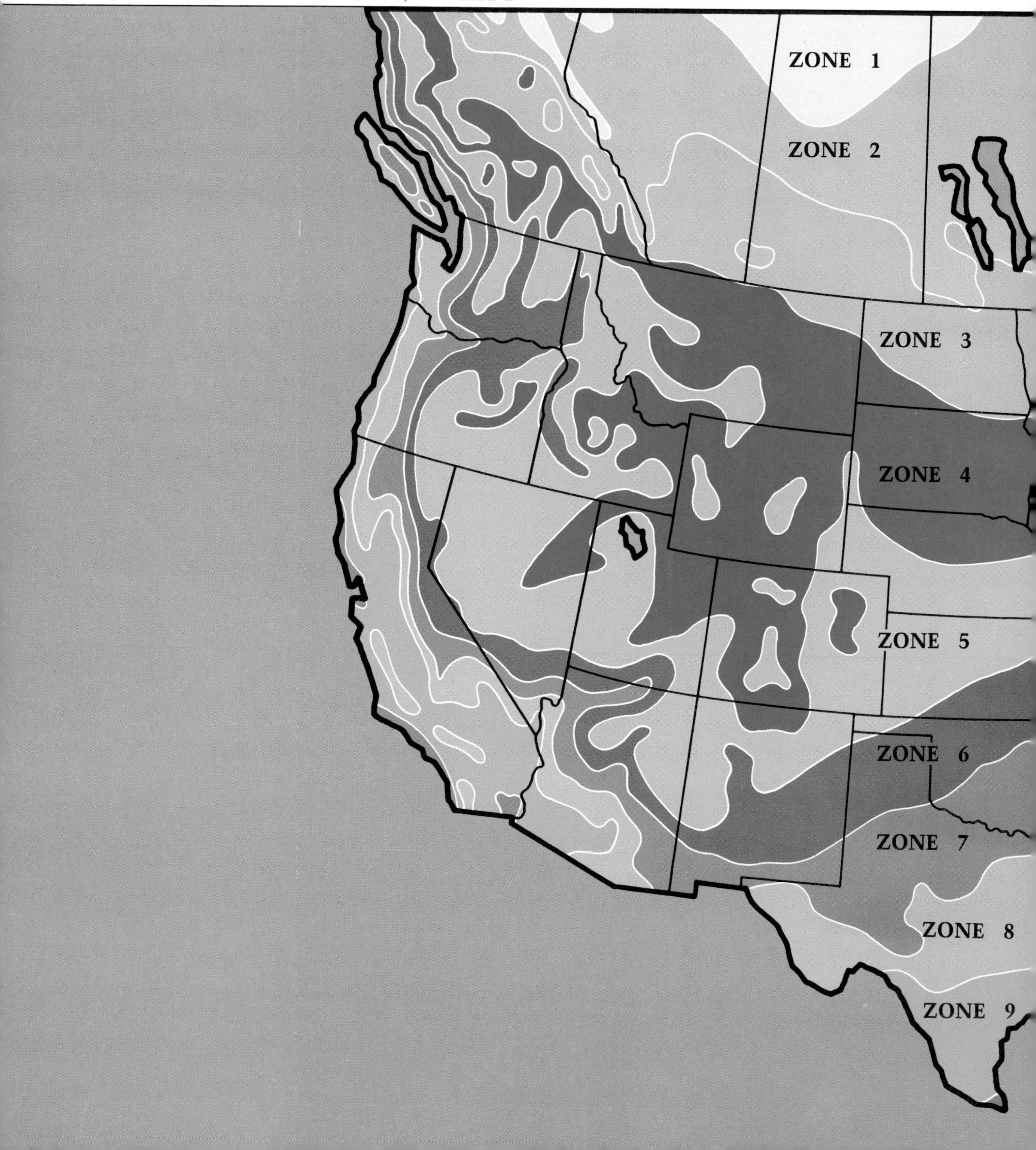

ZONE 1

ZONE 2

ZONE 3

ZONE 4

ZONE 5

ZONE 6

ZONE 7

ZONE 8

ZONE 9

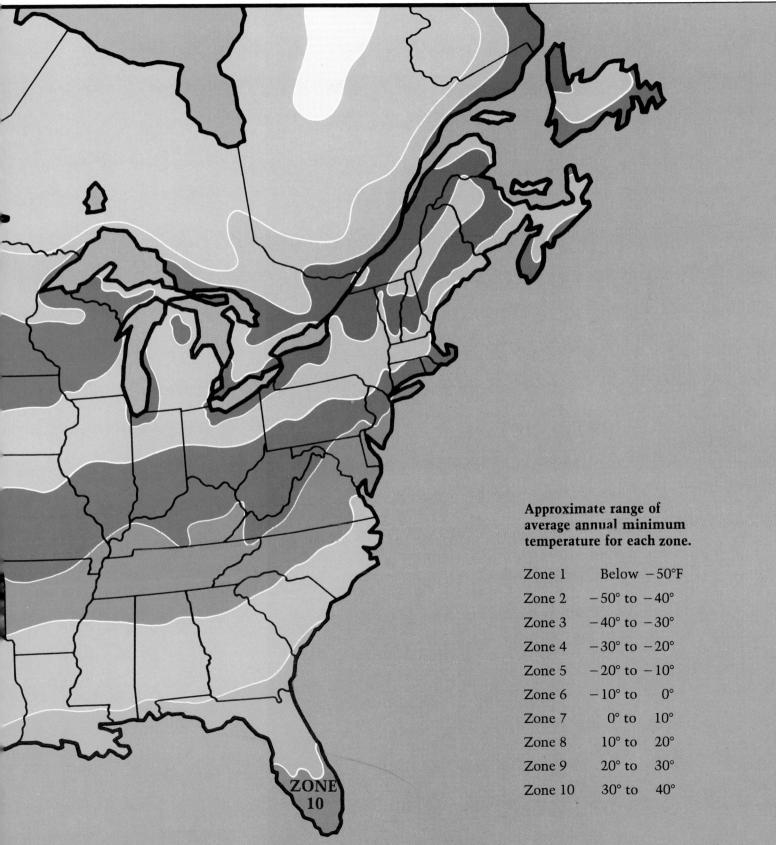

Approximate range of average annual minimum temperature for each zone.

Zone 1   Below −50°F

Zone 2   −50° to −40°

Zone 3   −40° to −30°

Zone 4   −30° to −20°

Zone 5   −20° to −10°

Zone 6   −10° to   0°

Zone 7   0° to   10°

Zone 8   10° to   20°

Zone 9   20° to   30°

Zone 10   30° to   40°

ZONE 10

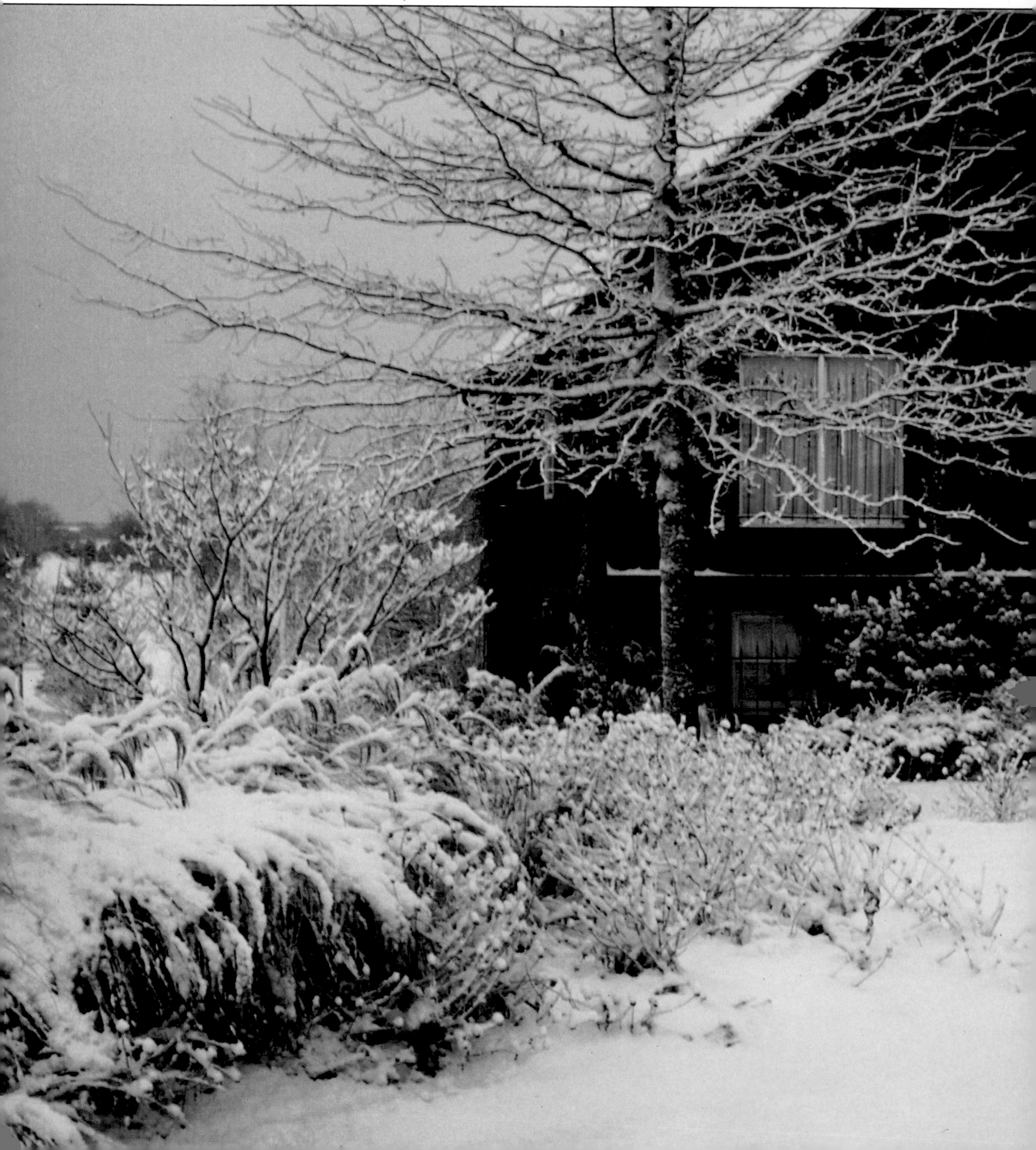

The snow load is not as heavy on the shrub planted next to the house because the eaves trap heat and melt snow. Even such a minor difference in temperature may be critical to the survival of a plant through a long, hard winter.

Cold and Microclimate

Because cold air is denser than warm air, it tends to sink and collect at the bottom of canyons and valleys. Often, frost pockets develop in a part of the garden where cold air flowing down a slope is trapped by a hedge or mass of shrubbery. In many cases, you can modify your garden to eliminate many of these frost pockets. Structural walls and plantings can be arranged to deflect the downhill flow of cold air around gardens and outdoor living spaces, providing shelter and protection.

In areas where the nights are often clear and dry, plants located under trees, eaves, or other overhangs are not as likely to suffer from cold damage as plants located out in the open. The heat that collects in the soil, plants, and structures during the day is lost during the night in the form of heat waves that radiate away from the earth's surface. However, when these heat waves encounter a tree, an overhang, or other overhead object, they are reradiated back to the earth's surface. Therefore, soil and plants that have something above them do not lose as much overall heat as plants out in the open. This same principle explains why plants out in the open are much less susceptible to frost during cloudy or foggy nights; the heat waves radiated from the soil and plants do not penetrate the cloud or fog layer effectively and are reradiated back to the ground.

Surrounding Structures and Plants

Buildings, automobiles, large expanses of concrete, and other heat-absorbing surfaces all contribute to making cities and towns warmer than outlying areas. Likewise, the warmest areas in the garden are often those beside paved surfaces such as sidewalks, driveways, patios, and sunny south and west walls. Not only do these surfaces reflect some of the sun's heat, light, and glare, but they also store heat during daylight hours and radiate it back to the atmosphere at night. Dark surfaces absorb more heat than light-colored ones.

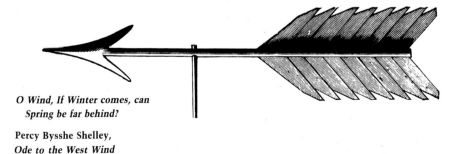

O Wind, If Winter comes, can Spring be far behind?

**Percy Bysshe Shelley,
Ode to the West Wind**

Shade

Shade is one of the most important elements of microclimate and, unlike some of the other components, is universal. It occurs in every garden where there is a plant or structure, and deserves special consideration. Shade dramatically alters the air and soil temperature, especially in dry areas, and often results in a humidity increase. Most important, shade, or the lack of it, dictates the types of plants that are suitable for any given spot in the garden.

Types of Shade

The word *shade* should never stand alone when it is used in reference to gardening. By itself, it has only the most basic definition—the relative absence of light—and provides little help for the gardener trying to figure out the best place for a shade-loving plant.

Any description of a particular type of shade is at best an approximation open to many interpretations. The only truly scientific measurement of light, or relative lack of light, is accomplished with a light meter. And though it is possible to describe different degrees of shade using exact footcandle measurements based on light-meter readings, most gardeners and horticulturists agree that to do so would be to make the problem more complex than necessary.

At the same time, there are distinct variations in shade, significant enough to make a difference in the type of plants that can be grown successfully in one set of conditions or another. To simplify the problem of describing different types of shade, we have grouped them in four categories. The Encyclopedia charts at the back of the book also contain information on light levels and shade tolerance categories, but the distinctions are not as fine as you'll find in this chapter. The plant lists on page 54–57 all carry a recommendation keyed to these classifications. Bear in mind that a garden is a place where rules can sometimes be ignored successfully, but some understanding of the types of shade commonly encountered is helpful.

Shade 1—Dappled Shade Dappled shade is produced by open trees, such as birch, that create a moving pattern of sunlight and shade across the ground and plants. This is a fairly bright situation and the lightest shade category, but direct sun on any given area is minimal for any length of time. This is also the type of shade that provides the widest range of gardening possibilities, because it is hospitable to a great many shade- and sun-loving plants. Lath houses also provide dappled shade.

The impatiens making up this colorful border thrive in the dappled shade cast by the birches and other nearby trees. Many plants that cannot tolerate long periods of direct sunlight are well-suited to dappled shade.

Top: The plants shown here are growing next to a north-facing fence, and are further shaded by trees—a typical, medium shade situation. Cyclamens, azaleas, primroses, coleus, and ferns are growing here. Bottom: a densely shaded planter bed.

Shade 2—Open Shade   Open shade is created by a northern exposure. A north-facing yard has open shade for as many feet out as shade is cast by an adjoining wall, fence, or building. The distance the shade is cast will vary with the season. Open shade provides bright light, but no direct sunlight. Fiberglass-roofed patios and whitewashed greenhouses under direct sun can also be considered as providing open shade. Proximity to a south-facing wall that reflects light will greatly increase brightness in an open-shade location.

Shade 3—Medium Shade   Medium shade is found in north-facing locations shaded by a structure and by trees—in other words, an open-shade situation where light is further obscured by foliage and branches. A similar degree of shade also occurs under decks and stairwells and in south-facing tunnel entrances with no direct sun.

Shade 4—Dense Shade   Dense shade is the deepest shade, found in north-facing tunnel entrances and north-facing side yards. Tall walls and fences block all but the narrowest strips of light. There will be some reflected light. These are the most problematic areas because plant selection is severely limited.

Gardening choices for areas of dense shade should be carefully considered in regard to how the area will be used. If it is rarely viewed, for example, something as simple as moss, stones, and gravel may be the best solution.

Know Your Garden Shade Areas

The gardener in search of plants to grow in a shaded location can take some practical steps to ensure matching the right plants with the right conditions.

First, when you are at the nursery or garden center, confine your initial selection to those plants already growing in shaded conditions. Almost every good-size nursery or garden center has a special place set apart for shade-loving plants. More often than not, the area is a large, enclosed lath house or screened-in area that simulates the growing conditions that are best for these plants.

Before talking with a nursery salesperson, know as much as possible about the various microclimates and conditions in your garden. The following points are important to consider.

If the planting area is under a large tree, the type of tree can make a big difference in the plants you can grow there. If the tree has a mass of surface roots, as sycamores, maples, and elms do, or drops leaves that are toxic to most plants, as the eucalyp-

tus does, you may be advised against planting anything under the tree. Or you may want to limit the plants to containers. If the tree is deeprooted, as are oaks and most conifers, but produces deep shade, you may be advised to do some selective thinning to allow more light onto the area below the tree.

If the shade in a planting area is produced by a structure, such as a house or fence, the situation is quite a bit different from that of a planting bed under mature trees. Planting beds on the north, northeast, and east sides of buildings and fences are frequently used as areas for growing shade plants. Although such areas are shaded, the amount of light they receive is usually fairly consistent, different from the play of sunlight and shadow produced by a canopy of leaves. Depending on the way your house is set on the lot and how far you are from the equator, the amount of morning sun the planting area receives can vary. For shade-loving plants, there is a notable difference between the intensity of the sun at ten o'clock in the morning and at noon, especially when light and heat are increased by a wall or fence in the background.

The old rule of thumb in such situations is that a great many shade-loving plants will tolerate the morning sun until noon, but after that success is variable. There are certainly many exceptions to the rule, but in general it is sound advice. Keep in mind, too, that as the sun changes its course during the year, the amount of light an area receives can change dramatically. North of the equator, the amount of sun an eastern exposure receives gradually increases as the sun approaches its peak at the summer solstice on June 22. In other words, a planting area may have the right conditions of light for shade lovers during fall, winter, and spring. But, by the middle of summer, the light intensity may increase to an unbearable level for many of the true shade-loving plants.

In assessing the amount of light a particular area receives, you may discover that you can plant part of the area with true shade-loving plants—plants adapted to open, medium, and dense shade—and another part with plants that tolerate some shade—plants adapted to half-day sun or dappled shade. All plant selections for a shaded area should be made carefully, with these important points in mind: Most sun-loving plants will accept some degree of shade during a portion of the day as long as they also receive the amount of direct sun they need. Shade-loving plants, on the other hand, will wilt, sunburn, or develop other signs of distress from too much direct sun (especially the hot late-afternoon sun) even though they receive adequate shade for the rest of the day.

The impatiens, primroses, and bergenia plants shown here are growing in dappled sunlight at the base of a tree. Using shade-loving annuals and perennials brightens otherwise uninteresting spots in the garden.

Garden Styles Well Suited to Shade

Woodland and oriental gardens are particularly well suited to the use of shade-loving plants. Possibly neither of these styles appeals to your personal taste, or they may not be feasible in your garden site; style is, after all, a personal statement. What the styles do show, however, is that creating a garden with a distinct theme enhances the impact of the garden itself.

The Woodland Garden   Woodland on your property, even the tiniest grove, places you among the most fortunate of gardeners. If there is no woodland but you are willing to invest some effort and time in creating the effect, you can still enjoy the style of shade garden that for many people is the most magical and the easiest to maintain.

A woodland garden includes a canopy of tall trees, a naturalistic or informal lower planting of shrubs and small trees, and a lush and colorful herbaceous carpeting of bulbs and perennials.

One of the special properties of woodland is the long dormancy of most deciduous trees in its high canopy. This period of leaflessness allows late winter and early spring bloomers to flourish in the weak sun of the early season, then lie protected or dormant through the shady hot months.

The shaded bog garden is a specialized woodland garden with a style all its own. A wet spot in your shade garden can be an asset. If your garden lacks a boggy spot, you can contrive a permanent seep to create one. Of course, a tiny pool or a short stream, perhaps with one or two large rocks and a recirculating pump, can create a focal point of great beauty with little water.

A woodland garden need not be large to be stunning. This small grove of trees with its understory of young camellia plants is a cool, refreshing contrast to the lawn and iris bed growing in direct sunlight. Eventually, the camellias will fill in and provide a dense green understory that will bloom every spring.

The Oriental Garden Gardens in the oriental style are to many people the subtlest and most beautiful. Because of its simplicity and informality, this style lends itself to nearly every garden space, including the shadiest. The thoughtful selection and arrangement of just a few simple materials can transform your large shaded area or tiny nook into a special place for serenity and contemplation.

If you walk into an oriental garden in the United States, you might automatically think of it as Japanese. It might be—but it could also be Chinese. The overwhelming likelihood, of course, is that the garden is American, with an oriental flavor. A true Chinese garden has precise, traditional combinations of rocks, water, and plants. A true Japanese garden has these combinations too, but also an intricacy of arrangement and symbolism that is obscure to most westerners.

To lovers of gardens and nature to whom the layers of elaborate symbolism and subtle meanings are perhaps inaccessible, Japanese and Chinese gardens can still be beautiful. Much that is Far Eastern can be adapted to an American garden.

Maybe you have only a dark, rather dank spot where you want a simple garden. If you are fortunate and live in an area where moss forms on trees and rocks, you might make a garden with a stone lantern (or a concrete facsimile); white river rocks, which will brighten the area and gather moss; a few larger rocks; and a few ferns that thrive in deep shade, such as maidenhair and holly ferns.

Many elements of an Oriental garden are illustrated here—water, a stone bridge and lantern, and ornamental, coniferous evergreens. A well-designed Oriental garden incorporates various shades of green. Using variegated and highly colored cultivars of junipers, *Chamaecyparis* species, *Cryptomeria* species, and *Thuja* species can create a peaceful and interesting Oriental garden.

Various dwarf ornamental conifers are naturals for a lightly shaded Far Eastern garden. You might work false cypress and Japanese cedar into whatever plan you develop.

Azaleas and camellias are oriental. In traditional Japanese gardens azaleas are used very sparingly for color. As long as you don't plant too many colors, you can include azaleas in your design without destroying the traditional oriental feeling.

If you want trees that will create shade, consider pines, flowering plums, cherries, crabapples, beeches, the larger Japanese maples, ginkgo, and saucer magnolia.

Whatever combinations you choose, remember oriental restraint and understatement. A Japanese maple, a few small evergreens, some tufts of dwarf bamboo, one flowering plant, pebbles, a flat, weathered bench, and a lantern might fill a large space adequately and beautifully. A tiny pool (perhaps a birdbath top) sunk among rocks and ferns, and a beautifully shaped, subtly pruned dwarf pieris, can create a world inside a tiny shaded courtyard.

Shade-Garden Specialties

The following lists of shade-tolerant plants are designed to help you select plants to fill special needs in your garden. Is your garden dry and very shady? Lightly shaded and moist? Are you looking for a bright-flowering annual to grow in medium shade? Consult these lists, then read about those plants that interest you in the Encyclopedia charts on pages 377–499. Use the lists to spark your imagination or to solve landscaping problems. Keep in mind that, in many cases, when a name appears on a list, only selected varieties (usually too numerous to mention in the list) may fit the given category. Some varieties may not flower or may flower poorly in the colder zones. Consult the Encyclopedia charts, seed catalogs, and local experts to help pinpoint the variety best suited to your needs.

Each plant on these lists is given a shade tolerance rating between 1 and 4 to indicate the degree of shade the plant can withstand. Ratings 1 and 2 are dappled and open shade, respectively; both of these fit under the definition of light shade in the Encyclopedia charts in the back of the book. Rating 3 is medium shade, and 4 is dense shade, both of which are described as deep shade in the Encyclopedia charts. For complete definitions of these categories, refer back to pages 46–48.

This shaded spot makes a cool, inviting retreat for relaxing on a hot summer day—an asset to any garden.

Plants for Very Deep Shade

Botanical Name	Foliage/Flower Color	Type of Plant
Asarum species	Deep green/brown	Ground cover
Aucuba japonica	Variegated/red berries	Shrub
Bergenia cordifolia	Light green/pink	Ground cover
Browallia speciosa	Deep green/blue, white	Annual
Clivia miniata	Med. green/orange	Perennial
Digitalis purpurea and hybrids	Med. green/yellow, buff, purple, white, pink	Perennial
Dryopteris	Med. green	Fern
Epimedium species	Med. green/white, pink, yellow	Ground cover
Fatsia japonica	Tropical appearance	Shrub
Gaultheria procumbens	Deep green/white; red berries	Ground cover
Hedera species	Lt.–deep green, yellow, white	Ground cover
Hosta species	Deep green/blue, white	Perennial
Hydrangea macrophylla	Lt. green/white, pink, red, violet, blue	Shrub
Impatiens wallerana	Med. green/mauve, pink, orange, white, red, rose, salmon	Annual
Kerria japonica	Lt. green/yellow	Shrub
Leucothoe fontanesiana	Bronze new growth, variegated	Shrub
Mertensia virginica	Deep green/violet, blue	Perennial
Mimulus species	Deep green/yellow, maroon	Annual
Pachysandra terminalis	Lt.–med. green/white	Ground cover
Pittosporum tobira	Dark green/white	Shrub
Polygonatum species	Med. green/white	Perennial
Polystichum species	Med. green	Fern
Pulmonaria saccharata	Deep green/all colors, bicolor	Perennial
Sarcococca ruscifolia	Med. green/white/blue berries	Shrub
Soleirolia soleirolii	Lt. green	Ground cover
Taxus species	Deep blue-green needles/red berries	Shrub

Plants for Very Deep Shade

Botanical Name	Foliage/Flower Color	Type of Plant
Torenia fournieri	Med. green/blue, yellow, violet	Annual
Tradescantia virginiana	Deep green/white, pink, blue, magenta, purple	Perennial

Annuals for Shade

Botanical Name	Flower Color	Shade Tolerance
Begonia × semperflorens-cultorum	White, pink, rose, red	1–3
Browallia speciosa	Blue, white	1–4
Campanula medium	Blue, pink, white	1, 2
Clarkia species (Godetias)	Pink, salmon, red, white	1, 2
Coleus hybrids	Blue; foliage red, purple, yellow	1–3
Impatiens balsamina	Red, pink, white	1
Impatiens wallerana	Mauve, pink, orange, white, rose, salmon, red, magenta	1–4
Mimulus species	Yellow, maroon	1–4
Myosotis sylvatica	Sky blue	1–3
Nicotiana alata	White, lime, pink, deep rose	1–3
Nierembergia hippomanica	Blue	1, 2
Salvia splendens	Red, white	1, 2
Torenia fournieri	Blue, violet, yellow	1–4
Viola hybrids	All colors	1–3

'Tangeglow', 'Superelfin Blush', and 'Futura Wild Rose' *Impatiens* from top to bottom.

Clivia miniata brightens up a shady spot.

Perennials for Shade

Botanical Name	Flower Color	Shade Tolerance
Acanthus mollis	White	1–3
Agapanthus species	White, blue	1–3
Anemone species	White, pink, red, purple, blue	1, 2
Aquilegia species and hybrids	All colors and combinations	1, 2
Aruncus dioicus	Ivory white	1, 2
Astilbe hybrids	White, pink, red	1–3
Brunnera macrophylla	Sky blue	1, 2
Caltha palustris	Yellow	1, 2
Chrysogonum virginianum	Yellow	1, 2
Cimicifuga racemosa	White	1
Clivia miniata	Orange	1–4
Dicentra species	Rose pink	1–3
Digitalis species and hybrids	Yellow, buff, purple, white, pink	1–4
Doronicum cordatum	Yellow	1, 2
Echinacea purpurea	Purple	1, 2
Helleborus niger	White	1, 2
Hemerocallis species and hybrids	Yellow, orange, red, pink	1, 2
Hosta species	Blue, white	1–4
Iris kaempferi	Blue, violet, white	1, 2
Ligularia dentata	Yellow	1, 2
Liriope species	Blue, white	1–3
Lobelia cardinalis	Crimson	1, 2
Mertensia virginica	Violet/blue	1–4
Ophiopogon japonicus	Blue	1–3
Polygonatum species	White	1–4
Primula species	All colors, some bicolor	1–3
Pulmonaria saccharata	Blue, silver-spotted foliage	1–4
Rehmannia elata	Rose-violet, spotted	1, 2
Tradescantia virginiana	White, pink, magenta, purple, blue	1–4
Trillium species	White, pink, maroon	1–3
Trollius europaeus	Yellow	1–3

Bulbs and Bulblike Plants for Shade

Botanical Name	Flower Color	Shade Tolerance
Begonia × *tuberhybrida*	White, yellow, bronze, pink, orange	1–3
Caladium hybrids	Foliage red, pink, white	1–3
Convallaria majalis	White, pink	1–3
Cyclamen species	White, pink	1, 2
Erythronium species	Yellow, pink, white	1–3
Fritillaria meleagris	Cream, maroon	1, 2
Leucojum species	White	1
Scilla	Blue, purple, pink, white	1, 2

Understory Trees

Botanical Name	Foliage/Flower Color	Shade Tolerance
Acer palmatum	Green	1, 2
Aesculus species	White, deep rose	1–3
Cercis species	Pink	1, 2
Cornus florida	White, pink	1
Hamamelis × *intermedia*	Yellow	1, 2
Ligustrum species	White	1–3
Tsuga canadensis	Brown cones	1

Kurume azaleas, boxwood, and dogwoods in bloom.

Flowering Shrubs for Shade

Botanical Name	Flower Color	Shade Tolerance
Abelia × *grandiflora*	Pinkish-white	1–3
Aesculus parviflora	White	1–3
Aesculus pavia	Red (deep rose)	1–3
Camellia japonica	White, pink, red	1–3
Camellia sasanqua	White, pink, red	1, 2
Clethra alnifolia	White	1, 2
Fuchsia species and hybrids	Red, pink, white, blue, purple	1–3
Hydrangea macrophylla	White, pink, red, violet, blue	1–4
Kalmia latifolia	Pink, white	1, 2
Kerria japonica	Yellow	1–4
Mahonia species	Yellow; blue berries	1–3
Pieris japonica	White, pink; red new growth	1–3
Rhododendron species and hybrids	All colors	1–3
Sarcococca ruscifolia	White; blue berries	1–4

Foliage Shrubs for Shade

Botanical Name	Height/Point of Interest	Shade Tolerance
Aucuba japonica	To 6'/brilliant variegation/red berries	1–4
Buxus sempervirens	To 10'/excellent for formal training	1–3
Calycanthus floridus	To 10'/fragrant maroon flowers	1, 2
Chamaecyparis species	To 5'/most elegant in habit	1, 2
Euonymus fortunei	To 2'/some with variegated foliage	1–3
Fatsia japonica	To 15'/tropical appearance	1–4
Gaultheria shallon	To 5'/red berries, white flowers	1–4
Ilex species	To 20'/red berries	1–3
Leucothoe fontanesiana	To 5'/bronze new growth; variegated	1–4
Ligustrum species	To 25'/white flowers if unpruned	1–3
Nandina domestica	To 8'/red-bronze foliage	1–3

Ajuga reptans.

Osmanthus species	To 10'/insignificant but fragrant flowers	1–3
Pittosporum tobira	To 10'/white flowers, orange berries	1–4
Taxus species	To 50'/deep blue-green needles, red berries	1–4
Vaccinium ovatum	To 12'/small white flowers, blue berries	1–3

Ground Covers for Shade

Botanical Name	Foliage/Flower Color	Shade Tolerance
Ajuga reptans	Variegated, green, bronze/blue	1–3
Asarum caudatum	Deep green/brown	1–4
Bergenia cordifolia	Light green/pink	1–4
Convallaria majalis	Deep green/white	1–3
Cornus canadensis	Deep green/white/red berries	1, 2
Duchesnea indica	Med. green/yellow/red berries	1–3
Epimedium species	Med. green/white, pink, yellow	1–4
Euonymus fortunei	Deep green, variegated	1–3
Festuca ovina glauca	Silvery blue	1, 2
Fragaria chiloensis	Deep green/white	1, 2
Gaultheria procumbens	Deep green/white/red berries	1–4
Hakonechloa macra	Variegated creamy white	1, 2
Hedera species	Deep–lt. green, yellow, white	1–4
Hosta species	All shades, variegated/white, blue	1–4
Liriope species	Yellow or white variegation/blue, white	1–3
Mahonia repens	Deep green, bronze/yellow	1–3

Mentha requienii	Light green/pink	1, 2
Ophiopogon japonicus	Deep green/blue	1–3
Pachysandra terminalis	Med.–lt. green/white	1–4
Pratia angulata	Med. green/white/violet berries	1–3
Sagina subulata	Lt. or dark green/white	1, 2
Soleirolia soleirolii	Lt. green	1–4
Vancouveria hexandra	Med. green/white	1–3
Vinca minor	Deep green/blue	1–3

Pratia angulata	Ground cover	1–3
Sarcococca ruscifolia	Shrub	1–4
Tradescantia virginiana	Perennial	1–4
Vinca minor	Ground cover	1–3

Shade-Tolerant Plants for Dry Spots

Botanical Name	Type	Shade Tolerance
Acanthus mollis	Perennial	1–3
Aucuba japonica	Shrub	1–4
Bergenia cordifolia	Ground cover	1–4
Cercis canadensis	Tree	1, 2
Cornus canadensis	Ground cover	1, 2
Duchesnea indica	Ground cover	1–3
Euonymus fortunei	Shrub or ground cover	1–3
Festuca ovina glauca	Grass	1, 2
Hemerocallis species and hybrids	Herbaceous perennial	1, 2
Kerria japonica	Shrub or vine	1–4
Ligustrum species	Shrub or tree	1–3
Mahonia species	Shrub or ground cover	1–3
Nierembergia hippomanica	Annual	1, 2
Polygonatum commutatum	Perennial	1–4

Shade-Tolerant Plants for Wet Spots

Botanical Name	Type	Shade Tolerance
Aesculus species	Shrub or tree	1–3
Aruncus dioicus	Perennial	1, 2
Asarum species	Ground cover	1–4
Astilbe species and hybrids	Perennial	1–3
Caltha palustris	Perennial	1, 2
Calycanthus species	Shrub	1, 2
Clethra alnifolia	Shrub	1, 2
Convallaria majalis	Perennial	1–3
Doronicum cordatum	Perennial	1, 2
Hemerocallis species and hybrids	Perennial	1, 2
Hosta species	Perennial	1–4
Ilex species	Shrub or tree	1–3
Iris kaempferi	Perennial	1, 2
Ligularia dentata	Perennial	1, 2
Lobelia cardinalis	Perennial	1, 2
Mahonia species	Shrub	1–3
Mertensia virginica	Perennial	1–4
Mimulus species and hybrids	Annual	1–4
Myosotis sylvatica	Annual	1–3
Pulmonaria saccharata	Perennial	1–4
Soleirolia soleirolii	Ground cover	1–4
Tradescantia virginiana	Perennial	1–4

Hosta sieboldiana.

Alcea rosea from *Flora Graeca*, vol. 7, tabula 662.

Annuals

To most gardeners annuals mean flowers, and lots of them—in every conceivable shape, color, and size. There are many flowering plants for garden use, but as a group, none is so willing to grow, easy to take care of, or inexpensive as the annuals.

The word *annual* is common enough; yet when it is used to describe a group of garden plants, few people could give you an exact definition. The key to the definition is in the word itself: Annual means yearly, and annual plants are those that complete their entire cycle within one year or less. Their pattern of growth is illustrated each year in the garden: They are usually planted in the spring, flower through summer and fall, and die with the first frosts in winter. Annuals are temporary plants, as opposed to permanent plantings of trees, shrubs, vines, and ground covers, but their brief stay is a brilliant one, making them among the most popular of all plant choices.

Other Flowering Plants

Flowering plants (excluding the woody shrubs and trees) are generally broken into three groups according to their life cycles: annuals, perennials, and biennials. Annuals, as we have mentioned, are temporary plants that live out their lives within one year. In all but a few cases in which they reseed themselves, new annuals must be planted each year.

Perennials, on the other hand, are more or less permanent plants in the garden. The stems and leaves may die back during the cold winter months, but the roots remain alive and send forth new and bigger plants each spring. If you are interested in knowing more about perennials, see Chapter 4, pages 83–107.

The third classification—biennials—tends to confuse most gardeners. Biennials are plants that take two years, or two growth periods, to complete their life cycle: The first year they grow from seed into a leafy plant; the second year they flower, set seed, and die. What is confusing is that many biennials, such as foxglove, sweet William, and money plant, are usually purchased as started plants in the nursery. In effect, the grower has taken care of the first phase of the biennial's life, and the gardener sees only the second phase, in which the plant flowers and dies at the end of the growing season in the same fashion as the annuals.

In favorable climates, some perennials and biennials will grow from seed to flower in a single growing season. These plants may be treated as annuals, and for that reason are included in this chapter.

Iceland poppies are biennials that are commonly grown as annuals.

Hardy, Half-Hardy, and Tender

Throughout this chapter we will refer to an annual as being
hardy, half-hardy, or tender. These categories refer to the
temperature ranges that various annuals need to germinate
(sprout from seed) and grow successfully. A plant's hardiness
refers not to its general strength or vigor, but to its specific
ability to withstand cold.

Hardy annuals can stand the most cold of all, taking light
frosts without being killed or badly damaged. The seedlings of
young plants of half-hardy annuals can tolerate long periods
of damp or cold weather, but can be damaged or killed by frost.
Most tender annuals are native to countries with mild climates.
They need warm soil to germinate, and usually a fairly long,
warm summer to produce the best display of flowers.

In addition to being vulnerable to cold, some tender annuals
cannot withstand periods of extremely hot or humid weather. In
the South and in low-elevation areas of the West, most tender
annuals "burn out" in midsummer. Successive plantings are
necessary to sustain full color throughout the summer. See
pages 80–81 for lists of hardy, half-hardy, and tender annuals.

Named Varieties

Beginning gardeners are often content simply to know the
common name of the annual, such as marigold or petunia. But
as you garden from one year to the next, you'll soon find that
one named variety outperforms another, and from that point
you'll be on a "first-name basis" with several members of a
particular group of annuals, asking for 'Royal Blue' alyssum or
'Queen of Hearts' dianthus, for example, instead of simply
for dianthus or alyssum.

Botanically speaking, there are two different groups of
varieties: Those that occur naturally in the wild are called
horticultural varieties, and those that are produced under controlled conditions by plant breeders are known as cultivated
varieties (frequently combined and shortened to "cultivars").
However, this technical distinction matters little to the home
gardener, whose main concern is to become familiar enough
with all the available varieties to know which ones will grow
best. As you are probably already aware, there are thousands
of named varieties of annuals. An organization known as the
All-America Selections does some of the experimenting and
comparing for you, making the job of choosing one named variety over another a little easier.

All-America Selections evaluates new vegetable and flower

varieties introduced by seed companies, universities, and private individuals. Some fifty official test gardens located throughout the United States and Canada are evaluated yearly by a council of judges.

The judges pay special attention to each entry's climatic adaptation, vigor, and length of blooming season. With test gardens in the different climates of the United States and Canada, the home gardener can be sure an All-America Selection is not only the best in its class, but is also adapted to a wide range of soils, climates, and cultural practices.

Above: During the growing season, the grounds of this large seed company are bright with many varieties of petunias and other annuals. Development of top-quality, new cultivars requires extensive and repeated testing. Left: A named cultivar such as *Helichrysum* 'Jewelled Mix' is the result of much testing.

This colorful, striking, mixed border contains forget-me-nots, English daisies, primroses, and tulips. Planting a mixed border requires a bit more planning and maintenance, but the resulting floral variety and changing foliage colors and textures are well worth the extra effort.

Designing Annuals with Other Plants

A border or bed planted entirely with annuals is rare. Because they are not permanent plants, gardeners usually combine annuals with other, more permanent specimens so that there will be something of interest all year.

Some of the most beautiful flower gardens include annuals and perennials or annuals and spring-flowering bulbs in the same bed. Both perennials and bulbs put on a spectacular show of blossoms—often in colors or forms not found in annuals. By combining the three, then, you not only lengthen the overall period of bloom but also create a scene rich in contrasting flower and foliage forms and expand the possibilities for color combinations.

Annuals As Fillers and Screens

There are many situations, especially in the making of new landscapes, in which nothing can fill the bill quite like annuals. If you've moved into a new house and just finished the initial landscaping, the garden is liable to look a little bare for the first year or two. In this case, annuals are indispensable. For a nominal investment, you can fill in among immature shrubs and trees with color spots of annuals and bring about a big improvement in a short time.

One of the most often overlooked plants for quick color are the annual flowering vines. For the most part, they grow at an almost unbelievable rate: the old-fashioned morning glory, the scarlet runner bean, and the sweet-scented moonflower (*Calonyction aculeatum*) can, under the right conditions, grow anywhere from eight to twenty-five feet in a single season.

As temporary screens against fences or shade-providers covering arbors or trellises, flowering vines are unequaled. In hot climates, some gardeners even save home cooling costs by using these vines to screen south and west windows. They can be planted alone or in combination with slower growing but more permanent vines.

Annuals in Containers

Annuals and containers were made for each other. Their fast and easy growth, glamorous display of color, and low cost make them an obvious choice for containers.

There need never be a dull season when you have a few pots of colorful flowers clustered around the door or the patio, or lining a walk. Although it's true that annuals are usually spring- and summer-flowering plants, it's easy to extend color into other seasons by planting them along with bulbs and perennials readily available at the nursery.

Experienced container gardeners favor containers in the larger sizes: The bigger they are, the more soil they will hold, which means less frequent watering for the gardener, more root space for the plants, and more chance to experiment with different combinations of flowering plants.

Choosing Annuals for Containers

When it comes time to pick out plants for your containers, there are some important points to keep in mind.

To get the most from your effort, choose annuals with the longest blooming periods.

Choose plants with a compact habit, those that do not need staking. (Of course, you can stake tall-growing annuals in

These sun-loving annuals are planted in shallow, but roomy, clay containers. Cockscomb, ageratum, marigolds, and geranium plants (often grown as annuals) bring summery color to this side patio, and the containers can be moved easily to other areas.

containers, but most gardeners find it a nuisance and look for lower-growing varieties of those plants.)

Plan to crowd the plants closer together than you would in the garden. Crowding gives a lush, full effect; but compensate for crowding by watering and feeding more often.

Decide whether you want flowers of all one kind in the container, or a few different kinds to create a living bouquet. The best bouquet plantings combine several different colors and plant forms. Plant an upright form, a bushy form, and a couple of trailing ones together, and in a few weeks you'll have the diversity of an old-fashioned garden, in miniature. An upright zinnia, a bushy marigold, and trailing lobelia makes a pleasing combination.

Container Basics

You can fill containers with garden soil, provided it is of good quality with excellent drainage properties; but keep in mind that whatever problems you've had growing plants in your garden soil will only intensify if you use that soil in containers, especially in the smaller pots. Repeated waterings tend to compact soil in containers to the point that there may be very little air space left, greatly slowing drainage. If your soil is marginally acceptable, you can improve it by mixing it in equal proportions with an organic soil amendment such as peat moss, compost, or ground-bark soil conditioner—to make a lighter, looser growing medium that is more conducive to growing plants in confined quarters. If your soil is downright poor, however, you'll make life easier by using one of the packaged soils sold under a variety of brand names.

If you're planting in clay pots, be sure to hose them down a couple of times to let some water soak in. Clay is very porous and will rob newly planted annuals of their first watering if not first allowed to absorb some water of its own. Cover the drainage holes (but don't completely block them) with broken pieces of pottery, irregularly shaped stones, or best of all, a small piece of fine-mesh screen.

Before planting in any container, thoroughly water the soil mass and allow it to settle. After settling, the soil should be one to three inches below the rim of the container, depending upon its size. There should be enough space between the rim and the soil so that one application of water will moisten the root-ball and drain all the way through. If the container is filled with too much soil, watering becomes a time-consuming and aggravating job. Several applications are required to ensure that the planter receives a complete soaking.

Petunias do not tolerate heavy, wet soil. The soil mix used here is light and drains well, yet retains enough water so that the container doesn't need constant watering.

These whimsical containers are planted with some flowers that are changed seasonally, such as marigolds, petunias, geraniums, and lobelia. They are carefully replaced so as not to disturb the perennials growing in the container.

Never apply water to container plants in a hard, unbroken stream. To protect surface roots and to keep the soil from splashing out, it's best to use a nozzle or water breaker that softens the flow to a gentle, rainlike pattern.

When you pick up healthy plants at the nursery, chances are they will continue to grow well, especially if you transplant them carefully and give them proper care. It is often in the first few days of ownership that plants are mishandled.

Watering and Feeding

Because of the limited amount of soil available to them, plants in containers need more attention than plants in the ground. In the hot summer months, daily watering is a common need, especially if the containers receive full sun. Since these repeated waterings leach nutrients out of the soil rather quickly, most container gardeners apply liquid fertilizers at half strength every two weeks, rather than full strength monthly, to compensate for this loss.

To keep container specimens looking their best, be sure to pinch off any dead flowers or leaves regularly.

Annuals in Hanging Baskets

There was a time when hanging baskets generally appealed to two types of gardeners: One was simply fascinated with hanging and trailing plants; the other had so little ground space that hanging baskets were one of the few ways to have some flowering color. While hanging baskets are the best way to display plants with a trailing habit, they are no longer limited to those varieties alone. The moss-lined wire basket has made it possible to grow almost any annual, no matter what its habit, as a hanging display.

Growing annuals in hanging baskets is a special form of container gardening. The basics of soil, water, and fertilizers are the same, but, depending largely on what type of basket you choose, there are some special considerations. Hanging containers vary immensely. They range from clay and plastic pots to wooden containers of all shapes, wicker and bamboo baskets, and moss-lined wire baskets.

Once you hang any container made of a porous material (clay, wood, wicker, or moss), additional surface is exposed to air circulation, and the wind, sun, and dry air evaporate water from the soil faster than from a container on the ground. In very warm, dry, or windy areas of the country, flowers can sunburn or dry out in a matter of hours. Gardeners compensate somewhat by hanging the baskets in areas protected from wind and

These moss-lined, wire baskets are planted with red and white fibrous begonias, pink impatiens, and coleus—all annuals that thrive in dappled sun or bright shade. Moss baskets are unique in that the entire basket surface can be planted with flowers. They dry out quickly, ensuring that plants will not suffer from overwatering; but during hot summer days, they may need to be watered twice daily.

A Garden should always look bigger than it really is.

Alexandre Le Blond,
The Theory and Practice of Gardening

afternoon sun. Plastic containers do a better job of retaining soil moisture, but many people find them aesthetically unappealing and thus not altogether appropriate for garden display.

Because hanging baskets dry out so quickly, the main consideration as you plan a hanging garden is how to water them on a regular basis. One of the best ways is to take the container down and set it up to its rim in a bucket of water until it is thoroughly soaked through. If you use this method, make sure your planted containers are light in weight; otherwise, hanging them securely may be a problem, and lifting them up and down for watering can be a backbreaking task.

Moss-Lined Baskets   What makes the moss-lined wire basket stand out from other hanging containers is that the sides as well as the top can be planted. This makes it possible to plant almost any annual you desire for large, profuse displays of hanging color.

To keep the basket neat and in full color requires continuous grooming. Remove all spent flowers, prune off any shoots that stray, and fertilize and water regularly, the same as you do with other container plants. You'll find that a few hairpins come in handy for securing errant shoots and vines to the moss.

Annuals from Seed

Starting any plant from seed is an immensely satisfying experience. It's even more enjoyable with annuals because they are generally easy to start, not overly particular about growing conditions, and best of all, can produce spectacular results in just a short time.

Seed Catalogs

The catalogs seed companies put out each year can be a great source of inspiration, ideas, and information for gardeners of every level of experience. Catalogs featuring spring- and summer-flowering annuals are mailed in the fall and winter months to those who request them, usually in plenty of time to place and receive orders before the planting season. On a drab winter day, the arrival of a seed catalog filled with colorful pictures and remarkable descriptions can be just what the gardener needs: hope and enticement toward an even more beautiful garden in the months ahead.

General Tips

After you buy and plant seeds, it may seem wise to save the leftovers from one year to the next; but in fact it's better to go ahead and plant them all, or give the excess to a gardening friend. Although it's true that some seeds remain viable for many years, the cost of fresh, guaranteed seed is so low that it really isn't worth risking the time and effort for a poor stand of weak seedlings.

The rule of thumb is to plant twice as many seeds as you think you will need. Some seeds just won't germinate. Some seedlings will be weak and need to be thinned out, or simply won't make it through the transplanting procedure.

Five Ways to Start Seeds

Over the years, gardeners have developed favorite ways of starting plants from seeds. The methods we will discuss here are: direct seeding; planting seeds in ready-made peat pots and pellets; the two-step method; using a seed-starting kit with artificial lights and soil-heating units; and last, planting in cold frames and hotbeds.

These methods combine different degrees of sophistication and different materials, but they all employ the same principles; namely, they provide an environment in which the seeds can readily germinate and grow steadily to a transplantable size.

Direct Seeding

Direct seeding—planting seeds directly into the soil where they will grow—is the most basic of all seed-starting methods; it is also the easiest.

The first thing to do is to make sure your soil is adequately prepared. Amend it with organic matter if necessary, and if soil acidity or alkalinity is a problem in your area, correct the pH. (For instructions on soil conditioning, see Chapter 14, page 343.) But be forewarned: Even if you have quality garden soil in good condition, it still will not be as fine textured as the packaged soil mixes recommended for starting seeds indoors. What this means is that the seeds will have a little tougher time germinating and getting going, in addition to having to put up with a more rigorous environment. The percentage of germination won't be as high as indoors (expect around 60 percent), and you'll have the additional task of distinguishing flower seedlings from weeds.

After planting, press the seeds into the soil using the flat side of a small board or the back of a hoe. A small board also serves as a "portable path" to walk on, enabling you to avoid walking over a newly seeded area.

Once the seedlings have developed true leaves, be sure to thin

Adequate soil preparation is the key to direct seeding. Once the seeds sprout and the plants begin to grow, initial soil preparation pays off in vigorous and healthy plant growth. In this picture, seeds are gently tapped from the packet into a shallow furrow.

them to the spacing recommended on the seed package. It's best to be ruthless at this stage to prevent future overcrowding. Use a pair of scissors to snip off the unwanted plants, rather than trying to pull them out.

Pros and Cons of Direct Seeding   The advantages of direct seeding include: minimal tool and equipment requirements; no transplant shock and a tendency for the plants to grow a little faster than transplanted seedlings; and a house free of pots, trays, lights, and the other paraphernalia of indoor gardening.

Disadvantages of direct seeding include: advisable only for seeds of a manageable size (minute seeds need the extra attention indoor culture provides); greater loss of seedlings to the elements, animals, insects, and inclement weather; and, most important, the requirement for careful attention to timing.

Peat Planters

The easiest method of starting seeds indoors requires buying some commercial products, most of which are made of compressed peat. Peat pellets, cubes, and strips are not very expensive and are available at most nurseries and garden centers and from mail-order garden and seed catalogs.

The only materials needed are the seeds, an appropriate number of peat planters, and some type of waterproof tray. First, read the information on the back of the seed packet; this will tell you how deep to plant the seed, whether it needs light or darkness to germinate, and the approximate length of time it takes to germinate.

Arrange the peat planters in the tray and fill the tray with water. If you have purchased the compressed peat pellets, within a few minutes the pellets will absorb the water and expand into small, self-contained "pots."

The peat moss and other organic materials that comprise the pellets are held in place with a thin plastic netting, easily penetrated by the roots. When it comes time to plant the annuals in the garden, you simply put the rooted plant, pellet and all, into the ground.

After the peat planters have absorbed the water, place two or three seeds in the small depression in the top of the individual planters, cover (or don't cover) according to the directions on the seed packet, and place the tray where it will receive the warmth necessary for the seeds to germinate.

Light and Heat   Seeds that do not need to be covered with soil are those that need light to germinate. The light source can

Many gardeners start seeds in peat planters available in a variety of shapes and sizes. A major advantage of using them is that when seedlings are ready to be transplanted, the entire peat planter can be put directly into the ground.

be natural sunlight, for as many hours per day as possible, or fluorescent light at the rate of twenty watts per square foot of lighted area, placed two to six inches from the top of the pellets and left on for twenty-four hours a day until the seeds sprout. Seeds that sprout best at soil temperatures of 75°F and higher, such as coleus and impatiens, react favorably when light tubes are placed only two or three inches above the seed.

Seeds that need a covering of soil require darkness for germination. After sowing and moistening this seed, cover the tray with a few layers of newspaper to exclude light or place flats in a dark closet. Peek under the papers, or in the closet, occasionally. As soon as the first sprouts appear, place the tray under fluorescent lights or in a spot where it will receive direct sun. Remember, all seeds, covered or not, must be kept evenly moist throughout the germination period.

To germinate, all seeds need some heat in the soil, in varying amounts. If your seeds have a high germination temperature requirement, give them extra heat. Warmth can be provided by heating cables (available from seed and garden catalogs and some garden centers) or by lights above the seeds. When temperatures higher than the cables can provide are needed, a piece of clear plastic, formed around the tray and the light like a tent, will hold in the accumulated heat. Another method of providing higher temperatures is to place the plastic-covered tray on top of a refrigerator or freezer; the heat from the motor keeps this spot warm practically twenty-four hours a day. With either method, be sure to remove the plastic at the first sign of tiny seedlings, and place the tray where it will receive light.

If you have the tray under a twenty-four-hour light unit, reduce the light to fourteen hours a day after the seedlings have emerged. Raise the unit to about eight inches above the seedlings. If you are growing them on a windowsill with natural light, no change in the amount of light will be necessary, but remember that the seedlings will grow toward the light source, so turn the tray around every day. On cold nights or stormy days, place an insulating shield between the plants and the cold windowpanes. A couple of layers of cardboard will work nicely.

Snip off—don't pull—all but the single strongest seedling from each pellet. If you try to pull the unwanted ones out, you may pull all the seedlings out simply because their roots are so closely intertwined. Now all you have to do is keep the pellets moist, turn the tray around every day, and watch the seedlings grow. By the time the seedlings are a few inches tall and the roots have come through the sides of the pellets, it should be time to plant them in the garden.

This seedling, started in a peat pot, is ready for transplanting. Seedlings started indoors, such as this one, must be "hardened off" before they can be transplanted. Gradual exposure to outdoor conditions over a week's time is usually necessary.

Hardening Off   The final step before planting the seedlings in the garden is to harden them off. Hardening off is a gardening term for gradually acclimatizing the seedlings to the outdoor environment. Remember, up until now they have been growing in very protected surroundings. To place them directly outdoors in the cool spring weather would probably be more than they could tolerate. Place the tray of seedlings outdoors for a few hours each day in a semiprotected spot. Lengthen the amount of time they stay out each day by an hour or so, and by the end of a week's time, they'll be ready for planting outdoors.

When transplanting seedlings started in peat planters into the garden, set the plants deep enough to cover the top of the pellet, cube, or strip with about half an inch of soil. If the top of the peat planter sticks up above the soil, it will act as a wick and dry out the rootball.

The Two-Step Method

In the two-step method of germination, flats, trays, or pots are filled with a growing medium and the seeds are sown closely together; then, after they have germinated and matured a little, they are transplanted into individual containers to give the roots more room to grow. You can purchase pots, flats, soil mix, and other seed-starting accessories at garden centers and nurseries. Most gardeners, though, augment what's available at the store with "recycled" material at home: plastic containers of all kinds, clay pots, flats, plastic pots, and cell packs left over from previous plant purchases. Foil trays—anything that holds soil—can be used as seed-starting containers provided you can also poke holes into them for drainage. Whatever you decide to use, be sure to keep everything as clean as you can. Start seeds in sterile milled (pulverized) sphagnum moss, or use one of the many packaged soil mixes, which are more likely than garden soil to be free of diseases.

Punch holes for drainage, fill the flats and other containers with the soil mix, wet it thoroughly (warm water helps), and firm it down lightly to form a smooth, even surface. You can scatter the seeds over the surface, or plant them in rows. If you plant in rows, use the edge of a ruler or other straight instrument to make depressions in the soil. Sow the seeds thinly, tapping them out of the packet; or use one of the commercially available mechanical seed sowers for an even spread.

Expert gardeners use an effective material called milled sphagnum moss to cover seeds. It has the ability to greatly reduce losses of seeds and plants by discouraging harmful fungi in the soil. You can order milled sphagnum moss by mail from

The materials needed for the two-step method of starting seeds are shown here: a plastic flat with drainage holes; an appropriate growing medium that drains well; a ruler for making straight, even furrows; and of course, seeds. These nasturtium seeds will be transplanted into small containers after they have developed into seedlings.

seed company catalogs. Note: It is not the same as the peat moss commonly available in bags or bales.

Follow the instructions for germinating given in the peat planter method (page 68). Once the seeds have germinated and produced their second set of true leaves, they are ready to be transplanted into their own containers. This step requires a little patience and dexterity. A flat, pointed stick (like a small plant label), an old teaspoon or fork, or some similar instrument should be used to separate the seedlings from each other and to ease them from the soil. The packaged soil mixes are quite light and porous, making this an easier task.

Have the new containers filled with moist soil before you start to transplant, and don't let the seedlings dry out between the time you remove them from the flat and the time they are safely in the new containers. Use a light touch even when you firm the soil around the roots of seedlings, because it's easy to squeeze air from the soil, turning the rootball into a soggy, compacted medium.

Keep the transplanted seedlings growing in a well-lit area until it is time to plant them outdoors. Follow the same hardening-off procedure outlined on page 70.

Seed-Starting Kits

Seed-starting kits are available from many mail-order catalogs. They usually contain all the necessary items—soil mix, small pots, trays, labels, fertilizer, and heating cables—in various combinations. Kits are available for either the peat planter or the two-step method. For the novice these kits are an especially good investment; in subsequent years, however, most gardeners modify the procedure to fit their own needs and, in effect, assemble their own "kits."

Cold Frames and Hotbeds

Cold frames and hotbeds are devices that provide some protection for seedlings outdoors. They are handy in the sense that they take the whole process outside, leaving the house free of gardening clutter.

A cold frame is basically a bottomless wooden box placed on the ground and filled with a good-quality soil mix. The dimensions of the box are up to the individual, but the sides need not be taller than eight or ten inches. The essential part of a cold frame is some type of transparent or semitransparent cover. In the past, the most common covers were sash windows, and more often than not, the size of the cold frame was dictated by whatever extra windows were available. Windows are still perfectly acceptable covers, but several of the new rigid or film plastic products make unbreakable covers, which are desired by many gardeners.

A cold frame looks like a large, covered flat and a small greenhouse. The best place to build one is close to the house in a location that receives plenty of sun. The cover should be adjustable to admit varying degrees of fresh, cool air. The gardener can start seeds in a cold frame in the same way seeds are started indoors, but it takes a little experimentation to keep the temperature at the right level.

In cold-winter areas, cold frames work best for the early starting of hardy and half-hardy annuals. The temperatures inside a cold frame are usually insufficient to germinate and protect seedlings of the tender annuals.

A hotbed is a variation of a cold frame. The structure of the unit is the same, but before the frame is filled with soil, electric heating cables are installed so that the hotbed can be used in colder weather or during long periods when there is insufficient warmth from the sun.

With electric heating units, the temperature in a hotbed is easier to control than that in a cold frame. Gardeners in extremely cold winter climates find that they get more use out of a hotbed than out of a cold frame, because they are not as dependent on the sun to warm the soil.

Getting Plants into the Ground

Every year people who love to grow plants wait for certain special days. Marked not on any calendar, but in the hearts of gardeners everywhere, these days are as distinct and special as Easter or Thanksgiving. On certain days in early spring, the sun shines sweetly, the birds sing, and the slowly warming soil lies waiting to be worked. Anyone who's ever had good garden soil under his or her nails finds it difficult to resist the temptation to get out of doors, armed with a shovel and trowel, to plant yet another garden.

By now you have already purchased transplants of the annuals you want to grow or have the transplants you started from seed hardened off (see page 70) and ready for the garden.

Transplanting into the Garden

Prepare your planting bed before you begin transplanting; make sure the soil is properly amended, cultivated, and well watered. Pick out the healthiest, youngest plants available for transplanting; they're bound to be vigorous.

Starting out with healthy plants ensures vigorous growth later on. Shop carefully when purchasing plants: Check them for insects and diseases, and avoid plants with yellowing leaves. Shown below are healthy, vigorous plants and useful tools for gardening in containers and planting beds.

This bed of pansies and calendulas is in full bloom. Because foliage growth slows during this time, a "bloom" food, or fertilizer low in nitrogen and high in phosphorous and potassium, will encourage continued flowering.

Water transplants before you remove them from their containers. Ideally, the soil should be moist but not soggy. A moist rootball will not fall apart or stick to the edge of the container.

If you're planting from flats, pull the plants gently apart; don't cut them apart with a knife or similar sharp instrument. Don't squeeze the soil or you will compact it and trap the roots inside a tight ball of soil. Plants in packs or containers should be thoroughly watered and allowed to drain for five to ten minutes before you try to take them out; otherwise the soil may crumble away from the roots.

To remove transplants from cell packs and market packs, just squeeze the bottom of each cell to force the rootball above the lip of the pack. Pinch off any long, coiled bottom roots. Plant the seedlings slightly deeper than they were in the container, firm the soil lightly around them with your hands, and give them a thorough watering with a watering can or soft-spray nozzle attached to a hose.

By taking the plants out of their containers one by one, you'll avoid problems with the rootball drying out and the plants wilting excessively. Some wilting is natural immediately after planting, but you can minimize it by planting during the cooler parts of the day (morning or evening) or by planting on overcast days. Wind can sometimes cause more problems than sun; protect newly transplanted seedlings with newspaper hoods or commercially available hotcaps for a day or two.

Fertilizing

In general, annuals are fairly undemanding when it comes to fertilizing. Many successful gardens of annuals get by without any fertilizer at all, but conscientious gardeners know that a few well-timed applications of fertilizer will result in healthier, more robust plants, and in most cases, more flowers. Certainly, these are reasons for considering fertilizing.

Feed annuals with a well-balanced fertilizer when you transplant them. Some gardeners also apply vitamin B-1 when transplanting to counteract transplant shock. Vitamin B-1 is controversial—some gardeners swear by it; others feel it makes no difference to the success or failure of their transplants.

Most fast-growing, short-season annuals can make it through a complete growing season on one application of fertilizer. However, any check in growth caused by insufficient nutrients can reduce the quality of the plant and its blooms, so it's usually better to make more than one application during the growing season, using less than the recommended amount and a weaker dilution. Whenever dry fertilizer is used, follow its application

Zinnias thrive in hot summer weather, but are more likely to dry out during this time. These zinnias show the benefit of careful watering.

Tall-growing sweet peas require staking. Here, they are secured to a cone-shaped twig trellis that they will eventually cover. Sweet peas, like all other annuals, will not form many new flowers if faded blooms are not pinched off. A weekly clean-up walk through the garden—pinching off dead blooms—will improve the garden's appearance and extend the blooming period.

with a good watering. Liquid fertilizer is best applied to damp (not dry) soil. The need for nitrogen is greater for plants in full sun than for those growing in the shade.

If your plants are producing lots of lush, green growth but few flowers, apply a "bloom" fertilizer containing only phosphorus and potassium—no nitrogen.

Pinching, Staking, and Grooming

Pinching out annuals when they are young, staking tall-growing annuals, and keeping flowering plants tidy and free of spent blossoms are all important activities. Remember, an annual lives in order to produce seeds for the next generation of plants. All of its energies are directed to the task of producing flowers that eventually will produce seeds. If you "deadhead"—pick the mature flowers and seed pods from the plant—the plant will produce more flowers in an effort to ultimately produce seeds. This practice keeps annuals in the flowering stage longer, and usually results in a greater number of blossoms.

Beginners' Mistakes

The most common mistake made by gardeners in general is planting tender transplants in the garden before the climate and soil have warmed sufficiently. It's a good idea to resist those first temptations and wait until the spring season has really arrived, if you want the best results from tender and half-hardy annuals. It's important to remember that soil temperature is usually around 10°F lower than the temperature of the air—the weather itself may fool you into planting too early. You can check soil temperatures with a soil thermometer and make sure when to plant.

Another common mistake is skimping on or ignoring completely the job of conditioning the soil. Unless you already have good-quality loam, the importance of improving your soil before planting cannot be overstressed. Add plenty of organic matter. If you do this on a yearly basis, you can work miracles even on problem soils. All your gardening efforts will be for naught unless you take this important initial step.

Planting sun-loving annuals in the shade and shade-loving annuals in the sun are common errors. The plants never quite do what they are supposed to and you can't figure out why until, finally, you go back and read the recommendations on the seed packet or in a gardening manual. Read as much as you can about individual annuals before you plant them; you'll be much better equipped to provide for their needs.

A flower bed located in the corner of a garden can be easily enlarged every year by digging up part of the lawn. Starting off with a small plot and gradually enlarging it is a manageable technique for the novice gardener.

Planting seedlings too close together increases the incidence of disease and inhibits the overall vigor and flowering of the plants. Give the plants enough room to grow to their full size and you'll receive more flowers and fewer problems. The garden may look a little sparse the first few weeks after planting, but remember, annuals are fast-growing plants.

Failure to pull weeds when they are small causes all kinds of problems in the annual garden. Weeds compcte for sunlight, nutrients, and water, robbing the annuals of their rightful share. The larger the weeds are, the more difficult they are to remove, and the more likely you are to use a hoe to remove them. If you must use a hoe or another sharp-bladed tool, respect the shallow roots of your annuals by chopping out weeds with short, shallow strokes. If you apply a mulch, as described in Chapter 14, page 359, many of your weed problems will disappear.

Planting taller-growing varieties of annuals in front of short ones not only blocks your view of the short varieties, but also throws the bed or border out of proportion. Granted, there are times when a plant grows larger or smaller than printed estimates, but more often than not it is the result of an oversight on the part of the gardener. The simple remedy is to know what to expect of your plants before you put them in the ground.

Beginning gardeners often complain that they started out too big the first year, and planted more than they could realistically take care of. It's far better to plant a reasonable-size garden the first year or two and gradually work into larger spaces.

Bringing Annuals Indoors

In some areas of the country with exceptionally mild winters, many annuals will continue to grow through the seasons. In areas with more severe winters, the first hard frost usually does a complete job of killing them to the ground. Some annuals, though, will respond well to being potted and brought indoors before the first frost. If placed in a location with plenty of light, cut back, and fertilized, these can reward the gardener with winter blooms until short days and the dry heat of the house make them decline.

When the weather warms the following spring, the overwintered plants can be returned to the outdoors, to grow on in containers or even be transplanted into the ground.

To keep it blooming as long as possible before the first fall frosts, this zinnia-filled container has been moved to a warm, protected spot receiving lots of direct sun.

An Annuals Inventory: Selected Lists

For that special purpose, problem, or form, the lists that follow will help you identify annuals that will meet your needs. Refer to the Encyclopedia charts, pages 377–499, for additional information on those plants that interest you. Remember that a plant's appearance on a certain list doesn't mean that all varieties necessarily fit that category. In many cases only selected varieties match the description.

Dahlia hybrid.

Annuals with Yellow, Orange, and Bronze Flowers

Alcea rosea (Hollyhock)
Antirrhinum majus (Snapdragon)
Calendula officinalis (Pot marigold)
Celosia cristata (Cockscomb)
Coreopsis tinctoria (Calliopsis)
Cosmos sulphureus (Orange cosmos)
Dahlia hybrids (Dahlia)
Dimorphotheca sinuata (Cape marigold)
Dyssodia tenuiloba (Dahlberg daisy)
Eschscholzia californica (California poppy)
Gaillardia pulchella (Blanket flower)
Gazania rigens (Gazania)
Gerbera jamesonii (Transvaal daisy)
Gomphrena globosa (Globe amaranth)
Helianthus species (Sunflower)
Impatiens balsamina (Balsam)
Lathyrus odorata (Sweet pea)
Limonium bonduellii (Algerian sea lavender)
Linaria maroccana (Toadflax)
Matthiola incana (Stock)
Mimulus × *hybridus* (Monkey flower)
Nemesia strumosa (Pouch nemesia)
Papaver species (Poppy)
Pelargonium × *hortorum* (Geranium)
Portulaca grandiflora (Rose moss)
Rudbeckia hirta var. *pulcherrima* 'Gloriosa Daisy' (Gloriosa daisy)
Sanvitalia procumbens (Creeping zinnia)
Tagetes species (Marigolds)

Thunbergia alata (Black-eyed Susan vine)
Tithonia rotundifolia (Mexican sunflower)
Tropaeolum majus (Nasturtium)
Verbena × *hybrida* (Garden verbena)
Viola × *wittrockiana* (Pansy)
Zinnia species (Zinnia)

Annuals with Cream to White Flowers

Ageratum houstanianum (Floss flower)
Alcea rosea (Hollyhock)
Antirrhinum majus (Snapdragon)
Arctotis stoechadifolia var. *grandis* (African daisy)
Begonia × *semperflorens-cultorum* (Wax-leaf begonia)
Callistephus chinensis (China aster)

Catharanthus roseus (Madagascar periwinkle)
Cleome hasslerana (Spider flower)
Dahlia hybrids (Dahlia)
Dianthus species (China pink; Sweet William)
Dimorphotheca sinuata (Cape marigold)
Eschscholzia californica (California poppy)
Gerbera jamesonii (Transvaal daisy)
Gypsophila elegans (Annual baby's breath)
Helichrysum bracteatum (Strawflower)
Iberis species (Candytuft)
Impatiens balsamina (Balsam)
Impatiens wallerana (Busy Lizzie; Impatiens)
Ipomea alba (Moonflower vine)
Lathyrus odorata (Sweet pea)
Lobelia erinus (Edging lobelia)
Lobularia maritima (Sweet alyssum)
Matthiola incana (Stock)
Nicotiana alba (Flowering tobacco)
Papaver species (Poppy)
Pelargonium × *hortorum* (Geranium)
Petunia × *hybrida* (Petunia)
Phlox drummondii (Annual phlox)
Salvia splendens (Scarlet sage)
Scabiosa atropurpurea (Pincushion flower)
Thunbergia alata (Black-eyed Susan vine)
Verbena × *hybrida* (Garden verbena)
Viola × *wittrockiana* (Pansy)

Moss basket planted with *Impatiens wallerana*.

Dianthus 'Baby Doll'.

Annuals with Red to Pink Flowers

Alcea rosea (Hollyhock)
Amaranthus species (Jacob's coat; Love-lies-bleeding)
Antirrhinum majus (Snapdragon)
Begonia × semperflorens-cultorum (Wax-leaf begonia)
Callistephus chinensis (China aster)
Capsicum annuum (Ornamental pepper)
Catharanthus roseus (Madagascar periwinkle)
Celosia cristata (Cockscomb)
Clarkia hybrids (Godetia; Farewell-to-spring)
Cleome hasslerana (Spider flower)
Coleus × hybridus (Coleus)
Consolida ambigua (Rocket larkspur)
Cosmos bipinnatus (Mexican aster)
Cuphea ignea (Mexican cigar plant)
Dahlia hybrids (Dahlia)
Dianthus species (China pink; Sweet William)
Dimorphotheca sinuata (Cape marigold)
Eschscholzia californica (California poppy)
Gaillardia pulchella (Blanket flower)
Gazania rigens (Gazania)
Gerbera jamesonii (Transvaal daisy)
Gypsophila elegans (Annual baby's breath)
Helichrysum bracteatum (Strawflower)
Iberis species (Candytuft)

Impatiens species (Balsam; Impatiens)
Ipomea × multifida (Cardinal climber)
Ipomea quamoclit (Cypress vine)
Lathyrus odorata (Sweet pea)
Lavatera hybrids (Tree mallow)
Linaria maroccana (Toadflax)
Matthiola incana (Stock)
Mimulus × hybridus (Monkey flower)
Nemesia strumosa (Pouch nemesia)
Nicotiana alba (Flowering tobacco)
Nigella damascena (Love-in-a-mist)
Papaver species (Poppy)
Pelargonium × hortorum (Geranium)
Petunia × hybrida (Petunia)
Phlox drummondii (Annual phlox)
Portulaca grandiflora (Rose moss)
Rhynchelytrum roseum (Ruby grass)
Salpiglossis sinuata (Painted tongue)
Salvia splendens (Scarlet sage)
Scabiosa atropurpurea (Pincushion flower)
Schizanthus × wisetonensis (Poor man's orchid)
Tropaeolum majus (Nasturtium)
Verbena × hybrida (Garden verbena)
Viola × wittrockiana (Pansy)
Zinnia elegans (Zinnia)

Centaurea cyanus.

Annuals with Blue, Violet, and Purple Flowers

Ageratum houstanianum (Floss flower)
Anchusa capensis (Cape forget-me-not)
Browallia speciosa (Sapphire flower)
Callistephus chinensis (China aster)
Campanula medium (Canterbury bells)
Centauria cyanus (Bachelor button)
Consolida ambigua (Rocket larkspur)
Convolvulus tricolor (Dwarf morning glory)

Cynoglossum amabile (Chinese forget-me-not)
Gomphrena globosa (Globe amaranth)
Heliotropium arborescens (Heliotrope)
Ipomea leptophylla (Bush morning glory)
Ipomea nil; I. purpurea; I. tricolor (Morning glory)
Lathyrus odorata (Sweet pea)
Limonium sinuatum (Notch-leaf sea lavender)
Lobelia erinus (Edging lobelia)
Myosotis sylvatica (Forget-me-not)
Nemophila menziesii (Baby blue eyes)
Nierembergia hippomanica (Cup flower)
Nigella damascena (Love-in-a-mist)
Petunia × hybrida (Petunia)
Salpiglossis sinuata (Painted tongue)
Salvia farinacea (Blue sage)
Salvia splendens (Scarlet sage)
Scabiosa atropurpurea (Pincushion flower)
Torenia fourneri (Wishbone flower)
Trachymene coerulea (Blue lace flower)
Verbena × hybrida (Garden verbena)
Viola × wittrockiana (Pansy)

Hardy Annuals

These frost-tolerant annuals can be sown outdoors in very early spring.

Arctotis stoechadifolia var. *grandis* (African daisy)
Brassica coerula (Ornamental cabbage and kale; best sown in summer for fall display)
Calendula officinalis (Pot marigold)
Centauria cyanus (Bachelor button)
Cheiranthus cheiri (Wallflower)
Clarkia hybrids (Godetia; Farewell-to-spring; tolerates light frosts)
Consolida ambigua (Larkspur)
Cynoglossum amabile (Chinese forget-me-not)
Eschscholzia californica (California poppy)
Grasses:
   Agrostis nebulosa (Cloud grass)
   Avena sterilis (Animated oats)
   Briza maxima (Quaking grass)
   Lagurus ovatus (Hare's tail grass)
Gypsophila elegans (Baby's breath)
Lathyrus odorata (Sweet pea)
Lavatera hybrids (Tree mallow)
Linaria maroccana (Toadflax)
Lobularia maritima (Sweet alyssum)
Nemophila menziesii (Baby blue eyes)
Nigella damascena (Love-in-a-mist)
Papaver nudicaule (Iceland poppy)
Papaver rhoeas (Field poppy)
Phlox drummondii (Annual phlox)
Reseda odorata (Mignonette)
Viola × wittrockiana (Pansy)

Tagetes patula.

Half-Hardy Annuals (Outdoor Sowing)

These annuals are easy to sow directly into the ground outdoors, but should not be sown until all danger of frost has passed.

Catharanthus roseus (Madagascar periwinkle)
Convolvulus tricolor (Dwarf morning glory)
Coreopsis tinctoria (Calliopsis)
Cosmos bipinnatus (Mexican aster)
Cosmos sulphureous (Orange cosmos)
Dianthus barbatus (Sweet William)
Dianthus chinensis (China pink)
Euphorbia marginata (Snow-on-the-mountain)
Helianthus species (Sunflower)
Iberis species (Candytuft)
Ipomea species (Morning glory; Cardinal vine; Cypress vine)
Mirabilis jalapa (Four o'clock)
Nicotiana alba (Flowering tobacco)
Portulaca grandiflora (Rose moss)
Ricinus communis (Castor bean)
Sanvitalia procumbens (Creeping zinnia)
Scabiosa atropurpurea (Pincushion flower)
Tagetes patula (French marigold)
Trachymene coerulea (Blue lace flower)
Tropaeolum majus (Nasturtium)
Zea mays var. *japonica* (Ornamental corn)
Zinnia species (Zinnia)

Half-Hardy Annuals (Indoor Sowing)

These annuals are best when started ahead indoors.

Ageratum houstonianum (Floss flower)
Alcea rosea (Hollyhock)
Amaranthus caudatus (Love-lies-bleeding)
Amaranthus tricolor (Jacob's coat)
Anchusa capensis (Cape forget-me-not)
Antirrhinum majus (Snapdragon)
Arctotis stoechidifolia var. *grandis* (African daisy)
Begonia × semperflorens-cultorum (Wax-leaf begonia)
Brachycome iberidifolia (Swan river daisy)
Browallia speciosa (Sapphire flower)
Callistephus chinensis (China aster)
Campanula medium (Canterbury bells)
Capsicum annuum (Ornamental pepper)
Catharanthus roseus (Madagascar periwinkle)
Celosia cristata (Cockscomb)
Cleome hasslerana (Spider flower)
Coleus × hybridus (Coleus)
Consolida ambigua (Larkspur)
Coreopsis tinctoria (Calliopsis)
Cosmos bipinnatus (Mexican aster)
Cosmos sulphureous (Orange cosmos)
Cuphea ignea (Firecracker plant)
Dahlia hybrids (Dahlia)
Dianthus barbatus (Sweet William)
Dianthus chinensis (China pink)
Dimorphotheca sinuata (Cape marigold)
Dyssodia tenuiloba (Dahlberg daisy)
Euphorbia marginata (Snow-on-the-mountain)
Gaillardia pulchella (Blanket flower)
Gazania rigens (Gazania)
Gerbera jamesonii (Transvaal daisy)
Gomphrena globosa (Globe amaranth)
Grasses:
 Coix lacryma-jobi (Job's tears)
 Pennisetum setaceum (Crimson fountain grass)
 Rhynchlytrum roseum (Ruby grass)
 Setaria macrostachya (Plains bristle grass)

Gerbera jamesonii.

Helichrysum bracteatum (Strawflower)
Heliotropium arborescens (Heliotrope)
Impatiens balsamina (Balsam)
Impatiens wallerana (Busy Lizzie; Impatiens)
Kochia scoparia (Summer cypress; Burning bush)
Limonium bonduellii (Algerian sea lavender)
Limonium sinuatum (Notch-leaf sea lavender)
Lobelia erinus (Edging lobelia)
Matthiola incana (Stock)
Mimulus × hybridus (Monkey flower)
Mirabilis jalapa (Four o'clock)
Nemesia strumosa (Pouch nemesia)
Nicotiana alba (Flowering tobacco)
Nierembergia hippomanica (Cup flower)
Pelargonium × hortorum (Geranium)
Petunia × hybrida (Petunia)
Rudbeckia hirta var. *pulcherrima* (Gloriosa daisy)
Salpiglossis sinuata (Painted tongue)
Salvia farinacea (Blue sage)
Salvia splendens (Scarlet sage)
Schizanthus × wisetonensis (Poor man's orchid)
Senecio cineraria (Dusty miller)
Tagetes erecta (African marigold)
Tagetes, triploid strains (Triploid marigolds)
Thunbergia alata (Black-eyed Susan vine)
Tithonia rotundifolia (Mexican sunflower)
Torenia fournieri (Wishbone flower)
Verbena × hybrida (Garden verbena)
Viola × wittrockiana (Pansy)

Tender Annuals

These annuals should not be set out or sown outdoors until the soil is thoroughly warm.

Amaranthus caudatus (Love-lies-bleeding)
Amaranthus tricolor (Jacob's coat)
Celosia cristata (Cockscomb)
Heliotropium arborescens (Heliotrope)

Annuals for Fragrance

Brachycome iberidifolia (Swan river daisy)
Cheiranthus cheiri (Wallflower)
Dianthus barbatus (Sweet William)
Heliotropium arborescens (Heliotrope)
Lathyrus odoratus (Sweet pea)
Lobularia maritima (Sweet alyssum)
Matthiola incana (Stock)
Mirabilis jalapa (Four o'clock)
Reseda odorata (Mignonette)

Perennials

To many people, perennials suggest images of old-fashioned gardens. In fact, perennials are old-fashioned, having been the favorites of many generations of gardeners. But they are also the favorites of many gardeners today, and for the same reasons as in the past: They are relatively easy to grow, last from year to year, and offer an abundance of flowers in an enormous array of colors and forms.

Perennials are plants that live more than two years. Many plants are perennial, including trees, shrubs, and bulbs; but the word as commonly used (and as we will use it in this book) refers to perennial flowering plants that are herbaceous, meaning that their stems are soft and fleshy, not woody like those of shrubs and trees. (Bulbs are classified separately because of their method of storing food.)

Woody shrubs and trees survive winters because their stems and trunks resist extreme cold. Herbaceous perennials survive varying degrees of winter cold by virtue of roots that are stronger and more vigorous than those of annuals and biennials. With the onset of cold, the tops of perennials die down but the roots remain alive in a dormant state, sending forth new foliage and flowers each year when the weather warms.

Perennial gardening has been beloved throughout history, so much so that it has been developed, particularly in the form of the perennial border, into a genuine art. In this section we will take a close look at the basic design principles that led to these remarkable gardens.

The Cottage Garden

The easiest way to begin learning to design a perennial garden is with the garden that shows the least design of all: the cottage garden. It is the English cottage garden—using the same plants as its more formal counterparts, but without any particular plan or reason—that is the forerunner of the most beautifully designed perennial beds and borders.

Cottage gardens are essentially the gardens of people who love plants for themselves and care little or nothing for the way they are organized. Plants are added to the taste and at the whim of the gardener; the only guiding principle is to have close at hand all of those plants the gardener loves, without much regard for such rules as placing taller plants in back or leading up to bright colors with more subtle ones. The effect is likely to be kaleidoscopic, with an old climbing rose; a clump of daylilies; a mat of nasturtiums; a towering stand of hollyhocks; and spots of cottage pinks, basket-of-gold, veronica, poppies, and other plants all growing on their own, without much focus. They are gardens of surprises, where such accidents of nature as the

How beautiful are the retired flowers! How they would lose their beauty were they to throng into the highway, crying out "Admire me, I am a violet! Dote upon me, I am a primrose!"

John Keats

encroaching of vigorous plants upon one another and the sudden appearance of plants the gardener doesn't recall planting are gratefully accepted. The true cottage garden has a wild and woolly look, but it is also a charming, engaging garden in which to lose oneself.

Designing the Perennial Garden

With flowering plants, the variations in size, shape, color, and texture pose the possibility of ending up with more of a devil-may-care look in your flower garden than you want. But if you take some time to plan out a garden design, you'll be sure to end up with a cohesive and beautiful garden.

Before you begin to design, take stock of your present garden. Some elements, such as your lawn shape, paths, trees, and background fences, are fairly permanent, and you'll need to work with them in developing your new design.

First, figure out from what angle you will view the garden most frequently. If you spend a lot of time indoors, you'll want to design your garden so that you can view it from one or more of your favorite picture windows.

Assess the flower beds in your yard, and determine which existing plants you'd like to keep. This will enable you to decide whether you want the straight lines and symmetry of a formal perennial bed or the curving, asymmetrical shapes and lines of an informal perennial garden. It's a good idea to invest some thought into the design of your perennial garden because, unlike annuals, perennials last for many years. For more information about garden design, see Chapter 1, page 13.

Left: This charming cottage garden is informal and unmanicured, yet has enough underlying design to keep it from appearing haphazard. Below: Carefully consider the design of perennial beds that will be seen from all sides, such as the one shown here. Try to create a bed that will look attractive and interesting from many perspectives.

The undulating curves of this
informal perennial border
add interest to the planting and
offer many different perspectives for viewing the plants.

Beds and Borders

The next step in designing a perennial garden is to decide
whether to plant beds or borders. A bed is a cultivated area
surrounded by a lawn, patio, or other open expanse. A bed
can be viewed from all sides, and must be planned accordingly.
Perennial beds are most suitable in large, open spaces; typically,
they are planted in parks, estates, and municipal grounds.

If you have a fair amount of space to fill, a perennial bed may
very well suit your needs. Beds are rectangular in a formal
style, or curving in an informal style.

A border is a cultivated area that bounds the perimeter of a
garden. Borders are often planted along walls, hedges, or
walkways in both formal and informal gardens.

Because borders don't cut into the garden, but help to define
it, they can be used in both formal and informal gardens.

Since they are usually planted against a wall or hedge, most
borders are accessible from one side only; for that reason, they
should be planted no more than five feet deep. Deeper borders
are very difficult to maintain because it is almost impossible to
weed, prune, or feed the plants in the back without stepping
on those in the front.

If you choose to plant a perennial border, you'll want to
consider another aspect of design, the background.

Backgrounds

For backgrounds, most of us must settle for whatever serves
currently to separate our property from adjacent properties. This
most often is a fence or wall, but may also be a hedge, shrubs,
or even buildings.

Among the most attractive backdrops for a secluded garden
perennial bed are stone or brick walls or weathered, natural-
wood fences. If you have a fence that is painted or stained
an unappealing color, keep in mind that if you repaint or restain
it, you may have to repeat the job every few years. Try to
choose paint closest to the color of the wood in its weathered
state. Medium-to-dark earth tones usually make the best
backgrounds for flowers.

Choosing Plants

You're finally ready to choose the plants for your perennial
garden. Some important elements to consider in choosing plants
are whether you have any favorites that you're intent upon
including in the design, and whether you want a garden full of
flowers that bloom all at once or waves of bloom throughout the
growing season. Some flower characteristics that you'll want

One of the keys to designing an attractive perennial bed is to choose plants whose varying characteristics complement each other. Here, contrasting foliage and flower shapes create textural variations.

to think about in planning your garden include color, height, spread, form, texture, and bloom season.

Color   One of the most important elements of a garden is color. Some color combinations work well together, others are boring or uninspiring, and some colors simply clash. A few basic color principles, described in Chapter 1 on pages 21–34, will help you to understand what colors can do for your garden.

Height   Perennials range in height from less than a foot to as tall as twelve feet. The ideal to strive for when designing perennial borders is to gradate the heights of the plants so that the shortest are closest to the front and the tallest are at the rear of the planting. When planning island perennial beds, place the tallest plants in the middle and the shortest plants along the edge of the bed. To give bed and border plantings more variation and excitement, plan a little inconsistency into the heights; for example, a few tall, spiky plants rising above some lower, mounded plants will create an interesting and more natural-looking border or bed.

Spread   An important element to consider when planning a garden is the mature spread of the individual plants. It's very easy to space plants too closely when planting the garden. When designed with the natural plant-spread in mind, the new garden looks sparse. But you'll appreciate your self-restraint later in the year when the perennial garden has filled in enough to look beautiful, but is not so closely packed that it looks like a jungle and is difficult to care for.

Form   Keep plant form in mind when planning the design of the perennial garden. Most perennials grow in five basic shapes: rounded, vertical, open, upright and spreading, and prostrate. The most interesting beds and borders are made of a combination of these plant forms.

Although their characteristics are too subtle to play a major role in design, you may want to think about flower forms. The forms that perennial blooms take are too numerous and complex to enumerate, but some of the common forms, and examples, are: the bell-shaped campanulas, daisylike shasta daisies or asters, spherical peonies, cup-shaped marsh marigolds, spurred columbines, frilly or lacy dianthus, star-shaped amsonia, and trumpetlike daylilies.

Bear in mind that the daisy family is so large that gardeners frequently find themselves with an overabundance of this shape. Generally, the most interesting gardens are those that offer variety in flower forms.

Texture   Plant texture refers to the appearance of the plant, not to how it feels to the touch. Plants with finely dissected, lacy leaves are considered fine textured. Large-leafed plants are considered to have a coarse texture.

You can use texture much in the same way as color to create spatial illusions. Coarsely textured plants are bold and appear to be much closer to the viewer than finely textured plants, even though both are planted side by side.

The annuals and perennials growing in these mixed border plantings give a lush, colorful effect. Initially, providing transplants with enough space in which to spread will eliminate overcrowding later in the season.

Bloom Season

Now we come to the most important aspect of perennial gardening: timing bloom. To design with perennials you must know when each plant will bloom and for how long. Different perennials bloom at different times throughout the season and for different periods of time. (Some, of course, do coincide.) These factors must be coordinated to produce the effects you

Planning for continuous bloom
keeps the garden from looking
tired or out of season.

PERENNIALS **91**

want. This is the most challenging, interesting, and exciting
feature of perennial gardening.

This coordination is necessary because, although there are
many exceptions, perennials generally bloom for two to four
weeks, a shorter duration than annuals, which generally
bloom throughout the season. To extend color over time, you
must select plants with varying blossoming times or durations
of bloom. (If faded flowers are cut back, most perennials will
bloom again. This second bloom will produce smaller flowers.)

Of course, you may want to select flowers that do bloom at
approximately the same time for a garden filled with color. This
is fine if you want a spectacular display and are willing to
settle for little or no perennial bloom the rest of the season. But
for a longer duration of color, you must plant for a continuous
succession of bloom, with new flowers appearing as others fade.
This will have a diluting effect on the overall garden color,
but it will also reveal the forms of the plants more clearly. In
general, even when you plant for a succession of bloom, there
will be three or four peak periods of bloom during the season,
interspersed with periods of quiet.

While it may be difficult to envision these changing patterns,
a time-lapse film of a perennial border taken from early spring
to late summer would clearly show one wave of flowers
replacing another.

With the varying blossoming times and duration of bloom,
the possibilities of the perennial garden are immense. When you
add the job of coordinating color to coordinating blossoming
time and duration of bloom, the possibilities become even
greater—so great that they may intimidate the beginning gardener. The question might be raised, Why bother with all this;
why not merely plant annuals for a full season of bloom? The
simple answer, apart from the uniquely attractive characteristics
and longer life of the perennials, is that the perennial garden
planned for a succession of bloom is always changing; in this
regard it is not one garden, but many gardens in one.

The Encyclopedia charts starting on page 377 are an ideal way
to find out a great deal about many different perennials in a
short time. They list all of the previously mentioned characteristics—cultural requirements, color, height, and bloom season—
for each plant. The lists beginning on page 105 will help you
choose perennials for specific characteristics and cultural
conditions. As you learn more about the individual plants, it's
good to keep a list of those you think may be ideal for your
garden, so that you'll have it handy when you begin laying out
your garden plan on paper.

Coordinating color and time of
bloom can be challenging
and sometimes complicated,
but the results are quite
rewarding.

The Mixed Border

In choosing plants for the perennial border, you are by no means limited to perennials entirely. In fact, if you want a fairly steady blaze of color, you'll have to add other plants, because perennials alone can't provide it.

Perennials do have the advantage of being permanent residents of the border, and thus provide its basic framework; but for the most part the warm-season annual flowers have a longer season of bloom. This makes them indispensable for color during "quiet" periods in the garden or to succeed faded perennial bloom.

Many of the most beautiful flower beds and borders in the world contain predominately perennial plants, but annuals, bulbs, flowering shrubs, and many other plants are equally important parts of the scene. If you limit yourself to perennials alone, you'll miss out on such powerful color combinations as pink coral bells and orange California poppies, orange nasturtiums and blue salvia, and rich purple heliotrope with dark rose penstemon.

Spring- and summer-flowering bulbs are also important to any flower border, if only for the variety of unusual flower shapes they provide: Daffodils, grape hyacinths, fritillaria, tulips, and crocuses are just a few of the spring-blooming bulbs that add excitement to the border well in advance of most perennial and annual bloom. The midsummer border can be made more interesting by adding any of the lily hybrids, the cactus-flowered dahlias, gladiolus, and the many varieties of allium.

The main drawback of an all-perennial border is that it is bare in winter. If you include a few hardy shrubs or small trees, you'll have something to look at during the cold months to testify that there is indeed a garden under all that snow or rain-soaked earth. When choosing shrubs and small trees for the border, it's best to pick those that will not overgrow their allotted space and to look for varieties with some interesting fall or winter characteristics, such as bright foliage, berries, or an attractive branch pattern when the plant is bare. Such trees include dwarf forms of crabapple or flowering cherry, Japanese maple, or the flowering chestnut. Dwarf hollies, the tree peonies, and dwarf junipers are only a few of the shrubs that are restrained in growth.

Dianthus, marigolds, astilbes, and daisies make a pretty mixed border. Planting a mixed border lets the gardener take advantage of the variety of colors, forms, and shapes of perennials, as well as the long-lasting bloom of annuals.

Left: *Iberis sempervirens.*
Below: Vita Sackville-West, an
English garden writer and
designer, created this all-white
perennial garden in the 1930s.

94   PERENNIALS

The Perennial Cutting Garden

Perennial flowers are among the most prized of all cut flowers,
lending themselves particularly to large bouquets of striking
impact. A dozen or so red-hot pokers in a tall glass cylinder,
masses of blue delphiniums in a copper kettle, or a combination
of sunflowers and coreopsis in a rustic wicker container are
just a few possibilities. For information on planning the garden
and cutting the flowers, see Chapter 1, pages 36–37.

Cutting gardens also serve as excellent places to hold perennials in reserve until you know where you want to plant them
in the landscape or garden.

A list of perennials that make outstanding cut flowers can be
found on page 107.

The Art of Perennial Gardening

There is a unique dimension to gardening with perennials that
for many gardeners greatly increases the pleasure of growing
them: They are plants with a rich heritage, one that dates back
through recorded history, and that attained rare heights in
nineteenth century England, when perennial gardening was
given new life and refined into an art.

For many generations of English gardeners, perennials have
been the backbone of the typical home garden. No particular
style or design was associated with these gardens, just a love
on the part of the gardener for the easily grown plants and their
beautiful flowers. These early perennial gardens were the
original cottage gardens.

The familiarity and ease of culture of perennials led to some
contempt for them during the Victorian era, when the demand
for exotic plants was at its peak. During this period, perennials
were relegated to the backstage, considered by many as coarse
"country cousins" of the more fashionable annuals that had
been introduced to England and America from faraway lands.

True to typical Victorian fashion, it became the popular form
of gardening among the wealthy to surround one's mansion with
lavish displays of tender annuals planted in severely geometric
patterns. Huge formal beds were imposed upon the landscape
almost like artist's canvases, and made ready for temporary
displays of color. Without regard for the individuality of the
plants, the annuals were mass-planted in elaborate configura-
tions designed primarily to be seen from an elevated viewing
position. Today you can see similar displays in public parks
and municipal gardens, where annuals are frequently used in
large beds to spell out words or to create specific designs. (It is

The garden is part of Sissing-
hurst Estate where she lived and
worked. The garden, still in
existence, uses plants of varying
shades of white, gray, and green.

also interesting to note that the term bedding plants originally referred only to annuals.)

Because these plants were gathered from countries with warm climates, they had to be coaxed into bloom in England in coal-heated greenhouses. It wasn't unusual for one display to be planted out, soon to be replaced with an entirely new one lest the owner and guests become bored by the same display. Obviously, this type of gardening demanded a great deal of time and money and a large staff of gardeners. As novel and exotic as the new plants were, their cultural requirements, as well as the prevailing style of planting them, put them beyond the reach of most gardeners.

Care of Perennials

Perennials, like most plants, require only the basics for good growth: a reasonably fertile soil, good drainage, sufficient sun and water, and a little tender, loving care. With a little attention to the basics in the beginning, most perennials will remain healthy for years.

Soil Preparation

If you live in an area with fertile, well-drained soil, consider yourself blessed, because there's nothing quite like having quality soil to garden in without expending any effort. But if you're not so fortunate, don't gamble on trying to garden without first improving your soil.

The best time to prepare your soil for perennials is a few months before you intend to plant. Any amendments you add to the soil have time to take effect during this waiting period. Most perennials are planted in fall or spring, so the soil should be prepared in the summer for fall planting, or in the fall for spring planting. Complete information on soil pH, fertilizers, and improving the soil can be found in Chapter 14, page 343.

Improving Your Soil   Improving clay or sandy soils is a straightforward task: Add plenty of organic matter to the top layer. Organic matter increases the soil's capacity to hold water and nutrients. It opens and loosens the soil and it breaks down into humus (the dark, decayed substance that gives soil its characteristic color).

Soil pH   It's a good idea to test the soil pH, especially if you live in an area with characteristically acid or alkaline soil. You can test the pH yourself with any of the kits available at garden centers, or you can have soil samples professionally tested.

Thorough soil preparation
makes it possible to crowd
plants a bit without detrimental
effects. This closely spaced
planting of coreopsis, achillea,
and centranthus is thriving—
fertilizer added to the soil
before planting provides adequate nutrients for healthy
growth.

Many county extension offices provide this service.

Most perennials grow best in neutral or slightly acid soil. If
your soil is quite acid, you can add ground dolomitic limestone
to correct the pH. If alkalinity is the problem, add soil sulfur
or ferrous sulfate. Have your county extension agent determine
the proper amount to add.

Fertilizer   Unless your soil is extremely fertile, it's a good idea
to incorporate a fertilizer into the soil during the soil preparation
process. Packaged dry fertilizers are the easiest to apply. Choose
a formulation such as a well-balanced 5–10–5 fertilizer.

Getting Ready to Plant

After clearing out the weeds and cultivating the soil amendments into the soil, you're ready to plant. If this is your first
experience with perennials, you'll probably want to begin
with started plants from the nursery, rather than with seeds. If
you're an experienced gardener and you enjoy growing plants
from seed, you might consider trying your hand at perennials.

Starting from Seed

Starting your perennials from seed is an intriguing and rewarding
venture, if you have the patience and the room to try it.
Planting seed has several advantages, not the least of which is
that it is the least expensive way to procure a large number
of plants. Another benefit is that you are not limited to the
varieties offered at your local nursery, or to those available
as plants from mail-order sources. Selections offered by nurseries
that specialize in perennials often include rare varieties you
may want to try.

Always buy the best-quality seeds you can find, and plant
them the year you receive them: The freshest seeds give the best
results. Some perennials are particular about the conditions
they need to germinate. Read the instructions included with the
seeds carefully and do your best to provide the conditions
called for.

Over a period of time, gardeners develop their own favorite
methods for starting seeds. The following is one way that works
well for many perennials.

Getting Started The equipment for seed germination should include a number of seed flats or trays with drainage holes, a top-quality growing medium such as milled sphagnum moss (not the product commonly seen in plastic bags, but one with an exceedingly fine texture), heating cables to provide warm soil (if necessary), and some type of fluorescent light unit whose height above the flats can be adjusted.

First, moisten the milled sphagnum in a plastic bag or other container, place it in the flats, and firm it down slightly to form a smooth, even surface. You can scatter the seeds over the surface or plant them in rows. Sow the seeds thinly, tapping them out of the packet slowly for an even spread.

The next steps depend upon the specific requirements of the seeds. Some need light and heat to germinate and others require darkness and fairly cool temperatures. Some have periods of dormancy that need to be overcome by chilling in the refrigerator. Some seeds, in order to germinate most quickly, need to be soaked or to have their seed coats filed. Be sure to check closely the instructions that come with the seeds.

Moisture is critical in seed germination, and it's best not to take chances. The best way to supply moisture is to water from the bottom, not the top. You can place the flat or tray in the sink or in a larger pan, such as a cookie sheet with sides; pour water into the sink or pan; and allow it to seep up into the soil. To maintain humidity, it's best to place a sheet of clear plastic over seeds that need light to germinate, and a sheet of black plastic over those that need darkness. Be sure, however, to remove the plastic as soon as the seeds start to sprout; otherwise, you'll be risking fungus disease that can kill the seedlings.

Maintaining moisture is especially critical with very fine, dustlike seeds, which have a tendency to dry out quickly.

Transplanting Seedlings Once the seeds have germinated and have produced their second set of true leaves, they are ready to be planted into their own containers. Small peat pots are best, as these can be planted directly into the garden. Fill them with good-quality packaged soil mix and wet it down before you start to transplant; be careful not to let the seedlings dry out between the time you remove them from the flat and the time they are safely in the new containers. This is one of the most common causes of plant loss.

Transplanting requires patience and dexterity. A flat, pointed stick, such as an old plant label, works well to separate the seedlings and to ease them into the new soil. Use a light touch when firming the new soil around the roots of seedlings; too

Some perennials are a little more difficult to start from seed than annuals, and many require special treatment for best germination. Carefully read the seed packet instructions before planting. Top: One simple and effective way to maintain soil moisture is to cover the flat with a plastic bag after watering. The seeds planted in this flat need darkness for best germination; a black plastic bag is ideal. Bottom: These seedlings are being carefully transplanted into individual containers.

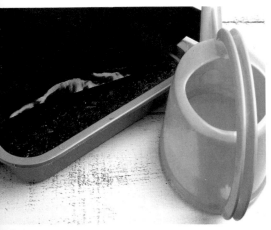

much pressure will squeeze the air from the soil, making it an unhealthy medium for the tender plants.

Many perennials do not take well to transplanting. Seeds of these should be sown directly into peat containers.

Seedlings in containers should be kept in a protected environment, such as a lath house or cool greenhouse, for several weeks. After they are established, they can be moved to a somewhat less protected environment; but they are still not ready for the full brunt of the elements. They will need more or less constant watering during warm summer months, and applications of an all-purpose complete fertilizer every four to six weeks throughout the growing season, to get them on their way. Within a year's time you should have quite a collection of healthy, good-size perennials ready to go into the garden.

Perennial seeds of course can be sown directly into the garden, but with varying degrees of success and usually with a very low percentage of germination. Following the previous instructions will greatly increase germination and allow you to control your supply of plants.

For more detailed information on starting plants from seeds, see Chapter 3, page 67.

Transplanting Dormant Plants

If you order dormant plants from a catalog, they should arrive sometime in early spring. They won't look like much, but they are alive and should be treated with care. If the weather does not permit planting immediately, keep them in a cool, dark spot and make sure the sphagnum moss surrounding them doesn't dry out.

When the time comes to plant them in the garden, remove them from their plastic coverings, shake the moss off carefully, and inspect the roots. Remove any that are dry and brittle or appear to have rotted. Then get them into the ground as quickly as possible: It doesn't take long for wind and sun to dry out the tiny roots that are essential to life during the critical first few weeks after transplanting.

Before planting, take a good look at your plan to make sure you know what plants you want in which locations and how far apart they should be spaced. Some gardeners place tiny stakes to indicate locations.

Dig the holes large enough so that the roots won't be cramped when you spread them out. The depth of the hole is determined by the root system of the plant. Generally speaking, the point where the roots meet the stem or crown should be placed right at ground level.

After you have inserted the plant in the hole, pack the soil around the root system gently. When the hole is filled, you can gently firm the soil around the roots to make sure there are no empty spaces between roots and soil. Water the plant thoroughly. This is also the best time to label plants for future reference.

Transplanting Started Plants

If you order started plants from a mail-order source or purchase them in six-packs or gallon cans from your garden center or nursery, the planting procedure is basically the same as for dormant plants.

Small plants in six-packs can be removed easily by pushing up on the bottom of the individual cell. Don't try to pull the plant out by the stem: It may not have an extensive root system and the top could break away from the roots. With a trowel, dig small holes roughly the same depth as the rootball. Take the plants out one by one and plant them slightly deeper than they were in the pack. Firm the soil and water thoroughly.

Larger perennials are usually planted in plastic or tapered metal cans. As long as the rootball is moist, you can remove them from their cans by placing your hand across the top of the can, turning it upside down, and shaking it slightly. If the plants are in straight-sided metal cans and you plan on planting them right away, have the cans cut at the nursery. If you intend to hold the plants awhile before planting, leave the cans intact and cut them later yourself with a pair of tin snips. (Cut cans are almost impossible to water thoroughly.)

Be sure to loosen the circling roots around the rootball and spread them before planting, so that they grow outward. If left uncorrected, circling roots will inhibit the plant's growth. If the plant is rootbound, score the rootball lightly with a fork or loosen it gently with your fingers before planting.

Staking

Staking is controversial among ardent perennial gardeners: Some dislike the task so much that they refuse to plant any varieties that need it. There are two types of plants that require staking: those with tall single stalks, such as delphinium, hollyhocks, and gladiolus; and those with many floppy stems, such as asters, chrysanthemums, coreopsis, heliopsis, and carnations.

Tall, thin poles, such as the commonly available bamboo stakes, make the best supports for the single-stem plants. Simply place the stake an inch or so from the main stalk and shove it

far enough into the ground to be stable. Attach the stalk to the stake with a plant tie, forming the tie into a figure eight, being careful not to cut into the stem but still allowing some natural back-and-forth movement.

The favored method for staking lower, bushier plants is to use the twining prunings from fruit or ornamental trees, cut into lengths of about sixteen to twenty inches. When the plants are about half that height, push the dried branches into the ground, placing several in a circular pattern around the clump. These provide a framework to support the plant and will become less noticeable as the plant grows and spreads over these supports.

These perennial sunflowers will grow to a height of eight feet. The twiggy stakes well anchored in the soil will provide ample support for the sunflowers as they grow, and eventually leaves will cover up the stakes.

As the years go by, most perennial plantings become overcrowded and should be divided. These astilbes are at their prime now, but will need to be divided soon.

Dividing

There are basically three reasons for dividing perennials: control of size, rejuvenation, and propagation.

The nature of most perennials is to grow larger every year, usually by spreading and making a larger clump. Left alone, the most vigorous growers can expand until they choke out many desirable plants. As the clumps expand, they also begin to compete with themselves; those plants on the outer edge thrive in fresh soil, but those in the center suffer from competition for moisture, nutrients, light, and air. You can end up with a healthy circle of plants around a dying center.

Except in areas of the country with extremely cold winters (temperatures of −10° to −20°F), fall is the best time to divide perennials. The general rule is to divide spring- and summer-blooming perennials in late summer or fall, and fall-blooming perennials in early spring, to give them a whole growing season to reestablish themselves. If you live in a climate with extreme winters, it's best to divide in early spring rather than subject newly planted divisions to the rigors of the weather.

Before you divide, decide what plants you want to save, which you want to dig out altogether, and which you want to replant elsewhere. To make digging and dividing easier, water the bed well a few days beforehand. Before you begin the actual dividing process, be sure to prune the perennials severely, to six inches from the ground. This will allow you to see exactly what you're doing.

The dividing process is simple. Dig the entire clump out as completely as possible. If the center of the clump has died out, divide the living portion into smaller clumps to replant where you like. Where roots are so ensnarled that you can't simply pull the plants apart, you can cut them apart, but this is likely to cause severe root damage. The best way to divide a stubborn clump is to insert two spading forks into it back to back, then press the handles toward each other, using the leverage at the tines to pry the clump apart.

The hole from which the clump was taken should be enriched with some organic matter and a handful of 0–10–10 fertilizer (or some similar formulation with no nitrogen). You can place one or more of the divisions in the hole and replant the rest elsewhere or give them away to gardening friends.

Perennials in Containers

Perennials make excellent container plants, especially when combined with annuals or bulbs. Such plantings provide a much longer season of color and a good contrast between foliage and flowers. As the early bulbs and perennials pass their prime, the annuals fill in and cover with a summer-long display of colorful flowers.

Some combinations with annuals, perennials, and bulbs that you might want to try are: dark pink penstemons and a lighter pink 'Cascade' petunia; perennial blue salvia with blue trailing lobelia, 'King Alfred' daffodils with basket-of-gold; and the bushy 'Connecticut Yankee' delphinium, blue hyacinths, white sweet alyssum, and 'Blue Mariner' petunias.

Container Culture

From a design point of view, containers offer the advantage of mobility. You can group containers around a patio or deck or about an entryway, adding color where you like and changing the color schemes and patterns as you wish. Containers also

Some perennials are well suited for container growing. The trailing growth habit of the Italian bellflower *(Campanula isophylla)* shown here makes it an ideal plant for a hanging moss basket.

can serve as holding areas for flowers you may wish to plant later in the garden.

Garden centers, nurseries, and variety stores offer a wide selection of containers in all sizes: clay and ceramic pots, wooden half-barrels, and plastic and wood pots and boxes. Experienced container gardeners favor the largest containers possible; the bigger they are, the more soil they hold, which means less watering for the gardener, more root space for the plants, and more room to experiment with different combinations of plants.

If you use clay pots, it's a good idea to wet them down thoroughly before planting. Clay is very porous and if dry will quickly rob newly potted plants of their first soaking. Cover the drainage hole (or holes) with broken pieces of pottery, irregularly shaped stones, or a small piece of fine-mesh screen. (It is not necessary to provide additional drainage with a layer of gravel or stones on the bottom.)

You can fill the containers with garden soil if your soil is a good loam with excellent drainage. If you've had problems growing plants in your soil, you'll only intensify the problems when you use that soil in containers. If your soil is marginally acceptable, mix it in equal proportions with an organic soil amendment such as peat moss, compost, or redwood soil conditioner, to make it a lighter, looser growing medium more conducive to the needs of plants in confined quarters. If your soil is actually poor, you'll be better off using one of the prepackaged soil mixes.

Thoroughly water the soil mass and allow it to settle before planting. After settling, the soil should be two to three inches below the container rim. There should be enough space between the rim and the soil so that one watering that fills the planter to its rim will moisten the rootball and drain through. If the container is too full of soil, the job becomes time-consuming and aggravating, requiring several waterings for a complete soaking.

Because of the limited amount of soil available to them, plants in containers need more attention than plants in the open ground. During the hot summer months, daily watering is commonly needed, especially if the containers are in a sunny or windy location. These repeated waterings leach nutrients out of the soil rather quickly. To compensate for this loss, most container gardeners favor applying a liquid balanced fertilizer at half-strength every two weeks.

To keep specimens looking their best, be sure to pinch off dead flowers and leaves regularly.

Perennial Performers

The following lists categorize some common perennials by color and use. Consult them to spark your imagination or to solve landscaping problems. Keep in mind that, in many cases, when a name appears on a list, only selected varieties (usually too numerous to mention in the list) may fit the given category. Consult the Encyclopedia charts (pages 377–499), seed catalogs, and local experts to help pinpoint the variety best suited to your needs.

Yellow Perennials

These plants include varieties with flowers in the color range from yellow-green and yellow to orange and bronze.

Achillea (Yarrow)
Alchemilla (Lady's mantle)
Anthemis (Golden Marguerite)
Aquilegia (Columbine)
Asclepias (Butterfly flower)
Aurinia (Basket-of-gold)
Caltha (Marsh marigold)
Chrysanthemum (Chrysanthemum)
Coreopsis (Calliopsis)
Delphinium (Delphinium)
Digitalis (Foxglove)
Doronicum (Leopard's bane)
Euphorbia (Spurge)
Gaillardia (Blanket flower)
Geum (Avens)
Helenium (Sneezeweed)
Helianthus (Sunflower)
Heliopsis (Heliopsis)
Helleborus (Christmas rose)
Hemerocallis (Daylily)
Iris (Iris)
Kniphofia (Torch lily)
Ligularia (Groundsel)
Lupinus (Lupine)
Lychnis (Campion)
Lysimachia nummularia (Moneywort)
Lysimachia punctata (Yellow loosestrife)
Paeonia (Peony)
Papaver (Poppy)
Penstemon (Beardtongue)
Primula (Primrose)
Rudbeckia (Black-eyed Susan)
Solidago (Goldenrod)
Thermopsis (False lupine)
Tradescantia (Spiderwort)
Trollius (Globe flower)

White Perennials

These plants include varieties with flowers in the color range from white to cream.

Acanthus mollis (Bear's breech)
Achillea ptarmica (Yarrow)
Anthemis (Golden Marguerite)
Aquilegia (Columbine)
Armeria (Sea pink)
Aruncus (Goatsbeard)
Aster (Aster)
Astilbe (False spirea)
Bergenia (Bergenia)
Campanula (Harebell)
Chrysanthemum (Chrysanthemum)
Cimicifuga (Bugbane)
Delphinium (Delphinium)
Dianthus (Pink)
Dicentra (Bleeding heart)
Dictamnus (Gas plant)
Digitalis (Foxglove)
Echinacea (Coneflower)
Filipendula (Queen of the prairie)
Geranium (Cranesbill)
Gypsophila (Baby's breath)
Hemerocallis (Daylily)
Heuchera (Coral bells)
Hibiscus (Rose mallow)
Hosta (Plantain lily)
Iris (Iris)
Kniphofia (Torch lily)
Liatris (Blazing star)
Lupinus (Lupine)
Lysimachia clethroides (Gooseneck loosestrife)
Monarda (Bee balm)

Coreopsis verticillata 'Golden Shower'.

Chrysanthemum × superbum

Paeonia (Peony)
Papaver (Poppy)
Penstemon (Beardtongue)
Phlox (Phlox)
Polygonatum (Solomon's seal)
Primula (Primrose)
Stokesia (Stokes' aster)
Thalictrum (Meadowrue)
Tradescantia (Spiderwort)
Veronica (Speedwell)

Red Perennials

These plants include varieties with flowers in the color range from red to pink and pinkish purple.

Achillea millefolium 'Fire King' (Fire king yarrow)
Aquilegia (Columbine)
Armeria (Sea pink)
Aster (Aster)
Astilbe (False spirea)
Bergenia (Bergenia)
Campanula (Harebell)
Chrysanthemum coccineum (Painted daisy)
Chrysanthemum hybrids (Hardy chrysanthemum)
Delphinium (Delphinium)
Dianthus (Pink)
Dicentra (Bleeding heart)
Dictamnus albus var. *purpureus* (Rose gas plant)

Digitalis (Foxglove)
Filipendula (Queen of the prairie)
Gaillardia (Blanket flower)
Geranium (Cranesbill)
Geum (Avens)
Grasses:
   Cortaderia (Pampas grass)
   Pennisetum (Fountain grass)
Gypsophila (Baby's breath)
Helleborus (Christmas rose)
Hemerocallis (Daylily)
Heuchera (Coral bells)
Hibiscus (Rose mallow)
Iris (Iris)
Kniphofia (Torch lily)
Liatris (Blazing star)
Lobelia (Cardinal flower)
Lupinus (Lupine)
Lychnis (Campion)
Lythrum (Purple loosestrife)
Monarda (Bee balm)
Paeonia (Peony)
Papaver (Poppy)
Penstemon (Beardtongue)
Phlox (Phlox)
Platycodon (Balloon flower)
Primula (Primrose)
Pulmonaria (Lungwort)
Scabiosa (Pincushion flower)
Sedum (Stonecrop)
Thalictrum (Meadowrue)
Tradescantia (Spiderwort)
Veronica (Speedwell)

Blue Perennials

These plants include varieties with flowers in the color range from blue and violet to lavender and bluish purple.

Amsonia (Blue star)
Anchusa (Bugloss)
Aster (Aster)
Baptisia (False indigo)
Brunnera (Siberian bugloss)
Campanula (Harebell)
Ceratostigma (Blue plumbago)
Delphinium (Delphinium)
Echinacea (Coneflower)
Echinops (Globe thistle)
Geranium (Cranesbill)
Hosta, selected species (Plantain lily)
Iris (Iris)
Lupinus (Lupine)
Mertensia (Virginia bluebells)
Phlox (Phlox)
Platycodon (Balloon flower)
Primula (Primrose)
Pulmonaria (Lungwort)
Salvia (Sage)
Scabiosa (Pincushion flower)
Stachys (Betony)
Stokesia (Stokes' aster)
Tradescantia (Spiderwort)
Veronica (Speedwell)

Lychnis chalcedonia.

Tradescantia virginiana.

Cool-Summer Perennials

These perennials are best when grown in climate zones that have cool summers, such as mountainous or coastal regions.

Aquilegia (Columbine)
Astilbe (False spirea)
Delphinium (Delphinium)
Dicentra (Bleeding heart)

Dicentra spectabilis.

Paeonia hybrid.

Helleborus (Christmas rose)
Ligularia (Groundsel)
Lupinus (Lupine)
Penstemon (Beardtongue)
Primula (Primrose)
Thalictrum (Meadowrue)

Fragrant Perennials

Some of the more fragrant perennials are included in the list below. An asterisk (*) indicates that the plant foliage is fragrant when crushed or bruised.

Achillea (Yarrow)*
Anthemis (Golden Marguerite)*
Artemisia (Wormwood)*
Cimicifuga (Bugbane)
Dianthus (Pink)
Dictamnus (Gas plant)
Filipendula (Queen of the prairie)
Hemerocallis (selected varieties) (Daylily)
Hosta plantaginea (Fragrant plantain lily)
Iris, bearded (Bearded iris)
Monarda (Bee balm)*
Paeonia (Peony)
Phlox paniculata (Garden phlox)
Primula (selected varieties) (Primrose)
Salvia (Sage)*

Perennials for Cutting

Not all of the perennials useful for cut flowers will be found in this list, only some of the best. The flowers of those plants marked with an asterisk (*) are especially suitable for drying and preserving.

Acanthus (Bear's breech)
Achillea (Yarrow)
Anemone (Anemone)
Anthemis (Golden Marguerite)
Aster (Aster)
Chrysanthemum (Chrysanthemum)
Coreopsis (Calliopsis)
Delphinium (Delphinium)
Dianthus (Pink)
Digitalis (Foxglove)
Echinacea (Coneflower)
Echinops (Globe thistle)*
Gaillardia (Blanket flower)
Geum (Avens)
Grasses: All
Gypsophila (Baby's breath)*
Helenium (Sneezeweed)
Helianthus (Sunflower)
Heliopsis (Heliopsis)
Hemerocallis (Daylily)
Heuchera (Coral bells)
Hosta (Plantain lily)
Iris (Iris)
Kniphofia (Torch lily)
Liatris (Blazing star)
Lupinus (Lupine)
Paeonia (Peony)
Papaver (Poppy)
Rudbeckia (Black-eyed Susan)
Scabiosa (Pincushion flower)
Solidago (Goldenrod)*
Stokesia (Stokes' aster)
Veronica (Speedwell)

Digitalis 'Foxy'.

Bulbs

Perhaps more than any other type of plant, bulbs have an everchanging, magical quality. The neatly packaged, unimpressive, dull brown bulbs that you take home from the nursery contain the promise of a fleeting, beautiful flower. The anticipation that accompanies the planning and planting of a bulb garden is satisfying in itself. And, what can compare to the delight of spotting the first daffodil leaftips poking through the soil on a frosty spring morning? Perhaps only the colorful splendor of a bulb garden in full bloom.

The bulb package nature designed millenia ago contains the embryo of the entire plant. Roots, stems, leaves, and flowers are stored in this form until conditions become favorable for growth.

Although bulbs become dormant every year, they burst forth with reassuring predictability time and time again.

Work in bulb selection and hybridization has developed features that were only latent in the wild forms, but the beauty of bulbs remains the same. We can still count on the coming of spring's first crocus, the fragrance of narcissus, the romantic lily-of-the-valley, the nostalgic gladiolus, the unsurpassed regal form of a calla, or the towering summer lily.

A Bulb by Another Name

For simplicity we've come to speak of any plant that stores its life cycle in an underground fleshy organ as a bulb. Actually, only some of these plants are true bulbs. Let's look briefly at the similarities and differences among these subterranean storage forms.

True Bulbs

Of the plants described in this book, only about half are grown from true bulbs. A true bulb consists of a tiny, fully formed plant within a package of fleshy scales. If you slice vertically through a tulip bulb at planting time, you can see a miniature life form with tiny flowers, stem, leaves, and roots that have been developing during the summer months.

The scales surrounding the embryo are modified leaves that contain all the necessary foods to sustain the bulb during dormancy and early growth. The scales may be loose and open, like a lily's, or tight and compact, like those of an onion. If a tight bulb is cut in half crosswise, the scales are visible as rings.

Around the scales, many bulbs have a paper-thin covering known as the tunic. At the bottom of the bulb is a modified stem, or basal plate, from which the roots emerge. This basal plate also holds the scales together. During the growing season,

And then my heart with
pleasure fills,
and dances with the daffodils.

William Wordsworth

Left: "Hyacinths" from *The Temple of Flora* by Robert Thornton.

Amaryllis blooms are showy and long-lasting. They are one of the largest of the true bulbs.

new bulbs (called bulblets or offsets) are formed from lateral buds on the basal plates. In some bulbs, like the tulip, the old bulb dies, leaving only the new ones. With other bulbs, such as the narcissus, the parent continues to grow and the bulblets can be separated from it to create new plants. A few bulbs (lilies, for example) form new bulbils in the leaf axils.

Corms

A corm is actually a stem that is modified into a mass of storage tissue. If a corm is cut in half crosswise, no rings are visible. The top of the corm has one or more growing points—or eyes—which are usually visible upon close examination. Corms are covered by dry leaf bases much like the tunic that covers many bulbs. There are no enlarged scales. Roots grow from a basal plate on the underside of the corm. As the plant grows, the corm shrivels away. New corms form on top of or beside the old one. In addition, some corms, such as gladiolus, form small cormels, or tiny corms, around the base plate or roots. While the large corms will produce flowers the following year, it will take two to three years before the cormels have developed sufficiently to bloom.

Tubers

The underground tuber is a solid mass of stem similar to the corm, but it lacks both a basal plate and the corm's tuniclike covering. Roots and shoots grow from growth buds, or eyes, scattered over the surface. As the plants grow, some tubers, such as potatoes, diminish in size and form new tubers, while others, such as ranunculus, increase in size as they store nutrients and develop new growth buds for the following year.

Cyclamens grow from tubers. Here, red and white cyclamen plants are growing with ferns and candytuft—a colorful planting for a shaded spot.

Tuberous Roots

These food storage units look like tubers, but are really swollen roots rather than stems. During growth, they produce fibrous roots to take in moisture and nutrients. New growth buds appear on the base of the old stem, where it joined the tuberous root. Roots can be divided by cutting off a section with an eye-bearing portion of the old stem attached.

Rhizomes

Sometimes known as rootstock, rhizomes are actually thickened, branching storage stems. They grow laterally just along or slightly below the surface of the soil. Roots develop on the lower surface, while buds along the top of the rhizome produce

Lilies-of-the-valley *(Convallaria majalis)* grow from rhizomes, and are a welcome sight when they bloom in spring.

the new plants during the growing season. Rhizomes may be propagated by cutting them into sections, making sure that each segment contains a growth bud, or eye.

While the various bulbous plants have their distinct differences, the common factor is their ability to store food to carry them over a period of adverse weather conditions until their aboveground growth begins again. This "dormancy" may be brought on naturally by winter or drought. In moderate-temperature climates, however, it may be necessary to enforce dormancy by withholding moisture or removing the bulbs from the ground for cold storage.

Bulbous plants are shown here by type from left to right: Daylilies (true bulb), gladiolus (corm), anemone (tuber), alstroemeria (tuberous root), calla lilies (rhizome).

Bulbous Plants by Type

True Bulbs:
Allium
Amaryllis
Camassia
Chionodoxa
Clivia
Eucharis
Fritillaria
Galanthus
Hippeastrum
Hyacinthus
Hymenocallis
Iris reticulata
Ixiolirion
Leucojum
Lilium
Lycoris
Muscari
Narcissus
Nerine
Ornithogalum
Oxalis
Scilla
Sprekelia
Tulipa
Zephyranthes

Tuberous Roots:
Alstroemeria
Begonia
Dahlia
Eremurus

Corms:
Brodiaea
Bulbocodium
Colchicum
Crocus
Erythronium
Freesia
Gladiolus
Ixia
Moraea
Sparaxis
Tigridia
Tritonia
Watsonia

Tubers:
Anemone
Caladium
Cyclamen
Eranthis
Gloriosa
Polianthes
Ranunculus
Sinningia

Rhizomes:
Achimenes
Agapanthus
Canna
Convallaria
Iris (rhizomatous)
Zantedeschia

Designing with Bulbs

Bulbs add qualities to the garden unparalleled by other plant forms. Consider the stately elegance of lilies in the summer or the delicate subtlety of lilies-of-the-valley in springtime. The first crocus or glory-of-the-snow lends a lively look to the early spring landscape, as do fall-flowering crocuses. What would formal gardens be without beds of tulips or hyacinths? And can you imagine informal cottage gardens without clumps of yellow daffodils? Dahlias, gladiolus, lilies, and a number of other bulbs add a wide range of bright, sunny colors to the summer-flowering garden.

Bulbs add variety and allow for seasonal change in a garden. These daffodils will finish blooming in a few weeks. After they begin to die back, other flowers can be planted in the same bed.

Before You Plant

If you decide to plant bulbs to create patterns, color combinations, or even whimsical pictures in the garden, carefully read the descriptions in catalogs or on labels in order to select those that will bloom simultaneously. A carefully planned design that blooms in stages can be terribly disappointing. It is difficult to be too exacting about bloom times, because every climate and microclimate affects bulbs differently, but you can get close enough to achieve the design you want.

Plant Bulbs Where You'll Enjoy Them

Position bulbs where they can be seen from inside the house as you dine or relax.

Plant clumps of fragrant bulbs near entryways or open windows to perfume interior spaces and welcome those who enter your home.

Consider planting a fragrant garden of hyacinth, narcissus, lily-of-the-valley, or other sweet-smelling bulbs beside your favorite backyard picnic area.

Plant Bulbs for Different Effects

Keep in mind that your garden will look more dynamic if you concentrate on a few kinds of bulbs than if you set out countless types. For an informal garden, bulbs usually look best planted in drifts or clumps of one variety rather than as isolated plants or in single rows. Use a select few favorite types of bulbs and create flowing patterns of color. Clumps or drifts of bulbs are more attractive when grouped close together so that the leaves of each bulb touch to form a solid cover.

Naturalized Landscapes

One of the most effective uses of bulbs in landscaping is naturalization—the impression that the bulbs have been scattered by Mother Nature's free hand. Usually, considerable space and a large number of bulbs are required to make naturalization effective. However, good results can be achieved with only a few dozen bulbs in a limited space, such as underneath a tree.

Naturalized bulbs look great on a grassy bank, the corner of a large lawn, spilling over from an adjoining field, along a country fence, or filling a wooded glade.

Daffodils naturalize very effectively. Here, they add interest and beauty to a grassy slope. The flower clumps will gradually enlarge over a period of time.

An advantage of naturalized bulbs is that they can be left undisturbed for years, although after a few years they may become overcrowded. Then you'll want to dig them up and separate the bulbs. If you plant the bulbs a bit deeper than normally recommended, they will divide more slowly and will not require separation as soon.

To achieve a natural look, it is best to scatter bulbs over the planting area by hand and then plant them where they fall instead of attempting to lay them out according to a plan.

Bulbs for Naturalizing

Allium species
Amaryllis belladonna
Anemone blanda, A. apennina
Brodiaea laxa
Camassia
Chionodoxa
Colchicum
Crocus
Cyclamen (hardy)
Eranthis
Erythronium
Fritillaria meleagris

Galanthus
Iris reticulata
Leucojum
Lilium tigrinum
Muscari species
Narcissus
Ornithogalum nutans,
  O. umbellatum
Scilla
Tulipa clusiana, T. kaufmanniana
  hybrids, *T. tarda*

Daffodils naturalized among a grove of trees add to the woodland effect.

The Mobile Bulb Garden

Many bulbs are particularly adaptable to container gardening. Among the advantages of growing bulbs in pots and other containers is the ability to bring them indoors at the peak of their bloom or enjoy them on the patio.

Container-grown bulbs can be moved about at whim to create instant landscape changes. Sink them in flower beds to add color, group them at an entrance to welcome visitors, position them outdoors where they can be enjoyed from inside, or bring them near an outdoor eating area for special enjoyment.

But remember that bulbs, like other plants, are not as hardy when they are planted in containers as when they are in the ground. Place the pots in a trench and cover them with straw, or move them to a protected location for the winter. For more instructions on the care of bulbs in containers, see page 126.

In addition, bulbs planted in pots can be "forced," or brought into bloom out of season, by creating conditions that bring them out of dormancy. Techniques are described on page 128.

Pots filled with flowering bulbs brighten up this entryway. Adding color to the garden, and indoors, is as simple as moving pots to where they're needed.

Bulbs for Containers
Achimenes
Agapanthus
Allium (short types)
Anemone blanda
Begonia
Caladium
Chionodoxa
Clivia
Crocus
Cyclamen
Eranthis
Eucharis
Freesia
Gladiolus (miniature)
Hippeastrum
Hyacinthus
Iris danfordiae, I. histrioides,
  I. reticulata
Lilium
Muscari
Narcissus
Nerine
Ornithogalum
Oxalis
Polianthes
Sinningia
Tulipa (early or midseason varieties)
Zantedeschia

Bulbs the Year Around

If you identify bulb gardening only with spring tulips, narcissus, and hyacinths, then you're in for a treat as you discover and grow bulbs during the other three seasons as well. Not only do bulbous plants herald the beginning of spring, leading the way in nature's annual parade of bloom, but they continue to appear throughout the gardening year to add their special charms to the landscape.

The outdoor garden can be filled or at least accented with bulbs from the last days of winter right on through fall. Flowering bulbs grown indoors as houseplants the year around can brighten the gloom of winter, or hardy spring bulbs can be brought into early bloom if you duplicate nature's cooling period and then add warmth. And gardeners who are fortunate enough to have a greenhouse can add even more colorful flowers throughout the year.

The bulb garden needn't end with the last of the spring tulips—using many other types of bulbs will allow for bloom throughout summer and fall.

Bulb Care

Bulbous plants are among the easiest plants to grow. They will bloom if you plant them in an average garden soil that has good drainage and water them throughout the growing season. You can even plant them in sand, pebbles, or marbles if you ensure a continuous supply of water. These marvelous little packages contain enough nutrients to bloom without any further help from you.

However, if you wish the bulbs to come back the following year, to persist in your garden for many years, or to naturalize and multiply themselves, they will probably need more care than just watering. Although bulbs thrive in many different types of soil, most bulbs need good drainage to prevent rotting. Drainage is most easily improved by adding an organic amendment to the soil.

The bulb contains all the nutrients needed to make a flower the first year, but after it blooms, the bulb is exhausted and must replenish its nutrient supply to bloom again the following year. This replenishment takes place during the "quiet period" after the flowers have faded. During this period, it is important to fertilize the plant properly to supply enough nutrients to make next season's flowers.

Most bulbs are almost pest free, but observing a few precautions will keep them healthy. If you know what problems to expect, you will be alert for potential trouble and can take corrective measures at the first sign of difficulty.

The basic elements of bulb care are simple and easy to apply. Observation of these basics will ensure a profusion of flowers for your garden, your patio, and your home.

Top: Bulbs are low-maintenance plants; the bed of tulips in this well-manicured garden needs much less attention than many of the other plants growing here. Bottom: These forced bulbs are growing in a container filled with small pebbles and water.

Selecting Healthy Bulbs

Success begins with good-quality bulbs. Always buy from a reliable source, whether you are shopping at local outlets or ordering from catalogs. As with other goods, you'll get what you pay for. It usually proves more economical to buy fewer bulbs of higher quality from a good source than to search out bargains. Normally, larger bulbs mean more or larger flowers.

When you buy bulbs locally, examine them closely. They should be firm and free from deep blemishes, cuts, or soft spots. They should feel heavy for their size, not light or dried up like a seed. It is very important that the basal plate be solid and firm. Small nicks and loose skins or tunics do not affect development; in fact, loose tunics help you spot harmful diseases.

Whether you purchase bulbs by mail or in person, plant them as soon as they reach home. If this is not possible, store the bulbs in a cool place, such as a refrigerator. Do not store them in closed plastic bags—bulbs need to breathe. Open the bags or transfer the bulbs to paper bags.

Choosing the Site

As it is for other plants in the garden, site selection is of primary importance to success with bulbs. Study the light requirements of the bulbs listed in the Encyclopedia charts, pages 377–499. Also read the instructions that come with the bulbs you purchase, then choose a spot in the garden that meets those specifications, even if it proves to be containers on the patio.

Top-quality bulbs produce the finest blooms. Select bulbs carefully, store them properly, and your reward will be a profusion of flowers as striking as these tulips.

Planting Suggestions

As a rule, always plant bulbs as soon as possible after receiving them to prevent drying out. Lilies are especially delicate and should go into the ground immediately. If you live in a warm climate, delay planting early-spring bulbs by keeping them refrigerated or stored in a cool place until warm weather is past.

Preparing the Soil

Bulbous plants adapt to many types of soil, but most prefer a loose, porous soil structure. With the exception of a few bulbs (such as Siberian iris, which tolerate swampy locations), bulbs must have good drainage. If you cannot provide good drainage by adding soil amendments, preparing a raised bed, or installing a system to carry away excess water, you'll have to choose another site.

Before planting bulbs, prepare the soil at the chosen site so that the tender roots can easily move through the growing medium and water will drain through easily. Heavy clay soils or extremely sandy soils can be improved by the addition of an organic amendment such as compost, humus, ground bark, sawdust, or peat moss. In the heavier soils, organic material improves drainage and allows air to move through the soil more readily. Organic matter incorporated into sandy soil holds moisture longer and keeps nutrients in the root zones.

In fact, organic matter will improve almost any soil. Add the amendment you select by spreading it over the surface of the area you intend to plant. Spread the amendment at least two, but not more than four, inches deep and work it into the soil with a rotary tiller or spade.

Fertilizing

When you plant bulbs, mix some bone meal or superphosphate into the soil at the bottom of the planting hole. Phosphorus, the plant nutrient supplied by both of these fertilizers, must be present deep in the soil, where the bulb roots are. Because phosphorus does not move readily through the soil as other plant nutrients do, it must be placed near the roots.

Fertilize the bulbs again when the foliage begins to emerge, usually in the spring. Spread a fertilizer containing nitrogen and potash on the ground around the plants and water it into the soil with a thorough irrigation. If the soil is exposed, stir the fertilizer into the top couple of inches before you water. The fertilizer label will tell you how much to use.

After this initial spring feeding, apply half the label amount of fertilizer every month until the foliage begins to yellow. If the

All bulbs benefit from proper soil preparation. These thriving ranunculas are no exception. Amending the soil with organic matter and adding fertilizer will greatly improve most soils.

bulb is one with evergreen foliage, continue the feeding program until fall; then begin again when growth resumes in spring.

Some bulbs, such as *Amaryllis belladonna* and colchicum, bloom after the foliage has died. Feed these plants only when the foliage is green. At this time they store all the nutrients they need to produce the flower.

The list on the following page gives recommended planting depths and spacings for a variety of bulbs. As a general rule, most bulbs are planted at a depth that is equal to three times their diameter at the widest point.

When planting a number of bulbs in one area, it will prove easier to dig up the area, set out the bulbs, and then cover them. When planting smaller quantities or in crowded areas among other plants, dig the hole with a special bulb planter or a trowel. Position the bulb, cover with soil, and compact the soil gently with your hands.

Space bulbs carefully. Give them enough room to grow well, but don't set them too far apart or the planting will look sparse.

Watering Bulbs

Unless the ground is rain soaked, water the planting area thoroughly after putting out bulbs. Winter or spring rains usually provide all the moisture needed until the bulbs sprout. If you live in a dry climate, you may need to provide additional water if the soil dries out.

When the plants are a few inches tall, begin watering to keep them evenly moist throughout the growing and blooming period. Bulb roots grow deep; watering should be thorough, not just a surface sprinkling. The amount of water, of course, depends on the weather and the rate of growth. Bulbs need a lot of water during active growth. Continue to water after the blooms fade, until the foliage turns yellow.

Bulb Planting Information

Bulb	Depth to Top of Bulb (in inches)	Spacing Between Bulbs (in inches)
Achimenes	½–1	1
Agapanthus	Just below surface	24
Allium (large bulbs)	6	12–18
Allium (small bulbs)	4	4–6
Amaryllis	1–2 (Zones 9 and 10) 9 (other zones)	12
Anemone (large types)	3–4	8
Anemone (small types)	3–4	2–3
Begonia evansiana	1–2	6
B. tuberhybrida	½	12–15
Brodiaea	4	3–5
Bulbocodium	3	4
Caladium	1	12–18
Calochortus	2	4–6
Camassia	3–4	3–6
Canna	1–2	15–18
Chionodoxa	4	1–3
Clivia	Just below surface	18–24
Colchicum	4	6–9
Convallaria	1	4
Crocus	4	2–6
Cyclamen (hardy)	2	6–8
C. persicum	Half of tuber above soil	12–18
Dahlia	2	15–30
Eranthis	4	3–4
Eremurus	6	18–36
Erythronium	4	4–6
Eucharis	Tips at soil level	2
Freesia	2	2–4
Fritillaria imperialis	6–8	12
Other Fritillaria species	4	3–4
Galanthus	4	2–4
Gladiolus	4–6	4–6
Gloriosa	4–5	8–12
Hippeastrum	Half of bulb exposed above ground	12–15
Hyacinthus	6	4–6

Bulb	Depth to Top of Bulb (in inches)	Spacing Between Bulbs (in inches)
Hymenocallis	3–5	12–15
Iris (bulbs)	4	4–6
Iris (rhizomes)	Just below surface	12
Ixia	4	3–6
Ixiolirion	4	3–4
Leucojum	4	4
Lilium	4–6	9–18
L. candidum	1	9–12
Lycoris	3–5	5–8
Moraea	3–4	12–24
Muscari	2	2–4
Narcissus (large)	6	6–8
Narcissus (small)	4	4–6
Nerine	4–6	6–8
Ornithogalum (large)	6	6–8
Ornithogalum (small)	4	3–4
Oxalis	4	4–6
Polianthes	3	6–8
Ranunculus	1½	3–4
Scilla peruviana	5–6	8–10
S. hispanica and S. nonscripta	4	6–8
Other Scilla species	4	3–6
Sinningia	1	1 per 6-inch pot
Sparaxis	2	2–3
Sprekelia	3–4	8
Tigridia	4	4–8
Tritonia	3–4	3
Tulipa	6	4–6
Watsonia	4	6
Zantedeschia	3–4	12–24
Zephyranthes	1–2	3

Maintaining Planted Areas

Mulching around bulb planting areas keeps the garden neat, prevents splashing of soil onto foliage during watering or rains, reduces weeding, and visually pulls the area together.

To keep bulb plants looking good, remove spent flowers with scissors. This causes no harm to the bulbs and channels the energy into storage of valuable nutrients instead of seed production.

However, leaves must be allowed to remain, yellow, and ripen. Do not cut or pull them off unless you plan to discard the bulbs after they bloom. If you plant bulbs in a ground cover, such as pachysandra or vinca, or in a perennial bed where flowering plants will distract attention from the fading foliage, no special attention will be necessary as the foliage ripens. If the yellowing leaves offend you, however, they can be folded and tied to make a neater package in the garden.

Once the leaves have turned yellow, the bulb has removed the nutrients and protein for use the following season and the leaves can be carefully pulled or cut off.

As the tulips in this bed begin to fade, they are carefully pruned off. Leaving dying blooms on the plants will give the planting an unattractive look even though many new blooms are present.

Planting in Containers

A porous growing medium is suggested for most bulbs that are
to be planted in containers. Choose equal parts garden loam,
coarse sand, and organic matter, such as peat moss or ground
bark, or purchase one of the soilless packaged mixes and add
a little builder's sand or perlite to make it looser. Freesia,
eucharis, ixia, moraea, and gloriosa require the addition of
ground limestone at a rate of three to five ounces per bushel.

Shallow (four to five inches deep) clay pots known as bulb
pans are the best choice for most bulbs, although lilies, hippeastrum, and other large bulbs don't fit in bulb pans and need
regular pots. Shallow barrels, ceramic planters, plastic pots, or a
host of other typical garden containers work satisfactorily.

Cover drainage holes with fine-mesh screen or pieces of
broken crockery; then add the soil and position the bulbs in the
pot, setting them closer than the planting spacing recommended
on page 124. When container grown, bulbs in groupings should
almost touch each other. Large bulbs such as lilies and hippeastrum are best planted individually in six- to eight-inch pots.
Plant tulips with the flat side of the bulb facing outward.

If the containers will be protected during winter or you're
planting in the spring after frost danger, set the bulbs with tips

Bulbs growing in containers
look best when they are planted
close together—much closer
than is appropriate for beds.
These daffodils were planted
with the bulbs almost touching.

just under the soil surface instead of at the depth suggested for garden planting. Fill the pot to the rim with loose soil. The first watering will settle the soil enough to make headspace for future waterings. Soak thoroughly after planting and place the pots in a cool area until the bulbs root.

If the potted bulbs are to be forced, store or bury as instructed below. If the bulbs are to be grown as greenhouse specimens or houseplants, after they are rooted and shoots emerge, place them where their light and heat requirements can be met.

If potted bulbs are to be grown outdoors in cold climates, plant them at the same time you would put out bulbs in the garden. If fall-planted, protect the bulbs in a cold frame or bury them in a trench as you would for forcing (page 132), leaving them covered until frost danger is past. If spring-planted, treat them the same as bulbs planted in the ground.

In warm climates (zones 8 through 10) you may need to use the trench method to provide the necessary cooling, as when forcing fall-planted bulbs.

Keep container-planted bulbs evenly moist throughout their growing and blooming period. Then reduce watering as bulbs begin their rest period.

Most bulbs grown in containers should be repotted annually, but some can remain in containers year after year, with winter protection provided in cold climates. They can go indoors, be buried in the garden and mulched, or be stored in a basement or garage where they won't freeze. These include achimenes, canna, clivia, lilium, and zantedeschia. Each year at the normal planting season, knock out some of the soil and add fresh mixture to the container.

This cyclamen is growing in a log planter outdoors in a very protected location. It is visible from indoors as well as outdoors.

Harvesting and Storing

Exercise care when you dig up bulbs to make room for other plants or when you dig those that are not hardy to your zone and must be stored for the winter. Likewise, be careful when you're planting in an area containing bulbs. The spading fork is the best digging tool, since it is less likely to slice through a bulb. Discard any badly wounded bulbs.

After digging bulbs, shake off loose soil and dry them for about a week in a shady, protected spot with good ventilation. Then brush off any remaining soil, and dust with a fungicide to help control rot and other diseases.

Store the bulbs in dry peat moss, perlite, vermiculite, or sand, in a porous bag or a shallow tray. This keeps them from drying out, yet allows them to breathe. Store them in a cool (35° to 50°F), dry place where they will not freeze.

These pots of flowering bulbs create a stunning indoor garden that will outlast most cut flowers. If you force your own bulbs indoors, you'll be able to watch their gradual development from day to day.

Bringing Bulbs Indoors

Flowering bulbs deserve close observation. The subtlety of individual forms, the complexity of their structures, their fragrances, their intense colors and delicate pastel hues are best appreciated at intimate range. While bulbs are beautiful in the landscape, it seems they reach their pinnacle indoors as cut blooms or "forced" for potted display.

Bulbs as Cut Flowers

Many bulbs produce long-lasting cut flowers. Select blooms that are just beginning to open, as well as a few buds that will open in a day or two, to prolong the bouquet. Leave behind as much foliage as possible on the plant to provide nutrients for the formation of next year's bulb. Removing flowers from the plant causes no harm to the bulb and may even make it stronger the following year, since it will not have to exert energy in the maturing and seed-producing stages of flowering. More information on planning and planting a cutting garden and caring for cut flowers can be found in Chapter 1, pages 36–37.

When you initially cut the flowers, don't combine tulips and daffodils in the same water. The sap of daffodils injures the tulips. If you wish to combine them in an arrangement, let each first sit in its own container of water for a few hours.

Although most bulbs enjoy deep water, narcissus seem to last longer if the water level is kept shallow, just a few inches at the bottom of the container. They drink a lot, so you'll need to check daily to maintain the water level.

Forcing Bulbs Indoors

Causing a plant to bloom at a time or under conditions that are not natural is called forcing. Hardy bulbs, listed on page 129, are particularly suited to this technique and can provide a succession of indoor color from January to April. Most gardeners force bulbs for potted display, but you can grow blooms in flats if the object is to have winter cut flowers that would be prohibitively expensive at your local florist's. If you wish, add the challenge of forcing blooms in time for a particular holiday, such as Valentine's Day or Easter.

Bulb Varieties for Forcing

Type of Bulb	Time of Flowering	
	January and February	**March and April**
Tulipa	Red—Bing Crosby, Olaf, Paul Richter Yellow—Bellona White—Hibernia Pink—Christmas Marvel Variegated—Kees Nelis	Red—Bing Crosby, Olaf Yellow—Bellona, Ornament White—Hibernia Pink—Peerless Pink Variegated—Golden Eddy, Edith Eddy
Hyacinthus	Red—Jan Bos Pink—Pink Pearl, Lady Derby White—L'Innocence, Colosseum Blue—Ostara, Delft Blue	Red—none available Pink—Pink Pearl, Marconi White—Carnegie Blue—Blue Jacket, Ostara
Narcissus	Yellow—Carlton, Unsurpassable, Dutch Master, Soleil d'Or Bicolor—Barrett Browning, Fortune, Ice Follies White—Mt. Hood, Paper-white, Chinese sacred lily	Yellow—Dutch Master, Soleil d'Or, Unsurpassable Bicolor—Barrett Browning, Magnet, Ice Follies White—Mt. Hood, Paper-white, Chinese sacred lily
Crocus	Purple—Remembrance, *Purpureus grandiflorus* White—Peter Pan Striped—Pickwick Yellow—none available	Purple—Remembrance, *Purpureus grandiflorus* White—Peter Pan Striped—Pickwick Yellow—Large Yellow
Muscari (grape hyacinth)	Blue—Early Giant	Blue—Early Giant
Iris reticulata	Blue—Harmony Yellow—Danfordiae Purple—Hercules	Blue—Harmony Yellow—none available Purple—Hercules

Adapted from Michigan State Extension Bulletin 593.

This forced hyacinth provides welcome indoor color during winter, a time of year when the outdoor landscape is often drab and uninteresting.

The most common hardy bulbs for forcing are daffodils, tulips, hyacinths, and crocuses. Others that can easily be forced include galanthus, Dutch iris and *Iris reticulata*, grape hyacinths *(Muscari)*, *Scilla tubergeniana*, eranthis, ornithogalum, and brodiaea.

Allium, camassia, *Scilla campanulata*, and lilies are among the difficult-to-force bulbs. They require specialized techniques and, usually, greenhouse conditions.

The four stages necessary for forcing hardy bulbs are: choosing the bulbs and, if necessary, preliminary storage; planting; cooling; and forcing them into bloom. The key to each is appropriate timing.

Choosing Bulbs for Forcing   Whichever kind of bulb you choose to force, be sure the variety you purchase is clearly marked "good for forcing," especially if, as is the case with tulips, hyacinths, and daffodils, a wide number of varieties are available. Some common varieties that are suitable for forcing are listed

on page 129. It's wise to order your selections well in advance—
in the spring if possible—to ensure their availability. Try to
have them delivered no earlier than mid-September.

If you receive an early shipment or for some reason can't plant
the bulbs immediately, store them in a cool (35° to 55°F) place.
A refrigerator is ideal. If they are packed in boxes or paper
bags, open them up to provide ventilation. Bulbs can be stored
this way for several weeks. Remember that bulbs are living
plants. Handle them carefully and avoid exposing them to
freezing temperatures.

Planting the Bulbs   Bulbs can be planted any time during
October or November to bloom from January through April.
They require a cooling period of about fourteen or fifteen weeks.
You can cool them for anywhere from thirteen to eighteen
weeks, but the stems will be short on those cooled less than
fourteen weeks and long on those cooled more than fifteen
weeks.

In general, plant around the beginning of October for January
flowers, the middle of October for February flowers, and
November for March and April flowers.

The planting mix serves to anchor the bulbs in place and to
hold moisture for rooting. The bulbs contain enough food for
the developing flowers and roots and shouldn't be fertilized
during the forcing process. They must have excellent, sharp
drainage or they will rot—but they should not be allowed to dry
out. A good soil mix is one part loamy soil, one part peat, and
one part sand. Use clean pots that have drainage holes in the
bottom. If you use clay pots, soak them overnight so they won't
draw moisture from the planting mix.

Fill each pot loosely with soil. The tops of the bulbs should be
even with the rim when placed in the pot. Don't compress the
soil or press the bulbs into it: The soil under the bulbs should
remain loose so that roots can grow through it easily. After the
bulbs are in, loosely fill the pots to the rim. The first watering
will settle the soil enough to provide a reservoir for future
watering. Water the pots to be sure all the soil is moist.

A six-inch pot or bulb pan can be planted with the following
quantities of bulbs: three hyacinths, six daffodils, fifteen
crocuses, or half a dozen tulips. When planting tulips, place the
bulb so that the flat side faces toward the outside of the pot.
The first large leaf of each plant will then face outward, creating
a uniform appearance. Be sure to label each pot as you plant it,
noting the name of the variety, the planting date, and the date
you intend to bring it indoors for forcing.

Cooling the Bulbs   All hardy bulbs need a period of cooling at temperatures between 35° and 50°F to prepare them for later leaf and flower growth.

Some bulbs, especially tulips that are sold in mild-climate regions, have been "precooled" by the producer. These can be planted and forced immediately, or they can be treated as uncooled bulbs and cooled all over again. If you want blooming plants later in the season, choose the second approach.

During this deceptively "quiet" cooling period, the plants' roots are forming, so pots must be kept moist. With well-drained soil, it's difficult to overwater; check weekly to see if the pots need watering.

Cooling methods vary, but any structure where temperatures can be kept at 35° to 50°F can be used. Many people find a root cellar or an unheated basement the most convenient; others dedicate an old refrigerator to this job.

In zones 3 through 6, pots can be cooled in a trench in the garden or in a cold frame. With either of these methods, it is important to keep the pots from freezing. A cold frame used for this purpose should be well drained and in a shady location. After the pots are placed in the cold frame, cover them with insulating material—sand, sawdust, straw, or similar mulches.

To use the trench method, dig a trench about six inches wider than the pots, deep enough for the pots to be below the frost line, and long enough to hold all the pots you wish to cool. Spread an inch of gravel or cinders on the bottom of the trench for drainage, and line the pots in the trench. Cover the pots with a few inches of sand and finish filling the trench with soil.

Just before freezing weather, cover the trench with an insulating mulch. Bales of straw are convenient.

For a succession of blooms, place pots in storage in the reverse order in which you wish to remove them.

If you anticipate that mice may make a home in the mulch and use your bulbs as food, top the trench with quarter-inch-mesh wire screen before applying the mulch. A diagram of where the pots are placed in the trench and which bulbs are in each will help you find what you want when you're ready to force each pot indoors. If the weather is dry, water the pots frequently.

Forcing the Blooms   At the forcing stage, the pots are brought out of their cooled environment into warmth and light, triggering the formation of leaves and flowers. From the time the pots are removed from storage, they will require about three or four weeks to bloom. Bulbs planted on the first of October can be brought indoors around Christmas. Bring in a few pots every week after that for a continuous supply of blooms.

For best results, give the bulbs a temperature of 60°F and direct sunlight. Rotate the pots regularly so that all the leaves receive an equal amount of light. Removing the flower buds from direct sunlight when they begin to color will prolong the bloom. Be sure to keep the soil moist throughout the entire forcing period.

If you're aiming for a specific flowering date and you see that growth is occurring too quickly, blooming can be delayed by moving the pots to a cool (40° to 50°F) room out of direct sunlight (but not in darkness). Reaccustom them gradually to sunlight when you want them to resume growth.

After blooming, hardy bulbs cannot be forced again. A few, such as daffodils, can be transplanted into the garden in spring, but it will take them two or three years to reach their full blooming potential again. Most, such as tulips and hyacinths, are best discarded after forcing.

Most bulbs cannot be forced more than once. These hyacinths will be replaced next year with new bulbs.

Rosa Gallica Aurelianensis   *La Duchesse d'Orleans*

Roses

The rose has long enjoyed universal appeal unequaled by any other plant form. The plants have been prized as ornamental shrubbery for centuries. And the flowers, bathed in the romantic language of love, are present on many important occasions of our lives.

Roses have been immortalized in every form of the arts. They are favorite subjects of painters, poets, playwrights, music composers, sculptors, craftsmen, and designers. Shakespeare probably spoke for most of the artistic community when he penned, "Of all the flowers, methinks a rose is best."

Roses have played important roles in history since ancient civilizations. Probably the most famous was in the English Wars of the Roses, when the House of York adopted a white rose as its emblem, opposed by the red rose symbol of the House of Lancaster. When the two families resolved their differences, a new Tudor rose that blended red and white became the national emblem of England. Roses have appeared on the emblems, awards, currency, and postage stamps of nations around the world.

Today the rose is certainly our most popular flower. More than fifty million American families have at least one rosebush under cultivation. In the majority of gardens, however, roses are not part of the total landscape design, but are grown primarily for their flowers.

A Guide to the Genus *Rosa*
Roses have always been a part of nature's landscape design. Fossil evidence shows that roses have been around for at least thirty million years. Some type of rose has been discovered growing wild in almost every habitable place in the northern hemisphere of our planet.

Botanically speaking, all roses belong to the genus *Rosa*, a member of the family *Rosaceae*. Relatives include almonds, apples, peaches, raspberries, and strawberries. The genus *Rosa* contains about two hundred species, with countless crosses that have produced thousands of cultivars, hybrids, and varieties.

Ancestors of the Modern Rose
The hybrid teas and other modern roses we grow today are the result of complex hybridization and interbreeding. The ancestors of our modern roses have a long history; some of them have graced gardens for thousands of years.

Left: *Rosa gallica aurelianensis* 'La Duchesse d'Orleans' by Pierre-Joseph Redouté.

*If Jove would give the leafy
  bowers
A queen for all their world of
  flowers,
The Rose would be the choice
  by Jove;
And reign the queen of every
  grove.*

Moore
The Queen of the Garden

China and Tea Roses

A big boost to European rose development arrived from China in the late 1700s and early 1800s. Forms of *Rosa chinensis*, known as China roses, made their debut, followed closely by the first tea rose, *R. odorata*. Chinas have small semidouble blooms in red or pink, with an occasional white streak, and a peppery fragrance. Tea roses smell much like freshly crushed tea leaves, and are medium-size to large, in pink, cream, and pale yellow. Both are everblooming, somewhat tender plants.

The addition of these repeat-blooming roses created much excitement among the breeders. Advancement was slowed because of the difficulty in crossing the genetic differences in the European and China roses. However, within a few years, many new forms of roses were developed.

Hybrid Perpetual Roses

The parentage of hybrid perpetual roses is complex, involving repeated intercrossing among the teas, Chinas, and others. Hybrid perpetuals became the rage of the mid-1800s, when at least four thousand varieties were introduced. Many are still available and worth growing because they are strong, hardy, vigorous plants, blooming profusely in the spring. Some repeat blooming occurs through the summer, producing large flowers of varied forms in shades of crimson, pink, purple, and white.

Hybrid Tea Roses

In 1867, J. B. Guillot of France bred 'La France', considered at first to be a more compact growing hybrid perpetual. Similar roses, however, appeared more and more frequently from breeding hybrid perpetuals and tea roses. Soon they were classified as hybrid tea roses.

Below: 'Chicago Peace', a hybrid tea rose, has large, double, pink and yellow flowers with a light fragrance. Right: 'China Doll' is a polyantha rose that blooms profusely.

In 1900, Joseph Pernet-Ducher added the yellow strain of *R. foetida* to the hybrid teas with his 'Soleil d'Or', opening many new possibilities for hybridizers. For a number of years his brightly colored roses were known as Pernetianas, but were absorbed into the hybrid tea class by the 1930s.

Hybrid teas have undergone constant improvements until they have become the rose of the mid-twentieth century. Flowers are borne singly on long stems or in small clusters. Colors range from whites through lavenders, pinks, yellows, oranges, and reds, with mixtures and blends in between. Most are fragrant. Plants are grafted onto vigorous shrub rootstock to produce salable plants faster in large quantities. They grow from two to six feet in height and are continuous blooming.

Polyantha Roses

The polyantha roses arrived on the French scene about the same time as the hybrid teas. They were derived mainly from *Rosa multiflora* and crossed with tea and China roses. The low-growing, continuous-blooming plants produce large clusters of small flowers in all the rose colors.

Floribunda Roses

Sometimes called hybrid polyanthas, the floribundas resulted from an early twentieth-century cross of the polyanthas and hybrid teas. As the name implies, they produce "flowers in abundance." Blooms resemble hybrid teas in form and color range, and are borne in clusters. Most plants are disease resistant, hardy, and low growing.

Floribunda roses have large clusters of flowers on short stems, and are among the best of the landscape roses. 'Spartan', shown here, is fragrant and disease resistant.

Climbing roses add old-fashioned charm to arbors, trellises, fences, and other garden structures. The large-flowered climber shown above is 'Lawrence Johnston'.

Grandiflora Roses

Grandiflora roses came into being about twenty-five years ago as an American classification to designate roses that are intermediate in habit between hybrid teas and floribundas. The flowers resemble those of hybrid teas, but are borne in clusters like those of floribundas. Growth habits resemble floribundas, and the plants are generally taller than hybrid teas.

Miniature Roses

In Europe in about 1815, *R. chinensis minima (R. roulettii)* was introduced as the first miniature rose. Miniatures were the rage in France, but fashion changed, and they quickly faded from sight. It wasn't until the late 1920s that the miniature was rediscovered growing in a window in Switzerland. In recent years these small plants with tiny flowers have become increasingly popular. Most bloom continuously and varieties appear in all the colors and forms of hybrid teas, with five to seventy petals. They have little or no fragrance.

Climbing Roses and Ramblers

Botanically tall-growing (six to twenty feet) plants of any one of the other types of roses are called climbing roses or ramblers. They are not true climbers, however, since they have no tendrils with which to attach themselves and must be tied to a support. In the wild, thorns act as tendrils. They may be everblooming or once-blooming each year, and come in a wide range of flower color, size, and form.

Designing with Roses

Whether you serve as your own landscape architect or use the services of a professional, consider some of the ways roses can fit into your landscape. The floribunda and miniature roses are shrubs that look well in a prominent spot in the garden. Hybrid teas and grandifloras need to be carefully planned into the landscape because they are grown for their beautiful flowers and are not as attractive in the landscape as are the floribundas and miniatures.

Roses As Space-Definers

Roses can be used to define space just like any other shrub. Use them as foundation plantings of various heights around the house; or plant them to form a living fence, hedge, or barrier to block a view, give privacy, or redirect traffic. The placement of roses can create illusions that carry the eye to another point, add extra height, or increase or decrease the depth of the garden.

This row of 'Europeana' floribunda roses makes a beautiful, fragrant hedge. Many roses used as landscape plants still yield bouquets of fresh-cut flowers.

Roses and Lawns

Plant beds of massed floribundas and miniatures to create a lush spot of color against a green lawn. Or add interest to your lawn by edging it with roses. Colorful rose blooms can fill in a corner to give the lawn a completed look.

Plant Roses Where You'll Enjoy Them

If you spend time entertaining outdoors, consider building raised or recessed beds into the patio or terrace to bring roses right into the entertainment area.

If you spend most of your time indoors, plant beds of roses so that they can be seen from your favorite picture window.

Consider planting a separate rose cutting garden. The hybrid teas and grandifloras, which are usually planted for their beautiful blossoms, are less attractive plants than some of the other landscape roses. The tea roses and grandifloras are ideally suited to the cutting garden, which is usually placed out of public view. Another benefit of the cutting garden is that you can lay it out so that it's easy to reach the individual plants, making it simpler to provide the extra care necessary to grow specimen blooms. This, in turn, allows you to leave flowers on your landscape bushes until they fade.

Good designing with any plant material requires an understanding of the particular plant's needs and potential. Study the characteristics of any given rosebush and how you can expect it to perform before determining where to place it in your landscape design. Consider its height, growth habits (bushy, spreading, upright), and foliage type and color. Rely on pruning to help control the fit of the plant into the garden design. And remember to choose varieties with long-lasting flowers.

Roses in Containers

When you grow roses in containers, you have total freedom to change the design of your landscape for special occasions, according to changes in the weather, or just on a whim.

Miniatures are obvious container-garden candidates, but full-size roses, even climbers and trees, can be successfully grown and moved in large pots or tubs.

Container gardening is the answer for people with limited space, balconies, decks, or terraces who still want to grow roses. Consider planting tree roses in containers near apartment windows for an eye-level splash of summer color. You can even brighten up an urban high-rise balcony with roses in containers. Train climbing roses on a wire fence to frame the cityscape and soften the harshness of adjacent buildings.

Left: 'Cecile Brunner' is one of the best known of the polyantha roses. Profuse, delicate pink, tiny blooms cover the plant throughout the season. It's a favorite for arbors and trellises. Below: Miniature roses, such as 'Tiny Flame' shown here, are perfect for containers.

Roses complement perennials and bulbs to give a charming cottage garden look, as shown by this planting of a rose with bearded irises and watsonias. Roses may need extra care when interplanted so closely; diseases are more likely to develop in such heavily vegetated plantings where air circulation is reduced.

Some Helpful Pointers

Choose your planting sites carefully. Sunshine, good drainage, and adequate air circulation are critical factors in rose growing. Give the bushes and roots plenty of room to develop.

Buy quality plants, and keep the quantity to a number that you can cope with, according to the amount of time and energy at your disposal. Be sure you are willing to provide the care that roses require all year long to produce a season of blooms— at least an hour or so of your time each week.

Remember that roses are deciduous, and for the winter months will be only naked silhouettes in most landscapes, or mounds of winter coverings in very cold areas.

Don't overplant. The purpose of good landscaping is to enhance the view, not overwhelm it. And don't forget the view from inside the house.

Rose Care

Many gardeners think of roses as difficult, fussy plants that demand a great deal of time and attention. It is certainly true that it takes some effort to grow good-quality roses, but the generous number of blossoms that a healthy plant produces is a sufficient reward for most gardeners.

In fact, a weekly or biweekly visit to the garden to fertilize, water, and spray your roses takes very little time. You'll probably find that these tasks turn into pleasant excuses to spend time in your garden.

Selecting a Site

Roses perform best when they receive full sunshine all day. If this is not possible, they should be planted where they will get a minimum of six hours of direct sunlight daily.

There should be air movement through the foliage to keep it dry and discourage diseases. Plant the bushes away from large trees or shrub masses, which will compete for nutrients, moisture, and sunlight.

Drainage is a critical factor for roses. If the desired site doesn't drain well, there are several ways to modify the area.

You can dig a large trench beneath the planting site and bury a drain tile or pipe in coarse gravel. Drain openings should be covered with asphalt roofing paper to prevent soil from washing in and clogging the holes. The pipe should be slightly slanted toward a ditch, storm sewer, or dry well.

An easier solution is to build a raised bed. In very moist areas build a bed at least ten to fifteen inches high. The side construction can be redwood or masonry framing, old railway

'McGredy's Sunset' (left) and 'Circus' (right) thrive in this sunny location with rich, well-drained soil—an ideal spot for roses.

ties, even stone or brick. In addition to giving excellent drainage, you'll find that raised beds make gardening chores easier.

Consider possible erosion problems before planting on a hillside or slope. Terracing—a modified raised-bed approach—can solve your problem.

Soils

Roses do well in a wide range of soils, but prefer loamy soil with high humus content, at least two feet deep. Amend the soil with organic matter, such as compost or leaf mold, dehydrated cow manure, peat moss, or shredded bark (all available from garden centers). Add three to four pounds of nourishing super-phosphate per hundred square feet of soil surface for stronger root development.

If you're planting bushes individually and the soil is good, dig holes fourteen to sixteen inches wide, and twelve to fifteen inches deep. Work organic matter into the excavated soil. Use the same principle for a large bed of roses.

Roses respond best in a slightly acid soil with a pH of 6.0 to 6.5. (For a complete description of soil pH, see Chapter 14, page 347.) Make a soil test to determine the acidity. If the soil is too acid (pH below 5.5), add five pounds of lime for each cubic foot of planting soil. If the soil is on the alkaline side (pH over 7.5), add soil sulfur at the rate specified by a soil testing company or by the label directions.

Roses need well-drained soil with lots of organic matter. Healthy growth with many blooms rewards the effort spent in preparing a rose bed properly.

Time to Plant

Start with strong-rooted, healthy plants with plump, fresh-looking canes.

Planting times for packaged or bareroot roses are:

Coldest winter

Temperature	Planting time
10°F	Any time bushes are dormant
−10°F	Fall or spring
Below −10°F	Spring only

Container-grown roses can be transplanted into the garden at any time from spring to fall.

If you're planting in the winter or early spring, get bareroot plants into the ground as early as the weather will permit. Early planting gives roots a chance to start growth before the tops break into leaf.

By the time you receive your roses, there's probably been some drying out in storage and shipping. To ensure a good start, either bury roots and tops in wet peat moss or sawdust for two or three days, or completely soak the plants in water overnight. Don't let roots dry out when planting. Carry them to the planting site in a wheelbarrow or bucket that is half-filled with water.

If you can't plant right away because of weather conditions or time schedule, wrap the entire soaked plant in wet burlap or newspaper. Store in a dark, cool spot (between 33° and 60°F). If you still can't plant after a week, soak the bushes again for an hour, rewrap, and store again for up to a week.

If you must keep roses even longer, soak once again and bury them in a trench at a forty-five-degree angle, covering the tops completely with a few inches of moist soil. They'll hold like this for up to five to six weeks. Or store them in a large container of moist peat moss in a shaded, protected area.

Planting Bareroot Roses   After preparing the hole as outlined earlier, prune the soaked rose plant to three or four strong canes, cutting about one-quarter inch above a good bud.

Next, prune the main root pieces to reveal white tissue. These cuts will cause scarring, which will promote increased root production.

Build a cone of soil mixture in the center of the hole to support the spread-out roots and hold the plant so that the bud union (the thick scar on the base of the trunk where the rose

was grafted to the rootstock) is at the proper level. The rule of thumb is that the bud union should be as much as two inches below the soil level in cold-winter areas. Place it at or slightly above soil level in mild-winter areas. Whatever method you choose, lay a pole or shovel handle across the hole to represent soil level when positioning the plant.

With the plant in position, add about two-thirds of the soil mix, then fill the hole with water. Let it soak in completely. Fill in around the roots with soil mix and firm gently.

Mound soil at least two-thirds the height of the plant. You may have to get extra soil for this. Moisten again. This mound gives protection from drying winds and warm sun, and provides enough moisture for the developing plant.

Leave the mound until new growth is one or two inches long, then carefully remove it to ground level and add mulch.

Left: Be sure to spread the roots of a bareroot rose over the soil mound in the planting hole. Use the handle of a shovel to determine the correct position of the bud union. Above: Wait until the new growth is several inches long before mulching.

Transplanting Roses

Transplant roses in the early spring or late fall when they are fully dormant, but while the ground is workable.

Prepare the new planting site as you would for planting container-grown or bareroot roses. Soak the soil around the rose bush overnight so that you can dig the plant with as much earth as possible to minimize root disturbance. Prune large bushes back to eighteen to twenty-four inches to make handling easier. Position the plant in the new hole and firm soil around the roots. Irrigate the plant just as you would for bareroot or container-grown plantings.

Label Your Plants

Roses arrive with name tags attached, but the wire attachment can damage the cane as it grows. Remove it at planting time, attach the label to a stake, and place the stake in the soil near the bush. Labels are available in many styles, plain or decorative.

In addition to placing a name tag near each plant in the garden, make a diagram of your landscape and write in the name of each rose, date planted, source, and any other information you wish to record. This may be valuable in the years to come, either to you or to someone who may later purchase your home.

Watering

One thing rose people do agree on is that you can't give a rose too much water. But a rose will not tolerate wet feet! Drainage must be excellent.

The frequency of watering, as well as the amount, depends on soil type, climate, and the growth stage of the rose. More water is needed when the soil is loose and sandy, when the air is hot and dry, or when the new plants are developing.

Normally a rose should receive the equivalent of one inch of rainfall per week, all at one time, starting in early spring and continuing through fall. Hot and dry weather may call for watering every three or four days, or more often during drought.

To keep track of your roses, identify them with permanent labels. Either remove the labels that come with the plants and attach them to stakes, or make your own labels.

For best performance, give roses growing amidst other plants the extra care they require. This cabbage rose *(Rosa centifolia)* must be watered more deeply and fertilized more frequently than the surrounding perennials.

Even when rainfall is plentiful, porous soils benefit from additional deep soakings.

In the early spring, water roses from overhead to prevent canes from drying while developing. When foliage growth begins, keep water off the leaves and apply directly to the soil for best results.

When you water, water well, soaking the soil to a depth of eight to ten inches. A light sprinkling is worse than no water at all. Frequent light applications result in shallow root systems, and increased susceptibility to drought conditions.

Rose growers differ in their methods of irrigation. Some people build a basin or dike around the entire bed. Others prefer a basin around each rose bush. Either way, the basin is flooded with water that slowly soaks into the soil. This is a good method in dry-summer regions.

The most efficient system is slow-drip irrigation at the base of the plants. A heavy stream of water from a hose is wasteful, because most of it runs off and what remains penetrates the soil only a few inches. A soaker hose provides deep soaking to moisten the soil to the required depth. Also, this system does not wet the foliage or spread the mulch, thus reducing disease. It saves you time, energy, and even money, because less water is used in the long run.

If you do choose to sprinkle, however, water early in the morning so that the leaves can dry before they are exposed to the hot midday sun. Be sure the sprinkler runs long enough to meet the eight- to ten-inch-deep soaking requirements. With this method you'll have to apply fungicides more frequently to guard against mildew and blackspot.

Controlling Weeds

Soil around roses requires just enough cultivation to eliminate weeds and prevent the light surface crusts that sometimes form. Cultivating soil to a very shallow level will prevent injury to roots that may be growing close to the surface. Deep cultivation can destroy feeder roots.

Weeds can be controlled by hand-pulling or by cutting them at the soil surface, eliminating cultivation if there's no problem with soil crusting.

Chemical weed control should be practiced according to directions on the manufacturer's weed-control product label. The easy way is to combine chemical weed control, nutrients, and pesticides in one application of systemic rose care. Be sure to follow the directions for suggested distances from fruit trees and vegetable gardens.

Feeding Roses

Roses are heavy feeders; they need regular applications of fertilizer for optimal growth.

The rate, frequency, and kind of fertilizer depend on the type of soil. Plants in sandy soils benefit from frequent applications; those in heavy soils may not need as much. A soil test can help determine the particular balance of nitrogen, phosphorus, and potassium you need. Or check with your county extension agent or nursery staff for recommendations of fertilizer ratio and application rates for your local area.

Begin your fertilizer program for newly planted bushes after the plants become established, about three or four weeks after planting.

Most rose growers agree on frequent fertilizer applications for all types of roses. Begin in early spring as the bush puts out leaves, then continue every six weeks, or even once each month, through late summer.

Some rose people advocate three applications per year for hybrid teas, grandifloras, and floribundas: (1) early spring just after pruning, when the bush begins to leaf out; (2) early summer, when the plant is beginning to flower; and (3) late summer, to carry it on through fall. In warm coastal areas an additional application in the fall may be necessary.

More so than many other landscape shrubs, hybrid roses must be fertilized regularly for top-quality flowers and healthy growth. Here, the floribunda rose 'John Church' shows the benefits of adequate fertilization.

Careful pruning in the early spring contributes to the showy display of summer flowers alongside this pathway. Tree roses, floribundas, and miniature roses are growing here. The tree roses require the heaviest amount of dormant pruning, the floribundas and miniatures, light dormant pruning.

Pruning Roses

An unpruned rose can grow into a mass of tangled brambles that produces small or inferior blooms. Proper pruning removes nonproductive or damaged wood, and leaves a few good canes as the foundation of a healthy bush. Pruning gives the rose plant an attractive shape and a size that fits into the landscape design. And bloom quality and quantity are improved by good pruning practices.

You'll need three types of cutting instruments: a fine-toothed curved saw for cutting woody tissue; pruning shears with one side for cutting and one for holding; and long-handled lopping shears for thick canes and for getting into hard-to-reach places. Make sure your tools have sharp blades and are well lubricated.

In addition, you'll need a pair of heavy-duty leather garden gloves and pruning paint to seal major cuts.

Make Cuts Correctly

Cut at a forty-five- to sixty-five-degree angle. Make all cuts down to a cane, to the point on the crown from which the cane originated, or to a strong outside (outward-facing) bud, or eye, on stem nodes. This eye is the origin of all new replacement growth. Make cuts about one-quarter inch above the bud. Don't leave stubs; they become entry points for disease organisms.

When using pruning shears, make sure the cutting blade is on the lower side to ensure a clean cut. The slight injury that results from pressure on the noncutting side should be on the top part of the cane, which will be discarded.

Pruning Bush Roses

Prune bush roses just before the rosebush breaks dormancy. The right time can fall anytime between January in warm areas to April in very cold zones. Check with your county extension service for suggested local dates.

Don't prune roses until you completely remove winter protections and frost danger is past. Prune when buds begin to swell and new leaves begin to develop. It's a good idea to wait until you see this new growth before pruning so that you can determine what part of the plant may have been killed during the winter.

Three Types of Bush Pruning   It usually takes several years to learn the best method for each variety of rose you prune. Don't be shy when it comes to taking off growth. Most roses are hardy shrubs and will bounce back with plenty of new growth after they've been pruned.

Heavy: The plant is cut back to three or four canes six to ten inches high in heavy pruning. This severe pruning method is practiced to produce showy blooms. Prune only vigorous, well-established bushes in this manner. Severe pruning of weak bushes sacrifices the plant's vigor and reduces the life span of the bush.

Moderate: In moderate pruning five to twelve canes are left, each about eighteen to twenty-four inches high. Moderate pruning develops a much larger bush than heavy pruning and is best suited to most garden roses.

Light: Light pruning involves a minimum of cutting, with plants remaining three to four feet in height. Light pruning produces a profusion of short-stemmed flowers on larger bushes. This method is practiced mainly with floribundas, grandifloras, first-year hybrid teas, species roses, and weak-growing varieties of all classes.

Bush Pruning Procedure You will find heavy pruning easier if the bud union is aboveground. If you have planted below the soil level, you might wish to remove soil from around the bud union during pruning so that you can see the origin of all canes.

First, remove any dead wood down to the nearest healthy, dormant bud. Make the cut at least one inch below the dead area. If no live buds remain, remove the entire branch or cane to the bud union.

Examine carefully for canker or other diseased areas. (See Chapter 14, page 365.) Cut down to a good bud at least an inch

Pruning can be a time-consuming task. Heavy pruning and careful pinching are required to produce large, long-stemmed roses.

Use long-handled, sharp shears to remove unwanted canes close to the bud union.

This climbing rose is growing on a narrow trellis. To maintain an attractive, full, but not sprawling, appearance, train climbers to fit the support on which they are growing.

below any evidence of disease. Although canes may look healthy, there can be a problem in the pith, the inside of the wood. Cut the top of each cane and check inside. Pith should be creamy white, not brown or gray. Prune down to healthy pith, or to the bud union if the pith is diseased all the way through.

Cut out weak, spindly, or deformed growth. This includes canes that grow straight out, then curve upward (doglegs). Remove canes growing toward the center of the bush. If two branches cross, remove the weaker one.

Remove all suckers (undesired shoots that grow above the bud union). Sucker foliage differs in color and form from the rest of the plant. If you do not remove suckers, they will soon dominate the plant. When cutting them out, take all of the sucker base from the crown area, along with a piece of the crown.

Next, thin out the remaining healthy canes to the desired shape and cut them down to the selected height. After severe winters, all the canes may have to be cut to within several inches of the bud union. In such cases you can't worry about shape; just save as much live wood as you can.

Pruning and Training Climbing Roses

Prune ramblers and vigorous climbing roses soon after flowering. Cut out diseased or dead canes and remove older gray canes, as well as weak new ones. Most climber canes are good for only two or three seasons. Save the green, healthy canes. Cut laterals back to eight to ten buds to shape the plant as desired. Be sure to remove any suckers.

Less vigorous climbers need to be trimmed each spring only to remove the wood that has been killed over the winter.

Hybrid climbers and everblooming large-flowered climbers are pruned while dormant. Do not take as much wood from the everbloomers as from the hybrids. Proceed as you would with bush roses: Remove dead and diseased canes; get rid of any sucker growth; and remove old growth or weak new growth. Retain three or four vigorous young canes.

Pruning Tree Roses

Standards, or tree roses, are pruned just like bush roses. Cut out dead or diseased branches and canes, leaving healthy canes pruned back to a good bud. Keep the shape as symmetrical as possible so that the foliage will fill out into a full, round shape.

You have twice as much chance for suckers with tree roses as you do with bush plants. They can grow from the rootstock or from the trunk stock. Cut them out as close to their base as possible to prevent regrowth.

Groom roses throughout the growing season—remove faded flowers, weak, crossing, and diseased shoots. When grooming hybrid tea roses, allow at least two five-leaflet leaves to remain on the shoot where you remove the faded rose.

Year-Round Pruning Care

Prune and groom roses as they grow. Continue all season to cut out weak and spindly shoots, suckers, and obvious signs of disease. Make an effort to remove old flowers as soon as they have passed their peak to encourage further bloom.

Hybrid tea flowers are produced in waves. Allowing the plant to set seeds increases the interval between periods of bloom. When removing fading flowers, don't just snip off the flower, but cut back to a five-leaflet leaf. Cuts at these major leaves result in stronger new foliage as the plant continues to develop. During the first growing season of a newly planted rose, just snip the flowers; a young plant needs all the leaves it can produce. In cold-winter areas, allow the seed pods (hips) to form on the final wave of bloom. Formation of hips slows down growth and hardens the plant for winter.

If you want to produce large exhibition blooms, disbud most of the side vegetative buds and flowers and allow only one or a selected few terminal buds to mature.

Keep flowers plucked off everblooming roses, but do not remove foliage, since reblooming occurs from the top leaves, immediately under the old flower cluster.

Winter Protection

Although there is controversy among the experts regarding the need for winter protection of roses, it's usually wisest to take the extra precaution. Many roses, including quite a few species, shrubs, and climbers, are naturally cold-hardy. But all newly planted or not-yet-established roses need to be mulched if you live in Zones 3 through 7. In areas where the winters are severe, roses may need to be tipped over and buried under protective mulch. Check with your county extension agent for help in determining what kind of protection is best in your area.

There are a number of newer hybrid teas marketed as sub-zero plants that will tolerate temperatures to 0°F with only a mulch around the base of the plant, but these need to be more thoroughly protected if temperatures fall below zero.

One of a plant's best defenses against cold weather is proper summer care. Vigorous bushes are able to withstand cold far better than unhealthy ones. Roses planted in locations that are protected by trees, large shrubs, or structures need less protection than bushes exposed to the elements.

Where temperatures drop to 10° to 15°F for as much as two weeks at a time, most bush roses are adequately protected by mounding the base of each plant with fresh, loose soil or compost that drains well. Immediately after the first frost, mound soil to a depth of six to eight inches around the plant. Some growers advise cutting back plants as much as sixteen to thirty inches before mounding. If you do this, be sure to clean up and dispose of all clippings to cut down the spread of disease. In any case, apply a final coat of dormant spray (an oil-based spray that kills overwintering pests and diseases) before mounding. At this time you can tie canes together to protect them from winds if you like.

Add hay or straw over the mound and exposed canes after the first hard freeze to protect against fluctuating temperatures, and freezing and thawing of soil around the canes.

There are rose caps available from horticultural houses, or you can devise your own cover. If you choose to use caps, prune the plant to fit underneath.

If you live in an area where salt is used on roads, protect your plants by spreading plastic over the soil after the first hard freeze, then cover with straw or hay.

Where temperatures dip below zero, additional protection may be required.

Remove winter coverings when all danger of frost has passed. The growth underneath is very tender, so keep some mulch material handy to cover plants in the event of a late frost.

Tree Roses

In mild-winter areas, wrap tree roses in straw and cover with burlap. No protection is necessary in temperate zones.

If temperatures drop as low as 10°F, you may want to tip the plants. In late fall dig under the roots on one side, until the plant can be pulled over onto the ground without breaking root connections with the soil. Stake the plant to the ground and cover the entire plant with several inches of soil.

In spring, after the soil thaws and frost danger is past, remove the soil and set the plant upright once again.

Climbing Roses

A burlap wrapping is adequate protection for climbing roses in mild-winter climates. But in areas with hard freezes, you can bury climbers the same way you would tree roses.

Miniature Roses

Miniature roses closely resemble standard-size roses in every aspect except for their diminutive size. Miniature roses have gained immense popularity in recent years and can be enjoyed both outdoors and indoors.

Outdoors, miniature roses can be grown in the ground or planted in a variety of containers, including hanging baskets.

The small varieties differ only slightly from large roses in care. Since they grow on their own roots and are not grafted to different rootstocks, you don't have to worry about bud unions when you plant. Whether you plant in a pot or in the ground, set the rosebush slightly deeper than it originally grew.

Most varieties should be spaced about ten to twelve inches apart. Make sure the roses are separated from large plants that can rob them of much-needed sunshine and moisture.

When you read catalog descriptions of miniature plant sizes, remember that these are based on indoor or greenhouse pot culture, where size is regulated by the restricted root growth. Although the flowers remain tiny, many of the miniature plants will grow quite large when planted in the ground, especially in temperate climates. If you want to keep the bushes small, you'll need to prune them back severely.

Pruning of miniatures is easy. In the spring just clip the plant back, like boxwood, into the desired shape and shake out the clippings. You can prune miniatures back to half their size.

These little plants are more cold resistant than most hybrid teas or other garden roses, and require little winter protection. In warm climates they even keep on blooming all year.

'Starina', a top-rated miniature rose, produces abundant double, orange-scarlet flowers, and vigorous, glossy growth.

Shrubs

As a group shrubs contain some of the most beautiful and dramatic plants available to the gardener. But because shrubs are so familiar, many of their special traits are frequently overlooked.

People tend to think of shrubs as obscure masses of green plants that don't have the flair or distinction of annuals, perennials, or bulbs. But the fact of the matter is, there are thousands of varieties of shrubs, all with their own unique features.

Shrubs come in every form and size imaginable, with an array of leaf shapes and textures that seems almost infinite. Some burst into seasonal bloom with exquisite, colorful flowers, while others remain a steady, stately green all year long.

Although shrubs are commonly used as backgrounds for other plants, they often deserve to be featured as garden highlights, with all their elegance on full display.

What Is a Shrub?

While there is no hard and fast definition of what constitutes a shrub, this one is commonly accepted: a woody plant with multiple stems or trunks that grows less than fifteen feet high when mature.

A woody plant has stems and branches that survive from one year to the next, and that do not die back to the ground after each growing season. Their woody nature distinguishes shrubs

Left: A boxwood hedge, rhododendrons, and azaleas make a backdrop for this classic garden bench. Opposite page: "The Narrow-leaved Kalmia" from *The Temple of Flora* by Robert Thornton.

from herbaceous plants, which are subject to winter damage and which die back to the ground each year.

The fact that shrubs have multiple stems or trunks sets them apart from trees, which usually have only a single stem or trunk. There are exceptions: Many shrubs can be deliberately trained to have only a single trunk. Shrubs trained in this way are called standards; basically, they are miniature trees, often used for a formal effect. Some trees also have multiple trunks, but they usually grow higher than fifteen feet.

What Is a Hedge?

Hedges are simply shrubs or other plants that have been put to special use: They have been planted closely together so that they form an unbroken line and in most cases are carefully trimmed. Formal hedges are similar to fences in their solid, even appearance.

Hedge shrubs come in three basic heights: low—twelve inches or less—for bordering flower beds and walks; medium—up to six feet—for marking property borders and as backdrops for other plants; tall—over six feet—for controlling wind and sun and screening out objectionable views.

Establishing and maintaining a good-looking hedge may require some effort, but for many people it is effort well spent. We will give you specific information about planting, trimming, and maintaining hedges in the following pages. In our general discussion of shrubs, however, we are referring to all shrubs, including those that are commonly used for hedge plantings.

Basic Shrub Forms

To pick the right shrub for each garden area, you should have some idea of the shrub's mature form. Often a shrub will look one way in a five-gallon can and quite another after it has been planted in the garden for a few years. Most shrubs have a naturally occurring form. Before you plant new shrubs, anticipate the mature form of the plant, and plan your garden so that each plant can develop naturally.

Commercial shrub growers have divided shrubs into eight forms: pyramidal; low-branching; roundheaded; prostrate or spreading; columnar; dense or compact; open; and weeping.

Any plant can be pruned and trained into almost any shape the owner desires. But remember, when you direct a plant's growth into a shape or form that is different from its natural inclination, you create more work for yourself. So, it's best to select shrubs that naturally grow into forms that please you.

Deciduous and Evergreen Shrubs

Shrubs may be deciduous or evergreen. Simply put, deciduous plants lose their leaves in the fall and grow new leaves in the spring. Many deciduous shrubs need a certain amount of winter chilling for best performance. Most of them can be grown in mild-winter areas, but they may not perform quite so successfully as they do in more intense cold.

In comparison, evergreen plants keep their leaves the year around. Evergreens can be classified into two major categories: broad-leafed and coniferous (cone-bearing).

Generally speaking, the broad-leafed evergreens tend to be more tender than deciduous shrubs, and find their widest adaptability in areas with reasonably mild winters. Coniferous evergreens grow satisfactorily in most climates—you will see them in almost every part of the United States.

The surest way to grow shrubs successfully is to choose varieties that you know are hardy for your climate—check the Encyclopedia charts (pages 377–499) for the zone hardiness of the plant before you buy it.

Many deciduous shrubs add color and texture to an otherwise drab winter landscape. The twigs and stems of this red-osier dogwood are a case in point.

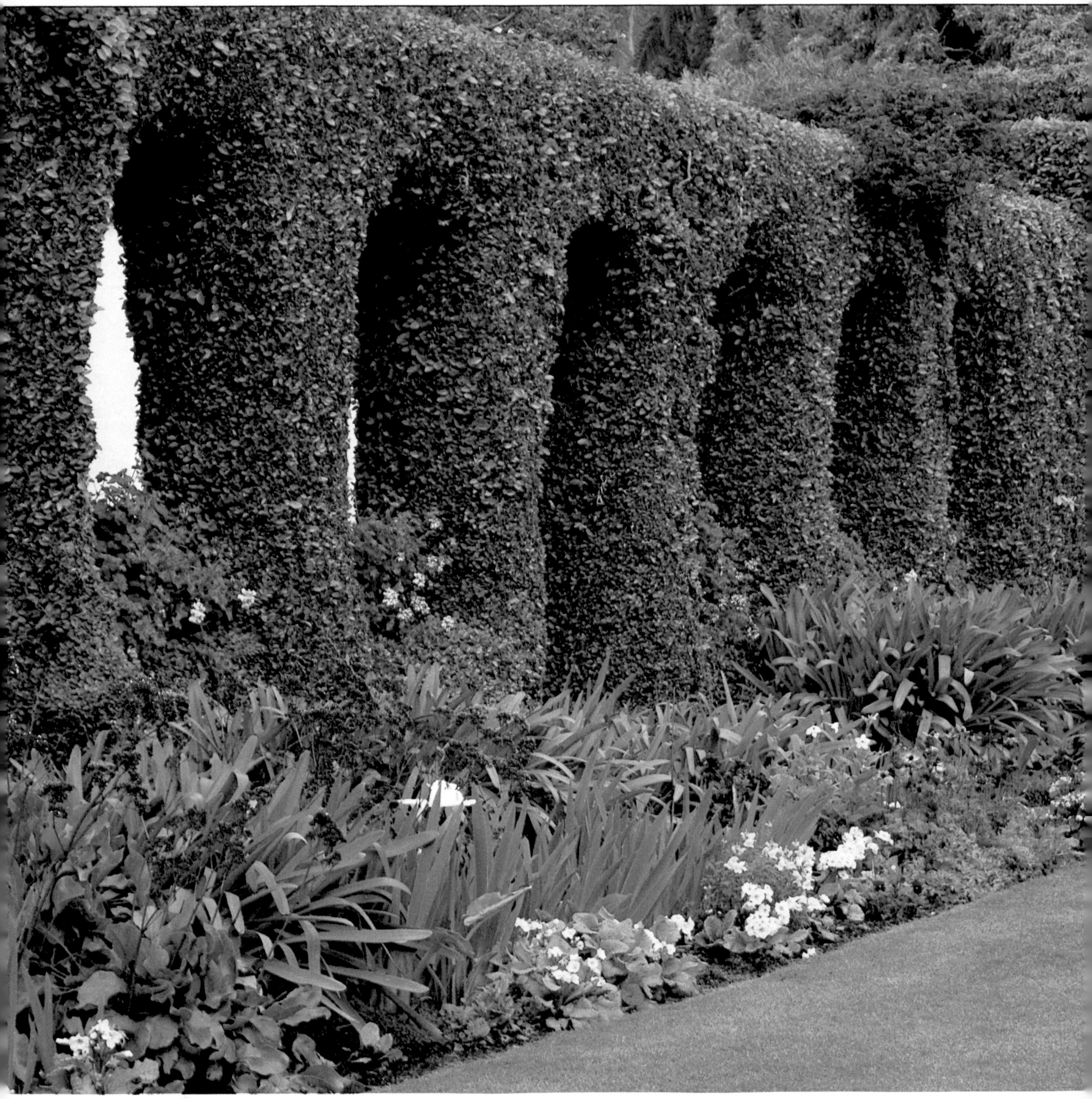

Designing with Shrubs

Good design in either a formal or informal garden requires balance. In a formal garden the balance seems obvious, although there may be more to it than immediately meets the eye. The balance in an informal garden is not as obvious, but is every bit as important. Balance leads to a sense of continuity between different kinds of plants. No matter what the garden style, balance can be achieved in the following time-honored ways.

First, plant taller growing varieties behind shorter growing ones. While rules were made to be broken, they should not be broken carelessly. There's no sense in planting short shrubs behind tall ones.

Second, place shrubs with lighter colored foliage in front of those with darker foliage. Gardeners usually find this arrangement of light leaves in front of dark leaves more pleasing. When the sun shines down on lighter green leaves against a dark backdrop, the color is particularly intense and striking.

Third, select background shrubs for their dark foliage, their base-branching form, and their leaf texture. Background shrubs are just that—backgrounds for more showy plants in front.

Fourth, limit the number of shrub varieties, not just in the background, but everywhere in the garden as well. There is sound reason for this contemporary trend. Grouping one plant variety makes a stronger design statement than planting individual specimens of assorted, unrelated varieties.

Shrubs for Color

Most people think only of flowers when they think of color in the garden. But while flowers, including flowering shrubs, may present the most obvious color, don't overlook the truly amazing variations of leaf color. There are so many different

Left: Creeping fig *(Ficus pumila)* is a woody vine often doubling as a shrub. Here it has the quality of a topiary: it has been carefully sheared to form an interesting backdrop for the perennial bed alongside. Right: Shrubs add many colors to the garden. From top to bottom: *Pinus mugo* var. *mugo*, *Euonymus japonica* 'Aureomarginata', *Juniperus horizontalis*, and *Nandina domestica* 'Nana purpurea'.

Frequent careful shearing maintains the fine texture of this juniper hedge.

shades of green that it would be difficult to go to a nursery and pick out five different shrubs of an identical color.

Besides the many hues of green, shrubs have gray, red, purple, yellow, and variegated foliage. And don't overlook the colors the seasons bring—the bare bark and branches of winter, the bright new growth and flowering of spring, the more muted tones of summer, and the fruits and changing foliage of fall.

Texture and Design

In the process of selecting shrubs, notice the different kinds of texture produced by a shrub's leaf size and pattern, and the texture that will be produced by the pattern of the bare branches, twigs, and bark during the dormant season. Are the leaves small and compact, giving a neat, clipped appearance? Or are the leaves large and uneven, creating a bold, informal feeling? Do the leaves have a coarse or fine pattern to them? What will the shrub look like in winter?

Judge the texture of a plant close up, then look at it again from forty feet away. Does the texture still look the same? Some shrubs lose their pleasing effect when they are planted too far away. Similarly, the texture of a large-leafed shrub may be out of scale when it is planted in a confined space or where viewing it up close is the only option. The general rule is to plant finely textured plants in front of more coarsely textured varieties.

Specimen Plants

Special effects can easily be achieved using unique shrubs known as specimen plants, or just specimens. Specimen plants draw attention to themselves. They usually have some feature or combination of features that sets them apart from other shrubs.

The uniqueness of a specimen shrub may be its form, flowers, berries, shape, color, texture, or rarity, as well as its personal significance. The number of specimens used in a single landscape is usually limited to one or two—any more than that and the special quality would be diminished.

Specimen plants depend a great deal for their specialness on the locations they are given in the garden. They should be carefully placed in spots where they can command center stage. For example, if a specimen's unique features need close viewing, place the plant by the front door or walkway so that it receives the attention it deserves.

Plan as You Buy

Achieving a pleasing, balanced planting of shrubs requires care. When you are at the nursery or garden center, take your time. Remember that once you get the shrubs in the ground, they are going to be there a long time (although they can be moved with relative ease the first year or two if necessary).

If you plan to buy more than one shrub, arrange your candidates together in one place at the nursery in much the same way as you want them to appear in your garden. How do they look together? Do their textures, forms, and colors complement each other? A certain amount of diversity is also necessary to create interest.

If you are adding new shrubs to established plantings, take samples of the existing plants with you to the nursery. As you pick out new plants, mentally reconstruct your garden as it is now. Will the additions fit into the picture, creating an interesting, balanced scene? (Also ask about the specific needs of the new plants you plan to buy. Do they require the same type of soil that your existing plants are growing in?)

Practical Considerations

As you design your ideal garden, keep in mind that shrubs can be practical as well as attractive. They can shield your yard from the wind, hide an unattractive ground area, or camouflage part of an oddly shaped building. In fact, they can vastly improve the environment in your garden in general. Here are some of the ways in which shrubs and hedges can do double duty.

The garden is best to be square, encompassed on all the four sides with a stately arched hedge . . .

Francis Bacon
Of Gardens

Next page: The meticulously pruned shrubs flanking the front door have a sculpted, architectural appearance, and when grown this way, become an integral part of the house's design.

Wind Control   The wind control properties of hedges and rows of trees have been known by gardeners and farmers for centuries. When the force of the wind is broken and diffused, the microclimate of your yard is improved. If you live in an area where afternoon winds are a common occurrence, a hedge can do a great deal to decrease the wind in your garden.

Privacy   There are many ways to achieve privacy in a garden, but none is as attractive as a wall of leafy green, with occasional splashes of color if desired. Besides formal, trimmed hedges, you can have less formal plantings of shrubs, left to grow in their own way. In localities where there are height limitations on fences between neighboring yards, a hedge is a good way to achieve the maximum in privacy.

Traffic Control   Shrubs can do a great deal to direct pedestrian traffic. Shrubs can also act as barriers, keeping people, bicycles, and cars from entering areas where they are not intended. Delicate plants should not be used; for best results use plants with thorns or prickly foliage. If you live on a street with heavy automobile traffic, you will probably want to choose dense shrubs to help deflect light from streetlights and headlights.

Below: Hedges provide as much privacy as a fence, and are usually more attractive. This hedge also creates a backdrop for the rose bushes growing in front of it. Right: A form of traffic control using shrubs.

How Shrubs Are Sold

Depending on the season, where you live, and the type of shrub, your nursery will carry shrubs in three different forms. You can buy them planted in containers, balled and burlapped, or bare root.

Container-Grown Shrubs

Shrubs are most commonly sold in containers. The containers may be metal, plastic, or wood, and are available in many sizes. Most shrubs are planted in one- or five-gallon containers. Specimen shrubs are sometimes sold in fifteen-gallon containers. The decision of whether to buy the smaller or larger size of container can be a difficult one. The key here is patience: It may be hard to buy a smaller size, knowing you will have to wait longer for the shrub to grow to ideal proportions. For that reason alone, many people will choose the five-gallon-size shrub, even though the cost is considerably higher.

Keep this formula in mind when it comes time to make your choices: It takes approximately eighteen months to two years for a one-gallon-size shrub to reach five-gallon size. But in two-and-a-half to three years, shrubs starting out in both one-gallon and five-gallon containers will have reached about the same size.

Make sure the container, no matter what it is made from, is in good shape when you purchase the shrub. Rusted metal, split plastic, or disintegrated wood usually means that the roots of the plant have grown into the ground soil at the nursery. When you take the plant away from its accustomed site, it's likely that it will suffer severe shock.

Shrubs in plastic cans can be slipped out easily without doing any damage to the root system, with the added bonus that the plastic container can be reused. Metal cans, except for those with sloping crimped sides, will have to be cut in order to get the plant out. You can cut them yourself or have it done when you're at the nursery. Large specimen shrubs in wooden containers require that the container be dismantled before planting.

Checking the Root System   The shrub should be well anchored in the container, but not to the point of being rootbound. Try gently lifting the plant by the trunk: If the soil moves at all, the plant has not had time to develop roots throughout the rootball.

But if the plant has been in the container too long, growth will have stopped and will be difficult to start again. Check for thick masses of roots on the soil surface or around the sides of the soil ball. Without pruning and straightening, the roots

When shopping for shrubs, choose plants carefully. It's much easier to start with a healthy plant than nurse a sick plant back to health after transplanting it.

will go on growing in the same circle and never expand into the garden soil. In the event of heavy winds, the plant may topple over because it is so poorly anchored in the soil. Even if it remains upright, the plant will just struggle along, growing within a small ball of soil the size of the original container, despite the good garden soil surrounding it.

Roots that are tightly wrapped around the stem are called girdling roots, and will restrict growth as they slowly choke the shrub. Avoid this shrub or cut the girdling root when you plant.

Wrong-Size Container   An oversize plant in a small can is sure to be rootbound, or has possibly sent its roots past the can, down into the soil below. In either case the plant should be avoided.

A small plant in a five-gallon can is as poor a buy as a large plant in a one-gallon can, but for different reasons. More than likely, the small plant in the five-gallon container was recently moved from a one-gallon can. In effect, you are paying a five-gallon price for a one-gallon plant. There's nothing wrong with nurseries transplanting one-gallon stock into five-gallon containers, but the plants should be held in a growing area until they reach five-gallon size before they are offered for sale. Tell-tale signs that plants have recently been potted into larger containers include: the relatively small size of the plant; a small rootball, disclosed by probing a little; and soft, loose soil (not yet packed down by repeated waterings).

Choosing container plants that are easy to reach in the plant shop or that have the most flowers will not guarantee a healthy garden. Pull the containers out and check a number of them before making a decision.

Balled and Burlapped Shrubs

Balled and burlapped shrubs can be bought and planted any time, but spring is the preferred season. To select a balled and burlapped plant, untie the top of the burlap and look carefully at the rootball; it should have a well-developed network of small, fibrous roots. Don't choose a shrub with a ball of soil that is loose, cracked, broken, or bone-dry.

In addition, check for roots circling back around the trunk—they can girdle the trunk after the shrub has been planted in the soil. To check for girdling roots, brush away the soil on top of the rootball or stick your finger in the top two or three inches near the trunk. You can usually see or feel girdling roots.

After you select the shrub that you want, retie the burlap and carry the shrub from the bottom of the rootball—don't use the trunk as a handle. Balled and burlapped plants are top heavy and not very stable. To keep them from falling over, tie or lean them against a wall or fence. Until planting, store the shrub in the shade, and keep the rootball moist.

Burlap is the traditional wrap, but many other materials are used. The advantage of burlap is that it rots readily, and can be left under the shrub when you plant it. Synthetic material must be removed before planting, since it does not decay.

Bareroot Shrubs

Bareroot plants are a good value if you know what to look for, and if you are in the mood to garden when others are still shaking off the winter doldrums. Bareroot plants are not only less expensive, but they also do not have to make the transition from nursery container soil to your garden soil and tend to establish themselves more rapidly.

Bareroot plants are available only during the dormant season, and they should always be planted before growth begins. For the best selection, shop at the beginning of the bareroot season—late winter or early spring. Many varieties of deciduous shrubs are available bare root, particularly roses and shrubs commonly used as hedge plants.

Before you buy a bareroot shrub, you should carefully examine its root system. Look for several good-size brown-colored roots growing in different directions at different levels from the main root. In most cases, the upper portion of the plant should be pruned before it leaves the nursery. If you cannot plant it right away, cover the roots with sawdust or damp earth to keep them from drying out. Dried roots quickly lose their ability to continue growing. Store the plants in a cool place to keep the buds from opening too early.

By lining the path alongside it, this small boxwood hedge directs traffic and encloses the mixed border of trees, shrubs, and perennials.

Selecting Hedge Plants

Evergreen shrubs, such as yew *(Taxus)*, holly *(Ilex)*, and the various varieties of boxwood *(Buxus)*, are among the most preferred varieties for hedges. Their slow growth may be a drawback to the gardener who wants quick privacy, but in the long run, slower-growing plants make a denser hedge that needs less pruning maintenance than some of the faster growing choices such as privet.

The deciduous plants commonly used for hedges are often available as bareroot plants. One of the most popular and best-looking hedge shrubs is the privet, botanically known as *Ligustrum.* There are many varieties of *Ligustrum,* but the one offered bareroot at your garden center will most likely be the one best adapted to your climate. Good-quality bareroot privets are usually from twelve to twenty-four inches tall, and should have sturdy stems and well-developed root systems.

If no bareroot plants are available at the time you want to start your hedge, the best bet is to buy one-gallon-size plants. The largest plant is not always the best buy, considering that you will immediately want to prune the plant heavily to force as many new shoots as possible from the base. Look for vigorous plants that are well branched.

If you want a neatly trimmed hedge, plants with large leaves will demand more specialized care than smaller-leafed varieties. The English laurel *(Prunus laurocerasus)* is a good-looking broad-leafed evergreen shrub sometimes used for hedges. The large size of its leaves, however, demands that as a hedge it be pruned selectively rather than sheared. Shearing plants with oversize leaves causes an abundance of imperfect, cut-up leaves.

The tall hedges shown here create a vista by drawing the eye towards the fountain, and they double as a fence, providing privacy.

Bringing Your Plants Home

When you purchase new shrubs, take a few precautions to ensure that the plants will survive until you are ready to plant them in the ground.

Because cut metal cans are almost impossible to water correctly, don't have a can cut unless you are going to plant the shrub that same day.

Don't attempt to bring a shrub home in a car in which the plant does not comfortably fit. Any plant, but especially a leafy one, can become rapidly windburned if left exposed in a speeding automobile. If you must take your new shrub home with you, protect it by wrapping it securely in cloth or some other protective material. Some nurseries and garden centers will deliver purchases free of charge. Take advantage of this service and both you and your new plant will benefit.

Planting Container-Grown Shrubs

In the past, early spring and early fall have been recommended as the ideal times for planting shrubs. Recent information suggests that this traditional advice may be a bit limiting. Actually, it is satisfactory to plant at any time, with the following exceptions.

Don't plant before the soil is workable. If you can't use a spade or cultivator easily, wait until the soil dries out somewhat.

Don't plant immediately preceding a period that will cause the shrub climate-related stress. Late spring and late fall can be times when the approaching heat or cold will place newly established plants under stress.

Preparing the Planting Hole

Dig the planting hole approximately twice as wide and to the same depth as the rootball, or one inch shallower. Plants have a tendency to sink after they have been planted, so if the hole is dug deeper than the original rootball, the plant may suffer from crown rot and root rot in the future. The rootball should be sitting on firm, undisturbed soil.

There is some question as to whether amending the backfill soil to make a transition soil will really help the plant establish itself. If the soil is not rock filled or all clay, it may be best to leave it alone and plant the shrub directly in it. This way the roots establish themselves in the native soil from the start, rather than adjusting to the amended soil only to be required to readjust months later when they grow into native soil.

If you are planting your new shrub in early spring or when you expect leaf growth to begin, now is a good time to apply a

complete fertilizer. Add dry types to the backfill soil according to the manufacturer's recommended ratios. As a rule of thumb, one to two tablespoons is adequate if you are planting a shrub from a one-gallon container, and one-quarter cup is all you need for plants in five-gallon containers. Stir it into the soil so that the rootball does not come into direct contact with straight fertilizer.

Removing the Plant from the Container
If the plant has been grown in a plastic container, it will slip out easily, especially if the rootball is damp. Whatever you do, don't break the rootball trying to get it out—you may permanently damage the root system. If the container is a straight-sided metal can and you are going to plant the shrub the same day you buy it, have the can cut at the nursery. If you are going to wait, even for a day or two, leave the can intact, and cut it at home with a large pair of tin snips or a can cutter like the type used at the nursery.

Most hedges do not produce conspicuous flowers, but this unusual camellia hedge is a lovely exception. When starting a flowering hedge, it's important to choose the same cultivars to ensure uniformity of flower color.

This camellia has been trained
into a stylized tree form.
This top-heavy growth pattern
is not natural for the camellia,
so the plant will require staking
for many years to prevent the
slender trunk from snapping.

Planting

Before placing the shrub in the hole, check the rootball. Cut or
pull away any circled, matted, or tangled roots so that they
radiate out from the rootball. Shorten the roots to the width of
the planting hole so that they will not be bent when planting.
Shrubs planted with their roots matted often remain that way;
the roots never venture into the surrounding soil.

Check the rootball depth in relation to the planting hole
depth and adjust if necessary. Position the shrub and fill the hole
with backfill soil to the level of the surrounding soil.

Build a shallow basin around the shrub so that irrigation
water will be concentrated in the area where it is needed most.
Be sure to build the basin so that the water drains away from the
stem of the plant. Thoroughly water the soil around the root
zone. Apply water until the soil is loose and muddy. Gently
jiggle the plant until it is positioned exactly as you want it. This
action will eliminate any remaining air pockets. Check again
to be sure water drains away from the stem of the plant. Use the
basin for primary watering until some roots have had a chance
to expand into the surrounding soil—usually around six weeks
after planting. If dry weather conditions require continued
irrigation, enlarge the basin at that time. However, if you live in
an area with sufficient summer rain or if you have installed
another irrigation system, you can break down the basin.

Staking and Pruning

Recent tests have shown that some back-and-forth movement of
the tops of plants actually results in faster and better-quality
growth. The only reasons to stake a newly planted shrub are if
the plant is top heavy or if it is planted in an area of high winds.
If staking is necessary, use two stakes on either side of the
shrub. To support the shrub, loosely tie it to the stakes with
something that will not damage the surface of the stem, such as
an old bicycle inner tube. Your nursery will have a supply of
other suitable materials.

Check ties frequently to make sure that they are not cutting
into the growing plant. Remove the stakes after the plant is
securely rooted in its new location, usually after the first year.

In the past it has been recommended that the top of the shrub
be lightly pruned to allow a period of strong root growth and
to balance the roots and the foliage. Recent studies have proven
this step to be ineffective. The best practice is to leave the
shrub just as it is unless its shape is poor; light pruning will
remedy this.

Watering After Planting

Keep a watch on the plant to see how much water it requires. If a newly planted shrub wilts during the hottest part of the day, the rootball is not getting enough water, even though the surrounding soil may appear wet. Even if it rains or if the plant is in the path of a sprinkler, you may need to water it by hand a few times a week for the first few weeks if the soil seems dry. But do not overwater. Too much water is as bad as too little.

Planting Balled and Burlapped Shrubs

In addition to the steps for planting container-grown plants, balled and burlapped shrubs require a few extra procedures.

Do not remove the burlap from the rootball, and be sure to handle the ball carefully. Set the plant in the hole and adjust the height of the rootball, as you would with a shrub from a container. If the burlap has been treated to retard rotting (ask at the nursery), it will have to be removed or have large holes cut in it.

After you've set the ball in the hole, untie the burlap from the trunk of the plant and pull it away from the top of the rootball. If the strings pull away easily, discard them; if not, leave them to rot in the soil. (Remove synthetic twine, since it does not decay.)

It's a good idea to do a little pruning to compensate for the roots that were lost when the shrub was dug up by the grower.

Cut or fold the burlap back so that it will be below the surface of the soil. Any exposed burlap acts like a wick, drawing water out of the soil, so be sure that all edges are buried. If the plant is wrapped in synthetic material instead of burlap, you must remove it completely.

Planting Bareroot Shrubs

The nursery will usually prune a bareroot shrub for you after it has been pulled from the holding bed. Sometimes one-third or more of the growth is cut back, but this results in a better looking shrub later.

Unless they are planted immediately after purchase, bareroot shrubs should be stored in a cool spot with their roots in moist soil, sawdust, or bark to prevent them from drying out.

Dig a hole large enough to accommodate the span of the roots without bending them. Also, prune off any broken or very long roots, and place the plant in the hole with the top root one inch under the soil level. Work the backfill soil between the roots with your hands, getting rid of any air pockets.

Since bareroot shrubs are always planted while they are

dormant, adding fertilizer is a wasted step. And, unlike other plants, a bareroot shrub will probably not need watering again until the spring. Nor do bareroot shrubs need staking, unless you have extremely high winds.

Planting Hedges

There are two basic ways to plant a hedge—you can dig a trench the length of the hedge, or you can dig individual holes. Although the methods are interchangeable, the trench method generally works best for bareroot plantings, and the individual-hole method works best for plants from containers. With either method, the previously mentioned planting steps apply. Generally speaking, the width of the trench should be two times the width of the rootball.

A double, staggered row of shrubs results in the more rapid growth of a thicker, denser, and wider hedge, but involves twice the initial expense and effort. If you plant a double row, stagger the plants so that no two plants are directly opposite each other.

The width of the spacing between individual plants will depend partly on the potential branch spread of the shrub variety and partly on how fast you want the hedge to fill in. Spacing can be from eighteen to thirty inches apart. Most gardeners recommend a spacing of eighteen to twenty inches within the row to avoid root crowding. Some dwarf varieties are planted twelve inches apart. Ask at your nursery for advice on your particular plant variety.

Whether planting container-grown shrubs, as shown here, or bareroot or balled and burlapped shrubs, proper soil preparation is a must.

Shrub Maintenance

One of the primary advantages of most shrubs is that they require so little maintenance. Give newly planted shrubs a little extra attention to ensure their establishment; then, after the first year, you can simply sit back and enjoy them.

Once a shrub is established in a location, its roots spread out through many cubic feet of soil. They may extend far beyond the limits of the branches and many feet down into deep layers of the soil. The large volume of soil that they "mine" for water and nutrients gives them more flexibility in their maintenance needs than flowers or vegetables.

Often, shrubs need no extra water or fertilizer at all, because their roots extend under the vegetable garden or the lawn, which you water and feed regularly, or just because their roots cover such a wide area that they are able to find enough naturally occurring food and water.

Slow-growing shrubs are particularly independent of fertilizers. Camellias often do well on the nutrients that are released as a mulch decomposes, and need no extra fertilizers.

Proper maintenance is nevertheless important for most shrubs and will result in beautiful plants year after year.

Remember to water thoroughly, add a layer of mulch to keep the roots moist, feed plants at the right time, protect them from severe weather conditions, and prune them occasionally.

Pruning Shrubs and Hedges

Pruning can direct the growth of shrubs, improve their health, and increase production of flowers and fruit. With pruning, you can direct growth to balance a lopsided shrub, keep a shrub small and compact, make one grow tall, or open another up.

The basics of pruning are really quite simple. You need to know what and how to prune, and when to do it. The information in this chapter is intended to remove any mystery that may surround the subject of pruning shrubs. Refer to Ortho's book *All About Pruning* for more detailed information on pruning all types of plants.

Pruning Styles

There are two basic styles of pruning: a natural style, which responds to the natural pattern of a shrub's growth, and a formal style, which includes espaliers, topiaries, hedges, and other severely shaped specimens.

The natural look is achieved by exploiting the natural growth habit of the shrub. The type of pruning that results in a natural shape is called thinning. See page 184.

Boxwoods grow slowly, but eventually fill in to form a handsome hedge.

Left: The hedges in this patio, with their straight lines and symmetrical design, are classically formal. Careful and frequent pruning is necessary to maintain them. Below: These hedges are also formally pruned, but in a softer, asymmetrical manner.

A formal effect is possible either with the ambitious use of pruning shears or by planting varieties of shrubs that are naturally neat and compact. If the shrubs in your garden are not naturally inclined to compactness, occasional heading back (see page 184) or frequent shearing will be necessary to create that tailored, formal look. If you shear plants, you should do it often so that only a little bit of growth is taken off each time.

Both formal and informal pruning styles can be used in the same garden to create an interesting and pleasing design, as in this front yard.

When to Prune

The appropriate time of year at which to prune a particular shrub depends on what type of shrub it is. Shrubs that are grown primarily for their flowers require greater attention to timing than either coniferous or broad-leafed evergreen shrubs.

Flowering shrubs divide into two groups: those that flower on old wood and those that flower on new wood. On this basis alone, you can determine when to prune your flowering shrubs.

How can you tell whether a shrub blooms on new or old wood? First, you need to know how to distinguish between the two types of growth. New wood is new stem growth that is produced during the current growing season. It is usually light green or pinkish in color. Old wood has been grown during a previous season. It is usually much darker in color than new wood, and is much more brittle. While a plant blooms, take a close look to see if the flowers form on new wood or old.

If you've just bought a shrub and it is not yet in bloom, or you've moved into a house with an established but dormant garden, the best advice is not to prune any shrub until you know whether it blooms or not, and if it does, on what type of wood.

Once you know what type of wood a shrub flowers on, knowing when to prune is easy. Shrubs (and trees, for that matter) that bloom in early spring bloom on old wood, and should be pruned a week or two after the flowers drop. If you prune them during the dormant season, you will remove the dormant blossom buds. Pruned at the correct time—in the spring or early summer—the plants have the rest of the season to produce more blossom buds for next year's display.

Shrubs that blossom in late spring or in the summer produce flowers on wood that was grown during the same growing season. The time to prune these shrubs is during the dormant season, or just before growth starts in very early spring. By so doing, you encourage more new stem growth and hence more blossoms.

Types of Pruning

When you remove any part of a plant, you are pruning. The two basic pruning methods are thinning and heading. Thinning, or thinning out, removes entire branches back to a main trunk, or major branches to the ground. Heading, or heading back, removes only part of a branch.

The important difference between thinning and heading is the effect of each on plants. When you thin, the shrub's energy is diverted to the remaining branches, which, in turn, grow more. The long-term result of thinning a shrub is that it will have

A steady hand and careful eye are a must when shearing an overgrown hedge. Frequent shearing maintains the straight, even lines of a hedge and makes the pruning task easier.

an open, natural look. Shrubs that are only thinned also become larger than shrubs that are headed back.

When you head back a branch, the plant will grow multiple branches where there was previously only one. Heading forces the dormant buds closest to a pruning cut to grow. Over the long term, heading results in a more dense shrub that has more branches but is smaller than a shrub that has been thinned. This type of pruning is most often associated with formal shapes.

Two special forms of heading are pinching and shearing. They have the same effect as other heading cuts but are accomplished in special ways.

Pinching is done with the finger tips. A pinch removes only the growing point of a branch, allowing the lateral buds near the end of the branch to grow. This usually results in two, three, or four growing points where there had been only one. Pinching is used to make a small plant bushy and thick or to redirect energy within the plant, guiding its growth as it develops.

Topiary is a very specialized pruning technique, most appropriate in a very formal landscape. Here, "poodles" and sculpted animals create a whimsical garden spot. Yew and boxwood are the most commonly used plants for this technique. Creating a complicated form with these slow-growing plants may take twenty years or more.

Shearing, or clipping, is like pinching in that only the growing points are removed. The difference is that shearing removes growing points en masse with hedge shears or power trimmers. The effect is the same—the plant responds by increasing the number of its growing points. Shearing is used to make hedges or topiary. Its use as a pruning method is associated with formal styles; just as thinning produces a natural, open shape, so does shearing produce a dense, sculptured shape.

Topiaries

Topiary is the art of shaping plants into geometrical and animal forms, creating living garden sculptures. The ideal plant choice for topiary work is a finely textured and hardy evergreen. The two varieties most often used in creating topiaries are boxwood and yew. Start with a young one-gallon plant with plenty of low branches that will fill out close to the ground. You must have a great deal of patience to create topiary. For example, if you want to make a simple double-ball shape, count on five years for boxwood and ten years for yew. If you want to shape a more complex animal form, count on twice that long.

The easiest topiary to shape is the double ball, or "poodle." After pruning the lower portion into a ball shape, select several strong branches and let them grow at least two feet above the first ball. Then strip the foliage off the bottom foot to form the separating stem, and begin to head the top foot of growth to encourage side branches that can be shaped into the second ball. See Ortho's book *All About Pruning* for detailed instructions.

Espaliers

Espaliers are shrubs or trees that are trained to grow flat against a vertical plane. Almost any shrub with fairly limber growth can be espaliered. All shrubs should have six inches between themselves and the wall or fence. Wire or wooden supports fixed at that distance will allow for both air movement and room for the branches to develop.

Start with a shrub that has a strong central stem. After planting the shrub, run the wires (or supports) horizontally at intervals of eighteen inches across the wall or fence. Cut the central stem off at eighteen inches, just below the height of the first wire. This will activate shoots to appear just below the cut. During the first growing season, allow only three new shoots to develop. Train two shoots horizontally onto the wire, and let the other one grow vertically as an extension of the central trunk. Rub off all the growth from the lower trunk.

Later on, cut the new trunk off a little below the second,

Carefully hand pruning
large-leaved hedges avoids
the butchered appearance that
can result from shearing.

thirty-six-inch-high wire. This will activate a second set of
shoots. Train these as you did the first set. Continue training
the shrub in this manner until all the wires are covered with
branches. When you have formed the frame you want, keep new
growth restricted with frequent pinching during the summer.

Hedges

Hedge plants should be pruned when they are first set out.
Bareroot plants, intended to produce a dense hedge, should be
pruned to about half their original height. Plants from containers, and other plants that will naturally produce an open
hedge, should be pruned back by about one-third, both the tops
and the sides.

Let a newly planted hedgerow grow without shearing for a
season to give the roots a chance to become established.

The second year, trim the hedge lightly to keep it dense as it
grows. Don't try to achieve the hedge height you want too
quickly. Continue to shear lightly to keep the hedge thick,
without gaps, as it grows to the desired height. Once the hedge
is as tall as you want it, your pruning technique should change.

Shear small-leafed hedges, such as boxwood or yew, whenever
they look ragged from uneven new growth, and cut off almost
all of the new growth. Just let the hedge retain a little bit of new
growth each time you shear by cutting about one-half inch
farther out than you cut at the last shearing. In this way, you
will avoid bare spots and clusters of cut branches. Allowing this
slow growth ensures that your hedge will always have a fresh
new layer of leaves. When, after ten or fifteen years of this slow
growth, the hedge becomes too large, cut it back very hard
early one spring and let it begin its slow growth again.

If you shear a large-leafed hedge, leaves will be cut in half,
giving the hedge a butchered look. So, if you have the time, it is
better to prune these hedges one branch at a time with a pair
of hand shears. Make your cuts inside the layer of foliage so that
they will be hidden, leaving uncut leaves on the surface.

To keep a hedge leafed out to the ground, shape your hedge so
that the top is narrower than the bottom, to let light reach the
entire side of the hedge. Leaves that do not get enough light will
drop off. Shaping a hedge in this way is especially important
on the northern side or on any portion of the hedge that is in
the shade of a tree.

Don't prune flowering hedges, such as this azalea hedge, once buds
form, or bloom will be greatly reduced.

How Often to Water?   A lawn has to be watered when the soil begins to dry out, before the grass actually wilts. At that stage, areas of the lawn will begin to change color, picking up a blue-green or a smoky tinge. An even more evident signal is a loss of resilience; the grass blades will not spring right back after you've walked on the lawn—footprints will remain a long time.

Soil moisture testers and coring tubes, available at most garden centers, are other ways to check for adequate moisture.

How long your lawn can go between waterings depends on several things. Roots grow only where there is water. If you constantly wet the top few inches of soil, roots won't venture any deeper. Eventually, the limited size of the root system will force you into watering more often. If roots go deep into the soil, they can draw on a larger water supply and the lawn can go much longer between waterings.

Soil conditions can also affect how often you need to water. Lawns in a sandy soil will need to be watered more often than those in a rich loam. Lawns in a clay soil will need water less often, and it will have to be applied at a slower rate to avoid wasteful runoff.

Different types of grasses have different water requirements, which also affect watering frequency. Local weather patterns are also important. Seasonal rain can play an integral part in a watering program. When it's hot and windy, it's obvious more frequent watering is required.

Mowing

Many people who want a handsome lawn don't realize just how important the job of mowing is. A lawn that is mowed when necessary and at the right height resists invasions of weeds, insects, and disease, and has a more lush, healthy look. Mowing infrequently, which often results in removal of too much grass at one time, will eventually produce a lawn with a thin, spotty, or burned appearance.

How Often to Mow?   How often your lawn needs mowing depends primarily on three things: the kind of grass, how often and how much you water and fertilize, and, of greatest importance, the time of year. The best rule of thumb is this: Mow when the grass grows to one-fourth to one-third taller than its recommended mowing height. In other words, if your lawn's mowing height is two inches, mow when it's about three inches high, thus removing one-third of the height of the grass blade.

The penalty for not following the rule is a stiff one. By letting grass grow too high and then cutting away half or more of it at

I have need of the sky,
I have business with the grass.

Richard Hovey
I Have Need of the Sky

once, you expose stems that have been shaded and are not adapted to strong sunlight. Grass leaves may be burned by the sun and turn brown. Mowing grass when it is too high results in deterioration of green leaf tissue at lower levels. More important, roots are severely shocked by a heavy mowing and may need several weeks to recover. Research has shown a direct relationship between height of cut and depth of roots. Roots of grasses properly mowed at correct heights will grow deeper. Deep roots are an important advantage and make lawn care many times easier.

The time of year has a large effect on the frequency of mowing. The cool-season grasses slow down or become dormant in hot summer weather. Mowing at this time will be infrequent—once every two or three weeks. During the cool months of spring and fall, most lawns will be growing at a maximum rate. These lawns will require mowing at least every week. Conversely, warm-season lawns will be growing their fastest during the summer months.

Lawn-Mowing Miscellany Be sure to pick up sticks and stones before mowing.

Don't cut wet grass; this can cause uneven mowing, the clippings are messy, and they can mat and suffocate the grass.

Alternate mowing patterns. Mowing the same direction every time tends to compact the soil and causes wear patterns.

Reel mowers are preferred for fine lawns. They cut the grass cleanly with a scissorlike action and smoothly follow surface contours. They perform poorly on tall grasses and lawns with high, wiry seed heads.

Sharp turns with a mower can cause uneven cutting. Make wide turns or use sidewalks and driveways, but be aware of rocks or debris on pavement areas.

If the ground is uneven from settling of the soil in some areas, scalping may result as you go over the high spots.

Lawns are heavy feeders during growth periods. Fertilize them regularly at such times.

The Nutrients a Lawn Needs

Lawngrasses live in what is basically an unnatural environment. They are crowded together and compete with each other, as well as with neighboring trees and shrubs, for water and nutrients. Because of this competition and the unnatural demands placed on them, lawns must be fertilized.

Properly fertilized, a lawn will maintain good color, density, and vigor and will not easily succumb to troublesome insects, weeds, or diseases.

Fertilizers   The most important factor to remember when fertilizing a lawn is to use a complete fertilizer. A complete fertilizer is one that contains all three of the primary nutrients: nitrogen, phosphorus, and potassium. Usually a lawn needs three to five times as much nitrogen as phosphorus and two times as much potassium as phosphorus. (Although nitrogen and potassium are needed by the plant in similar amounts, some nitrogen is leached from the soil.)

Calcium, sulfur, and magnesium are also needed in relatively large amounts. These are not found in a fertilizer that is labeled as complete. Calcium is either present in adequate quantities in the soil or is added through periodic applications of lime. Dolomite (or dolomitic limestone) supplies magnesium as well as calcium. Most sulfur reaches a lawn through air, water, or organic matter.

Micronutrients are elements needed in small amounts. If your lawn does not green up with an application of nitrogen, the problem may be a shortage of iron. This is particularly true in areas where soil pH is high. (For an explanation of soil pH see Chapter 14, page 347) Yellowing can also be caused by a sulfur deficiency, and acidic soils with a pH less than 5. A soil test may help solve these types of soil-related problems.

When to Fertilize   Few gardeners need to be reminded to feed their lawns in spring. It helps a lawn get a head start on pests, weeds, and the summer heat that's soon to come.

By midsummer, heat and light intensity slow down the growth of the cool-season grasses. They usually remain green but are essentially dormant. With only a few exceptions, cool-season grasses should not be fed in midsummer.

The most important time to fertilize cool-season grasses is in the fall. Fall fertilization keeps the grass growing green and longer into cold weather. Fall feeding also gives the lawn a chance to store food that will allow a fast start in the spring.

Growth of the warm-season grasses peaks in midsummer and

then tapers off in fall, continuing at a slower pace until frost. The first sign of spring green comes when the soil is still cold. This is the time when lawn food with quick-acting forms of nitrogen pays off, making grass fully green sooner.

Warm-season grasses can also benefit from fall fertilization, with two exceptions. If winter weeds are a problem, their growth will be further stimulated by the feeding.

A heavy fertilization may also promote a flush of succulent growth that leaves the grass more susceptible to cold injury.

Lime   In areas of the country with heavy rainfall, soils are typically acid. Grasses grow poorly in highly acid soils because of nutrient imbalance and toxicity. Acid soil is corrected by adding lime.

The only sure way to know if your lawn needs lime is through a soil test. If the pH is below 4.5, you need to add enough lime to raise the pH to 6. However, liming is a way of life in many areas. In those areas, you already know your soil needs lime.

The easiest and best form of lime for lawns is ground dolomitic limestone. Your soil test will provide recommended rates. Lime is best applied with a mechanical spreader.

Cool-season grasses do not require fertilization during the summer when their growth rate slows. During this time, they just need to be watered.

Ground Covers

Ground covers include all kinds of plants—low-growing perennials, shrubs, familiar herbs, and sprawling vines—and are valued for their ability to spread rapidly, grow close to the ground, and create a thick, low-maintenance covering that binds the soil. They can be deciduous or evergreen, broad leafed or needle leafed, and can range in size from plants a few inches high to shrubs that reach three or more feet. Generally, the smaller the plant, the more versatile it is as a ground cover.

Choosing a Ground Cover

Once you've decided to fill an area with ground cover, the question is, which one? There are hundreds of possibilities. The variety in color, texture, and size is tremendous. You want a ground cover to be attractive, but even more important, it must be suitable for the particular site you want to plant.

Be sure you know the growth habit, mature size, and water requirements of a ground cover before you plant it. Use the information provided in the Encyclopedia charts beginning on page 377 to become familiar with some of the many plants available and their specific growing requirements. Then select a ground cover that best suits your needs.

Below: Succulents make beautiful and interesting ground covers for sunny slopes, dry sandy soils, and many warm coastal areas. Many succulents produce brilliantly colored flowers, and their thick, fleshy leaves are available in unusual shades of blue, gray, and coppery green. Right: When in bloom, *Hypericum calycinum* is one of the showiest of ground covers.

Hostas make an excellent ground cover for a shaded area. These plants grow very close together and compete heavily for nutrients; they must be fertilized occasionally to remain healthy.

When to Plant

The time to plant a ground cover varies across the country. In warm areas, ground covers can be planted almost anytime as long as water is available to young plants through their establishment period. Generally, either a spring or fall planting is best. These are the times of least environmental stress, when the shock of transplanting is most easily endured.

In cold-winter areas, ground covers planted in the spring are usually more successful. Fall plantings are most likely to suffer from the "heaving" caused by alternate freezing and thawing of the soil. Young plants may be literally pushed out of the ground. With their roots exposed, they quickly die. If you must plant in fall, do it as early as possible.

Where freezing soil is not a problem, a fall planting can be very successful; winter rains and cool temperatures help plants to adjust to their new home. And when spring comes, they are already established and begin to cover the ground more quickly. In dry-summer areas, avoid planting in midsummer, unless you're prepared to spend a lot of time watering.

Planting

Ground covers are plants that naturally grow in very close proximity, creating severe competition for space, nutrients, and water. A good soil helps overcome these adverse conditions. As a rule, soil for ground covers should be prepared as carefully as soil for a fine lawn, as described on page 222. There's no hard and fast rule for estimating the number of plants for a given location. The number depends on the effect you want to achieve and how fast you want that effect. Naturally, the closer you space the plants, the faster they will cover the ground completely.

In arranging the plants, some gardeners opt for staggered rows; others, for straight. One advantage of staggered-row planting on slopes is that it helps prevent erosion by not allowing water to run off in a straight line.

The soil has been carefully prepared for this new planting of pachysandra. The plants have been closely spaced because pachysandra fills in slowly.

Spacing Guide for Ground Covers

Inches Between Plants	Square Feet 64 Plants Will Cover	Square Feet 100 Plants Will Cover
4	7	11
6	16	25
8	28	44
10	45	70
12	64	100
15	100	156
18	144	225
24	256	400

Formulas to Determine Square Feet
Circles: Area = diameter squared × 0.7854
Triangles: Area = ½ base × height
Rectangles: Area = base × height

The Problem of Weeds

Weeds can quickly overrun any planting and turn an enthusiastic gardener into a frustrated one. The most critical time is just after planting, particularly in the spring. You'll need to keep a close eye on newly planted ground covers until they are dense enough to shade the ground and choke out weeds.

Mulches will help stave off the weed population. They should be applied only after the soil has warmed in the spring. A generous quantity (three to five inches thick) will stop many of the most troublesome annual weeds and make it easier to pull out the ones that do sprout.

Eliminating the No-Maintenance Myth

Often ground covers are mistakenly thought of as no-maintenance plants. This philosophy pervades all areas of ground-cover culture: in the preparation of a location, and in watering, fertilizing, and pruning. Perhaps because ground covers are the problem solvers—growing in areas where a lawn wouldn't be found—they are often allotted second-class status. But ground covers have the same fundamental needs as any plant.

There are, of course, ground covers that can grow in less than ideal soil, and still others that can grow on a steep slope better than anywhere else. But ground covers deserve your best efforts. Even if you give them just half the attention you give your lawn, you'll be happily surprised at the results. Given adequate care, they blanket the ground with striking color or foliage instead of just barely covering it.

Watering

Young plants should be given special attention. A steady watering program is important so that root systems develop fully. There is no rule such as "Water once a week in the summer"—there are too many variations. You have to watch the plants and make sure water is getting to the roots. After the plants are growing, your program should be adjusted to one of deeper and less frequent watering.

Mowing

You probably expected to leave your lawn mower in the garage when you planted a ground cover. But there is one consolation: Ground covers need to be mowed only to rejuvenate new growth, usually just once a year.

Mowing, or any method of cutting back old growth, is very important to the appearance of a ground cover. As with watering, there is no firm schedule to abide by: When a ground cover is beginning to develop thatch, or when the foliage loses its fresh look, it's time to clip off the old growth. Generally, the best time to trim is just before the plant's normal growth cycle. This would be in spring for most ground covers, just as the weather begins to warm.

Hand Pruning

Some ground covers can be improved by pruning rather than mowing. Using pruning shears on a plant such as wintergreen (*Gaultheria* sp.) helps to maintain compact and dense growth.

Left: Maintaining the clean, curving line of this *Drosanthemum* planting requires some effort, but the results are stunning. Many ground covers tolerate poor soil and growing conditions and look adequate, but a regular maintenance program will produce lush, vigorous growth. Above: This planting of Hahn's ivy must be hand pruned to keep it in bounds.

Selected Ground Covers for Special Situations

Because ground covers display such a wide range of cultural requirements and growth habits, some are naturally better suited than others to specific landscape situations. The following lists are designed to help you choose plants to meet the particular needs of your home landscape. The lists are not exhaustive but represent some of the most common ground covers.

Ground Covers for Full Sun

Achillea tomentosa (Woolly yarrow)
Arabis (Rock cress)
Arctostaphylos uva-ursi (Kinnikinnick)
Artemisia schmidtiana (Angel's hair)
Baccharis pilularis (Dwarf coyote brush)
Ceanothus (California lilac)
Cerastium tomentosum (Snow-in-summer)
Cotoneaster, low-growing
Cytisus (Broom)
Helianthemum nummularium (Sun rose)
Juniperus (Juniper)
Lantana
Phlox subulata (Moss pink)
Phyla nodiflora (Lippia)
Pyracantha koidzumii 'Santa Cruz' (Santa Cruz pyracantha)
Rosa (Rose)
Rosmarinus officinalis 'Prostratus' (Dwarf rosemary)
Santolina chamaecyparissus (Lavender cotton)
Sedum (Stonecrop)

Ground Covers for Sun or Partial Shade

Aegopodium podagraria (Goutweed)
Ajuga (Bugleweed)
Bergenia
Campanula (Bellflower)
Cyrtomium falcatum (Holly fern)
Dichondra micrantha (Dichondra)
Epimedium (Barrenwort)
Fragaria chiloensis (Wild or sand strawberry)
Hedera helix (English ivy)
Hypericum calycinum (Aaron's beard)
Liriope spicata (Lilyturf)
Mahonia repens (Creeping mahonia)
Ophiopogon japonicus (Mondo grass)
Paxistima canbyi (Canby; Pachistima)
Polygonum (Knotweed)
Sagina subulata (Irish and Scotch moss)
Trachelospermum (Jasmine)

Ground Covers That Tolerate Deep Shade

Adiantum pedatum (Five-finger fern)
Asarum (Wild ginger)

Arctostaphylos uva-ursi.

Trachelospermum asiaticum.

Pachysandra terminalis.

Athyrium goeringianum (Japanese painted fern)
Convallaria majalis (Lily-of-the-valley)
Dryopteris (Wood fern)
Epimedium (Barrenwort)
Galium odoratum (Sweet woodruff)
Hedera helix (English ivy)
Pachysandra terminalis (Japanese spurge)
Sagina subulata (Irish and Scotch moss)
Sarcococca hookeriana humilis (Small Himalayan sarcococca)
Viola odorata (Sweet violet)

Drapers and Trailers
Arctostaphylos uva-ursi (Kinnikin-nick)
Artemisia (Dusty miller; Wormwood)
Asparagus densiflorus 'Sprengeri' (Sprenger asparagus fern)
Campanula (Bellflower)
Cerastium tomentosum (Snow-in-summer)
Cotoneaster, low-growing
Euonymus fortunei (Euonymus, in variety)
Hedera (Ivy)
Juniperus (Juniper, low-growing)
Lotus berthelotii (Parrot's-beak)
Rosmarinus officinalis 'Prostratus' (Dwarf rosemary)
Trachelospermum jasminoides (Star jasmine)
Verbena peruviana (Peruvian verbena)
Vinca minor (Periwinkle)

Ground Covers That Tolerate Traffic
Ajuga (Bugleweed)
Chamaemelum nobile (Chamomile)
Dichondra micrantha (Dichondra)
Duchesnea indica (Mock strawberry)
Juniperus horizontalis 'Blue Rug' (Blue rug juniper)
Phyla nodiflora (Lippia)

Duchesnea indica.

Sagina subulata (Irish and Scotch moss)
Veronica repens (Speedwell)
Zoysia tenuifolia (Korean grass)

Lawn Alternatives (Large Areas)
Aegopodium podagraria (Goutweed)
Ajuga reptans (Bugleweed)
Arctostaphylos uva-ursi (Kinnikin-nick)
Baccharis pilularis 'Twin Peaks' (Dwarf coyote brush)
Coronilla varia (Crown vetch)
Dianthus deltoides (Maiden pink)
Dichondra
Duchesnea indica (Mock strawberry)
Euonymus fortunei (Wintercreeper)
Festuca ovina glauca (Blue fescue)
Fragaria chiloensis (Wild or sand strawberry)
Hedera (Ivy)
Hypericum calycinum (Aaron's beard)
Juniperus (Juniper, low-growing)
Lantana
Liriope spicata (Lilyturf)
Lonicera japonica (Honeysuckle)
Pachysandra terminalis (Japanese spurge)
Phyla nodiflora (Lippia)
Polygonum cuspidatum compactum (Fleece flower)
Potentilla (Cinquefoil)
Sedum (Stonecrop)
Trachelospermum (Jasmine)
Vinca (Periwinkle)
Zoysia tenuifolia (Korean grass)

Columbinam appellant. Alij: militia
riam. Alij: verti pedium. nuncupit.
Nascitur ubiqȝ. in planis. ʒ in aquosis
locis.

Prima virtei   ad uulnera.
ʒ pariotidas.
Herbe verminace
radix. in collo ligata. mirifice sa

Herba verminacia epacis dolore
solstitio lecta. ʒ in puluem reo
igne robusto: dabis coclearia quin
er uino quam optimo cyatos tribu
potu sumpta: mirifice creditur p
sicere. ʒ recers pro aliiqȝ virib; sic
bis. ad calculosos sanandos. a
Herbe verminacie radix conti
cum mulso optimo tepido da
credibilrer cal culosis succurrit: s
quicquid ē uidetur quod urinā in
dit ad trahendum celerit producer
Herbe verminacie ad capras d
corona facta: in capice impo
dolorē capitis tollit. ad serpentis m
ertum verminaciā cum folijs
ʒ radicibus quisquis onustat
emeramqȝ secum portauerit: ab
serpentibus tutus erit.

Herbs

A walk through a garden planted with herbs is like a world tour. Plants we use as herbs and spices have been gathered from the temperate and tropical zones of both hemispheres. Many of our favorite seasonings and fragrances from the arid regions of the Mediterranean and the humid tropical islands grow alongside natives from North America.

When you survey the spice shelves, you're looking at exotic products from all corners of the globe. Many flavorings and fragrances we now take for granted were once costly treasures or just not available at any price. Throughout the centuries herbs and spices have had their ups and downs, periods of great demand followed by dwindling interest. The New World was discovered by Europeans searching for new trade routes to the spice-producing areas of Asia. Native American herbs and spices were among the first New World treasures taken back to Europe. Despite that, even into the twentieth century, most Americans were unfamiliar with herbs other than the ubiquitous parsley, mint, and a few other basics. Recently, however, there's been a tremendous escalation in the popularity, production, and distribution of herbs and spices as garden seed, plants, and dried products.

Defining the Terms

Chefs, perfumers, chemists, and horticulturists can give you helpful information, but in the end, no certified expert can tell you more about the varied natural substances collectively labeled herbs and spices than you'll discover through your own senses and experiences.

Botanically speaking, the word *herb* is derived from the Latin *herba*, which means grass or green crops. Most herbs are herbaceous plants—that is, plants whose stems are soft and succulent rather than woody; such plants die down to the root after flowering, or die back entirely. In ordinary language, the word *herb* refers to any of that host of plants, both herbaceous and woody, whose leaves, flowers, seeds, roots, bark, or other parts we use for flavor, fragrance, medicines, cosmetics, or dyes. Thus, herbs are a very general and comprehensive group of plants that includes many weeds, grasses, and hardy vegetables, along with flowers, shrubs, and trees.

The word *spice* comes from the Latin *species*, which means ally. Spices may be thought of as the allies or complements of other food substances. They're really defined by how we use them and how they stimulate our senses. A spice may be any flavored or aromatic substance obtained from seed, root, fruit, flower, or bark that is used in the same way as an herb.

Above: Apothecary jars with colorful herbs. Left: A detail from a thirteenth-century English herbal depicting a verbena plant.

Left: Many herbs are suitable
for growing in traditional geometric patterns.

HERBS   **245**

Often entire plants are regarded as herbs, while only the useful
parts or derivatives of plants are true spices. The climbing
orchid, *Vanilla planifolia*, for example, is not itself a spice. Only
its long, podlike fruit—fermented, cured, and marketed as a
vanilla bean—and the extract prepared by macerating the bean
in an alcohol solution are spices. On the other hand, the
entire sprig of parsley, leaves and stem, is the herb parsley. In
fact, the stems of many herbs are richer in the essential oils
than their leaves.

Growing Herbs

In spite of all the lore surrounding the use of herbs and spices,
growing them is no more difficult than growing ordinary flowers
and vegetables. We'll discuss the ideal conditions for optimum
growth, but keep in mind that you can have success with annual
herbs by planting and growing them along with your other
annual vegetables and flowers.

It would be impossible to satisfy the ideal conditions for all
the herbs in the small garden space usually devoted to them,
but you can count on plenty of seasonings if you consider herbs
as a group and think of them as part of the vegetable garden.
With many herbs, such as mint, bee balm, and tarragon, the
problem is keeping them under control once they're in the
garden.

Most of the plants classified as herbs are hardy, easy to grow,
practically immune to diseases and pests, adaptable to many
types of soil and growing conditions, and quite tolerant of
drought and neglect. Of course, like any group of plants, they'll
reward you well if you pay attention to their simple needs.

Like most herbs, sweet woodruff *(Galium odoratum)* can
be enjoyed in several ways; it
makes an attractive ground
cover and its leaves can be used
to brew herbal tea.

Borage *(Borago officinalis)* prefers full sun and well-drained soil. Since most herbs need similar conditions, choose a sunny spot and amend the soil to improve drainage (if necessary) before you plant an herb garden.

The Outdoor Garden

Whether you have a few plants growing near the kitchen door, rows of herbs among the vegetables or cutting flowers, or a large formal herb garden, the techniques of outdoor gardening remain the same in most climates.

Selecting the Best Exposure

Most herbs and spices require full sunlight for at least five to hours a day. Quite a few are tolerant of partial shade and some forest natives enjoy the shade. Check the individual plant requirements in the Encyclopedia charts on pages 377–499.

Preparing the Site and Soil

Most herbs and spices prefer well-drained soil. Exceptions to the rule include horseradish, ginger, sweet flag, and woodruff, which all enjoy moist, rich soil around their roots. A few plants even grow directly in water. But for the vast majority of herbs and spices an ideal planting site would be a gentle incline with sandy soil.

If your garden doesn't have good natural drainage, you have two options: a raised bed and soil amendment.

Raised beds have been a part of herb gardening since ancient times. All you need is something that will hold about six inches of soil above the normal ground level. Railroad ties, fence posts, cement blocks, or stones can be used as the bed walls, or you can use redwood boards held in place with 2×4s. A wood railing nailed to the top will let you sit while you maintain and harvest the herbs or just enjoy their textures and fragrances.

Once you've built the bed, fill it with fresh soil. If it is a small bed, you can purchase one of the packaged synthetic soils formulated to provide good drainage and balanced support for the roots.

If you do not want a raised bed for your herbs, you can improve drainage and soil by amending the planting area to a depth of about a foot. See Chapter 14, pages 354–359, for information about amending soil.

Planting the Garden

Seed and transplants of common herbs are available at garden centers, nurseries, and plant shops or from mail-order suppliers. You'll have to order the more unusual varieties from specialized catalogs or secure them from herb-growing friends.

If you need only a few plants, it's easiest to buy little ones from a local source. They're ready to transplant for an almost instant herb garden.

Left: Many herbs grow slowly; after soil preparation and planting, it will take some time before the plants fill in and complete the design. Below: In areas where only one or two herb plants are wanted, buy them from a nursery and transplant them.

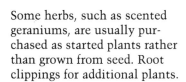

Some herbs, such as scented geraniums, are usually purchased as started plants rather than grown from seed. Root clippings for additional plants.

If you want a head start on the season, you can begin seeds indoors in late winter. However, most seeds thrive better if sown in the garden as soon as all danger of frost is past and the soil begins to warm up. Some seeds that require a long germination period can be planted in the late fall for the following growing season. Follow the planting times recommended on the seed packets for your local climate.

Herbs look best and grow well when planted in large expanses or clumps rather than neat rows. Rake the freshly prepared bed and scatter the seeds evenly over the area. Cover with soil to the depth recommended on the seed packet—usually twice the seed diameter. Firm the topsoil with your hands or a board and sprinkle the planting area with water.

Always label all seedbeds as soon as you've planted them so that you'll know what is growing where.

If you want to plant seeds in rows, make shallow furrows in the prepared soil with a rake. Sow seed in the furrows at the distance suggested on the packet. Firm and moisten as above.

If your garden is plagued by birds, cover the planting area with screening until the seeds germinate. Keep the soil moist, but never soggy, throughout germination. Normally annuals take about two weeks and perennials about three to four weeks or longer to germinate; check the seed packet.

You can stretch the harvest season of some short-cycle herbs such as coriander and borage by making successive sowings several weeks apart.

When the little plants are up and have formed two pairs of true leaves, thin out overcrowded areas. The thinnings of culinary herbs are delicately flavored and can be used in foods, or you can transplant healthy thinnings to another spot in the garden or to containers.

When the plants are several inches tall, they may benefit from a covering of mulch. Mulches keep weeds under control, set off the herbs visually, retain moisture, and keep the soil at a cool and even temperature. Organic materials such as bark chips, chunky peat moss, pine needles and straw, and small gravels are natural companions to herbs. Plastic sheeting isn't good around herbs because it tends to retain too much surface moisture and doesn't allow enough air circulation.

Watering and Feeding

Frequent light spraying with the garden hose is a poor method of watering because it supplies moisture only to the topsoil. Herbs need deep soaking that penetrates the ground at least twelve inches. Use a hand-held hose if you have the patience, but a soaker hose is more convenient and effective. Let it run for a couple of hours each time you water, preferably in the morning so that the plants will have time to dry off before dark.

Avoid overwatering, but at the same time, never allow the soil to dry out completely. For routine watering some gardeners use this rule of thumb: Don't water until you see a few leaves beginning to wilt, then water thoroughly. A more accurate test is to insert your finger into the soil; if it's beginning to dry out a half-inch below the surface, it needs water.

Although herbs don't need the large amounts of fertilizer that many other plants do, they respond to moderate feedings once or twice a year. Feed in the spring with a balanced fertilizer such as 5–10–5 and again in late summer to help carry the herbs on through fall. Too much fertilizer makes the soil overly rich and results in lush foliage that has only small amounts of fragrant oils. However, some plants—such as the flowering shrubs—require more and heavier feedings than most other herbs for optimum growth.

Next page, left page: French lavender prefers dry soil. This aromatic plant makes a lovely addition to any garden, and its leaves and flowers can be used in cooking. Dried lavender is often used to make sachets and potpourris. Right page: Calendulas grow best in a bright, sunny exposure, well-drained soil, and with light feedings.

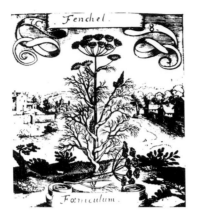

*Anything Green that grew out
of the mould
Was an excellent herb to our
fathers old.*

Rudyard Kipling

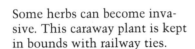

Some herbs can become inva-
sive. This caraway plant is kept
in bounds with railway ties.

Protecting Herbs in Winter

After the leaves of perennial plants wither in the fall, cut the
stalks down to ground level. In very cold regions, evergreen
perennials can be dug up, potted in containers, and moved
indoors before frost.

With a little extra attention to the less hardy varieties, the
herb gardener in the North can be just as successful as one in a
kinder climate. The annual herbs grow fast enough to mature
in a short season and most perennial herbs are winter hardy.

Rosemary, bay, lemon verbena, sweet marjoram, and some of
the thymes are not hardy and can be brought indoors to winter
over; they all make attractive houseplants in the process.

Some people like to extend the season for fresh herbs by
digging annuals that are still productive from the outdoor garden
and potting them for growing indoors.

When you move herbs indoors, wash them in soapy water to
get rid of aphids, spider mites, and other insects that may be
hiding and could wreak havoc with other houseplants.

In regions where the ground freezes, mulch over the outdoor
perennial herb garden after the first freeze. Plants should remain
frozen all winter and not be subjected to alternate freezing and
thawing. Cover thickly with straw, leaves, marsh or salt hay,
or evergreen boughs to allow air to get through. Leave the
mulch on until all frost danger is past.

Confining the Spread of Herbs

If you want just a small area of tarragon, mint, or another herb
that spreads rapidly, plant the herb in a clay pot with soil about
an inch below the rim, then sink the pot deep enough into the
ground to leave the soil level in the pot even with the surface of
the ground.

Instead of pots, you can sink a wooden box, header boards, or
metal strips six to eight inches into the soil.

The Container Herb Garden

Herbs and spices are good candidates for container gardening. They're easy to grow, adaptable, and enjoy the good drainage that pots and other containers allow. Often herbs look more attractive displayed in containers than lost or tucked away in the garden. Best of all, potted herbs give you the versatility to meet their cultural needs throughout the year. The containers can be shifted all around the garden, deck, or patio as sun patterns change with the seasons. For gardeners with limited space, growing herbs in containers is an obvious convenience.

In a sunny window, under artificial lighting, or with a combination of the two, herbs can keep on growing indoors all winter. Then they can go outdoors when the weather warms up, or if their simple growing requirements can be met, remain indoors the year around.

This wire basket lined with sphagnum moss has been planted with several herbs commonly used in spaghetti sauce—a convenient set-up for the cook.

Herbs play an essential role in good cooking. Whether freshly harvested or preserved, herbs enhance the flavor of all types of food.

Harvesting Herbs and Spices

For most herb and spice gardeners, the greatest fun comes in the harvest. Snip bits of French tarragon and parsley to add to a simmering dish. Cut a bouquet of yellow tansy flowers to dry for a centerpiece. Pinch leaves of rose geranium to add to sweet sachet or float in finger bowls for a special dinner. Clip a cup of chamomile flowers to brew afternoon tea. Catch the seed from a sesame flower just before it bursts open. Or gather big bunches of sweet marjoram just before it blooms.

Harvesting Through the Season

Most culinary herbs can be used from the time you start thinning the seedlings. The flavor is already there. Snip and clip leaves and sprigs as you need them throughout the growing season. Use scissors, a sharp knife, or your fingernails to take sprigs from a few inches down the stem, just above a set of leaves. Be sure not to take too much growth at once while the plants are young and developing or you may weaken them. Select healthy leaves and pluck out yellow or dead ones at the same time to keep the plants continuously groomed.

As you snip and clip, you are also determining the shape of the growing plant, so harvest judiciously. You benefit from enjoying the fresh herbs, and the plants respond with lusher and fuller growth.

Leaves that are to be eaten fresh as salad greens—rocket, sorrel, borage, burnet, nasturtium—should be gathered when quite young and tender. Old leaves get too tough to eat.

Herbs that send up grassy leaves or stalks directly from the ground—chives and parsley—should be cut just above ground level. Don't just cut off the tops or you'll ruin the plant's appearance and growth habit.

Keep an eye out as you pinch through the season. Take out flower buds of tender perennials to increase edible leaf production. If allowed to flower early, these herbs will grow tough as the seeds are set. If you want flowers or seed heads on some plants, let some stems develop through their full cycle. Of course, you'll want to let one or two plants go to seed so that they will self-seed the garden or give you seed to harvest and store for planting next season.

Harvesting for Preservation

Now that you've taken bits and pieces of fresh herbs to use all during the season, you can start the special harvest for preserving. With most herbs it comes just when the flowers are about to open and the oils are most heavily concentrated.

Of course, there are exceptions. Sage should be cut when the buds appear, and you should wait until the blooms are full to gather hyssop, oregano, and thyme. Cut parsley, borage, salad burnet, and winter savory when the leaves are young.

Harvest early in the morning after the dew has dried but before the hot sun brings out the oils. Some annuals harvested in early summer may grow enough for a second major harvest provided you don't take too much the first time. In the first harvest, cut them several inches above ground. For fall-harvested annuals, cut all the way to the ground.

Lavender, marjoram, rosemary, and other shrubby perennials should be cut back to about half the length of the year's growth.

Harvest flowers for drying and fragrances when they have just opened and are fresh looking.

Seed heads are ready when they turn color, as they do just before they open and scatter their seed on the ground. Harvest heads on a warm, dry day by cutting off the entire head or stem and dropping them into paper bags.

Bring all cut herbs indoors out of the sun as soon as possible after harvesting. Keep the different kinds separated and rinse quickly in cool water to remove the dirt. Shake off excess water, drain well, then spread on a flat surface. Pick over and discard bad leaves or petals.

At this point label each bunch. If the garden is cooperative and everything doesn't come at once, harvest and prepare only one or two herbs a day.

Preserving Herbs

Drying is the time-honored method of preserving most leaves, seeds, and flowers. We offer three variations on the drying theme. A few herbs can be preserved in salt and quite a few take well to freezing. Others can be preserved in vinegar. Select the methods that seem best for you.

Herbs to be used in cooking should be dried as whole as possible to retain flavor.

Hang Drying

The old method of hang drying is still the most colorful way of drying the harvest. All you do is take a bunch of one kind of herb, tie the ends of the stems together with string, and hang them upside down in a place that's warm, dry, and away from direct sunlight. Hang them free where air can circulate all around to prevent mildew. If the room is dusty, place the bunch in a paper bag that's been perforated all around for air circulation. Tie the bag around the stems. This is a good method

Above: Garlic braided together and hung to dry. Left: A dry, dark shed is ideal for drying herbs, but a closet or an attic is a good substitute.

for drying seed heads: As the seeds fall they are caught in the bottom of the bag.

Depending on the weather, hanging herbs usually take about two weeks to dry. They should be crisp and crackly to the touch. Store in labeled jars or bags.

To dry whole onions, shallots, or garlic, simply store in a mesh bag or wire basket. Or make a decorative braid to hang: Leave stems on the bulbs and clean off ugly leaves and the first skin layer; braid strands, beginning with three bulbs. Continue braiding and adding bulbs. Tie off the end with twine. Hang in a dry, well-ventilated place. Cut off bulbs and use them as needed.

Quick Drying

If you want to dry herbs in a hurry, spread the leaves on a cheesecloth-covered rack in the oven at its lowest temperature. Leave the oven door open and stir the leaves until they are crisp. They'll be ready in a few minutes.

Tray Drying

For small quantities of herbs or short pieces of stems and seed heads, drying trays are handy. A simple box constructed of 1 × 1-inch lumber with screen mesh or cheesecloth stapled to the bottom works fine. Make the boxes small enough to hold just a few leaves—ten inches square is a good size. Put a one-inch block at each corner if you want to stack several boxes.

Let the leaves stay on the stems or strip them off. Make one layer in each tray. Stir the contents gently every few days to ensure even drying. Most herbs dry crisp within a week or ten days. Remove the leaves from the trays when they are crisp.

Dry the seed heads the same way, then gently rub the capsules through your hands. A fan on low speed or a natural breeze will blow away the chaff as you drop seed into the tray or a bowl.

Freezing

Freezing is recommended for a few of the tender herbs, including basil, burnet, fennel, tarragon, chives, dill, and parsley. Simply tie a small bundle of the herb together and blanch it by dipping it head-first into boiling water for a few seconds. Cool the bundle immediately by plunging it into ice water for a couple of minutes. (Blanching isn't necessary for basil, chives, and dill.) Remove leaves from the stems and put them into plastic bags, label, and freeze.

Freezing is a good way to save the herbs that you pick and don't use fresh during the season. Just chop the leaves before freezing and store in bags as much as you'll use at one time.

Salt Curing

Some of the tender herbs—such as basil, burnet, dill, fennel, and parsley—can be packed down in salt. Wash and drain, remove leaves from their stems, and place them in alternate layers with plain table salt in a container, beginning and ending with salt layers. Fill the container completely and cover with an airtight lid. Label and store in a cool, dark place.

Packing in Vinegar

The French tightly pack tarragon leaves in little jars, then completely fill the jars with vinegar. You might try this method with other leafy herbs as well.

A convenient method of drying herbs, the tray dryer is neat and simple to use. This three-layer tray dries a fairly large amount of herbs, and takes up very little space.

Herbs can be preserved by various methods. Before using them in cooking, measure them properly, taking into consideration the method used in preserving them.

Storage and Shelf Life

To retain their flavor, dried herbs should be kept as whole as possible and stored in airtight containers away from the heat of the stove and moisture. Some people advocate dark jars, cans, or ceramic containers. Clear jars or bottles—even plastic bags—are equally effective as long as they are kept out of the sun or other bright light.

When stored in a cool, ventilated place, leafy herbs can be expected to retain freshness for an entire year. Seeds and roots will keep somewhat longer, depending on the sturdiness of the crop.

Commercially available herbs and spices will last six months or slightly longer before beginning to lose their flavors. They should be stored exactly like homegrown products.

Frozen herbs retain texture and flavor much longer than one might expect. They'll keep indefinitely but are best used within one year. Once they have been thawed, they cannot be refrozen.

Using Preserved Herbs

To use dried herbs you'll need to break them up finely to release their stored flavor. You can simply pulverize them between your fingers as you add them to a dish or use a mortar and pestle to grind them as finely as you wish.

Since oils become concentrated in the drying process, you'll find that it usually takes less of the dried product in a recipe than it does of the fresh herb. However, the strength of the dried herb depends on how it was harvested and preserved, how it has been stored, and how long you've had it on the shelf. The old rule of thumb is: ¼ teaspoon dried, finely powdered herb = ¾ to 1 teaspoon dried, loosely crumbled herb = 1½ to 2 teaspoons fresh chopped herb.

Other equivalents to keep in mind:

- 1 clove fresh garlic = ½ teaspoon garlic salt (reduce other salt in the recipe to compensate)

- 1 teaspoon dried dill seed = 1 head fresh dill

- 1 tablespoon dried onion flakes = 1 medium-size raw onion

When you use salt-cured herbs, remove the amount of leaves you'll need and rinse away the salt just before adding them.

To use frozen herbs, remove only the amount you'll be using. Add them frozen to foods to be cooked; let herbs thaw before adding to cold foods.

If you've preserved herbs in vinegar, remove the desired amount, rinse, chop, and add to the recipe.

Using Fresh Herbs

Gather herbs from the garden as you need them. Wash them quickly in cold water when you bring them in and discard any bad leaves. Keep garden or produce-market herbs crisp for several days by storing them in sealed plastic bags or containers in the refrigerator.

Mince or chop small amounts when you need them. Flavors are quickly lost as volatile oils are released by heat. Add herbs to a hot dish at the last minute, unless it's a simmering stock.

Edible Flowers

Perhaps you can't eat the daisies, but there are quite a few other blooms from the garden that have numerous culinary uses. When you gather flowers for eating, choose perfect, blemish-free specimens that have not been sprayed with any chemicals. Wash them quickly in cool water to remove dust and then cut away the green stems to the base of the flower. Chill flowers in the refrigerator in a bowl of water or in a plastic bag to keep them fresh and crisp. Add to dishes at the last minute. Use sparingly to make them seem quite special.

Choose whole flowers or mince petals to garnish canapés, toss in salads, float on drinks, sprinkle on soups, cook in eggs, finish off vegetable dishes, and brighten desserts.

Among the flowers you can pick to eat are borage, calendulas, carnations and pinks, chives and onions, fennel, geraniums, nasturtiums, rosemary, roses, salad burnet, and violets. Calendulas, like safflower petals, are good substitutes for saffron.

Nasturtiums are colorful, decorative flowers, and are also edible. The mild-tasting petals can be used in salads.

Bouquets Garnis

A bouquet garni or fagot is a combination of several herbs—usually bay, thyme, and parsley or chervil—simmered in dishes as they cook. Fresh herb sprigs are simply tied with string and dropped into the cooking pot. Leaves or dried herbs are wrapped inside a four-inch square of cheesecloth, which is tied with string to form a bag. You might use a fine-wire-mesh tea ball.

Here's a classic bouquet garni for soup, fish, or meat stocks.

Fresh:
2 sprigs thyme
5 or 6 sprigs parsley
1 bay leaf

Dried:
1 bay leaf
1 tablespoon *each* tarragon and parsley
1 teaspoon *each* rosemary and thyme

Many recipes, such as the spicy crab-and-shrimp boil that's unique to Louisiana, call for a special bouquet garni. A favorite New Orleans combination includes the following:

Louisiana Bouquet Garni
1 teaspoon *each* whole allspice, thyme, celery seed, and
  black peppercorns
½ teaspoon *each* cayenne and whole cloves
5 bay leaves, broken
3 dried hot chile peppers

Bring about 4 quarts water to a boil and add a seasoning bag containing the above, along with salt and sliced lemons. Boil for about 10 minutes before adding shellfish.

Combining Herbs

Herbs are usually used in combination. When you blend your own, it's a good idea to remember that strongly flavored herbs such as marjoram, rosemary, sage, and tarragon are best used alone or in combination with several milder herbs whose flavors blend easily. In most instances avoid the conflict of two strongly flavored herbs that compete for attention.

The classic herb mix of French haute cuisine is known as *fines herbes*. This is a delicate combination of three or four herbs, preferably fresh, used to flavor many dishes. The usual portions are equal parts parsley, chervil, chives, and tarragon. Other mild herbs may be substituted or added.

Stoveside Herbs

The creative cook will want to have herbs and spices within arm's reach for inspired last-minute additions to foods under preparation.

You'll probably enjoy hanging small bunches of drying herbs near the stove to pick as needed. Use them within a couple of months because the flavor is rapidly lost when they are exposed to air and heat. Festive strands of dried peppers, garlic, and onions last longer than herbs.

Perhaps you'd enjoy a collection of potholders stuffed with dried rosemary or other herbs. When they touch a warm dish or pan, the fragrance is released in the kitchen. There are fabric prints of botanical herbs, or use any cloth that matches your kitchen. Don't forget herbed potholders when you want to give a special gift.

Sprigs of herbs can be conveniently hung in the kitchen, or grown in pots on a kitchen windowsill or just outside the door.

Left: A field of wild mustard.

Flavored Vinegars

One of the most pleasurable things you can do with herbs and spices is to create flavored vinegars. Colorful and varied vinegars in interesting bottles are not only visual assets to the kitchen shelves, but nice to have on hand when you want to perk up a salad dressing or add zest to dishes calling for vinegar. It's like having a good choice of wines to call on.

You can use almost every herb and spice, alone or in combination. Experiment with small quantities of various mixes to find flavors you enjoy. Pretty bottles with a sprig of herb immersed in the vinegar make welcome gifts. Take a corked bottle of flavored vinegar instead of wine to your next dinner party. Your hosts will be delighted.

The flavoring procedure is simple. Just add 4 ounces of fresh herb or spice, or 2 ounces of the dried version to each quart of cold vinegar. Leave for five to six weeks to develop flavor. (Your palate will let you know if you need to add more or less next time.) Then strain the vinegar into clean bottles, or leave fresh herb twigs in for show. Cap tightly and store. You can seal with hot wax to which pungent powdered cinnamon has been added.

As the base you can use any of several store-bought vinegars—white, wine, cider, or malt. The white vinegar will let the flavor of the herb or spice shine through. Other vinegars add their own characteristics to the end product.

If you want flavored vinegar in a hurry, bring the vinegar and spices to a boil and simmer for about twenty minutes. Pour into bottles and cap. It's ready to use without waiting for it to mellow.

Herbed vinegars are easy to make, and special gifts to give. Many different herbs can be used for herbed vinegars.

Herb Garden Themes

Of the many ways herbs and spices can be grouped, their uses and pleasures for us come first. The accompanying plant lists describe a few theme gardens, along with plants for special purposes.

Shakespeare Garden

Listed below are herbs mentioned in the writings of William Shakespeare. All were popular in Elizabethan England.

Artemisia absinthium (Wormwood)
Aquilegia spp. (Columbine)
Brassica juncea (Mustard)
Calendula officinalis (Calendula)
Chamaemelum nobile (Chamomile)
Dianthus caryophyllus (Carnation)
Dianthus deltoides (Maiden pink)
Fragaria chiloensis (Strawberry)

Hyssopus officinalis (Hyssop)
Laurus nobilis (Bay)
Lavandula spp. (Lavender)
Melissa officinalis (Lemon balm)
Mentha spp. (Mint)
Myrtus spp. (Myrtle)
Origanum majorana (Marjoram)
Petroselinum crispum (Parsley)
Poterium sanguisorba (Burnet)
Rosa spp. (Rose)
Rosmarinus officinalis (Rosemary)
Satureja spp. (Savory)
Thymus spp. (Thyme)
Viola tricolor (Johnny-jump-up)

Good Cook's Garden
The plants on this list are indispensable ingredients in the kitchen. You may want to plant them near the kitchen door to save steps.

Allium ampeloprasum (Leek)
Allium ascalonicum (Shallot)
Allium cepa (Onion)
Allium sativum (Garlic)
Allium schoenoprasum (Chives)
Anethum graveolens (Dill)
Angelica archangelica (Angelica)
Anthriscus cerefolium (Chervil)
Armoracia rusticana (Horseradish)
Artemisia dracunculus (Tarragon)
Borago officinalis (Borage)
Brassica juncea (Mustard)
Carum carvi (Caraway)
Chrysanthemum balsamita
  (Costmary)
Coriandrum sativum (Coriander)
Cuminum cyminum (Cumin)
Eruca sativa (Rocket)

Hyssopus officinalis (Hyssop)
Laurus nobilis (Bay)
Lavandula spp. (Lavender)
Levisticum officinale (Lovage)
Marrubium vulgare (Horehound)
Mentha spp. (Mint)
Nasturtium officinale (Watercress)
Ocimum basilicum (Basil)
Origanum marjorana (Marjoram)
Origanum vulgare (Oregano)
Petroselinum crispum (Parsley)
Pimpinella anisum (Anise)
Poterium sanguisorba (Burnet)
Rosa spp. (Rose)
Rosmariunus officinalis (Rosemary)
Salvia officinalis (Sage)
Satureja spp. (Savory)
Sesamum indicum (Sesame)
Tropaeolum majus (Nasturtium)

Tea Garden
Almost every herb and spice can be made into a tea. These are especially good and will make attractive plantings as well. If your climate is quite warm, add the Oriental tea plant and ginger.

Aloysia triphylla (Lemon verbena)
Anethum graveolens (Dill)
Angelica archangelica (Angelica)
Borago officinalis (Borage)
Chamaemelum nobile (Chamomile)
Chrysanthemum balsamita
  (Costmary)
Foeniculum vulgare (Fennel)
Galium odoratum (Sweet woodruff)
Gaultheria procumbens
  (Wintergreen)

Jasminum spp. (Jasmine)
Levisticum officinale (Lovage)
Marrubium vulgare (Horehound)
Melissa officinalis (Lemon balm)
Mentha spp. (Mint)
Monarda didyma (Bergamot)
Myrrhis odorata (Sweet cicely)
Nepeta cataria (Catnip)
Ocimum basilicum (Basil)
Origanum majorana (Marjoram)
Petroselium crispum (Parsley)
Rosa spp. (Rose)
Rosmarinus officinalis (Rosemary)
Salvia officinalis (Sage)
Tanacetum vulgare (Tansy)
Thymus spp. (Thyme)

Garden of Fragrances
A walk through a garden designed for fragrances is a delight to all the senses. Not only do these plants smell great but they're visually pleasing, some of them taste good, and you can't resist touching the leaves as you listen to the birds and bees enjoying them, too.

Achillea millefolium (Yarrow)
Acorus calamus (Sweet flag)
Aloysia triphylla (Lemon verbena)
Angelica archangelica (Angelica)
Artemisia abrotanum (Southernwood)
Artemisia dracunculus (Tarragon)
Chamaemelum nobile (Chamomile)
Chenopodium bonus-henricus (Good-
  King-Henry)
Chrysanthemum balsamita
  (Costmary)
Convallaria majalis (Lily-of-the-
  valley)
Galium odoratum (Sweet woodruff)
Heliotropium arborescens (Heliotrope)
Hyssopus officinalis (Hyssop)
Jasminum spp. (Jasmine)
Lavandula spp. (Lavender)
Melissa officinalis (Lemon balm)
Mentha pulegium (Pennyroyal)
Mentha spp. (Mint)
Monarda didyma (Bergamot)
Myrrhis odorata (Sweet cicely)
Nepeta cataria (Catnip)
Ocimum basilicum (Basil)
Origanum majorana (Marjoram)
Origanum vulgare (Oregano)
Pelargonium spp. (Scented geraniums)
Rosa spp. (Rose)
Rosmarinus officinalis (Rosemary)
Salvia officinalis (Sage)
Satureja spp. (Savory)
Tanacetum vulgare (Tansy)
Thymus spp. (Thyme)
Viola odorata (Violet)

Mentha species.

The Flowering Garden

A well-planned garden of herbs and spices can provide a lot of flowers for fragrances, cutting, drying, eating, garnishing, or just enjoying. Many other herbs flower, but should be harvested just before flowers open.

Achillea millefolium (Yarrow)
Anethum graveolens (Dill)
Angelica archangelica (Angelica)
Anthriscus cerefolium (Chervil)
Borago officinalis (Borage)
Brassica juncea (Mustard)
Calendula officinalis (Calendula)
Carthamus tinctorius (Safflower)
Chamaemelum nobile (Chamomile)
Chrysanthemum balsamita (Costmary)
Convallaria majalis (Lily-of-the-valley)
Coriandrum sativa (Coriander)
Cuminum cyminum (Cumin)
Dianthus caryophyllus (Carnation)
Dianthus deltoides (Maiden pink)
Galium odoratum (Sweet woodruff)
Helianthus annuus (Sunflower)
Hyssopus officinalis (Hyssop)
Inula helenium (Elecampane)
Lavandula spp. (Lavender)
Levisticum officinale (Lovage)
Monarda didyma (Bergamot)
Nigella sativa (Fennel flower)
Pimpinella anisum (Anise)
Rosa spp. (Rose)
Rosmarinus officinalis (Rosemary)
Tanacetum vulgare (Tansy)
Taraxacum officinale (Dandelion)

Chenopodium bonus-henricus.

Thymus spp. (Thyme)
Viola odorata (Violet)
Viola tricolor (Johnny-jump-up)
Zingiber officinale (Ginger)

Gray and Silver Garden

A quiet garden of subtle shimmering foliages is a pleasant place to visit, especially on a moonlit evening. Gray foliage highlights the colors of the flowers of these plants and their companions, and provides contrast in vivid flower beds.

Achillea millefolium (Yarrow)
Aloe vera (Aloe)
Artemisia abrotanum (Southernwood)
Artemisia absinthium (Wormwood)
Dianthus caryophyllus (Carnation)
Lavandula spp. (Lavender)
Marrubium vulgare (Horehound)
Mentha suaveolens (Apple mint)
Mentha × *rotundifolia* (Pineapple mint)
Origanum vulgare (Oregano)
Pelargonium × *fragrans* (Nutmeg geranium)
Rosmarinus officinalis (Rosemary)
Salvia officinalis (Silver sage)
Teucrium chamaedrys (Germander)
Thymus nitidus (Silver thyme)

Indoor Garden

When you plan an indoor herb and spice garden, start with these easy-to-grow plants. If there's insufficient sunlight, group them in an attractive unit under wide-spectrum artificial light.

Allium schoenoprasum (Chives)
Aloe vera (Aloe)
Aloysia triphylla (Lemon verbena)
Anethum graveolens (Dill)
Anthriscus cerefolium (Chervil)
Artemesia dracunculus (Tarragon)
Borago officinalis (Borage)
Foeniculum vulgare (Fennel)
Hyssopus officinalis (Hyssop)

Foeniculum vulgare.

Laurus nobilis (Bay)
Lavandula spp. (Lavender)
Levisticum officinale (Lovage)
Melissa officinalis (Lemon balm)
Mentha pulegium (Pennyroyal)
Mentha spp. (Mint)
Ocimum basilicum (Basil)
Origanum dictamnus (Dittany of Crete)
Origanum majorana (Marjoram)
Origanum vulgare (Oregano)
Pelargonium spp. (Scented geraniums)
Petroselinum crispum (Parsley)
Poterium sanguisorba (Burnet)
Rosmarinus officinalis (Rosemary)
Rumex scutatus (Sorrel)
Salvia officinalis (Sage)
Satureja spp. (Savory)
Thymus spp. (Thyme)
Zingiber officinale (Ginger)

Tanacetum vulgare.

This page: *Pisum ochrus* from *Flora Graeca*, vol. 7, tabula 89. Opposite page: Cabbage and stock make an attractive combination.

Vegetables

Almost every gardener has grown a vegetable garden at one time or another. Whether they plant only a child's simple patch of radishes and carrots, or enough vegetables to feed an entire neighborhood, most gardeners can't resist the challenge—and rewards—of vegetable growing. There are as many ways to grow a vegetable garden as there are gardeners. The choice of what to plant is a highly personal one, reflecting the interests, knowledge, and imagination of the gardener.

You may want your garden to be purely practical, or beautiful, or a mixture of both. Some gardeners plant only the most reliable, "success guaranteed" performers, carefully laying out their plots to maximize production. Others remember the unstructured beauty of grandma's garden with fascination, and base their plans on that recollection. And some gardeners are full of surprises, always changing their gardens as their own whims change.

Vegetable gardening is not quite the same as growing vegetables. Vegetable gardening implies straight rows and an orderly sequence of operations: planning for space, choosing varieties, figuring planting dates, and anticipating harvests. It can be a challenging and exciting exercise, especially for the beginner.

Growing vegetables, on the other hand, means that you can squeeze your plants into any free corner, set them among flowers and ornamentals, or just plant them for their own special kind of beauty. 'Salad Bowl' and 'Ruby' lettuce are beautiful with Iceland poppies. Try an attractive combination such as yellow violas with parsley. Mixed and planted about ten inches apart, they make a beautiful sight in spring, with the yellow violas shooting up through the green mountain of parsley. Whether your garden site is as small as a box or as big as a house, growing vegetables can be a creative and satisfying pastime.

Success with Vegetables

It's well known that home-grown produce is superior to store-bought corn, snap beans, peas, and all vegetables that lose their fresh quality soon after picking. This is because vegetables that must be picked green to allow for shipping time lack the taste and quality of ripe, home-gardened produce.

But home-grown vegetables are not automatically superior. Only when the best varieties are planted, given the right amount of water and fertilizers, and harvested at the right time will the taste be something to brag about.

In this chapter you will read about how to improve your soil, select plants, plant seed, water, fertilize, and otherwise care for vegetable plants. All these procedures are important, and your mastery of them will ensure a bumper crop.

Take your climate into account when selecting vegetable seeds and seedlings since most vegetables have been hybridized for specific climatic adaptations. Choosing varieties suitable to your area will help ensure a bountiful crop.

Know Your Climate

More than any other type of plant, vegetables have been bred for specific climatic factors. You can buy tomato varieties that fruit early, melon varieties for short, cool summers, varieties of lettuce that tolerate a fair amount of hot weather—the list is endless. That's why a knowledge of your climate and microclimate is essential to choosing vegetable varieties best suited to your garden. See Chapter 2 (pages 39–45) for a discussion of climatic and microclimatic influences in your garden.

Soil

It is the rare gardener whose soil is deep, fertile, easy to work, and easy to manage. Most home gardeners do not have ideal soil; many have problem soils that are either too heavy and poorly drained or too coarse or sandy. Almost any problem soil can be improved by adding the proper amendments, an important aspect of vegetable gardening. Of course, vegetables will grow in poor soil, but the improved taste and quality of vegetables grown in amended soil are well worth the time and expense invested in soil preparation.

Improving Your Soil

You don't need to improve the entire garden area—it's enough to add organic amendments to only those areas in which you intend to plant. For further discussion of soil amendments, see Chapter 14, page 343.

Raised Beds

Even with the addition of soil amendments, some vegetable gardens will still benefit from the use of raised beds. The basic advantages of raised beds are that you can choose which kind of soil to fill the bed with, greatly improve soil drainage, and increase the amount of soil available to plants that would otherwise have to grow in shallow soil. To avoid depriving the plants of water or nutrients, you can build a raised bed and fill it with a loose, fast-draining soil mix.

If your area typically receives heavy spring or fall rains, you should definitely consider using raised beds. Since water drains quickly in a raised bed, the roots won't be harmed by water-logged soil that would otherwise suffocate them.

You can also use raised beds to lengthen the vegetable-growing season. In the spring, they warm earlier than the surrounding soil, since air circulation is freer in looser soil.

This raised bed, filled with two varieties of lettuce, onions, and violas, is attractive as well as functional. The plants are easier to tend because of the raised height, and the soil mix is high in organic matter and drains well—an ideal composition for most vegetables.

Above: This side yard has been carefully planned to accommodate a variety of vegetables. Successive plantings will keep fresh vegetables on the table all season long. Right: 'Sugar Snap' peas make an excellent choice for the gardener with limited space. Because they are vines, they can be trained up a trellis or fence, a method requiring only a little room.

Before You Plant

It's easy to get carried away when choosing vegetable seeds at the nursery. The attractive seed racks with their colorful seed packets are irresistible. Almost all of the delicious-looking vegetables displayed on the packets appear to be just right for your garden and your palate.

All too often, the eager gardener returns home with a bag full of seed packets to find that there is not nearly enough room in the garden to accommodate the seeds. In fact, many of the seeds are not really right for the garden, and no one in the family actually enjoys most of the vegetables the eager gardener has purchased.

Take time to plan your vegetable garden, and it will reward you with the right kinds and proper amounts of vegetables.

Determine how much space you actually have to work with, and figure out which vegetables you and your family will enjoy eating. Make sure that you know approximately how large the plants will grow so that you'll be able to allot the appropriate amount of space. Find out how many plants of each kind you will actually need to feed your family so that you won't overplant or underplant.

You can find this kind of information on the seed packets; read them carefully before you buy them. If you order your seed through mail-order catalogs, read the catalog descriptions carefully. You may find more vegetable varieties offered through a seed catalog than are usually available at a garden center.

Planning for a Continuous Harvest

Vegetable gardens bring many joys, but they also bring problems. One of the most typical (and most frustrating) occurs when everything ripens at once—a classic illustration of the perils of "too much, too soon." It isn't easy to plan for a continuous harvest of fresh vegetables, especially for the beginner. And the limited-space gardener has a more difficult challenge than the gardener with a large yard.

If you're fortunate enough to have plenty of room, you can block out space for the spring garden and leave some space empty in readiness for the summer garden. This way, you can plan and plant the summer garden without interference from the spring garden.

But a city gardener with a twenty- by thirty-foot area needs to plan for both the spring and summer gardens (and also for the fall-winter garden in warm-winter areas). Clutching a dozen packets of seeds, each holding enough seed to plant 50 or 100

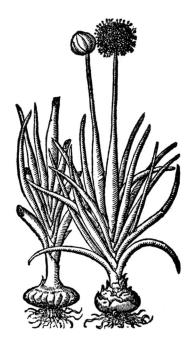

This matter of vegetable rank has not been at all studied as it should be. Why do we respect some vegetables, and despise others, when all of them come to an equal honour or ignominy on the table?

C.D. Warner
My Summer in a Garden

feet of row, the small-space gardener waxes optimistic and pictures row upon row of beautiful, healthy plants.

But although it might seem as if twenty or thirty heads of lettuce couldn't possibly produce enough salads for the whole family, when the thirty heads all mature within a ten-day period, you'll know you planted too many.

A dozen cabbage plants don't seem excessive in their little nursery trays. But they'll make thirty to forty pounds of cabbage when mature, which is more than enough for most families. To avoid those excesses, take into account the length of the harvest period when planning your garden, and make successive plantings through the season.

Length of Harvest Period

Fortunately, not all vegetables have short harvest periods; but if you choose two or three of the short-harvest varieties, you can extend the harvest period. Check how many days it takes for the vegetable to reach maturity. There are early, mid, and late cabbages. Each variety takes a different number of days to reach maturity.

These vegetables have long harvest periods:

Green beans begin producing after fifty to sixty days and continue until frost.

Eggplant begins in sixty to seventy days and lasts until frost.

Peppers begin after sixty to eighty days and last until frost.

Summer squash is harvestable after fifty to sixty days and keeps going until frost.

Tomatoes begin anywhere from fifty to ninety days after planting and last until frost.

In contrast, a vegetable like corn is picked within a two-week period. And the radish harvest lasts only about two weeks. The shorter the duration of the harvest, the more important small, successive plantings are.

Some root crops will last a long time in the soil, including carrots, beets, parsnips, and salsify. Of these, carrots and beets provide a succession of harvests. You can begin harvesting when they are baby-size and continue up to maturity. Then they will last in the soil for periods of weeks or months, depending upon your climate and the time of year.

Perennial vegetables—asparagus, rhubarb, and Jerusalem artichoke (same as sunchoke)—come back year after year. Their duration of harvest is measured in seasons.

Succession Plantings

The way to a continuous harvest is to make successive plantings of small quantities. For example, if you first plant lettuce in March, you can make another planting in April, and another in May. Successive plantings of snap beans, four to six weeks apart, will give you fresh beans for five months or more. But to get a continuous harvest of a vegetable, you must plant the second crop before you harvest the first.

Chart Your Plantings

When you chart a succession of plantings on paper, the goal of a long harvest season comes within reach. It's easier than you might think. Planting times are determined by only four factors: when the soil is workable in spring; the date of the last spring frost; the date of the first fall frost; and the average time the soil freezes, if ever.

Next, look up the vegetables you would like to grow; note when they should be planted and the average number of days to harvest. Using these figures in combination, you'll know what to plant when, about when it will be ready to harvest, and when to replant for a steady harvest. Once you've charted your plantings in this way, you can easily make adjustments that will lengthen the harvest season.

Tomatoes have a long harvest period and many will bear fruit for several months. 'Tiny Tim', the variety shown here, is ideal for growing in containers.

Seeding

Seeds may be sown directly into the prepared garden soil, or they may be started in containers indoors or in another controlled environment to be transplanted into the ground later.

Direct Seeding

Direct seeding is one of the easiest and most basic of all seed-starting methods; it is the only method that can be used for certain vegetable seeds, such as beets, parsnips, carrots, and other root crops. Cabbage and its relatives, lettuce, onions, and melons, can also be direct seeded, although they may also be started indoors in containers. If you live in an area with a long growing season, or you don't have the room or inclination to start seeds indoors, direct seeding the appropriate vegetables is the ideal method. See Chapter 3, pages 67–68, for complete instructions on direct seeding.

Don't Rush the Season   It's critical to the success of your vegetable garden that you let the soil warm up enough before planting. Seeds planted in soil too cold for germination will decay rather than sprout, or when they do sprout, their overall vigor will be reduced.

Weeds   Weeds will inevitably appear soon after you plant vegetable seeds. Unfortunately, weed seedlings tend to compete with vegetable seedlings. Every time you work the soil, you inadvertently bring weed seeds up to the surface, where they find excellent conditions for germination. If you're a first-time gardener, you may wonder whether your seed packet didn't, in fact, contain 50 percent weed seeds. With today's highly developed techniques of cleaning vegetable seed, the chance of weed seed appearing in any of these seed packets is negligible. There are a thousand times more weed seeds in the soil than you'll ever find in a packet of seed.

Growing Transplants

For root crops, you sow seeds directly where you want them to grow. But for tomatoes, peppers, and eggplants, you almost always have to start the seeds indoors in containers and grow them to transplantable size. Many other vegetables can also be grown indoors as transplants.

Growing transplants indoors is an ideal method for the gardener who lives in an area with a short growing season. Not only does growing transplants save time, but it also gives the plants a head start before frost danger is over and before the soil

Above: The tomato seedlings
are growing in peat pots.
Peat pots are easy to use; and
when the seedlings are ready for
transplanting, the entire peat
pot can be planted too. The
roots will grow through it and
the pot itself will eventually
degrade. Right: Cold frames give
tender seedlings a headstart
on the growing season.

is workable. In this way, transplants can actually lengthen the
growing season by one or two months.

Transplants are also not as susceptible to some of the hazards
common to tiny seedlings, including birds, insects, heavy rain,
and weeds.

You can buy transplants or start your own. Which route you
choose depends on whether the varieties you want are available
at your garden center and whether the idea of starting from
scratch appeals to you.

There are four different methods for starting transplants
indoors: planting seeds in ready-made peat pots or pellets; the
two-step method; using a seed-starting kit with artificial lights
and soil-heating units; and planting in cold frames and hotbeds.
See Chapter 3, pages 68–73, for descriptions of these methods.

Mulching

Your vegetable-garden mulch may be made of organic material (such as leaves, peat moss, straw, manure, sawdust, ground bark, compost, and the like) or manufactured materials (such as polyethylene film, aluminum foil, or paper).

Organic Mulches

An organic mulch offers many advantages, but it needs to be applied at the right time. If applied in early spring, for example, it will slow up the natural warming of the soil as spring advances. Thus it will become an insulating blanket, reducing solar radiation into the soil and increasing the chance of frost hazards. Therefore, summer is the best time to add organic mulch, when the soil is already sufficiently warm.

These lettuce plants are heavily mulched with straw. Mulching benefits any vegetable garden; among other functions, mulches conserve soil moisture, reduce soil crusting, and prevent weed germination.

A thick layer of straw makes a good mulch for these bean plants. Straw, considered a coarse, organic mulch, must be layered three to four inches for maximum benefit.

Mulch Thickness   Apply organic mulches one to two inches thick for fine materials (for example, sawdust) and up to four inches thick for coarse materials (such as straw). If your sawdust is untreated, increase the amount of fertilizer regularly used for the crop by 25 percent to reduce the loss of nitrogen from the soil.

A one-eighth-inch-thick mulch of vermiculite, bark, or sawdust will prevent soil crusting and reduce the need to water frequently.

Manufactured Mulches

Some gardeners cover soil rows with burlap sacks immediately after planting and sprinkle them as necessary. With sacks, however, there is always the danger of forgetting them for a few days just at the time the seedlings are emerging.

Clear plastic makes a good mulch but, again, watch closely for the emergence of seedlings and remove the plastic as soon as the seedlings show. When using clear plastic, make a shallow trough and plant seeds at the bottom; then cover the trough with the plastic at an angle so that water can run off it. The seeds and soil must have ventilation. You may need to punch holes in the plastic to allow some air circulation. Clear plastic enables the gardener to direct seed hard-to-germinate seeds like tomato, pepper, and eggplant. The plastic cover prevents evaporation, heats the soil twenty to thirty degrees higher than air temperatures, and makes the seed germinate fast. It also helps prevent loss of the seedlings from disease. Plastic should be removed after germination to control weeds.

Water

Few gardening subjects stir up as much confusion and controversy as this familiar liquid. How much water should be applied? When? How often? If your tomato blossoms drop or your carrots come out stumpy, you may be warned about overwatering. If your lettuce tastes bitter, you may be cautioned against giving an uneven supply of water.

Since every gardener has a different answer, how can you tell what's too much and what's too little? There are no exact formulas, but the basic rule of thumb is to water thoroughly, filling the root zone. Then let the soil dry out a bit, and when it looks as if it needs it, water again.

How can you tell what "thorough" watering means in your specific garden? Apply what you think is a sufficient amount of water. Then, using a spade or shovel, dig up the top three or four inches of soil and take a look. Did the water penetrate to that depth? If it did, you are watering properly. If not, you need to water longer.

You can get a feel for how long to wait between waterings by observing the appearance of your soil and using your hands to feel it.

It doesn't matter when during the day you water; any time will do. However, many experts suggest the early morning, which offers two advantages. First, the plants will lose less water to evaporation. Second, the plants will stay dry at night and thus be less susceptible to attack by disease-causing organisms.

Furrow Irrigation

The most commonly used method of watering vegetables may well be furrow irrigation. It is frequently preferred by gardeners who have a variety of vegetables crowded into a small area. Overhead sprinklers cannot be selective enough to avoid those vegetables that do not like wet leaves. Furrow irrigation confines the water to the plant's root zone, and also inhibits weed growth in unwatered areas.

When you lay out your furrow irrigation system, keep the furrows as level as possible. Too much slope will cause the water to flow too rapidly, and some areas may receive too little water. You can, if you have the room, place the furrows to allow dry walkways between paths.

Drip Watering

The idea of making a little water go a long way is nothing new, especially in areas with a limited supply of water. What are new, however, are some irrigation techniques and equipment.

Most gardeners are familiar with furrow irrigation. It requires a minimum of equipment and is especially beneficial for plants that cannot tolerate wet foliage.

The drip/trickle system of irrigation is now available to the home gardener, after years of testing in thousands of acres of orchards, row crops, and nursery operations. Although these systems are not totally foolproof, their potential advantages are so great that it seems worthwhile to experiment with them in the home garden. Drip irrigation drops the water onto the ground through one or more emitters located adjacent to each tree or plant.

Sprinklers

There are two kinds of sprinklers—underground sprinkler systems with sprinkler heads above ground and hose-end sprinklers. The underground systems are good for large gardens, because they provide even coverage with a minimum of guesswork. If installed on a timer, they will water with convenience and regularity. For smaller gardens, you can use underground systems or try hose-end sprinklers. The latter will cost less, although they offer less convenience. They come in many sizes and shapes. Choose the one best suited to your area, the one that will use water most efficiently.

Fertilizers

On a daily basis, plants require only a small amount of nutrients, but that amount must be available just when the plants need it. Certain slow-growing plants allow some leeway—you don't need to fertilize until you see the lower leaves begin to yellow. But vegetables won't let you be this casual. Right away, they demand adequate nutrients in the soil to see them through to harvest. An insufficient amount of nutrients will retard growth, and this, in turn, will reduce both quality and yield.

How Much Fertilizer?

When you apply fertilizers to your vegetables—whether fish emulsion, blood meal, commercial liquid, or commercial dry fertilizers—be sure to follow the label directions on the package, bag, or bottle. Don't try to outguess the manufacturer. If you must err, err on the side of too little. Too much of any fertilizer, even manure, is dangerous.

When using large amounts of fertilizer for such heavy feeders as cabbage and onions, apply half the amount before planting, and then side-dress with the remainder once growth is under way.

Check the timing for applying fertilizer to each vegetable. The first application is crucial with many crops, since it can protect early, vigorous leaf growth.

Normally, lettuce plants do not require as much fertilizer as other vegetables; but any vegetable grown in crowded conditions, as shown below, requires heavier feeding.

The rewards of a regular fertilization and irrigation program are beautifully illustrated here—a succulent turnip ready to be harvested.

Give less nitrogen to plants grown in partial shade than to the same kind of plants grown in full sun.

Increase the amount of fertilizer when plants are crowded by narrow spacing between rows and when plants are grown in a random pattern in a small plot.

Vegetables in Containers

All of us might like to have a large country-style garden, but most people don't. Nevertheless, small-space gardeners are a determined breed. "Gardeners will garden," a veteran small-spacer once said. "It's that simple." Productive vegetable gardens have been grown on rooftops, balconies, decks, and in other nontraditional locations.

Of necessity, the gardener without a vegetable garden can neither overplant nor waste the harvest. No time is spent guessing how much a twenty-foot row of beets will produce; instead, seeds are simply sown a container or two at a time.

Some determined gardeners combine resources with their friends and neighbors to make a community garden, an undertaking that's simultaneously practical, social, and educational— practical because it makes good use of vacant lots found in urban areas, and lets the gardeners grow food close to where it is used; social because it offers a great way to get to know your neighbors; and educational because of the gardening knowledge that's shared.

Versatility is the hallmark of the container gardener. On balconies, decks, or patios, vegetables can grow in boxes, tubs, bushel baskets, cans, and planters of all shapes and sizes. Any of these containers will work—the depth of the box is what's critical.

The major considerations to keep in mind are portability, frequency of watering, and fertilizing. The shallower the box, the more frequent is the need for water and fertilizer.

When watering plants in containers, keep applying the water until it drains out the bottom, which will leach nitrogen and potassium through the soil mix. This may seem like a waste of fertilizer, but it offers a distinct advantage by preventing harmful salts from building up in the mix.

For the following vegetables, the boxes should have these minimum depths:

Four inches deep: Lettuce, radishes, beets, and all the low-growing herbs.

Six inches deep: Chard, kohlrabi, short carrots such as 'Baby Finger', and turnips.

Eight inches deep: Bush beans, cabbage, eggplant, peppers, and bush cucumbers.

Ten inches deep: Cauliflower, broccoli, and brussels sprouts.

Twelve inches deep: Parsnips, salsify, long-rooted carrots, and tomatoes.

The choice of which vegetables to plant in container gardens also depends on which ones give the highest return per square

Almost any vegetable can be grown in a container. This artichoke is no exception. Its striking gray foliage contrasts strongly with the dark color of the sturdy redwood container. It makes an attractive specimen plant, and its unopened flower heads will find their way onto your dinner table!

foot of space—in other words, on which ones can be spaced most closely in the row. Some vegetables in this group are carrots, beets, chives, leaf lettuce, mustard, green onions, radishes, and turnips.

For a continuous harvest, you might plant a total of six boxes early; two more three weeks later; and the last two boxes approximately two weeks after that.

How vegetables grow in your climate will dictate your choice of late spring and fall plantings. Box plantings make it easy to think of harvests in terms of the number of meals instead of the total quantity of plants.

Compact Varieties

Gardens that cannot grow out can grow up. A fence five feet high and twenty feet long provides a whopping one hundred square feet of growing space. It can be covered with vines of beans, cucumbers, tomatoes, squash, or gourds without infringing on much of the ground space. Pole beans yield more per plant than bush beans; upright planters produce a row's worth of strawberries, lettuce, or herbs. The needs of small-space gardeners have not gone unheeded by vegetable plant breeders; they have come up with many miniature and bush varieties of favorite vegetables.

"L'Imperatrice" (plum)
from *Pomona Londinensis* by
William Hooker.

Fruits & Berries

Strictly speaking, a fruit is the seed-bearing portion of any plant, but the term commonly suggests the delicious edible fruits that grace our tables—apples, pears, peaches, plums, and berries of all kinds. In this chapter you'll find descriptions and basic information about all the most popular fruits and berries suitable for growing by the home gardener.

Many gardeners share the misconception that producing a good fruit crop requires the knowledge and skill of an expert orchardist. In fact, extensive maintenance and culture are necessary only for maximum commercial production. The home gardener can get by with less complicated spraying, feeding, and pruning programs. Your chances of growing good fruit are greater today than ever before. We now have improved varieties with better fruiting, disease resistance, and tolerance of special soil and climate conditions.

Fruits in the Landscape

Gardeners who grow fruits and berries at home will tell you that the fresh-picked taste is more than enough reason to grow them; but fruit plants also enhance the landscape—even in a small yard or garden.

Not long ago a gardener with an average-size lot had to be content with very little in the way of fruit—perhaps a single apple tree in the center of the lawn and a grapevine growing over an outbuilding or arbor. But as the average lot has grown even smaller, modern horticulture has met the challenge. Fruit trees are now available in a range of sizes that permits using them in the smallest yards and gardens. Modern dwarfing techniques and simplified methods of training allow you to grow as many as a dozen fruit trees in one small garden and still have plenty of sunny space available for vegetables or flowers.

A Sample Garden

When you landscape with fruit, you combine beauty with practicality. You may not want a garden composed entirely of fruit, but you may wish to add a few fruit-bearing plants to enhance your surroundings.

Fruit trees can serve many functions. For example, apple trees make superb shade trees anywhere in the yard if you prune them to a branch high enough to allow passage underneath. A large crabapple tree or a spreading cherry will also provide good shade.

Any fruit tree you like can be used as a focal point or accent in the yard or garden. The most striking trees in bloom are apples, cherries, quince, and the showier flowering peaches.

Fruit and berry plants are attractive in the landscape and produce a delicious harvest.

Crabapples are especially effective. These hardy trees are the most widely adapted of all flowering trees and offer abundant displays of red to pink to white blossoms followed by brilliantly colored fruit. As a rule they require some winter chilling, but many varieties bloom beautifully even in mild climates. Some crabapples have fragrant blossoms; others have red to purple foliage. Citrus trees, where they can be grown, also have attractive foliage, showy fruit over a long season, and a wonderful fragrance.

These are just a few ideas for planting with fruit. Other possibilities depend on climate, soil, available varieties, and your personal taste.

Fruits and Berries for Your Garden

A large variety of fruits and berries can be grown in the United States. The general discussion of each type of fruit plant in this section will guide you toward the plants best suited for your area. Information about pruning is discussed in this section, but for descriptions of specific pruning methods, see page 315.

Many different fruit trees can be enjoyed in small gardens. This dwarf apple tree has been trained to grow on a trellis. Use the dwarf varieties in gardens that cannot incorporate larger, standard-sized trees.

Bear in mind that when a fruit is recommended for one area, that does not necessarily mean it can't do well in others. Climatic conditions vary so widely that any such recommendations must be general. Local geographical features and other factors that affect climate, as well as special treatment from the gardener (for example, providing sheltered areas or winter protection), can support plants that generally are not expected to do well in a given region. If you are attracted to a particular variety but are uncertain whether you can grow it in your garden, check with your local nursery staff, county extension agent, or gardening neighbors.

Apples

There are well over a thousand varieties of apples available today. Many of these have been developed through the painstaking, time-consuming efforts of apple breeders. Their work takes time, and many seedlings that are developed prove to be inferior to their parent trees.

The extensive work on dwarfing rootstocks for apples has produced plant sizes ranging from a four-foot bush to a thirty-foot spreading tree. Fruit trees can be dwarfed further through the various methods of pruning, girdling, scoring, and training. Apples can now grow flat on a wall or trellis, as hedges, or in fanciful three-dimensional shapes.

Thinning is crucial with many apple varieties. If left alone, the trees set too many fruits and the heavy crop can snap branches. Even more important, many apple varieties tend to bear every other year. If you leave too much fruit, you encourage this alternate bearing. The following year you many find that your tree bears only a handful of apples because the large crop of the previous year has depleted the tree's reserves.

The easiest way to thin is to wait for the natural drop of young fruit in June, then thin the remaining fruit so that there is a single apple every six inches along the branches. Each spur may have a cluster of fruit. A single fruit is less likely to become diseased, so leave only the largest fruit on each spur.

Apples form at the tip of last year's spur growth, and the spur itself then grows a bit more, off to the side of the fruit. Each spur bears for ten years or more, so don't tear it off when you pick.

Apples are only partially self-fertile, but many varieties set a good crop without a pollinator. Any two kinds that bloom together offer cross-pollination, except for a few such as 'Gravenstein', 'Winesap', and 'Stayman'. These will not set a crop at all if you plant them with no other source of pollen. Also, if

Apples are probably the most widely grown of the fruit trees. Varieties adapted to many different climates are available. Top: 'Ruby Red Rome'. Bottom: 'Law Red Rome'.

you plant only a very early and a very late variety, they will not cross-pollinate. Check with your local extension office for a list of varieties and their need for pollinators.

All apples need some cool winter weather, but there is an enormous range in this requirement, so varieties are available for any climate except subtropical and low desert regions.

Apricots

The selection of apricot varieties is limited in the colder regions of the country, because apricots bloom early and may suffer frost damage. In recent years, however, breeders have produced a number of hybrids with hardy Manchurian apricots, and now varieties such as 'Moongold' and 'Sungold' will fruit fairly regularly even in the northern plains. The choice of varieties widens in milder regions, and more tender varieties, such as 'Moorpark', will bear even in the eastern states.

Dwarfed apricots on special rootstocks produce fair-size trees, and a full-size tree will fill a twenty-six-foot-square site; but you can train the tree to branch high and use it in the landscape as a shade tree. Trees are fairly long-lived and may last from fifteen to thirty years, depending on location and care.

For best production, prune apricots heavily. For a crop of larger-sized apricots, thin fruits when they are small.

Apricots appear on the previous season's shoots, but the bulk of the fruit appears on four-year-old spurs on older wood, and the spurs drop soon after. To encourage spurs, pinch the lateral shoots when they are about three inches long.

Heavy pruning is essential to apricot production. Without it apricots will be borne only high in the tree.

Remove one-third of the new wood each year by both thinning and heading. See Chapter 8, pages 213–214, for explanations of these procedures.

Many apricots are self-fertile, but in colder regions it is usually best to plant a second variety for pollination to encourage the heaviest fruit set possible.

Blackberries

Blackberries and raspberries are closely related and have similar growing requirements, but blackberries are larger and more vigorous, and some varieties are less cold hardy. Blackberries come in two fairly distinct forms—erect and trailing—and have a number of different names.

The ordinary blackberry is a stiff-caned, fairly hardy plant that can stand by itself if properly pruned. The trailing kind is generally called a dewberry, and it is tender and grown mainly in the South. In addition, trailing plants from the Pacific Coast are sold under their variety names; for example, 'Boysen' and 'Logan'. These varieties will freeze in the East and the North without winter protection.

Blackberries like a light, well-drained soil with a high moisture-holding capacity. Do not plant them where tomatoes, potatoes, or eggplant have grown previously, since the site may be infected with verticillium wilt and the berries will succumb to the disease.

Blackberries fruit on twiggy side branches growing from canes of the previous season. The canes fruit only once and must be removed every year so that new canes replace them. All blackberries are self-fertile.

If you disturb or cut roots of blackberries, they will sucker badly. If you want more plants, chop off pieces of root beside the parent plants and set them in the new planting site like seed. If you don't want more plants, mulch the planting instead of cultivating for weed control. Blackberries can be more troublesome than any other cultivated plant and, if abandoned, can quickly grow out of control.

Blackberries are subject to enormous numbers of pests and diseases. Save yourself trouble by buying certified plants and keeping them away from any wild plants.

'Logan' blackberry. Blackberries will quickly overtake a garden if their rampant growth is not controlled.

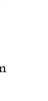

Left: Cover blueberry plants with netting to keep birds from feeding on the ripening fruit. Right: Blueberry 'Dixi'.

Blueberries

Blueberries demand the right climate and planting soil, but need very little care if you provide suitable conditions. They are a bit hardier than the peach, they need a fair amount of winter chill, and they will not grow well in mild-winter climates.

Blueberries like soil rich in organic material such as peat—very acid, but extremely well drained. Such soils are usual in areas of high rainfall, which is lucky, since the berries need constant moisture, but they cannot tolerate standing water.

When you plant blueberries, choose two varieties for cross-pollination. Approximately the same varieties are used throughout the country, since the conditions for growing them are so similar.

Blueberries suffer from very few difficulties, but birds will take them all unless you net the plants. If the berries are very small one year, thin out the oldest shoots. If the berries are large, skip the thinning.

Always taste blueberries before picking. Some look fully mature when still quite acid.

Cherries

Cherries come in three distinct forms, with many varieties in each. The sweet cherry sold in markets is planted commercially in the coastal valleys of California, in the Northwest, and near the Great Lakes. Sour cherries, or pie cherries, are good for cooking and canning. These are the most reliable for home gardeners, and there are many varieties developed for special conditions. Duke cherries have the shape and color of sweet cherries and the flavor and tartness of sour cherries.

All cherries require considerable winter chilling, which rules out planting in the mildest coastal and Gulf climates; but they are also damaged by early, intense cold in fall, and by heavy rainfall during ripening. Sweet cherries are especially tricky for the home gardener, but try them wherever summer heat and winter cold are not too intense.

Cherries come in many sizes. Bush varieties reach six to eight feet tall and spread about as wide. The dwarf sour cherries grow to about eight feet, but have a single trunk. Standard sour cherries and sweet cherries on dwarfing roots both reach fifteen to twenty feet. A standard sweet cherry is the largest and can equal a small oak in size if the climate permits. Such cherries can serve as major shade trees.

All cherries bear on long-lived spurs. Those on tree cherries can produce for ten years and more, and begin to bear along two-year-old branches. Count on the first crop in the third or fourth

'Montmorency' is a widely grown sour cherry. Its bright red fruit has firm yellow flesh and is crack resistant. Various strains have different ripening times and fruit characteristics.

year after planting. Bush cherries may bear sooner.

After the tree begins to bear, prune out only weak branches, those that develop at odd angles, and those that cross other branches. Be sure to head back the leader and upright side branches to no more than twelve to fifteen feet, so that the mature tree can be kept at about twenty feet.

Sour cherry trees differ from the sweet cherries in that they tend to spread wider and are considerably smaller.

Most sweet cherries need a pollinator. 'Windsor' and 'Black Tartarian' are good pollinators and bear well, but always plant at least two varieties, or use a graft on a single tree. Sour cherries are self-fertile, as are bush cherries.

Citrus

In much of the West and South there's nothing unusual about an orange tree outside the front door, bearing its load of golden fruit. But even where winter cold makes it impossible to put citrus in the ground, a smart gardener can manage some of the pleasure of the perfumed flowers and juicy fruits by planting in containers.

Citrus varieties can be grouped in two ways in relation to climate. First, for the gardener whose winter temperatures drop below 15°F, the question is: Is the plant hardy enough? Of course you can always grow dwarfed varieties in containers and haul them off to shelter for the winter. The second question is: Will it get hot enough long enough for the fruit to develop sugar? Inadequate summer heat means sour fruit, so even in areas where the plants grow outdoors, a cool summer may make your mandarins very puckery. However, that doesn't matter at all for sour fruit like lemons, 'Rangpur' limes, and so forth, and sour mandarin is just as pretty on the tree and produces fine juice for drinks. The most climatically limited fruit is the grapefruit from the garden; you need desert heat.

All citrus are touchy about their roots and lower trunk. The plants need a soil with constantly available moisture, but wet soil and poor drainage will be fatal in a short time.

Whether the plant is in a container or in the ground, never bury its lower trunk. If the plant is pruned so that the trunk is exposed to the sun, paint it with white interior latex paint to prevent sunburn.

Standard trees can reach thirty feet tall and spread equally wide. Dwarfed trees are a lot more manageable.

There really isn't much pruning to do on citrus trees. Pruning should consist of removing any damaged branches (cut off winter-killed branches only after new growth is sturdy) and

Below: This dwarf 'Washington' navel orange produces seedless fruits with a thick skin that peels easily; it also makes an attractive container plant. Right: Citrus are self-fertilizing and, unlike many other fruit trees, do not need to be thinned for abundant fruit production.

clipping off dead twiglets inside the tree. Sometimes an extra-vigorous shoot suddenly sprouts beyond all the other branches. Reach in and break it off at the base.

Citrus requires no attention to pollination. All kinds are self-fertile, and some need no pollination at all, forming seedless fruit without it.

Don't worry about thinning fruit unless you think a branch is about to break.

Crabapples

Fine for jellies or as pickled whole fruit, crabapples are also the most decorative of fruit trees. The varieties sold for their flowers also have edible fruit, but the large-fruited varieties are better if your aim is to grow the fruit for jelly.

Crabapples range from small, ten-foot trees to spreading trees twenty-five feet tall. The large-fruited kinds are larger trees.

Crabapples fruit on long-lived spurs, generally producing clusters of several fruits on each spur. Since crops are heavy, you can cut back new wood without losing anything. No thinning of the crop is necessary.

Crabapples are self-fertile, but you can graft several kinds that bloom at different times to extend the flowering season.

Crabapples need much the same care as apples. This crabapple in full bloom promises an ample crop.

Currants and Gooseberries

Currants and gooseberries both belong to the genus *Ribes*. The difference between the two is simply that gooseberries have spines and currants do not.

You won't often see these fresh fruits in the market, since crops from the limited commercial plantings go to processors for commercial jellies and canned fruits. But since the plants are ornamental, easy to care for, and productive, northern gardeners can tuck a few among other shrubs for their bloom, fruit, and fall color. Fall and winter planting is a good idea, since the plants leaf out early. In cold climates, plant right after the leaves drop and the roots will be established before winter. If your summers are hot, plant them against a north wall. In most areas, plant in the open, but be sure soil moisture is constant. Set the plants a little deeper than they grew in the nursery.

Pruning is necessary only if the plants produce very small fruit one year. If this is the case, prune out older shoots and tangled branches.

Figs

Although the fig is generally thought of as a subtropical fruit suited mainly to mild winters, some varieties will bear in milder climates of the Northwest and Northeast. If a freeze knocks the plant down, it will sprout again quickly.

In warm regions the fig bears big, juicy fruit in early summer, then sets a heavier crop of small fruit, perfect for drying, in the fall. In cooler climates fruit set occurs only once, in the early summer. The fig lives for many years, loves clay soil if drainage is good, and needs little attention. You have a choice of dark fruit with red flesh or greenish yellow fruit with bright pink flesh.

In cold-winter regions, fig shrubs reach ten feet tall and spread that much or more. In warm regions trees reach fifteen to thirty feet and spread wide and low, but you can easily cut them back or confine them.

Currants are beautiful plants. Their fruit can be eaten fresh or preserved in jams and jellies.

Because fig trees bear fruit on wood one year old or older, pruning is necessary only to shape a tree for its health and for convenient picking.

Most home garden varieties need no pollination; however, the California commercial fig, 'Calimyrna', does need pollinating and should not be planted in the South.

Grapes

The American grape entered our history more recently than the vine of Europe, but it has already played an important role, since its roots saved the European grape from extinction during the *Phylloxera* plague of the last century. This plague attacked the roots of the European grape and threatened to destroy it; the only remedy was grafting these grapes to American rootstocks that were resistant to the disease. More recently, American grapes have been developed into sturdy hybrids that carry European wine grapes far north of their original climate area.

Grapes send their roots deep where they can, and they prefer a soil that is rich in organic material. The site should have good air circulation, because grapes are subject to disease where air is stagnant.

Grapes all require heavy pruning to produce fruit, but after the first three growing seasons, different types of grapes need different pruning. Wine grapes and muscadines usually need spur pruning, in which all growth is limited to two lateral branches, one on either side of the trunk. All side branches from these two laterals are cut to two buds in fall or early winter. Two new shoots grow on each spur you leave, and each spur produces a cluster or bunch of fruit.

Some grapes do not produce fruit on shoots that grow too near the main scaffold. 'Thompson Seedless' and many American grapes, such as 'Concord', are among these and you must cane-prune them. Instead of cutting short spurs in winter, leave two new canes—that formed the previous growing season—on either side of the trunk. Cut one cane to two buds and leave the other long. After fruit forms from side growth along this longer cane, clip the cane off. Again, choose two new canes (that grew from the previous year's short, two-bud cane) and trim one to two buds, leaving the other long. This is done to branches on both sides of the trunk. You thereby encourage two new canes that will bear fruit the following year. Both spurs and canes grow from a permanent trunk, or trunk plus arms (side branches), that you train on a trellis or arbor.

Grape plants do not require a pollinator to set fruit because they are all self-fertile.

Harvest grapes by taste and appearance. When you think a bunch looks ripe, taste a grape near the tip. If it's good, cut the whole bunch.

Sometimes grapes never taste sweet, no matter how long you wait. That simply means that you have planted the wrong variety for your area. Either move it to a hot spot against a south wall or to a westward-facing corner, or switch to a variety that is adapted to your climate.

If vines are overcropped with too many bunches of grapes, the grapes will never get sweet. This can be remedied in future years by more extreme pruning in the dormant season or by thinning the grape bunches to balance the leaf area with the grape berry load.

Nectarines

The nectarine is simply a fuzzless peach. Peach trees sometimes produce nectarines as sports, and nectarine trees will produce fuzzy peach sports. The two plants are nearly identical, and nectarines require the same care as peaches.

Peaches

The peach is one of the most popular of homegrown fruits. Both peaches and their close relatives, the nectarines, are at their best when tree ripened, so a home gardener's time and effort are rewarded by a product that money can't buy.

Peaches cannot tolerate extreme winter cold or late frost, so in the northern plains states and northern New England, peaches are purely experimental.

Peaches are borne on the last year's wood, so it is necessary to

'Bonanza' is a popular genetic dwarf peach variety. Genetic dwarfs are excellent for small gardens and can even be grown in containers.

prune every year to stimulate new growth for the following year's flowers and fruit.

The standard tree on a peach rootstock grows to about eighteen feet tall and fifteen feet wide.

Once a crop sets on a peach tree, you may not even see the branches through all the fruit. Thin out the fruit when it reaches thumbnail size. For early-season peaches, leave six to eight inches of space between each fruit; for late-season peaches, leave four to five inches between each fruit. If a frost knocks off much of your crop, leave all the remaining fruits, even if they're clustered. What is important is the ratio of leaf surface to peaches, so a sparse crop will do equally well in singles or bunches.

Only a few peach varieties need a pollinator. Normally the trees are self-fertile, although bees are a big help in pollen transfer.

Be sure to choose varieties that suit your climate: Some peaches have been bred for short, mild winters and may bloom too early or may freeze in the North. Be sure to buy hardy varieties for the North.

Pears

Pears, especially dwarf pears, are a fine choice for the home gardener. The plants take well to formal or informal training. The trees are attractive even in winter, they require little pruning after they begin to bear, they begin to bear early, and the fruit stores fairly well without any special requirements.

Standard pears will spread twenty-five feet across and grow as tall or taller. A dwarf in natural shape needs a space about fifteen feet square, but you can espalier a pear, using very little space.

Pears bear on long-lived spurs, much as apples do. These spurs last a long time if you're careful not to damage them when picking the fruit. You usually don't need to thin fruit, but if a very heavy crop sets, remove fruit that is damaged or very undersized. Do the thinning a few weeks before harvest.

All pears need a pollinator. Use almost any other pear. However, the variety 'Bartlett' is a poor pollinator for 'Seckel'.

Most fruits are best when picked ripe, or nearly so. Pears are the exception. A tree-ripened pear breaks down and turns soft and brown at the core. Always harvest pears when they have reached full size but are still green and firm. Hold them in a cool, dark place if you intend to eat them within a few weeks. For longer storage, refrigerate the harvested fruit, and remove it from cold storage about a week before you want to use it. For fast ripening, place several pears in a plastic container.

'Comice', a late-season pear, is sweet, aromatic, and juicy. Like all pears, 'Comice' must be harvested when the fruit is green and firm.

'Bosc' pears are among the finest of pears both for eating fresh and for canning. The flesh is firm, crisp, and sweet.

Colorful fall foliage and orange-gold fruit make the persimmon a striking autumn tree. 'Hachiya', shown here, is a large, popular, Oriental persimmon.

Persimmons

The American persimmon, *Diospyros virginiana*, grows as a native from Connecticut to Kansas and southward, but it won't take the extreme cold of the northern plains or northern New England. It has small, edible fruits up to two-and-a-half inches in diameter.

The large persimmon found in the market is the Oriental persimmon, *Diospyros kaki*, and its many varieties. It can be grown in the southern states and on the West Coast. The tree grows well in any well-drained soil and makes a fine medium-size shade tree with large leaves that turn a rich gold to orange-red in the fall.

A heavy crop of two-inch fruit hangs on into the first frosts and is orange with a red blush. Eat it when it softens, or use it as you would applesauce or bananas.

Persimmons are often allowed to grow naturally, forming globe-shaped trees up to twenty-five or thirty feet high. They can be pruned back in spring to keep them smaller. Little pruning is necessary, however. Train the young tree to three widely spaced scaffolds and leave it alone thereafter.

Fruit is borne on new wood. On a naturally shaped tree it will set on the outer portion.

American persimmons are normally dioecious, meaning that some trees are male, producing pollen but no fruit, while others are female. You will need a female tree for fruit and a male close by for pollen.

Oriental persimmons set fruit without pollination. The large fruits are three to four inches in diameter and are usually picked in the fall before the first frost. Store them in the refrigerator and eat them only after they soften. 'Fuyu' is the one persimmon that is not astringent when firm. You do not need to soften it before eating.

Plums

Of all the stone fruits, plums are the most varied. They range from hardy little cherry plums and sand cherries, to hybrids with the hardiness of natives, to sweet European plums and prunes, to sweet or tart Japanese plums. Plums bear for ten to fifteen years and sometimes more.

Standard plum trees take space. Expect your tree to fill an area fifteen to twenty feet square. Bush and cherry plums can be used in smaller spaces and reach six feet or so, but may spread as wide or wider. A dwarfed European plum on 'Nanking' cherry roots will reach ten to twelve feet in height.

Tree plums don't lend themselves to confinement, so use bush types if your space is limited.

Japanese plums are relatively large, soft, and juicy. The plants are more tender than European plums, although selected varieties are grown in the milder northern regions.

Plums fruit on wood produced the previous year and on spurs on older branches. The branches are particularly prone to split when the trees are mature and bearing heavy crops.

There are many plum varieties, but they fall into two groups—European and Japanese—based on the length of the fruiting spurs. The fruit of the European varieties is small, usually egg-shaped, and often dried to make prunes. Spurs may reach three feet long, much longer than the three-inch spur of the Japanese types. Since the fruit buds are so spread out, far less thinning is needed and the long, bushlike mass of spurs does not require the severe pruning given Japanese varieties. The oldest shoots should be trimmed off to encourage new growth after about four years of bearing.

Most varieties of European plums are self-pollinating.

Japanese varieties include most of the dessert plums found at the market, such as the 'Santa Rosa' and 'Satsuma'. These have large, soft, juicy fruit and are less hardy than the European varieties. Some Japanese plums grow upright and some spread out, but all fruit in this group is borne on stubby spurs no longer than three inches. These spurs will bear for six to eight years.

Remove one-third of the new wood each year by thinning and heading. This heavy pruning is necessary to produce larger fruit. Keep long, thin branches headed to give the tree a stubby, wide shape.

Most Japanese varieties are self-pollinating, but all plums set fruit better with a pollinator.

Pomegranates

Pomegranates are often thought of as a tropical or desert fruit, but in fact they withstand winter temperatures down to about 10°F. While they do ripen their fruit best in very hot, arid climates, you can harvest edible fruit in cooler areas. They are ideal plants for the desert Southwest because they tolerate considerable drought. Rain or irrigation can cause pomegranates to split if either occurs close to harvest time.

You can grow pomegranates as fountain-shaped shrubs or as single- or multiple-trunk trees. They reach about ten to twelve feet tall under ideal conditions but often remain smaller. A shrub can spread from six to eight feet across. Since they fruit on new growth, you can prune them back heavily without loss of flowers or fruit. You can prune as you like to shape the plants, but no pruning is necessary if you choose to let your tree grow naturally.

The trees are self-fertile, which means that even a single specimen growing alone will bear fruit.

And there grow tall trees blossoming, pear-trees and pomegranates, and apple-trees with bright fruit, and sweet figs, and olives in their bloom . . .

HOMER
The Odyssey
(Translated by Butcher and Lang)

Above: This 'Heritage' raspberry is everbearing, producing one crop in the fall, and another the following summer. Unlike other bramble fruits, raspberries pull free of their core. Below: Black raspberries.

Raspberries

Raspberries are the hardiest of the cane berries, and perhaps the most worthwhile home-gardened crop because prices for the market fruit are so high. Also, market raspberries are subject to a long handling period during which the fruit loses its finest flavor. Home-gardened fruit can be picked and eaten at its peak.

What makes a raspberry a raspberry is the fact that it pulls free of its core when you pick it. Other bramble fruits take the core with them. The red raspberry is the most popular, but raspberries grow in a variety of colors and plant forms—red and yellow fruits growing on trailing plants, and purple and black fruits growing on stiff plants. Do not try both red and black raspberries in the same garden. Reds sometimes carry a virus that they can tolerate but that is fatal to blacks. Virus-free stock will spare you this trouble.

Raspberries do not like spring and summer heat; the red varieties will grow in areas with warm springs and summers, but only in the coastal or mountain regions. The black (blackcap) varieties are the least able to tolerate mild climates. The prime berry country in the coastal states is western Washington around Puget Sound, and the Willamette Valley of Oregon.

On most raspberries, the fruit forms on side shoots along canes that grew the previous year. Everbearing varieties are the exception. They produce a crop in the fall at the end of new canes, and then another along the side shoot in the early summer of the following year.

New canes should be laid carefully along the rows until it's time to prune away old canes, then these new canes should be lifted and trained for the next year's crop.

Raspberries do not need a pollinator and they are extremely hardy, so no special protection is needed except in the coldest mountain and plains climates.

Strawberries

If you have grown strawberries for any length of time, you know that flavor and yield are not predictable, but vary from year to year depending on spring growing conditions. Also, if you have gardened in several locations, you know that the best variety in one place may be only fair in another. A good nursery can be a big help, since the staff keeps abreast of developments in plant breeding and offers plants that should succeed.

Strawberries are without question the easiest berry to work into any space you may have available. On a south-facing apartment terrace you can produce a crop in containers such as strawberry jars or moss-lined wire strawberry trees.

Plant strawberries in soil with good drainage; mound the planting site if you're not sure about the drainage. When planting, position the new leaf bud in the center of each plant so that the bud sits exactly level with the soil surface.

To encourage vigorous growth of regular varieties, remove blossoms that appear the year the plants are set out. The year that everbearing kinds are planted, remove all blossoms until the middle of July. The later blossoms will produce a late-summer and fall crop.

Winter protection is needed where alternate freezing and thawing of the soil may cause the plants to heave, breaking the roots. Place a straw mulch three or four inches deep over the plants before the soil is frozen hard. Remove most of the mulch in spring when the centers of a few plants show a yellow-green color.

All strawberries are self-fertile and need no other pollinator.

Probably the most commonly grown berry, and certainly a favorite for eating fresh and cooking, strawberries can be grown throughout the country—many varieties are available. 'Olympus' shown above.

Top: Bees and other insects are essential to the pollination of many fruit trees. Don't apply insecticides when trees are in full bloom and bees are pollinating. Right: One pollinator variety among all these trellised apples will pollinate the entire row.

Fruit Care

Despite all the advances brought to us by plant breeders and growers, good performance of any fruit plant still requires proper care. In this section we discuss how fruit plants produce fruit; how they grow; and what you need to know to get them started and to keep them healthy, beautiful, and productive.

Pollination

You may feel that once you plant a tree you've done your part and the rest is up to nature. This idea can easily lead to fruitless plants. A bountiful crop of fruit depends upon pollination. With a few exceptions (certain figs, for example), fruit will not form unless pollen from the male parts of a flower is transferred to the female parts of a flower. The pollinating insects for most fruits are bees, and the pollen that bees carry must be of the right sort. Most of us know that apple pollen, for example, will never pollinate a pear blossom; few of us realize that apple pollen will not always pollinate an apple blossom.

The Right Combinations   Some plants are self-pollinating
or self-fertile. This means that their flowers can be fertilized
by pollen from flowers either on the same plant or on another
plant of the same kind. Self-fertile plants will produce fruit even
if they are planted far away from any other plant of their kind.
Among the self-fertile plants are some apples, pears, and plums;
most peaches and apricots; and all sour cherries, blackberries,
citrus, crabapples, figs, grapes, raspberries, and strawberries.

Other plants set fruit only when they receive pollen from a
plant of a different variety. When a plant's pollen is ineffective
on its own flowers, it is called self-sterile. This group includes
many apples; all sweet cherries; and some pears, peaches,
apricots, and plums. A plant that will fertilize a self-sterile plant
is called a pollinator.

A fruit plant that needs a pollinator needs it close by. The
maximum distance is one hundred feet, but the closer the
better. Never assume that because you have a bearing fruit tree
you can plant a new tree of a different variety nearby and be

assured of a crop. Plants must bloom at about the same time for successful cross-pollination; for example, an early self-sterile apple will not bear fruit unless the pollinator is another early apple variety.

Some plants bear male and female flowers on separate plants. Kiwi fruit are a good example of this. You must have both a male and a female plant in your yard, and bees to pollinate the flowers, in order for the female to set fruit.

Soil

Some fruits, such as pears, will tolerate dense, airless, soggy soil. Apples and crabapples will take short periods of airless soil, but apricots, cherries, figs, nectarines, peaches, plums, grapes, and currants all need fair drainage. Strawberries, cane berries, and citrus need good drainage, and blueberries must have perfect drainage.

In gardens with extremely dense soil you can still plant fruits that prefer porous soils by using containers or raised beds. A raised bed for a standard fruit tree should be three feet deep and six feet long by six feet wide. For more information about soil preparation, see Chapter 14, page 343.

Planting

Nurseries and garden centers sell bareroot plants, plants with the rootball wrapped in burlap (called balled and burlapped), and plants growing in containers.

Most deciduous fruit plants are sold bare root. Evergreen plants are sold either balled and burlapped or in containers made of plastic, pulp, or metal. Balled and burlapped plants are sold at the same time as bareroot plants and should go into the ground or their permanent containers quickly. Those sold in containers are available all year around.

When planting a tree from the nursery, remember never to plant if the soil is very wet. Working wet soil packs it, driving out the air and trapping the roots.

A good rule of thumb is to dig the planting hole twice the width of the rootball. It's also important to plant high. The planting soil should be mounded above the normal soil line. The most fragile part of a woody plant is the crown, that section where the roots branch and the soil touches the trunk. The crown must be dry most of the time, especially in spring and fall. Raised planting minimizes crown rot (which can be fatal to the plant) by making it impossible for water to puddle near the trunk. If you plant at soil level, you invite disaster because the soil in the planting hole will settle and so will your plants.

Planting Grafted Dwarf Fruit Trees   Be especially careful when planting grafted dwarf fruit trees. Dwarfing rootstocks cause dwarfing because the rootstocks are not vigorous or deep rooted. Trees on the smallest stocks may blow over unless they have support. Many growers now place the bud of the fruiting variety high on the rootstock, up to six or eight inches above ground. This bud union shows later as a bulge with a healed scar on one side. Plant the tree with the union about two inches above the soil. This is deeper than it grew in the nursery and accomplishes two things: First, the deep planting makes the tree a little more stable; and second, the rootstock is less likely to send up suckers from underground. Be careful never to bury the bud union in soil or mulch at any time during the life of the tree. If moist material touches the union, the upper fruiting part will root and its vigorous root system will produce a full-size tree instead of the dwarf you bought.

Feeding

Feed a newly planted tree with a starter solution of high-phosphorus liquid fertilizer to encourage new root growth. Never give nitrogen fertilizer to a newly planted tree. Nitrogen will stimulate leaf growth, which is undesirable until the roots become established. Fertilize with nitrogen when the leaves begin to expand. Keep fertilizers away from the trunk of the tree.

Although one or two feedings are often recommended, we suggest feeding equal amounts of chemical fertilizers four times at evenly spaced intervals between early spring and late June. Water very deeply after feeding. For more information about fertilizers, see Chapter 14, page 354.

Watering

Standard fruit trees need deep watering. Dwarf trees on shallow-rooted stocks may not need as much, but they must have a constant moisture supply. At planting time, if the garden soil is dry, soak the hole itself before you put in the plant. Finish by soaking from the top of the planting mound, creating a depression to hold the water.

After planting, and before new growth begins, do not water again unless the soil seems dry. The roots are not growing actively at this time, and soggy soil will invite rot. When new growth begins, let the top inch or so of soil dry; then give the plant a thorough soaking. Be sure to water at the top of the planting mound. This is especially important with balled and burlapped plants, since the soil in the rootball may not take up water unless the water is applied directly.

This dwarf apple tree is espaliered against a heavy wire fence. The last of three different apple varieties has recently been grafted to the top of the tree.

When first-season growth is abundant and plants are growing well in midsummer, stop watering from the top of the mound. Dig a shallow ditch around the base and soak the soil about every two to three weeks, or whenever the top inch or two of soil dries out.

After the first season, make a shallow ditch about six to twelve inches wide around the plant and just outside the tips of the branches. Move the ditch outward as the plant grows. Soak thoroughly about once every three or four weeks. This is a rough guide. Your tree may need water more often in very sandy soil, less often in heavier soil. Always dig down a few inches into the soil first to see if watering is necessary.

Your aim in watering is to soak the soil long enough for moisture to reach the deep roots. On standard trees the deepest roots may penetrate the soil to a depth of many feet. On dwarf trees the deepest roots may extend only thirty to thirty-six inches beneath the surface.

Trees in a lawn area should have a deep soaking about twice a summer in addition to normal lawn-watering.

Basic Fruit Pest Control

Complete control of insects and diseases on susceptible fruit crops requires a thorough and comprehensive spray program. Proper timing, good coverage of foliage, and correct chemicals are essential. The following spray program should meet the essential needs of fruit trees that commonly have pest problems.

Apples, Crabapples, and Pears   *Winter:* Before leaves are out, apply a dormant oil spray to control scale, mites, and other pests. This can be the most important spray of the year. Follow the directions on the label fully and completely for best results.

Spring: The next important spraying time is when fruit buds show pink at the tips. Spray with an insecticide such as diazinon to control aphids, leaf rollers, and many other pests, and with a fungicide such as captan to control apple scab, fruit spot, and bitter rot. When three-quarters of the petals have fallen, spray an insecticide again to stop codling moth, which appears at this time. Where apple scab is a problem, consistent use of a fungicide such as captan is necessary for control.

Summer: The first summer spray is ten to fourteen days after petal fall. Use an insecticide, fungicide, or both, as your trees require. For perfect fruit, continue to spray through the summer with insecticide and fungicide as needed.

Fall: Spray as necessary, but follow label directions carefully regarding time intervals between spray treatments and harvest.

Apricots, Cherries, Nectarines, Peaches, and Plums   *Winter:*
Apply the same treatment as for apples, crabapples, and pears.
Where peach leaf curl is a problem, timing is very important.
Lime sulfur sprays should be applied in October or November
after leaf drop. In areas of heavy winter rainfall, do this before
rains begin. Apply another full-coverage spray in late winter
before buds begin to swell. Note: If buds have begun to swell or
open, it is too late to obtain satisfactory control, as infection
has already occurred. For best results, spray in the fall and late
winter.

Spring: When blossom buds show color—pink for peaches, red
for apricots, popcorn stage for cherries, and green-tip stage for
plums—spray with an insecticide such as diazinon to control
insect pests. A fungicide such as captan is often needed for
brown rot control. Spray an insecticide and fungicide again when
three-quarters of the flower petals have fallen.

Summer: Apply the same treatment as for apples, crabapples,
and pears.

Fall: Apply the same treatment as described for apples,
crabapples, and pears.

Pruning

Plants will live, grow, and bear fruit without ever being pruned,
but experience has shown that good pruning is the most
effective means to head off trouble, improve your fruit production, and keep plants in excellent condition.

No other plants in the garden depend on pruning as much as
fruit trees. Unfortunately, fruit trees vary widely in the most
effective means of pruning. If you want to grow beautiful apples
or peaches, you must learn the difference between pruning an
apple tree and a peach tree.

The objective in pruning a fruit tree is to produce an abundance of good-quality fruit throughout the branches, including
the lower and interior ones. An unpruned peach or nectarine
tree will bear fruit mostly on branch tips, and the leaves that
produce the sugars that nourish the plant and accumulate in the
fruit will grow only where they receive sufficient light. An
unpruned tree with heavy growth in its interior, restricting light
and air circulation, is more susceptible to fungus diseases. In
addition, heavy loads of fruit at branch tips can make harvest
difficult and can cause splitting and breaking of branches,
producing wounds that invite pests and disease.

If you find yourself in a quandary about where to begin,
remember that you can't hurt a plant by cutting out dead,

Top: A 'Yellow Delicious' dwarf
apple before it has been pruned
in the fall. Middle: The plant
after it has been properly
pruned. Bottom: Before fruiting
in the spring.

This 'Mutsu' apple has been
pruned into a classic vase shape.

diseased, or damaged wood, or wood that crosses and rubs
against other wood (which can cause wounds susceptible to
infection).

Remember that any heavily pruned tree sends out abundant
new growth in the spring. If a tree bears on one-year or older
wood, heavy winter pruning will cut back fruit production the

following spring. If it bears on new wood, heavy pruning will stimulate fruit production the following season. Pruning always removes some fruiting wood, but an unpruned tree may bear too heavily and may produce small fruit and almost no new growth. Proper pruning produces even crops over many seasons.

Pruning Methods

Commercial fruit growers prune fruit trees in three ways, and each has its own advantages. Some growers use the older method called vase pruning. Another popular method is modified central-leader pruning. The third method, delayed open-center pruning, combines both techniques. Remember that dwarf trees will require less severe pruning because they are smaller.

Vase Pruning By vase pruning the tree is shaped to a short trunk of about three feet with three or four main limbs, each of which has fully filled-out secondary branches. This shape creates an open center that allows light to reach all branches.

   Vase pruning is always used with apples, apricots, crabapples, plums, and peaches, and often with pears and sour cherries.

Modified Central-Leader Pruning By the modified central-leader technique the tree is shaped to one tall trunk that extends upward through the tree, emerging clearly at the top. This shape makes a strong tree, but since the center is shaded, less fruit is produced. Sweet cherries, sour cherries, and pears are pruned in this manner. The smallest dwarf apples are also pruned to this shape.

Delayed Open-Center Pruning The third method, delayed open-center pruning, produces both the strength of a central trunk and the sun-filled center of a vase-shaped tree. A single trunk is allowed to grow vertically until it reaches six to ten feet tall. It is then cut off just above a branch. Main scaffold branches (side branches that form the framework of the tree) are then selected and pruned to form a vase shape. Subsequent prunings follow the vase method. Trees that are pruned by the vase method can be pruned by the delayed open-center method to create a more upright, taller tree.

   Productive fruit trees require that a definite method of pruning be established from the moment the tree is planted. Such pruning and training will keep the tree balanced in form and—very important—balanced in new and young wood. Left unpruned, the tree will become dense with weak, twiggy growth and overloaded with small, less healthy fruit.

This apple has been trained into a striking espalier. This technique requires careful pruning over several years.

Houseplants

People have been cultivating plants indoors for thousands of years. Long ago, the Egyptians, Assyrians, Babylonians, Chinese, Greeks, Romans, Incas, Aztecs, and countless other civilizations put plants in containers and brought them onto terraces and into their homes. By the early eighteenth century more than five thousand species of tropical and semitropical plants were in cultivation indoors all over the world. During the nineteenth century, improvements in plant transportation methods made even more species widely available, especially to the Victorian English, who were enthralled with growing plants everywhere—in greenhouses and conservatories, parlors, bedchambers, sunrooms, and libraries.

People still are enthralled with displaying plants indoors, but no longer do we find many homes decorated in the ostentatious formal manner so popular with the Victorians. The plants we grow are much more numerous and diverse, and include countless hybrids different from those they grew. The ways we display them reflect our simpler modern tastes and the need to blend our houseplants with contemporary interior designs. Today, we see kitchen windows brimming with potted begonias, or living rooms graced by ficus trees. Hanging baskets of grape ivy, philodendrons, and Boston ferns decorate many windows. And in interior spaces where sunlight never reaches, fluorescent and direct incandescent lights provide life-giving rays for plants.

What Is a Houseplant?
Houseplants differ from outdoor plants only in their location. They were not originally developed to grow indoors; rather, many were derived from ancestors native to the shade of tropical forests. In that habitat, temperature changes are seasonal, heavy rainfall and high humidity are normal, and the ground is rich in nutrients from decayed leaves shed by the thick vegetation. Houseplants are wild plants that have been domesticated.

Plants for the Indoor Landscape
Indoor landscapes are as varied as the individuals who create them. Some people grow only a few plants and spread them throughout the house; others prefer a busy and vibrant atmosphere featuring groups of many different plants in all shapes and sizes. One gardener may blend foliage and flowering plants to create a splash of color against a backdrop of green. And then there's the plant collector who concentrates on growing one type of plant, such as cacti or orchids, and designs around it.

In all cases, what makes indoor gardens work both functionally and aesthetically is forethought and planning.

Left: "The Oblique-leaved Begonia" from *The Temple of Flora* by Robert Thornton. Above: A chrysanthemum and paper-white narcissus brighten up this entryway.

Basic Considerations

As you set out to create your own individual indoor landscape, ask yourself the questions that follow; they'll familiarize you with some basic design considerations. The way you answer them will help you determine what plants to select and how best to use their individual features to complete your design.

Know Your Plants' Needs What is the environment in the room or rooms in which you want to grow plants; how does it meet the cultural requirements of your houseplants?

Although this question may not appear to concern design, it overrides every other consideration. A sickly plant is unsightly wherever it grows and however it is used.

Take note of the temperature, humidity, and light conditions in your home and try to choose only plants that thrive in those conditions.

Balance Scale and Shape A large, branching fiddleleaf fig may overpower a small sitting room; a single fern or prayer plant will go unnoticed in the corner of a large, open interior. Generally, a large plant looks most appropriate placed in a room spacious enough to balance its size. A small plant, on the other hand, is best displayed in a spot where its delicate features can be seen and appreciated.

Create Focal Points Displayed in a decorative hanging basket, the arching leaves and shoots of a large spider plant will attract attention to a dull corner at the far end of a room. The same plant tucked into a corner near an entryway would be missed by most. As you would your best pieces of furniture, display your houseplants where they will add the most to the total decorating scheme.

Right: The plants in this room are well balanced visually and include two large rubber trees, a mistletoe fig, a croton, and a zebra plant. Left: The weeping fig and cape primroses create a focal point next to the doorway and also draw your eye to the strong, curving lines of the stairway.

Plan Compatible Plant Groupings   A massive collection of different types of plants accumulated randomly can easily make a cluttered, ineffective display. A well-planned grouping, however, can be compelling and impressive. Choose plants that are compatible culturally and work together aesthetically to create dynamic, unified compositions.

Relate Leaf Shape, Plant Form, and Color to Decor   Certain plants look better than others when combined with the particular design features of a room. Almost all plants look best with an undecorated wall for a background. Bright or large-leafed foliage provides a nice contrast to small, delicate wallpaper and fabric patterns. Boldness of form and leaf pattern enhance design schemes with neutral tones and solid colors.

Use flowering plants to pick up the hues present in the furnishings and walls. The shapes of the blooms can reflect and accent the patterns in wallpapers and upholstery, especially if they feature a flower design.

Use Attractive Containers   Containers are important to a plant display: Choose them carefully to enhance the plant's appearance and its compatibility with the design of the room. For example, a ceramic American Indian pot makes a nice home for a cactus in an adobe-style house, but the same pot planted with a delicate fern might look awkward.

The Houseplant Environment

All of the elements of a plant's environment must be in balance to ensure continuing health and growth. A knowledge of how light, temperature, humidity, and air circulation affect plants will help you determine which plants are right for your home.

Light

Light is a critical factor in growing plants indoors. Without adequate light, plants cannot photosynthesize enough food for growth to occur. As an indoor gardener, you should consider both the amount of light available and the length of time it is present in your home.

The intensity and the duration of light both vary considerably within a home, not only from room to room but also within

Many houseplants need bright indirect light. This ficus has been placed next to a mirror to increase the amount of light it receives.

A graceful row of dracaena plants divides this large room into a sitting area and a study. Houseplants are quite effective room dividers—even barriers— and provide a much softer effect than shelves and partitions.

Although this office has no windows, skylights provide enough light to grow many light-loving houseplants.

one room. For example, light is less intense at a window with shades or curtains than at an unobstructed window. In the same room another window may permit more intense light to enter, but for a shorter time. Light at a single window will vary in intensity and duration if trees or other obstructions outside block the sun's rays at certain times of the day or year. Furniture and reflective surfaces within a room can alter light as well. All of the conditions in your home that affect light should be taken into consideration when you grow houseplants.

Most houseplants benefit from receiving as much indirect light as possible, rather than direct sun. Only a few benefit from more than one to two hours of direct sun in the summer.

Seasonal Light   With different seasons the angle of the sun changes, so intensity varies. Summer sun shines almost perpendicular to the earth, striking it with maximum intensity. In contrast, our winter sun hovers low in the sky, even at noon. Its rays travel on a slanted path and consequently pass through more dust and moisture in the air, which scatters or diffuses the light and reduces its intensity. At noon on a clear day in midsummer, when the sun shines directly overhead, the level of illumination is much higher than it is in December. On a rainy day in winter it may be only one-twentieth the light intensity of summer. Given this reduced light intensity, it's easy to understand why so many plants grow very slowly during the colder months of the year.

Most houseplants will welcome at least a few hours of full winter sun. However, in the warmer seasons the situation changes and you should be cautious about the amount of light that reaches your plant.

All of the care you give your plants must coincide with the seasonal increases and decreases in light intensity. During summer, when light is brightest and heat is highest, all plant life processes speed up and plants absorb more water, more minerals, and more carbon dioxide. Therefore, you must provide them with more moisture and fertilizer. During winter, when light is less intense and photosynthesis slows, a cutback in moisture and fertilizer is in order.

Where you live also affects how much light you receive. For example, sunlight in the Rockies during winter is much more intense than in New England because the higher elevation means thinner air and less light diffusion through the atmosphere. In winter, the sun rises and sets farther to the south of the United States. Consequently, Florida and other southern states receive more bright light than northern states.

Other Factors Affecting Light   Even within your local area, light intensity will vary, and not just because of the seasons. Smoke from local industry may make sunny days hazy. Clouds or fog will cut down light. Trees and shrubs that shade your home reduce the amount of light that passes through your windows. Screened windows, doors, or porches reduce light by as much as 30 percent. A white house next door or a light-colored cement driveway will reflect sunlight, increasing the intensity of the light your rooms receive. Snow will reflect a great deal of light, especially on a sunny day.

Too Little or Too Much   Too little light causes a plant to elongate and lose leaves that it can no longer support due to diminished photosynthesis. As the plant attempts to gather

This dining room receives little natural light so plants that tolerate low-intensity light have been selected for this space. Both the Kentia palm and the Chinese evergreen will thrive here; however, the African violets must be rotated occasionally to a brighter spot to keep them blooming.

more light, the spaces on the stems between the leaves (called internodes) lengthen and the leaves grow broad and thin.

You can correct a low light situation in several ways. Increasing the duration of light helps compensate for low intensity, so simply move the plant to a window that admits light for a longer time. If possible, move the plant to a sunnier window, or place it near reflective surfaces such as white or light-colored walls. In extreme situations, you can even place mirrors, foil, or white backdrops about the plant. Bear in mind that these changes will help only if the added light is intense enough to stimulate photosynthesis.

Too much light causes plants to wilt and their vibrant green color to fade. Young, thin leaves are affected first because they cannot hold much water. Inexperienced indoor gardeners often miss the problem by attributing the symptoms to a lack of nutrients. Before you rush to fertilize a drooping plant, check its light requirements and how they are being met. Keep in mind that excessive light intensity is most likely to occur at midday. Some plants may even wilt slightly during this time and recover later in the day.

Another thought to keep in mind is that plants grow in the direction of the strongest light source. You may notice that after a period of time your plants appear to be "leaning" toward the window. They are actually growing toward the light and it is a good idea to rotate the plants occasionally so that they maintain a balanced shape.

In this section we have been discussing natural light. Remember that you can use artificial lighting to supplement natural light—and grow plants in places that otherwise would be impossible. For information on artificial lighting, see Ortho's book *All About Houseplants.*

Temperature

Temperature interacts with light, humidity, and air circulation to directly affect plant metabolism. Most indoor plants adapt to the temperatures normally found in homes, around 70°F days and 65°F nights. At night many plants benefit from a ten-degree drop in temperature. This gives them a breather from the rapid rate of transpiration during the day, when temperatures are higher and water loss is greater. Overnight, any water deficit in the leaf cells is made up as the roots take up water.

If you assume from the reading on your thermostat that your house or apartment temperature is uniform, you are likely to be in for a surprise. Generally variations occur even within each room. Use a thermometer to check the temperatures of

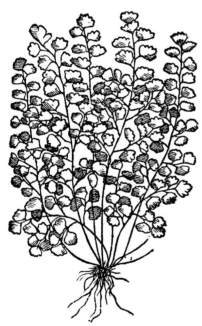

*Who loves a garden loves a
  greenhouse too.
Unconscious of a less
  propitious clime,
There blooms exotic beauty,
  warm and snug,
While the winds whistle, and
  the snows descend.*

Cowper

Choosing You...

soils, time to d...
easier to buy r...
and some are f...
from your loca...
appropriate for...
adequate drain...
not drain well,...
or with perlite,...

Houseplant (...

Houseplants ar...
concept to rem...
roots of the pla...
search deeper o...
depends totally...

How and Whei...

More houseplar...
other cause, an...
underwatering...
forces roots to s...
unable to carry...
the result is wil...
assume immedi...
grow as you hac...
if the plant is su...

Water needs a...
have specific pr...
habitats. The li...
plants will furth...
much moisture...
container it gro...
absorbed quickl...
you can't keep ...
then it needs re...
plant's growth c...
will absorb mor...

Your job is to...
simplest and mc...
your finger into...
feel the degree o...
between your th...
you'll be able to...
soil feels.

Acclima...

When yc...
adjust to...
case of sl...
meticulo...
cial greer...
reduced l...

This ac...
week leav...
acclimati...
the plant...
condition...
light and...
If possible...

Humidity

Humidity refers to the moisture content of the air. It is expressed as relative humidity: a percentage of the maximum amount of water vapor the air can hold at a given temperature.

Nearly all houseplants prefer a humidity level of 50 percent or higher, but in drier climates it is practically impossible to create this level of humidity in a home. As a result, many houseplants suffer from low humidity. This is especially true in winter, when dry home heating robs the air of moisture. At this time of year, humidities of 4 to 10 percent are common.

A cool vapor humidifier is one excellent way to increase the humidity in your home. Portable units can be placed wherever they are needed. Or you may want to have a humidifier installed as a part of your home's central heating system. These units are relatively inexpensive, and may be well worth the cost because humidified air is more comfortable for people as well as for plants. Such systems should have the capability of raising the humidity by 25 or 30 percent, even on the coldest winter days.

Misting, unless done several times a day, only temporarily raises the humidity around plants. If the room humidity is low, the moisture will evaporate quickly. Humidifying the air and keeping plants adequately watered are the only ways to ensure that they have sufficient moisture.

Air Circulation

Air circulation is as important to plants as it is to people. Just as you enjoy fresh air, it also helps plants to thrive. Soft breezes of warm, humid air supply necessary oxygen and moisture. When plants are cramped together so that air cannot circulate among them, or are placed in an environment that lacks circulation, fungus disease is much more likely to occur.

The movement of dry air over leaves is another matter; this can cause moisture stress and leaf burn, especially in direct sun. Sudden changes in air movement and temperature do not benefit plants, either. These can send plants into shock, a state of decline brought about when chemical growth processes stall or stop due to radical environmental changes. Be careful if you keep your plants near a window, especially during the winter, when cold drafts and frosted windowpanes can cause harm.

Pollutants in the air can also harm plants. Fumes from burning propane or butane gas are likely to cause flowering plants to drop their buds. They can also cause leaves to yellow and drop off. Fumes from burning natural gas are not harmful to plants.

Dust and dirt can accumulate on houseplant leaves, clogging

A shower c
quickly cle
this scheffl

Most houseplar
drained soil mi
retains enough
doesn't dry out

Flowering houseplants, such as
this chrysanthemum (bottom)
and lipstick plant (top) must
be fertilized with low-nitrogen,
high-phosphorous fertilizers
for best bloom.

How and When to Fertilize

Nitrogen, phosphorus, and potassium are the three major
nutrients needed by plants. Fertilizers come in many different
formulations; for example, those designed for flowering plants
usually contain less nitrogen than phosphorus and potassium,
because nitrogen encourages foliage growth but at some expense
to flowering.

In addition to foliage growth, nitrogen contributes to the deep
green color of plants and to stem growth. Phosphorus encourages bloom and root growth, and potassium contributes to stem
strength and disease resistance. In addition to these primary
nutrients, plants also need a variety of nutrients in smaller
quantities, including sulfur, calcium, and magnesium, and
minute quantities of iron, zinc, manganese, copper, chlorine,
boron, and molybdenum.

As well as being manufactured in many formulations,
houseplant fertilizers are available in many forms: water-soluble
pellets, powders, liquids, dry tablets and sticks to insert in the
soil, and time-release pellets. The variety can be confusing,
and value does vary widely. Any reliable plant seller will help
you choose the best fertilizer for your needs.

In applying fertilizers, always read the label first and follow
the directions carefully. Don't succumb to the notion that more
is better. It takes only a little extra fertilizer to burn a plant's
roots or leaves. A good method is to use half the recommended
amount twice as often.

Container plants need regular feeding only when they are in
active growth. Dormant or sick plants never benefit from the
addition of fertilizers. Dormant plants are in a natural state
of arrested growth and fertilizer is not needed. Wilting, yellowing, pallid plants that are suffering from something other than
lack of fertilizer will decline even more rapidly if you feed them.
These plants are in a state of shock and may even die if fed.

Before turning to fertilizers, review the care requirements of
the plant and determine whether you have been meeting them
properly. If you have been fertilizing regularly and the plant
isn't growing, it's likely that the plant is dormant or sick.

Good Grooming Techniques

Plants in containers need regular pruning and trimming to keep
them manageable in size and attractive in shape. Good grooming also reduces the possibility of disease and helps flowering
plants produce better blossoms. There are two methods for
shaping plants: pinching and pruning.

Pinching When you use your thumb and forefinger to remove the young tip growth of a stem, you are pinching the plant. This simple operation forces the plant to branch out below the pinch and become fuller and bushier.

Consider a young coleus plant, one started from seed or a cutting. If you do not pinch the plant during its active growth period, it will have one stem that grows straight up and eventually will become gangly, weak, and unattractive. To avoid this, nip out the growing tip as soon as the plant has four to six leaves. This will cause dormant buds to spring into active

Many houseplants can be easily propagated by pinching. Philodendron tips pinched from an overgrown plant will root easily in water. Secure a leaf from a piggyback plant in damp potting soil, and it will soon root.

growth. Where you had one stem, now you'll have two or more. After two or three weeks, pinch the tips of these new stems, and soon you'll have a bushy plant. Pinching is a handy skill to have in gardening. It works well for virtually all plants, but especially for soft-stemmed plants such as wax-leaf and angel-wing begonias, young geraniums, and coleus.

Pruning   Pruning is a slightly more complex operation that can shape a plant attractively and invigorate it. Pruning refers to removing young woody stems. When part of a plant is removed, the energy invested in sustaining that part is directed toward the rest of the plant. A sickly plant may be revived by pruning, and flowering plants encouraged to bloom.

If a stem is removed at its point of origin, the result is to open up space within the stem framework. New growth will take place in the stems remaining or from the base of the plant. If the stem is cut off above a leaf, one or more dormant growth tips will begin to grow near the pruned tip to make the plant denser.

Cleaning

Plant foliage must be cleaned occasionally to rid the plant of insects, eggs, and mites. Cleaning also clears the stomata of dust, facilitating the intake and release of gases, and allows the maximum amount of light to reach the plant.

Wash large-leafed plants with a damp cloth or sponge. Use a very mild solution of dishwashing soap and water to make the job easier. The soap will not harm plants, but oil can cause problems by clogging leaf pores.

Always be careful in cleaning your houseplants not to spread pests or disease from an infested plant to others. For example, if you are using a rag and clean a plant suffering from mites, disinfect the rag with a one-to-ten solution of household bleach and water before cleaning other plants.

Care During Rest Periods

Nature's cycle for seasonal plant growth applies to indoor plants in somewhat the same way it applies to others: Shorter days and cooler temperatures often bring about a period of dormancy. Centrally heated indoor environments with artificial light offer the potential to create an endless summer for plants. However, some plants under regulated artificial light and temperatures still have resting periods when growth slows and when, consequently, they need less food and water. It is most important that you realize when your houseplants are resting— or need rest. This most likely will occur after a flush of new

Proper grooming is beneficial to both small and large house-plants. These tall fishtail palms are pruned and cleaned regularly, as are the smaller plants beneath them.

growth or a period of heavy flowering. Symptoms may include the absence of new growth, a drooping appearance, and yellowing, falling leaves.

When these symptoms appear, do not apply any fertilizer. Allow the plant to dry out a bit; don't keep it constantly damp. Tropical plants are especially apt to go dormant if situated where temperatures stay generally below 70°F. Cold temperatures, wet soil, and continued fertilization can devastate your houseplants when they're dormant. When seasons change and your plant needs a rest, do not repot it. If you think repotting is necessary, wait until the plant puts out some new leaf buds and shows signs of active growth.

Tuberous and bulbous plants often die back to the ground when they rest. In cultivation we simply withhold fertilizer and water. However, not all bulbous plants die down. Potted agapanthus, for example, stays leafy and green all year, sending up flowers after a period of active growth.

Tropical foliage plants are responsive to warm, moist air rather than to seasonal periods of long and short days. These plants will grow very slowly in winter unless your home is unusually warm and humid. Also, in these energy-conscious days when many thermostats are being lowered a few degrees, the growth of almost all houseplants will slow down in the colder months.

Left: Poinsettias are usually treated as temporary plants and discarded after the holidays. But they will survive to the following year if given a rest period in the spring. Below: Daffodils and other bulbous plants gradually die back after they bloom.

Garden Care

You can buy the highest quality plants and seeds, and spend a small fortune on a beautiful landscape design, but these efforts alone won't assure you of a successful garden. Healthy, growing plants will be your reward only if you pay attention to their cultural needs. A basic knowledge of soil preparation, fertilizers, mulching, and watering, as well as of weeds and of plant pests and diseases, will give you the background necessary to plan your own plant care and maintenance program.

Soil

Soil is a word that means different things to different people. The engineer, the farmer, and the home gardener all have a special relationship with soil, and the type of information each needs may be quite different.

The information in this chapter is intended for the home gardener, who most often thinks of soil as a substance in which to grow plants. Because few people are blessed with the "rich, well-drained garden loam" referred to so often on the back of seed packets, most gardeners must improve their soil in one way or another.

Don't try to live with a problem soil—nothing can dampen the enthusiasm of a gardener more quickly than a soil that doesn't allow healthy plant growth.

It should be noted, though, that some plant can be found for almost any kind of soil. The results would be a garden dictated not by the gardener's desires, but by the natural limitations of that gardener's soil. On the other hand, almost any kind of soil can be modified to grow any plant that's right for the climate. Most successful gardeners try to find satisfying combinations of plants that require a minimum of soil improvement for good growth. And for all but the worst soils, changing the soil so that it supports a wider variety of plants is not a particularly extensive or complicated process.

What Is Soil?

Every soil consists of mineral and organic matter, water, air, and living organisms. The proportions may vary but the major components remain the same. Ideally, soil serves as an anchorage for the plant roots and as a reservoir for water, air, and nutrients.

Every soil has these elements: depth, fertility, texture, and structure. A good garden soil has a topsoil that is several feet deep; is reasonably fertile; has a good balance of sand, silt, and clay particles (texture); and has just the right amount of air space between those particles to promote both good drainage

Left: "Superb Lily" from *The Temple of Flora* by Robert Thornton. Above: Scarecrows do not scare off birds very well, but they make charming additions to a vegetable garden.

and water retention (structure). In addition, it has an acceptable pH (the acid-alkaline balance) for healthy plant growth.

Very few soils are absolutely ideal. In most cases, however, there are relatively simple solutions to soil problems. And because of the complex nature of soil, when you improve one aspect of it, you usually eliminate several other problems.

Soil Testing

The most accurate way to find out what kind of soil you have is to take samples from the areas in which you intend to plant and have them tested in a soil laboratory. For information on how to take samples and where to have them tested, contact your local county extension agent. Some states offer a free soil-testing service.

You can get a general idea of the quality of your soil by doing some relatively simple tests yourself that will provide you with rudimentary but helpful information.

Testing for Texture   Texture is the relative proportion of sand, silt, and clay particles in a soil. To test, dig several holes six to eight inches deep in the area where you expect to plant. Fill a quart jar about two-thirds full of water. Add soil from one of the holes until the jar is almost full. Then add about one tablespoon of water softener. Screw the lid on the jar and shake vigorously. Then let the soil settle. In a short time the heaviest sand particles will sink to the bottom, making the sand layer visible. The next layer to form will be the silt layer, and finally the extremely small clay particles will settle on the top. The clay particles are so small that the molecular action of the water alone may keep them in suspension indefinitely. The experiment should be ready to read in two to three hours.

Carry out this same test using soil from each of the different holes you dug in the garden. Then chart each test by marking off the thickness of the layers on a piece of paper held up to the jar. Estimate the percentage of clay by comparing the width of that layer to the sand and silt layers. Compare the proportions of the elements using the following information:

Your soil is sandy if there is less than 5 percent clay.

Your soil is sandy loam if there is 5 to 10 percent clay.

You have a medium loam if there is 10 to 20 percent clay.

Your soil is clay if there is 25 to 30 percent clay.

You have a heavy clay soil if there is 35 to 50 percent clay.

Right: Good soil is essential to growing top-quality flowers, fruits, and vegetables. Few gardens are naturally favored with ideal soil, but most soils can be greatly improved by adding the proper soil amendments before planting. Below: Many experienced gardeners can determine a soil's texture by squeezing a fistful of soil.

Watering

Watering isn't difficult to do properly, and it's easy to give general advice on the subject, but offering specific advice is very difficult. This is because there are so many variables to be considered: soil type and slope, humidity, type of plant grown, weather, season, light intensity, wind, temperature, whether the soil is covered with a mulch, and on and on.

All these factors are best known to the individual gardener. So the first word of advice to you, the gardener, should be: "Know your garden." This means, for example, the characteristics of its soil and plants, and how its location affects your watering practices. With this personal knowledge, you can develop an art of watering that transcends technical advice.

Water and Soil Character

It's impossible to talk about watering without talking about the characteristics of the soil being watered. The characteristics of your own soil are the most important factors influencing your watering practices. If you've improved your soil to the point that it has the characteristics of a loam, more than half the watering battle is already won. Most plants grown in a good loam soil are far more tolerant of a range of watering practices, good and bad, than if they were grown in either clayey or sandy soils, both of which are notoriously difficult to water properly. This isn't to say that you can't learn to handle a clay or sand soil successfully—many gardeners have—but it's a challenging procedure involving much trial and error.

The ideal garden soil absorbs nearly all the water that falls on it, holds a large quantity within its fine pores, allows any excess to drain away, and is protected by surface mulches from excessive evaporation.

It is harder to establish proper water–air–plant relationships in a clay soil, because water enters the small soil pores slowly; overwatering causes flooding, which deprives plant roots of oxygen, and the soil compacts easily. The gardener who manages a clay soil must learn to provide alternate wetting and partial drying of the soil. The drying will allow air into the soil.

Sandy soils provide fast drainage and good aeration, but they do not retain much water. They must be watered often.

Generally speaking, the coarser the particles that make up a soil, the less water the soil will hold. Sandy soils (they have the coarsest particles) hold only about one-quarter inch of water per foot of depth. Sandy loams usually hold about three-quarters of an inch of water per foot; fine sandy loams hold about one-and-a-quarter inches; and silt loams, clay loams, and clays hold

about two-and-a-half to three inches of water per foot of depth. Although these are rough figures, they clearly show that different soil types demand different watering schedules.

The addition of organic matter to any of the soil types mentioned above will have the effect of equalizing their water requirements. Large amounts of organic matter may increase the water-holding capacity of the sandy soils, and "open up" heavier silt loams and clay soils to allow more air and water to enter.

How Important Is Water?

Applying water correctly is essential for a healthy, successful garden. Don't forget, though, that the best watering practices in the world will not make up for deficiencies of mineral nutrients, lack of weed control, or the plant variety's lack of adaptability to your climate. There is little point in supplying water to plants that are unable to make productive use of it because of poor soil or poor soil management.

The oscillating sprinkler system shown here works fine for this vegetable garden, but a large variety of watering methods and mechanisms are also available. Analyze your garden's watering needs and your own preferences before choosing a system.

Amount and Timing

While it is difficult to give general advice on specific watering practices, a couple of time-honored rules should be followed. The first concerns the amount of water to apply at any one time, and the rule is simple: Fill the root zone, then allow the soil to dry out somewhat before the next watering.

If you water thoroughly and too frequently, there's a good chance that you'll cut off the supply of air in the soil by filling all of the air spaces with water. Then root growth stops; the longer the air is cut off, the greater the root damage. Damaged roots can be invaded by decay-causing microorganisms in the soil, and the plant can be killed easily by root rot.

On the other hand, if you water too lightly and frequently, the water never has a chance to move very far into the soil. Plant roots grow only in areas where moisture, nutrients, and air are available. The soil surrounding the roots may be nutrient rich and contain plenty of air, but without moisture, roots will not grow there. The result of shallow watering is shallow-rooted plants. If you miss a couple of waterings, a shallow-rooted plant cannot tap reserves of water deeper in the soil. Consequently, the plant will not survive even brief periods of drought or high temperatures.

The general rule of thumb is: When you water, water well and learn how long it takes for your particular soil to dry slightly between waterings.

One of the general questions about watering is: When is the best time of day to water? There are plenty of local prejudices and differing schools of thought on this subject, but common sense may be the best advice of all. You can reduce plant diseases and lose less water to evaporation by watering in the early morning. The reasoning behind this is clear: Leaves (including blades of grass) that stay damp through the night are more susceptible to attack by disease-causing organisms. By watering them in the morning hours, you give plants a chance to dry off before nightfall.

How Much Is Enough?

There are several answers to the how-much-is-enough question. Lawns, shallow-rooted annual flowers and vegetables, mature trees and shrubs, container-grown plants, and other plants in various stages of growth all have different water needs, and the climate has a lot to do with it. But if you remember the general advice—to water thoroughly when you do water—you'll have few water-related problems.

How can you tell if you're watering thoroughly? The best way

Proper irrigation can mean the difference between a beautiful, healthy lawn and a spotty, unattractive lawn that succumbs easily to disease and weed invasion. Irrigating to the proper soil depth is critical.

The measure of water application is usually determined in inches of water applied per hour. An easy way to determine how many inches of water per hour your sprinklers emit is illustrated here. Set out buckets or containers in a grid pattern in the area covered by the sprinkler, and check the amount of water in the containers at thirty-minute intervals. Time your watering periods accordingly.

Types of Fertilizers

Fertilizers can be made either from organic materials or from commercially produced substances, in both liquid and dry form.

Dry Fertilizers   Dry fertilizers are available in powders, granules, and pellets. In most cases, dry fertilizer is the most convenient kind to use. It can be scattered on the ground and watered in, cultivated into the soil, or buried deep in the root zone.

Some dry fertilizers are soluble in water and become instantly available to plants. This type usually leaches from the soil in a few weeks and must be reapplied regularly.

Other dry fertilizers are insoluble in water, but become available to plants over a period of time. These are known as slow-release fertilizers. When nitrogen is in its most common form, urea formaldehyde, bacterial action in the soil slowly releases the nitrogen into a soluble form available to plants. Other slow-release fertilizers use different methods of releasing nitrogen. These fertilizers remain effective in the soil for six weeks to two years, depending on the type. They can be applied less often, but are more expensive than the soluble forms.

The amount of slow-release nitrogen in the fertilizer is shown on the label as part of the nitrogen analysis; it is called water-insoluble nitrogen and is shown as a percentage of the total fertilizer. A fertilizer with 10 percent nitrogen might be 8 percent water-soluble, and 2 percent water-insoluble nitrogen.

Liquid Fertilizers   Liquid fertilizers may be bought in liquid or powdered form, but both must be dissolved in water before use. You can mix either kind in water in a watering can and apply it directly to the root zone or put a concentration into a hose-end sprayer and spray it on your plants.

Liquid fertilizers are often preferred for container plants, for which light but frequent feeding is desirable. They are also useful in drip-irrigation systems, where they can be metered into the watering system and fed to the plants with regular irrigations.

Liquid fertilizers and soluble powders are also used for foliar feeding, a method by which a dilute fertilizer solution is sprayed directly onto the leaves. Foliar feeding is useful when very quick results are desired, or when a soil problem inhibits the uptake of nutrients by the roots. Any excess fertilizer falling to the ground also becomes available for absorption by the roots, resulting in a "double action" feeding.

A healthy, blooming garden is the result of good planning, careful planting, and a regular fertilization program.

Organic Fertilizers   Organic fertilizers are derived from plant or animal sources. Manure, compost, seed meals, blood meal, and fish meal are all organic. Fish emulsion is a liquid organic fertilizer; most of the rest are sold in dry form. Most of these fertilizers are expensive, but they last for a long time in the soil, and the nonnutrient part of the fertilizer improves soil structure.

When you need to purchase a fertilizer, take the time to read the labels. They will tell you what each fertilizer does and when to apply it, which will help you purchase exactly the right fertilizer at the right time. And the directions on the package will help you to determine how much fertilizer to apply.

Compost

The black, crumbly, organic residue called compost comes from garden waste material that has broken down over time.

Compost is a highly useful soil amendment and mulch. Whatever method of composting you use, the main objective is to arrange the waste material in such a way that the soil organisms that break down the waste can thrive and multiply. These organisms need moisture, air circulation, and food.

Making Compost

To build a compost pile, use a mixture of green and dry materials. Green material decomposes rapidly. Grass clippings, lettuce leaves, pea vines, and other succulent materials contain sugar and proteins that provide excellent nutrients for the organisms. On the other hand, dry materials such as sawdust, dry leaves, small twigs, and prunings contain very little nitrogen and decompose very slowly when composted alone. By mixing green and dry materials, your pile will compost at just the right rate.

The size of the woody material in the pile will affect the rate of decomposition. If dry leaves and other dry materials are put through a shredder rather than added to the pile as is, they will decompose faster. Shredding also creates a fluffier mixture, making air and water penetration more efficient. You can buy or rent a shredder, or you can just use a rotary mower to shred leaves. If you produce grass clippings in large quantities, mix them thoroughly into the composting material. Otherwise they will begin to form a soggy mass, putrefy, produce unpleasant odors, and attract flies. After you've mixed the grass into the compost, spread a layer of soil or old compost over the top.

The compost is ready for use when it has cooled, has a dark and rich color, is crumbly, and has that good earthy fragrance.

For the sake of convenience you can divide the compost

pile into three piles. The first is for the daily collection of waste products—refuse from the vegetable harvest, wastes from the kitchen, coffee grounds, eggshells, small prunings, and so on. The second is for the fast-working compost; add nothing to this pile, and make sure to turn it frequently. The third pile is for finished compost.

Mulching

Mulching is one of gardening's oldest techniques. Until fairly recently, only natural mulches were used. In the past few years, however, university researchers, commercial farmers, and home gardeners have experimented with black and clear polyethylene film as a mulch and have achieved good results. The plastic mulches may have great advantages in increasing crop yields and in weed control, but their virtues in no way deny the value of a natural organic mulch; it's up to the gardener to decide which is better in any given situation.

Many materials are used both as mulches and as soil amendments. The difference between a soil amendment and a mulch is not in the nature of the material but in the method of application. A soil amendment is incorporated into the soil to improve its texture and structure; a mulch is applied in a fairly thick layer on top of the soil, and although it performs many of the functions of an amendment, mulch has a number of other positive effects.

Top: A compost structure with three bins is efficient and convenient. Bottom: Measure the soil amendment to be sure you have added enough.

Reasons for Mulching

Mulches serve to keep wind and sun from baking the soil and causing it to form a crust; they help control weeds and protect the soil from pedestrian traffic. Mulches help conserve water, reduce runoff, and moderate soil temperatures. Organic mulches keep the soil surface cool in the summer, and clear plastic mulches help warm the soil in winter. Mulches applied during winter help keep the soil from alternately freezing and thawing.

Natural mulches include such materials as fir bark, compost, hay, dried lawn clippings, peat moss, leaf mold, pine needles, and sawdust. Natural mulches are usually raked over the area to a thickness of several inches. Depending upon the type of mulch, this thickness varies from one to four inches.

Man-made mulches include such materials as black, clear, and sky-blue polyethylene film, aluminum foil, paper coated with aluminum foil, and biodegradable paper. These materials are usually available in large rolls and are rolled out and secured along the edges with pins or stakes.

Weeds

A weed can be loosely defined as any plant growing in the wrong place. The finest lawngrass plant is a weed when it grows in the perennial garden, and dandelions are purposely cultivated in some of the best vegetable gardens.

For the most part, weeds are annual or perennial herbaceous plants that spread rapidly by seeds or underground stems or roots. These seeds, stems, or roots sprout to produce new plants.

Weeds compete with other plants by crowding them out and using up water and nutrients. Weeds can be divided into two major categories: broadleaf and narrowleaf. Broadleaf weeds, such as dandelions, have more obvious, showy flowers. Their leaves have a network of small veins originating from a principal point or vein at the leaf base; this vein often divides the leaf in half. Grassy weeds are the narrowleaf type. They usually have hollow stems and long, narrow leaf blades with parallel veins. Foxtail and crabgrass are common narrowleaf weeds.

These miniature, raised beds of strawberries have been mulched with black plastic. Redwood chips cover the walkways between the beds. Both the plastic and the chips reduce weed growth; the black plastic also warms the soil.

Opposite page: A weed-free garden is much more attractive; and of course the plants perform better because they don't have to compete with weeds for nutrients, light, and water. This page: Rototilling is a good, initial weed eradication measure, but after the garden has been planted, other methods must be used for weed control.

Cultural Weed Control

Good cultural techniques can reduce the growth of weeds in your garden. Keep your plants healthy and vigorous by giving them the proper care; this will help considerably in weed control. Healthy plants can crowd out and compete with weeds much more effectively than sickly, slow-growing plants. This is especially true in lawns, ground covers, and annual and perennial beds, where the plants shade out weeds because they are spaced closely together.

Mulching will prevent weed seeds from germinating, and turning the soil over by tilling or hoeing will kill many weeds. Just spending an hour or so each week picking weeds when they're young can cut down the time you spend later in the season digging out mature weeds that are ready to seed or have already reseeded themselves.

Chemical Weed Control

It is important to recognize the difference between broadleaf and narrowleaf weed types. An herbicide (weed killer) that kills weeds with narrow leaves may not even affect the broadleaf weeds. Also, it is particularly important to pay strict attention to label instructions. Many weed killers or pest controls are only effective within certain temperature ranges and at specific stages of plant maturity.

Herbicides are either preemergent, meaning they kill weed seeds before they germinate, or postemergent, meaning they kill weeds after they've germinated. The postemergent types are further categorized as either contact or systemic. Contact herbicides kill the aboveground plant parts. Systemic herbicides actually move through the plant's entire system, killing both the aboveground plant parts and the roots. Systemic herbicides are most effective when the plant is actively growing.

504

Herbicides may be very general and nonselective, killing both weeds and desired plants, or they may be very specific to the types of weeds they kill.

Weed Control in Lawns Broadleaf weeds in grass lawns are usually controlled with a postemergent systemic herbicide. Narrowleaf weeds are more difficult to control in a grass lawn. Most of them must be spot treated with a postemergent contact herbicide. You can reseed or resod the dead spots after treatment. One of the best weed controls is simply to maintain a healthy, vigorous lawn.

Weed Control in Annual Beds Because most annuals have a short life, growing quickly from seeds to bloom, many weeds can be controlled by applying preemergent herbicides to the soil before planting annual transplants. Before planting an annual bed, kill existing weeds by cultivating and treating with postemergent contact or systemic herbicides.

Weed Control in Vegetable Gardens Weeds often grow most abundantly in vegetable gardens, where the ample amount of water and fertilizer provides an ideal environment. Herbicides must be used carefully around vegetables and other edible plants; as a result, the use of herbicides in vegetable gardens is limited. Remove existing weeds by cultivating with a sharp hoe. Cut off the weeds just below the soil line, rather than trying to dig them from the ground. To remove small weeds close to vegetable seedlings, pinch them off, or cut them at the ground line with scissors. Prevent weeds from returning by treating the soil with a preemergent herbicide. A preemergent herbicide can be used in the vegetable garden but only when the vegetables are listed on the product label.

Weed Control in Perennial Beds Before establishing a perennial bed, kill all existing weeds with a contact or systemic herbicide. Once the flower bed is established, use a preemergent herbicide to keep the area weed free.

Weed Control Around Trees and Shrubs Weed control under trees and shrubs is usually simpler and easier than weed control in other areas because the trees and shrubs shade the soil, reducing the vigor of the weeds. If the area has been neglected for some time and is full of perennial weeds, kill them with a systemic or contact spray. Light, shallow cultivation and mulching under trees will help keep the area weed free.

Among the most easily seen of insect pests, caterpillars are the larvae of moths and butterflies and have voracious appetites. Here, a caterpillar feeds on a petunia leaf.

Pests and Diseases

Much popular garden literature enthusiastically claims certain plants to be "pest free" or "trouble free". In fact, no plant is immune to all plant pests and diseases, although some plants are less inclined to such problems.

Keep a careful eye on your garden for early signs of infestation or infection. The following descriptions of common pests and diseases will help you identify possible problems. Maintaining your plants in good health and following good sanitation practices (cleaning up plant debris, renewing mulches) will greatly reduce the incidence and severity of plant problems.

Before spraying, be sure to read the pesticide label. Make sure your plant and the problem you're treating are listed on the label. It's essential to follow directions carefully, or you may wreak havoc on your plants. Because insect emergence dates vary throughout the country, check with your local extension office for specific spray dates and reapplication periods.

Pests

Most pests are insects, technically belonging to the class Insecta. Many other animals, such as spider mites, snails and slugs, and mice, are also considered pests because they feed on or damage plants in some way. In this section, you'll find a listing of plant pests common to many kinds of plants.

Aphids often go unnoticed. They are usually found on the undersides of leaves and can cause extensive damage.

Aphids   Aphids are small, soft-bodied insects that feed on plant sap. They may be yellow, green, red, purple, brown, or black, and are visible on plant leaves, stems, and flowers. Some aphids are covered with a white, waxy coating.

Hosts: Flowers, trees, shrubs, vegetables, herbs, and occasionally houseplants.

Damage: Leaves, flowers, and fruit become distorted, yellowed, and curled; plant growth is stunted. Aphids produce honeydew, a clear, shiny, sticky fluid that coats plant parts.

Control: Spray with insecticides containing malathion or acephate. Ladybugs feed on aphids.

Flea beetle.

This insect, a larva of an
Oriental fruit moth, bores into
twigs, stems, and tender shoots.

Beetles   There are many different species of beetles that feed on
a wide variety of plants. Both the adult beetles and the larvae,
called grubs, can be damaging. The adult beetles feed on leaves,
succulent stems, flowers, and fruits, and the grubs usually
feed on plant roots and sometimes on the undersides of leaves.
Some common beetles include Japanese beetles, elm-leaf beetles,
and flea beetles.

Hosts: Flowers, lawns, trees, shrubs, vegetables, and herbs.

Damage: Leaves and flowers are riddled with holes, chewed, or
skeletonized. Holes may be chewed in fruit. In the cases of
flowers and vegetables, plants may be stunted and wilted from
root damage.

Control.   Control adult beetles by spraying with diazinon or
carbaryl. Control grubs in the soil by treating the soil with
diazinon. Beetles may be handpicked from plants.

Birds   Many types of birds feed on vegetable and flower seeds
and seedlings, and on fruits and berries, especially cherries
and grapes.

Control: Exclude birds with wire or fabric cages placed over
newly planted areas. You can also make cages or protective
coverings with cheesecloth or plastic bird netting. Prevent birds
from digging up seed by laying hardware cloth over the seedbed.
Keep birds from feeding on fruit and berry plants by throwing
nets (available in garden centers) over the tree or bush. Be sure to
secure the net tightly around the trunk or the base of the plant.

Borers   Most borers are the larvae of beetles or moths that
tunnel in wood or soft stems. Borers are usually pale and resemble worms or hairless caterpillars.

Hosts: Trees, shrubs, flowers, and vegetables.

Damage: Holes are present in trunks or branches, or in the
softer stems of flowers or vegetables. Foliage on the affected
stems or branches may be wilting and yellowing.

Control: The best control for borers in most herbaceous plants
is sanitation; cut out and destroy infested stems and remove
dying plants. To control borers with contact insecticides such as
carbaryl you must usually apply insecticides before the borers
enter the plant.
    Borers in woody plants are difficult to control. Long-residual

types of insecticides, such as lindane, are commonly used against borers once they've tunneled into the wood. Carbaryl will control borers before they've burrowed into the wood. Weakened and diseased trees and shrubs are especially susceptible to borer attack; to help prevent infestation, keep plants healthy and vigorous.

Bugs   Several species of bugs are commonly found in the garden, including squash bugs, stinkbugs, plantbugs, and lacebugs. Bugs feed on leaves, flowers, and fruits.

Hosts: Vegetables, flowers, trees, and shrubs.

Damage: Leaves, flowers, and fruits are speckled, mottled, spotted, or distorted.

Control: Spray with insecticides containing malathion, carbaryl, or acephate (Orthene[R]).

Caterpillars   Caterpillars are the larvae of moths and butterflies, and include such garden pests as gypsy moths, codling moths, cutworms, tent caterpillars, leaf rollers, leaftiers, certain borers, leaf miners, hornworms, and loopers. (Moths and butterflies do not feed on plants, but may drink nectar from flowers.) Caterpillars may be smooth, hairy, or spiny. Depending upon the species, caterpillars feed on leaves, stems, flowers, fruits, and in some cases, roots.

Hosts: Flowers, vegetables, herbs, trees, shrubs, and lawns.

Damage: Leaves, flowers, stems, and fruit are chewed; leaves are rolled or are sheared from the plant. Caterpillars and cocoons or pupae may be visible on the plant.

Control: Spray with insecticides containing carbaryl, diazinon, or acephate. The bacterial insecticide *Bacillus thuringiensis* may be used.

Lacebugs.

Tobacco hornworm.

Western tent caterpillars.

Cutworms   Cutworms are fleshy, hairless caterpillars that are serious pests of vegetables and flowers, and sometimes of vines and trees. Surface cutworms and climbing cutworms hide in the soil during the day and emerge at night to feed. Subterranean cutworms spend their lives in the soil. They feed on the roots and underground stems of plants.

Hosts: Flowers, vegetables, trees, vines, and lawns.

Damage: Leaves are sheared from plants; seedlings are toppled over or entirely eaten. When plants are inspected at night with a flashlight, cutworms may be seen curled around the base of plants or feeding on the lower leaves.

Control: Treat soil with an insecticide containing diazinon. Cultivate the soil thoroughly in late summer to fall to expose cutworm eggs, larvae, and pupae.

Leafhoppers   Leafhoppers are tiny, green, wedge-shaped insects that hop or fly away quickly when disturbed. They feed on plant sap and excrete honeydew, a clear, sticky fluid that coats leaves, flowers, and fruits.

Hosts: Flowers, vegetables, trees, shrubs, and lawns.

Damage: Leaves and stems are stippled, stunted, and distorted. In some cases, infested leaves turn brown and curl upward.

Control: Spray with malathion, diazinon, or acephate.

Leaf miners   Leaf miners are insect larvae that feed inside a leaf. They may be the larvae of flies, moths, or beetles.

Hosts: Flowers, vegetables, herbs, trees, and shrubs.

Damage: Winding trails, blotches, and sometimes blisters develop on leaves and flowers.

Control: Leaf miners are difficult to control once they are inside the leaf. A systemic insecticide containing acephate will control leaf miners inside the leaves of nonedible plants, and sprays containing diazinon will control leaf miners on edible crops when applied before the leaf miners tunnel into the leaf.

Leafhopper.

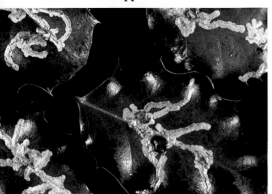

Leafminer damage on holly.

Mealybugs on coleus.

Spider mite webs.

Mealybugs on schefflera

Mealybugs   Mealybugs are oval, white insects that cluster in white, cottony masses on stems and leaves. Mealybugs suck plant sap.

Hosts: Houseplants, flowers, trees, and shrubs.

Damage: Infested plant parts may be distorted, yellowed, and stunted. Honeydew, a clear, shiny, sticky fluid excreted by mealybugs, may cover the plant.

Control: Spray with an insecticide containing malathion, diazinon, or acephate (Orthene[R]).

Mites   Mites are tiny pests that are related to spiders. In fact, some mites are commonly called spider mites. Many mites produce webbing that covers the undersides of infested leaves and other plant parts. Mites feed on plant sap.

Hosts: Houseplants, flowers, vegetables, herbs, trees, and sometimes lawns.

Damage: Leaves and flowers are stippled, discolored, and yellowing; infested plant parts may die.

Control: Spray with an insecticide containing dicofol, diazinon, or malathion.

Gray squirrel.

Cactus scale.

Rodents   Several rodents, including mice, moles, and pocket gophers, are common garden pests. Mice feed on bulbs and tender vegetables and flowers, and may severely damage young trees by gnawing on the bark and roots. Moles seldom feed on plants, but their tunneling uproots plants and loosens the soil around plant roots so that they dry out and die. Moles are especially notorious for the unsightly ridges they create in lawns. Pocket gophers eat roots and bulbs, and pull plants into their burrows. They can kill shrubs by eating most of the roots and girdling the underground part of the trunk or stems.

Control: Keep mice out of the garden by fencing them out, protecting tree trunks with hardware cloth cylinders, and placing traps or poisoned bait along mouse runways. Eliminate moles and pocket gophers by using traps. An active cat will help eliminate rodent problems.

Scales   Scales are insects that resemble small bumps; they may be brown, reddish, or gray in appearance, or they may be covered with a white, waxy material. The adult scale insect produces a protective shell. Adult scales are immobile and remain in one place sucking plant sap. Young scales are active, have no shell, and can move around the plant.

Hosts: Houseplants, trees, and shrubs.

Damage: Infested foliage turns yellow and may die; scale insects may entirely cover trunks and branches; plants may be covered with a sticky, clear, shiny honeydew.

Control: Suffocate adult scales and scale eggs by spraying with a dormant oil spray. Spray with an insecticide containing acephate or diazinon when the immature scales are present.

Snails and Slugs   Snails and slugs feed on a wide variety of garden plants. Snails and slugs are mollusks and need to be moist at all times. They avoid direct sun and dry places, and hide during the day in damp places.

Hosts: Flowers, vegetables, herbs, trees, shrubs, and lawns.

Damage: Snails and slugs shear leaves from stems, and may shear off and devour entire seedlings. They feed on all succulent plant parts, such as flowers, tender shoots, leaves, and sometimes fruit.

Control: Handpick and destroy snails and slugs. Clean up debris that might harbor snails. Control them with an insecticide containing metaldehyde or methiocarb (Mesurol[R]).

Thrips   Thrips are tiny, slender insects that infest the flowers, leaves, fruit, and shoots of all kinds of plants. They damage plants by rasping the plant tissue and then sucking the released sap.

Hosts: Houseplants, flowers, vegetables, trees, and shrubs.

Damage: Dead spots; distorted blossoms and leaves; and flecked, streaked foliage that may be dotted with black, shiny spots are signs of infestation.

Control: Spray with an insecticide containing acephate, malathion, diazinon, or carbaryl (Sevin[R]).

Whiteflies   Whiteflies are tiny, white, winged insects that flutter around infested plants. They cluster on the undersides of leaves, and feed on plant sap.

Hosts: Houseplants, flowers, vegetables, trees, and shrubs.

Damage: Leaves are mottled and yellowing.

Control: Spray infested plants with an insecticide containing acephate, diazinon, or malathion.

Thrips damage.

Whiteflies.

Botrytis on strawberries.

Diseases

Most plant diseases are caused by parasitic fungi or bacteria. Descriptions of some of the most common plant diseases follow.

Botrytis   Botrytis is a plant disease caused by a fungus. It is also known as gray mold. Brown spots and blotches develop on infected leaves and flowers, and eventually a fuzzy brown or grayish mold develops. Infected leaves and flowers may be soft and rotted. The disease is most severe in wet, humid conditions.

Botrytis on begonia.

Hosts: Houseplants, flowers, and vegetables.

Control: Keep leaves and flowers as dry as possible, and pick off and destroy dead leaves and flowers. Spray with a fungicide containing maneb or mancozeb.

Cankers   Cankers are dark, sunken areas on trunks or branches. Often, a sticky sap oozes from cankers. They are caused by fungi and bacteria that infect the soft tissue just underneath the bark. Bark that has been damaged by sunscald, cold injury, pruning or insect wounds, or mechanical injury is especially susceptible to canker development. If the canker girdles a branch, the branch dies; if the trunk is girdled, the whole tree or shrub dies.

Canker on sycamore.

Hosts: Trees and shrubs.

Control: Remove badly infected branches, and cut out cankers. Keep tree wounds from pruning or mechanical damage to a minimum; use the proper equipment and work carefully.

Crown Gall   Crown gall is caused by bacteria that live in the soil. The bacteria enter the plant through wounds, and cause rough, corky galls to form on the roots, crown, and sometimes on the stems. Infected plants are often weak, stunted, and more susceptible to other sources of plant stress, such as drought and winter injury.

Crown gall on rose.

Hosts: Trees and shrubs.

Control: Even though infected plants cannot be cured, they usually survive for many years. The plants look better if stems with galls are pruned off. Galls on roots and trunks are much more difficult to remove; professional horticulturists or landscape contractors should be consulted for such a job.

Crown and root rot on apple.

Crown and Root Rot   Crown and root rot are usually caused by any of a number of organisms that live in the soil. Fungi and bacteria decay the roots and crown, causing wilting, leaf yellowing, and dieback. Crown and root rot are most prevalent in heavy, poorly drained soils.

Hosts: Houseplants, flowers, vegetables, trees, and shrubs.

Control: Remove dead and dying plants; plants that are not so severely affected may possibly be saved by improving the soil drainage. Be sure not to overwater plants.

Damping-off   Damping-off is a fungus disease that attacks germinating seedlings. The fungi decay the seedlings just before or after they emerge from the soil. Damping-off is favored by wet soil high in nitrogen.

Hosts: Flowers and vegetables.

Control: When watering seedbeds, allow the soil surface to dry slightly between waterings. Add nitrogen fertilizers *after* the seedlings have produced their first true leaves. Coat seeds with captan before planting or spray captan on the soil and work it into the upper two inches.

Damping-off on snapdragon seedlings.

Honeydew and sooty mold.

Honeydew   Honeydew is a sweet, sticky, shiny substance that is often found on leaves, flowers, and sometimes on fruit and twigs. It is secreted by aphids, mealybugs, whiteflies, and certain scales. Often, a black, sooty mold grows on the honeydew, causing the affected foliage to appear black and dirty. The sooty mold fungus does not infect the leaf, but grows superficially on the honeydew.

Hosts: Houseplants, flowers, vegetables, trees, and shrubs.

Control: Honeydew can be wiped off with a wet rag or hosed off. Eventually, it will be washed off by rain. In itself, it does not damage the plant, but indicates that damaging insects are present. Check for these insects and control them.

Leaf Spots   Leaf spots are usually caused by fungi. In most cases, leaf spots do not seriously damage the plant; the spotting is unsightly but not harmful. Some leaf-spot fungi cause leaf yellowing and death, and may eventually kill the plant. Leaf-spot fungi are most active in mild, damp weather.

Hosts: Houseplants, flowers, vegetables, trees, and shrubs.

Control: If spotting is not severe, pick off infected leaves and flowers. If spotting is severe, spray with a fungicide containing basic copper sulfate, captan, maneb, or mancozeb.

Leaf spots on liquidambar.

Powdery mildew on rose.

Rust on snapdragon.

Powdery Mildew   Powdery mildew is a fungus disease that produces a very characteristic grayish white coating on infected leaves, stems, and flowers. Infected plant parts may turn yellowish or reddish and drop. New growth that is infected often becomes stunted and distorted.

Hosts: Flowers, vegetables, trees, and shrubs.

Control: Spray with a fungicide containing triforine, benomyl, dinocap, or cycloheximide.

Rusts   Rust is caused by a group of fungi that produces rust-colored or brown pustules on plant foliage. Plants infected with rust are often weak and stunted, and severely infected plants may die. Rust thrives in wet conditions.

Hosts: Flowers, vegetables, trees, shrubs, and lawns.

Control: Spray with a fungicide containing folpet, triforine, mancozeb, or zineb. Keep the foliage as dry as possible. When possible, plant resistant varieties.

Wilt Disease   Wilt refers to the diseases caused by the many different species of the fungi *Verticillium* and *Fusarium*. The disease affects the water-conducting vessels in plant stems, and results in wilting, stem and leaf discoloration, and the death of many plants.

Hosts: Flowers, vegetables, trees, and shrubs.

Control: Once these fungi have infected the plant, you cannot halt the progression of the disease. Diseased flowers and vegetables often last through the season if they are cared for properly. Replace infected plants with varieties that are resistant to these fungi. If you want to use susceptible plants, eliminate the fungi from the soil by fumigating.

Wilt on sumac.

Hypericum olympicum from *Exotic Botany* by Smith and Sowerby.

Encyclopedia Charts

The plants in this encyclopedia are listed in alphabetical order. Ornamental plants are listed by their botanical names. This practice is common in horticultural books because many plants have several common names, and different plants are frequently called by the same common name. If you don't know a plant's botanical name, look it up in the List of Common Names on the next page. Food plants—fruits, berries, herbs, nut trees, and vegetables—are entered in the encyclopedia by their common names, so they do not appear in the List of Common Names.

Zones The climatic zones listed follow the United States Department of Agriculture system. The zones are based on average winter low temperatures. The zone system is widely used because low winter temperatures limit where many plants can be grown. No zones are given for annuals, biennials, or annual vegetables because they do not usually live through the winter. Find your zone on the map on pages 42 and 43.

Flowers The two columns showing flower color and bloom time are only filled in if the flowers on that plant are of significant interest. If there are no flowers, or if the flowers are insignificant, the columns are left blank.

Bulbs In the encyclopedia all bulblike plants are referred to as bulbs even though some grow from tubers, corms, rhizomes, or tuberous roots. To find out which of these bulbous types a plant grows from, see the list on page 112.

Shade Two types of shade are referred to in the encyclopedia: *light shade* and *deep shade*. In the chapter "Climate, Microclimate, and Shade," we describe four types of shade: *dappled shade, open shade, medium shade,* and *dense shade*. The first two are included in *light shade;* the latter two are included in *deep shade*.

Grass height The heights given for turfgrasses are the recommended mowing heights.

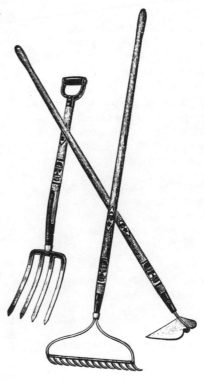

List of Common Names

Because the common names of plants vary from one part of the country to another, ornamental plants are listed in this encyclopedia by their botanical names. If you don't know the botanical name of a plant, look up the common name you know in the list below. Food plants—vegetables, herbs, and fruit trees—are listed in the encyclopedia by their common names, so they don't appear in this list.

A

Aaronsbeard: *Hypericum calycinum*
Abelia: *Abelia × grandiflora*
Adriatic Bellflower: *Campanula elatines garganica*
African Daisy: *Arctotis stoechadifolia, Osteospermum fruiticosum*
African Lily: *Agapanthus africanus*
African Marigold: *Tagetes erecta*
African Sumac: *Rhus lancea*
African Violets: *Saintpaulia* species
Airplane Plant: *Chlorophytum comosum*
Akebia: *Akebia quinata*
Alaska Cedar: *Chamaecyparis nootkatensis*
Alder: *Alnus*
Alder Buckthorn: *Rhamnus frangula*
Algerian Ivy: *Hedera canariensis*
Alkanet: *Anchusa officinalis*
Almond: *Prunus triloba*
Aloe Vera: *Aloe barbadensis*
Alpine Cinquefoil: *Potentilla cinerea*
Aluminum Plant: *Pilea cadierei*
Amaryllis: *Hippeastrum* species
Amazon Lily: *Eucharis grandiflora*
American Arborvitae: *Thuja occidentalis*
American Elm: *Ulmus americana*
American Filbert: *Corylus americana*
American Holly: *Ilex opaca*
American Hophornbeam: *Ostrya virginiana*
American Hornbeam: *Carpinus caroliniana*
American Linden: *Tilia americana*
American Olive: *Osmanthus americanus*
American Sweet Gum: *Liquidambar styraciflua*
Amsonia: *Amsonia tabernaemontana*
Amur Corktree: *Phellodendron amurense*

Amur Honeysuckle: *Lonicera maackii*
Amur Maple: *Acer ginnala*
Amur Privet: *Ligustrum amurense*
Angelica: *Angelica archangelica*
Anglojap Yew: *Taxus × media*
Annual Baby's Breath: *Gypsophila elegans*
Annual Delphinium: *Consolida ambigua*
Annual Phlox: *Phlox drummondii*
Annual Ryegrass: *Lolium multiflorum*
Apricot: *Prunus armeniaca*
Aralia: *Fatsia*
Arabian Star-of-Bethlehem: *Ornithogalum arabicum*
Arborvitae: *Thuja*
Arrowhead Vine: *Syngonium podophyllum*
Artichoke: *Cynara scolymus*
Ash: *Fraxinus*
Asiatic Jasmine: *Trachelospermum asiaticum*
Asparagus Fern: *Asparagus densiflorus* 'Sprengeri'
Astilbe: *Astilbe* species and hybrids
Atlas Cedar: *Cedrus atlantica*
Austrian Briar: *Rosa foetida*
Austrian Pine: *Pinus nigra*
Autumn Crocus: *Colchicum luteum*
Autumn Elaeagnus: *Elaeagnus umbellata*
Autumn Zephyr-lily: *Zephyranthes candida*
Avens: *Geum hybrids*
Azalea: *Rhododendron*

B

Baby Blue Eyes: *Nemophila menziesii*
Baby's Breath: *Gypsophila*
Baby's Tears: *Soleirolia soleirolii*
Bachelor's-button: *Centaurea cyanus*
Bahia Grass: *Paspalum notatum*
Bailey Acacia: *Acacia baileyana*
Bald Cypress: *Taxodium distichum*
Ball Fern: *Davallia mariesii*
Balloon Flower: *Platycodon grandiflorus*
Balsam: *Impatiens balsamina*
Bamboo Palm: *Rhapis excelsa*
Banks Rose: *Rosa banksiae*
Barberry: *Berberis*
Basket Of Gold: *Aurinia saxatilis*
Basswood: *Tilia americana*
Bay: *Laurus*
Bear's Breeches: *Acanthus mollis*

Bearberry Cotoneaster: *Cotoneaster dammeri*
Bearberry Manzanita: *Arctostaphylos uva-ursi*
Bearded Iris: *Iris*
Beauty Of The Night: *Mirabilis jalapa*
Beautybush: *Kolkwitzia amabilis*
Bee Balm: *Monarda didyma*
Beefsteak Begonia: *Begonia × erythrophylla*
Beefsteak Plant: *Iresine herbstii*
Beefwood: *Casuarina cunninghamiana*
Belgium Indica Hybrid: *Rhododendron*
Belladonna Lily: *Amaryllis belladonna*
Bellflower: *Campanula*
Bells-of-Ireland: *Moluccella laevis*
Bentgrass: *Agrostis palustris*
Bergamot: *Monarda didyma*
Bermuda Grass: *Cynodon dactylon*
Bermuda Grass: *Cynodon* species
Big Leaf Lilyturf: *Liriope muscari*
Big Tree: *Sequoiadendron giganteum*
Big-leaf Linden: *Tilia platyphyllos*
Bigleaf Hydrangea: *Hydrangea macrophylla*
Birch: *Betula*
Bird's Nest Fern: *Asplenium nidus*
Biscay Heath: *Erica mediterranea*
Bishop's-hat: *Epimedium grandiflorum*
Black Alder: *Alnus glutinosa*
Black Gum: *Nyssa sylvatica*
Black Locust: *Robinia pseudoacacia*
Black Snakeroot: *Cimicifuga racemosa*
Black Tupelo: *Nyssa sylvatica*
Black Walnut: *Juglans nigra*
Black-eyed Susan: *Rudbeckia fulgida*
Black-eyed Susan Vine: *Thunbergia alata*
Blanket Flower: *Gaillardia × grandiflora*
Bleeding Heart: *Dicentra spectabilis*
Blood-red Geranium: *Geranium sanguineum*
Bloodleaf: *Iresine herbstii*
Blue Fescue: *Festuca ovina glauca*
Blue Gum: *Eucalyptus globulus*
Blue Lungwort: *Pulmonaria angustifolia*
Blue Plumbago: *Ceratostigma plumbaginoides*

Blue-leaf Plantain Lily: *Hosta sieboldiana*

Bluebeard: *Caryopteris × clandonensis*

Bluebells: *Scilla*

Bluegrass: *Poa pratensis*

Blunt-leaf Plantain Lily: *Hosta decorata*

Borage: *Borago officinalis*

Border Forsythia: *Forsythia × intermedia*

Boston Fern: *Nephralepsis exaltata*

Bottlebrush: *Callistemon*

Bowie Oxalis: *Oxalis bowiei*

Boxwood: *Buxus*

British Columbia Wild Ginger: *Asarum caudatum*

Broom: *Cytisus*

Brown-eyed Susan: *Rudbeckia hirta* var. *pulcherrima*

Buckeye: *Aesculus*

Buckthorn: *Rhamnus alaternus*

Bugbane: *Cimicifuga racemosa*

Bugle: *Ajuga*

Bugloss: *Anchusa officinalis*

Bugloss: *Anchusa azurea*

Bunchberry: *Cornus canadensis*

Bunya-bunya: *Araucaria bidwillii*

Bur Oak: *Quercus macrocarpa*

Burkwood Daphne: *Daphne × burkwoodii*

Burkwood Viburnum: *Viburnum × burkwoodii*

Burning Bush: *Euonymus alatas*

Burro's Tail: *Sedum morganianum*

Bush Cinquefoil: *Potentilla fruticosa*

Buttercup: *Ranunculus*

Butterfly Bush: *Buddleia davidii*

Butterfly Flower: *Schizanthus × wisetonensis*

Butterfly Iris: *Moraea iridoides*

Butterfly Weed: *Asclepias tuberosa*

Button Fern: *Pellaea rotundifolia*

Busy Lizzie: *Impatiens wallerana*

C

California Poppy: *Eschscholzia californica*

California Privet: *Ligustrum ovalifolium*

Calla Lilly: *Zantedeschia aethiopica*

Callery Pear: *Pyrus calleryana*

Calliopsis: *Coreopsis tinctoria*

Camass: *Camassia*

Camellia: *Camellia japonica*

Camphor Tree: *Cinnamomum camphora*

Canadian Or Eastern Hemlock: *Tsuga canadensis*

Canary Island Pine: *Pinus canariensis*

Cannas: *Canna*

Canoe Cedar: *Thuja plicata*

Canterbury Bells: *Campanula medium*

Cape Marigold: *Dimorphotheca sinuata*

Cape Primrose: *Streptocarpus* species

Caraway: *Carum carvi*

Cardinal Flower: *Lobelia cardinalis*

Carnation: *Dianthus caryophyllus*

Carob: *Ceratonia siliqua*

Carolina Hemlock: *Tsuga caroliniana*

Carolina Jasmine: *Gelsemium sempervirens*

Carolina Silverbell: *Halesia carolina*

Carpathian Harebell: *Campanula carpatica*

Carpet Bugle: *Ajuga reptans*

Cast-iron Plant: *Aspidistra elatior*

Catnip: *Nepeta cataria*

Caucasian Wormwood: *Artemisia caucasica*

Cedar: *Cedrus*

Cedar Of Lebanon: *Cedrus libani*

Centipede Grass: *Eremochloa ophiuroides*

Century Plant: *Agave americana*

Chamomile: *Chamaemelum nobile*

Checkerberry: *Gaultheria procumbens*

Cherry Laurel: *Prunus caroliniana*

Cherry Pie: *Heliotropium arborescens*

Cherry Plum: *Prunus cerasifera*

Chervil: *Anthriscus cerefolium*

China Aster: *Callistephus chinensis*

China Pink: *Dianthus chinensis*

Chinaberry: *Melia azedarach*

Chinese Elm: *Ulmus parvifolia*

Chinese Evergreen: *Aglaonema modestum*

Chinese Forget-me-not: *Cynoglossum amabile*

Chinese Hibiscus: *Hibiscus rosa-sinensis*

Chinese Holly: *Ilex cornuta*

Chinese Juniper: *Juniperus chinensis*

Chinese Lantern: *Abutilon hybridum*

Chinese Lilac: *Syringa × chinensis*

Chinese Parsley: *Coriandrum sativum*

Chinese Photinia: *Photinia serrulata*

Chinese Pieris: *Pieris forrestii*

Chinese Snowball Virburnum: *Viburnum macrocephalum*

Chinese Sweet Gum: *Liquidambar formosana*

Chinese Witch Hazel: *Hamamelis mollis*

Chokeberry: *Prunus virginiana*

Christmas Cactus: *Schlumbergera bridgesii*

Christmas Rose: *Helleborus niger*

Cider Gum: *Eucalyptus gunnii*

Cigar Tree: *Catalpa bignonioides*

Cilantro: *Coriander*

Cinquefoil: *Potentilla*

Cinquefoil: *Potentilla fruticosa*

Climbing Lily: *Gloriosa rothschildiana*

Clock Vine: *Thunbergia alata*

Cloudland Rhododendron: *Rhododendron impeditum*

Coast Live Oak: *Quercus agrifolia*

Coast Redwood: *Sequoia sempervirens*

Cockscomb: *Celosia cristata*

Cockspur Thorn: *Crataegus crus-galli*

Coleus: *Coleus × hybridus*

Colorado Spruce: *Picea pungens*

Columbine: *Aquilegia*

Columbine Meadowrue: *Thalictrum aquilegifolium*

Comfrey: *Symphytum officinale*

Common Bald Cypress: *Taxodium distichum*

Cootamunda Wattle: *Acacia baileyana*

Coral-bells: *Heuchera sanguine*

Coriander: *Coriandrum sativum*

Corn Plant: *Dracaena fragrans*

Cornish Heath: *Erica vagans*

Corsican Hellebore: *Helleborus lividus corsicus*

Corsican Mint: *Mentha requienii*

Coyote Bush: *Baccharis pilularis*

Cottage Pink: *Dianthus plumarius*

Cottonwood: *Populus deltoides*

Crabapple: *Malus* species

Cranberry Cotoneaster: *Cotoneaster apiculatus*

Crape Myrtle: *Lagerstroemia*

Creeping Bent Grass: *Agrostis palustris*

Creeping Charlie: *Pilea nummularifolia*

Creeping Fig: *Ficus pumila*

Creeping Gardenia: *Gardenia jasminoides* 'Prostrata'

Creeping Juniper: *Juniperus horizontalis*

Creeping Lilyturf: *Liriope spicata*

Creeping Mahonia: *Mahonia repens*

Creeping Red Fescue: *Festuca rubra*

Creeping Thyme: *Thymus serpyllum*

Crested Iris: *Iris cristata*

Crocus: *Crocus* species

Croton: *Codiaeum variegatum*

Crown Imperial: *Fritillaria imperialis*

Crown Of Thorns: *Euphorbia milii*

Cucumber Tree: *Magnolia acuminata*

Cup Flower: *Nierembergia hippomanica*

Cussick Camass: *Camassia cusickii*

Cutleaf Japanese Maple: *Acer palmatum dissectum*

Cyclamen: *Cyclamen persicum*

Cypress: *Cupressus*

D

Daffodil: *Narcissus*

Dahlberg Daisy: *Dyssodia tenuiloba*

Daisy: *Chrysanthemum*

Danford Iris: *Iris danfordiae*

Darwin Barberry: *Berberis darwinii*

Dawn Redwood: *Metasequoia glyptostroboides*

Daylily: *Hemerocallis* hybrids

Delphinium: *Delphinium elatum*

Delphinium: *Consolida ambigua*

Deodar Cedar: *Cedrus deodara*

Devil's Ivy: *Epipremnum aureum*

Devilwood Osmanthus: *Osmanthus americanus*

Dichondra: *Dichondra micrantha*

Dogwood: *Cornus florida*

Donkey's Tail: *Sedum morganianum*

Douglas Fir: *Pseudotsuga menziesii*

Drooping Leucothoe: *Leucothoe fontanesiana*

Dumb Cane: *Dieffenbachia* species

Dusty Miller: *Senecio cineraria*

Dwarf Alberta Spruce: *Picea glauca* 'Conica'

Dwarf Blue Fescue: *Festuca ovina* 'Glauca'

Dwarf Flowering Almond: *Prunus glandulosa*

Dwarf Morning Glory: *Convolvulus tricolor*

E

Easter Cactus: *Schlumbergera bridgesii*

Eastern Poplar: *Populus deltoides*

Eastern Red-cedar: *Juniperus virginiana*

Eastern Redbud: *Cercis canadensis*

Edging Lobelia: *Lobelia erinus*

Empress Tree: *Paulownia tomentosa*

English Hawthorn: *Crataegus laevigata*

English Holly: *Ilex aquifolium*

English Ivy: *Hedera helix*

English Laurel: *Prunus laurocerasus*

English Lavender: *Lavandula spica*

English Lavender: *Lavandula angustifolia*

English Oak: *Quercus robur*

English Primrose: *Primula vulgaris*

English Yew: *Taxus baccata*

Eucalyptus: *Eucalyptus cinerea*

European Alder: *Alnus glutinosa*

European Ash: *Fraxinus excelsior*

European Beech: *Fagus sylvatica*

European Cranberry Bush: *Viburnum opulus*

European Hackberry: *Celtis australis*

European Hornbeam: *Carpinus betulus*

European Linden: *Tilia* × *europaea*

European White Birch: *Betula pendula*

Evergreen Candytuft: *Iberis sempervirens*

Evergreen Pear: *Pyrus kawakamii*

Everlasting: *Helichrysum bracteatum*

F

False Aralia: *Dizygotheca elegantissima*

False Spiraea: *Astilbe*

Fancy-leaved Caladium: *Caladium* × *hortulanum*

Father Hugo Rose: *Rosa hugonis*

Fawn-lily: *Erythronium* species

Fescue: *Festuca*

Feverfew: *Chrysanthemum parthenium*

Fibrous-rooted Begonia: *Begonia* × *semperflorens-cultorum*

Fiddle-leaf Philodendron: *Philodendron bipinnatifidum*

Fiddleleaf Fig: *Ficus lyrata*

Field Poppy: *Papaver rhoeas*

Fig: *Ficus*

Filbert: *Corylus*

Filbert: *Corylus maxima*

Fir: *Abies*

Firethorn: *Pyracantha*

Five-finger Fern: *Adiantum pedatum*

Five-leaf Akebia: *Akebia quinata*

Five-stamen Tamarisk: *Tamarix ramosissima*

Flame Violet: *Episcia cupreata*

Flameleaf Sumac: *Rhus copallina*

Flaming Katy: *Kalanchoe blossfeldiana*

Florist's Cyclamen: *Cyclamen persicum*

Florist's Eucalyptus: *Eucalyptus cinerea*

Flowering Almond: *Prunus triloba*

Flowering Ash: *Fraxinus ornus*

Flowering Cherry: *Prunus serrulata*

Flowering Crabapple: *Malus floribunda*

Flowering Dogwood: *Cornus florida*

Flowering Gum: *Eucalyptus ficifolia*

Flowering Kale: *Brassica oleracea acephala*

Flowering Quince: *Chaenomeles speciosa*

Flowering Spurge: *Euphorbia corollata*

Flowering Tobacco: *Nicotiana alata*

Forget-me-not: *Myosotis sylvatica*

Fortnight Lily: *Moraea iridoides*

Foster Tulip: *Tulipa fosterana*

Fountain Grass: *Pennisetum alopecuroides*

Four O'clock: *Mirabilis jalapa*

Foxglove: *Digitalis purpurea*

Fragrant Plantain Lily: *Hosta plantaginea*

Fragrant Viburnum: *Viburnum farreri*

Franklinia: *Franklinia alatamaha*

Fraser Photinia: *Photinia* × *fraseri*

Freesia: *Freesia refracta*

French Marigold: *Tagetes patula*

Friendship Plant: *Billbergia nutans*

Fritillary: *Fritillaria*

Fruitless Mulberry: *Morus alba*

Fuchsia: *Fuchsia* × *hybrida*

G

Gable Hybrids Azalea: *Rhododendron*, Gable hybrids

Garden Chamomile: *Chamaemelum nobile*

Gardenia: *Gardenia jasminoides*

Garland Flower: *Daphne cneorum*

Gas Plant: *Dictamnus albus*

Geranium: *Pelargonium* × *hortorum*

Giant Arborvitae: *Thuja plicata*
Giant Onion: *Allium giganteum*
Giant Redwood: *Sequoiadendron giganteum*
Gladiolus: *Gladiolus hybridus*
Globe Amaranth: *Gomphrena globosa*
Globe Flower: *Trollius europaeus*
Globe Thistle: *Echinops exaltatus*
Gloriosa Daisy: *Rudbeckia hirta* var. *pulcherrima*
Glory Lily: *Gloriosa rothschildiana*
Glory-of-the-snow: *Chionodoxa luciliae*
Glossy Abelia: *Abelia* × *grandiflora*
Glossy Privet: *Ligustrum lucidum*
Gloxinia: *Sinningia speciosa*
Godetia: *Clarkia* hybrids
Gold-moss Stonecrop: *Sedum acre*
Golden Calla: *Zantedeschia elliottiana*
Golden Fleece: *Dyssodia tenuiloba*
Golden Marguerite: *Anthemis tinctoria*
Golden Polypody Fern: *Polypodium aureum*
Golden-chain Tree: *Laburnum* × *watereri* 'Vossii'
Goldenrain Tree: *Koelreuteria paniculata*
Goldenrod: *Solidago* hybrids
Goldentuft: *Aurinia saxatilis*
Goldflower St. Johnswort: *Hypericum* × *moseranum*
Good King Henry: *Chenopodium bonus-henricus*
Gooseneck Loosestrife: *Lysimachia clethroides*
Grape Hyacinth: *Muscari botryoides*
Grape Ivy: *Cissus rhombifolia*
Grecian Laurel: *Laurus nobilis*
Green Ash: *Fraxinus pennsylvanica*
Greig Tulip: *Tulipa greigii*

H
Hackberry: *Celtis*
Hardy Aster: *Aster* species and hybrids
Hardy Chrysanthemum: *Chrysanthemum* hybrids
Hardy Fuchsia: *Fuchsia magellanica*
Harvest Brodiaea: *Brodiaea coronaria*
Hawthorn: *Crataegus*
Heart-leaf Bergenia: *Bergenia cordifolia*
Heart-leaf Philodendron: *Philodendron scandens*
Heath: *Erica*

Heather: *Calluna vulgaris*
Heavenly Bamboo: *Nandina domestica*
Hedge Cotoneaster: *Cotoneaster lucidus*
Hedge Maple: *Acer campestre*
Heliotrope: *Heliotropium arborescens*
Hemlock: *Tsuga canadensis*
Hen And Chicks: *Sempervivum tectorum*
Herbaceous Peony: *Paeonia* hybrids
Hinoki False Cypress: *Chamaecyparis obtusa*
Holly: *Ilex*
Holly Olive: *Osmanthus heterophyllus*
Hollyhock: *Alcea rosea*
Hollyleaf Cherry: *Prunus ilicifolia*
Honeylocust: *Gleditsia*
Honeysuckle: *Lonicera*
Hophornbeam: *Ostrya virginiana*
Hornbeam: *Carpinus caroliniana*
Horse Chestnut: *Aesculus hippocastanum*
Houseleek: *Sempervivum tectorum*
Hyacinth: *Hyacinthus orientalis*
Hybrid Witch Hazel: *Hamamelis* × *intermedia*
Hydrangea: *Hydrangea macrophylla*

I
Iceland Poppy: *Papaver nudicaule*
Impatiens: *Impatiens wallerana*
Incense Cedar: *Calocedrus decurrens*
Inch Plant: *Tradescantia* species
Indian Bean: *Catalpa bignonioides*
Indian Strawberry: *Duchesnea indica*
Inkberry: *Ilex glabra*
Irish Moss: *Sagina subulata*
Iron Cross Begonia: *Begonia masoniana*
Italian Alder: *Alnus cordata*
Italian Alkanet: *Anchusa azurea*
Italian Buckthorn: *Rhamnus alaternus*
Italian Bugloss: *Anchusa azurea*
Italian Cypress: *Cupressus sempervirens*
Italian Grape Hyacinth: *Muscari botryoides*
Italian Ryegrass: *Lolium multiflorum*
Ivy: *Hedera*
Ivy Geranium: *Pelargonium peltatum*

J
Jaburan Lilyturf: *Ophiopogon jaburan*
Jade Plant: *Crassula argentea*
Jade Tree: *Crassula argentea*
Japanese Anemone: *Anemone* × *hybrida*
Japanese Aralia: *Fatsia japonica*
Japanese Aucuba: *Aucuba japonica*
Japanese Barberry: *Berberis thunbergii*
Japanese Black Pine: *Pinus thunbergiana*
Japanese Boxwood: *Buxus microphylla* var. *japonica*
Japanese Cedar: *Cryptomeria japonica*
Japanese Crape Myrtle: *Lagerstroemia fauriei*
Japanese Dogwood: *Cornus kousa*
Japanese Euonymus: *Euonymus japonica*
Japanese Flowering Cherry: *Prunus serrulata*
Japanese Flowering Crabapple: *Malus floribunda*
Japanese Garden Juniper: *Juniperus procumbens*
Japanese Holly: *Ilex crenata*
Japanese Holly Fern: *Cyrtomium falcatum*
Japanese Honeysuckle: *Lonicera japonica*
Japanese Iris: *Iris kaempferi*
Japanese Jasmine: *Jasminum mesnyi*
Japanese Kerria: *Kerria japonica*
Japanese Larch: *Larix kaempferi*
Japanese Maple: *Acer palmatum*
Japanese Pagoda Tree: *Sophora japonica*
Japanese Pieris: *Pieris japonica*
Japanese Pittosporum: *Pittosporum tobira*
Japanese Primrose: *Primula japonica*
Japanese Privet: *Ligustrum japonicum*
Japanese Quince: *Chaenomeles japonica*
Japanese Red Pine: *Pinus densiflora*
Japanese Rose: *Rosa multiflora*
Japanese Skimmia: *Skimmia japonica*
Japanese Snowbell: *Styrax japonicus*
Japanese Spirea: *Spiraea japonica*
Japanese Spurge: *Pachysandra terminalis*
Japanese Tree Lilac: *Syringa reticulata*
Japanese White Pine: *Pinus parviflora*
Japanese Witch Hazel: *Hamamelis japonica*
Japanese Yew: *Taxus cuspidata*

Japanese Zelkova: *Zelkova serrata*
Jasmine: *Jasminum*
Johnny-jump-up: *Viola tricolor*
Jonquil: *Narcissus jonquilla*
Juneberry: *Amelanchier arborea*
Juniper: *Juniperus*

K

Kaffir Lily: *Clivia miniata*
Kaffirboom Coral Tree: *Erythrina caffra*
Kale: *Brassica oleracea acephala*
Kangaroo Vine: *Cissus antarctica*
Kashgar Tamarisk: *Tamarix hispida*
Katsura Tree: *Cercidiphyllum japonicum*
Kentia Palm: *Howea forsterana*
Kentucky Bluegrass: *Poa pratensis*
Kinnikinick: *Arctostaphylos uva-ursi*
Kirk's Coprosma: *Coprosma × kirkii*
Korean Barberry: *Berberis koreana*
Korean Grass: *Zoysia tenuifolia*
Korean Lilac: *Syringa oblata*
Korean Mountain Ash: *Sorbus alnifolia*
Korean-spice Viburnum: *Viburnum carlesii*
Kousa Dogwood: *Cornus kousa*
Kumquat: *Fortunella* species

L

Laceleaf Japanese Maple: *Acer palmatum dissectum*
Lady Banks Rose: *Rosa banksiae*
Lamb's Ear: *Stachys byzantina*
Lantana: *Lantana montevidensis*
Larch: *Larix*
Large Fothergilla: *Fothergilla major*
Larkspur: *Consolida*
Late Lilac: *Syringa villosa*
Laurel Bay: *Laurus nobilis*
Lavalle Hawthorn: *Crataegus × lavallei*
Lawson Cypress: *Chamaecyparis lawsoniana*
Leatherleaf Mahonia: *Mahonia bealei*
Leichtlin Camass: *Camassia leichtlinii*
Lemon Balm: *Melissa officinalis*
Lemon Bottlebrush: *Callistemon citrinus*
Lemon Verbena: *Aloysia triphylla*
Leyland Cypress: *× Cupressocyparis leylandii*
Lily: *Lilium*

Lily Magnolia: *Magnolia quinquepeta*
Lily-of-the-Nile: *Agapanthus africanus*
Lily-of-the-valley: *Convallaria majalis*
Lilyturf: *Liriope*
Lippia: *Phyla nodiflora*
Lipstick Plant: *Aeschynanthus speciosus*
Littleleaf Linden: *Tilia cordata*
Live Oak: *Quercus virginiana*
Loblolly Pine: *Pinus taeda*
Lombardy Poplar: *Populus nigra 'Italica'*
London Plane Tree: *Platanus × acerifolia*
Longleaf Pine: *Pinus palustris*
Loquat: *Eriobotrya japonica*
Love-in-a-mist: *Nigella damascena*

M

Madagascar Periwinkle: *Catharanthus roseus*
Madonna Lily: *Lilium candidum*
Madrona: *Arbutus menziesii*
Madrone: *Arbutus menziesii*
Magic Flower: *Achimenes*
Maidenhair Fern: *Adiantum pedatum*
Maidenhair Tree: *Ginkgo biloba*
Maltese Cross: *Lychnis chalcedonica*
Manchu Cherry: *Prunus tomentosa*
Manchurian Lilac: *Syringa patula*
Manzanita: *Arctostaphylos*
Maple: *Acer*
Marigold: *Tagetes patula*
Marsh Marigold: *Caltha palustris*
Marvel Of Peru: *Mirabilis jalapa*
Mascarene Grass: *Zoysia tenuifolia*
Matricaria: *Chrysanthemum parthenium*
Maytens Tree: *Maytenus boaria*
Mexican Aster: *Cosmos bipinnatus*
Mexican Orange: *Choisya ternata*
Mexican Sunflower: *Tithonia rotundifolia*
Michaelmas Daisy: *Aster* species and hybrids
Mimosa: *Albizia julibrissin*
Mirror Plant: *Coprosma repens*
Mock Orange: *Philadelphus coronarius*
Mock Strawberry: *Duchesnea indica*
Modesto Ash: *Fraxinus velutina 'Modesto'*
Mollis Hybrid Azaleas: *Rhododendron × kosteranum*

Monarch Birch: *Betula maximowicziana*
Mondo Grass: *Ophiopogon japonicus*
Moneywort: *Lysimachia nummularia*
Monkey Flower: *Mimulus × hybridus 'Grandiflorus'*
Monterey Cypress: *Cupressus macrocarpa*
Monterey Pine: *Pinus radiata*
Moonflower Vine: *Ipomoea alba*
Morning-glory Vine: *Ipomoea tricolor*
Mosaic Plant: *Fittonia verschaffeltii var. argyroneura*
Moses-in-the-cradle: *Rhoeo spathacea*
Moss Pink: *Phlox subulata*
Moss Sandwort: *Arenaria verna*
Mossy Stonecrop: *Sedum acre*
Mother-in-law's Tongue: *Sansevieria trifasciata*
Mother-of-thousands: *Tolmiea menziesii*
Mountain Laurel: *Kalmia latifolia*
Mugo Pine: *Pinus mugo var. mugo*
Myrtle: *Myrtus communis*

N

Naked Lady: *Amaryllis belladonna*
Nanking Cherry: *Prunus tomentosa*
Naples Onion: *Allium neapolitanum*
Nasturtium: *Tropaeolum majus*
Natal Plum: *Carissa grandiflora*
Neapolitan Cyclamen: *Cyclamen hederifolium*
Nerve Plant: *Fittonia verschaffeltii*
Netted Iris: *Iris reticulata*
Noble Fir: *Abies procera*
Nordmann Fir: *Abies nordmanniana*
Norfolk Island Pine: *Araucaria heterophylla*
Northern Bayberry: *Myrica pennsylvanica*
Northern Catalpa: *Catalpa speciosa*
Norway Maple: *Acer platanoides*
Norway Pine: *Pinus resinosa*
Norway Spruce: *Picea abies*
Notchleaf Sea Lavender: *Limonium sinuatum*

O

Oak Leaf Ivy: *Rhoicissus capensis*
Oakleaf Hydrangea: *Hydrangea quercifolia*
Old-fashioned Weigela: *Weigela florida*
Oleander: *Nerium oleander*

Olive: *Olea europaea*
Orchid Tree: *Bauhinia variegata*
Oregano: *Origanum vulgare*
Oregon Boxwood: *Paxistima myrsinites*
Oregon Grape: *Mahonia aquifolium*
Oriental persimmon: *Diospyros kaki*
Oriental Poppy: *Papaver orientale*
Ornamental Cabbage: *Brassica oleracea acephala*
Ornamental Pepper: *Capsicum annuum*
Osage Orange: *Maclura pomifera*
Oswego Tea: *Monarda didyma*

P Q

Pagoda Dogwood: *Cornus alternifolia*
Painted Daisy: *Chrysanthemum coccineum*
Painted Tongue: *Salpiglossis sinuata*
Pampas Grass: *Cortaderia selloana*
Pansy: *Viola × wittrockiana*
Paper Birch: *Betula papyrifera*
Parlor Maple: *Abutilon pictum*
Parlor Palm: *Chamaedorea elegans*
Parrot's-beak: *Lotus berthelotii*
Paulownia: *Paulownia tomentosa*
Peace Lily: *Spathiphyllum* species
Pelaragonium: *Pelargonium domesticum*
Pepperidge: *Nyssa sylvatica*
Peppermint: *Mentha × piperita*
Perennial Ryegrass: *Lolium perenne*
Perennial Salvia: *Salvia × superba*
Periwinkle: *Vinca*
Persian Buttercup: *Ranunculus asiaticus*
Persian Lilac: *Syringa × persica*
Peruvian Verbena: *Verbena peruviana*
Petticoat Daffodil: *Narcissus bulbocodium*
Petunia: *Petunia × hybrida*
Phlox: *Phlox paniculata*
Photinia: *Photinia × fraseri*
Piggyback Plant: *Tolmiea menziesii*
Pin Oak: *Quercus palustris*
Pincushion Flower: *Scabiosa caucasica*
Pink: *Dianthus*
Pink Clover Blossom: *Polygonum capitatum*
Pinkshell Azalea: *Rhododendron vaseyi*
Pistache: *Pistacia chinensis*

Pittosporum: *Pittosporum tobira*
Plane Tree: *Platanus × acerifolia*
Plantain Lily: *Hosta*
Plume Celosia: *Celosia cristata*
Poinsettia: *Euphorbia pulcherrima*
Polyantha Primrose: *Primula × polyantha*
Polyanthus Narcissus: *Narcissus tazetta*
Pomegranate: *Punica granatum*
Poor Man's Orchid: *Schizanthus × wisetonensis*
Poplar: *Populus*
Poppy: *Papaver*
Poppy Anemone: *Anemone coronaria*
Port Orford Cedar: *Chamaecyparis lawsoniana*
Possum Oak: *Quercus nigra*
Possumhaw Holly: *Ilex decidua*
Pot Marigold: *Calendula officinalis*
Pothos: *Epipremnum aureum*
Prayer Plant: *Maranta leuconeura*
Primrose: *Primula*
Primrose Jasmine: *Jasminum mesnyi*
Privet: *Ligustrum*
Privet Honeysuckle: *Lonicera pileata*
Purple Loosestrife: *Lythrum salicaria*
Purple-coneflower: *Echinacea purpurea*
Pussy Willow: *Salix discolor*
Pygmy Date Palm: *Phoenix roebelenii*
Pyrethrum: *Chrysanthemum coccineum*
Queen's Tears: *Billbergia nutans*

R

Rabbit's Foot Fern: *Polypodium aureum*
Ramanas Rose: *Rosa rugosa*
Red Alder: *Alnus rubra*
Red Ash: *Fraxinus pennsylvanica*
Red Buckeye: *Aesculus pavia*
Red Cedar: *Thuja plicata*
Red Chokeberry: *Aronia arbutifolia*
Red Escallonia: *Escallonia rubra*
Red Fescue: *Festuca rubra*
Red Horsechestnut: *Aesculus × carnea*
Red Maple: *Acer rubrum*
Red Margined Dracaena: *Dracaena marginata*
Red Oak: *Quercus rubra*
Red Pine: *Pinus resinosa*
Red-hot Poker: *Kniphofia uvaria*

Red-osier Dogwood: *Cornus sericea*
Redwood: *Sequoia sempervirens*
Rex Begonia: *Begonia × rex-cultorum*
River Birch: *Betula nigra*
Rock Cotoneaster: *Cotoneaster horizontalis*
Rock Cress: *Arabis caucasica*
Rock Maple: *Acer saccharum*
Rock Rose: *Cistus* species
Rocket Candytuft: *Iberis amara*
Rocket Larkspur: *Consolida ambigua*
Rocky Mountain Juniper: *Juniperus scopulorum*
Rosary Vine: *Ceropegia woodii*
Rose: *Rosa*
Rose Daphne: *Daphne cneorum*
Rose Moss: *Portulaca grandiflora*
Rose Of Sharon: *Hibiscus syriacus*
Royal Paulownia: *Paulownia tomentosa*
Rubber Plant: *Ficus elastica*
Russell Lupines: *Lupinus, Russell* hybrids
Ryegrass: *Lolium multiflorum*

S

Sand Strawberry: *Fragaria chiloensis*
Sapphireberry: *Symplocos paniculata*
Sargent Cherry: *Prunus sargentii*
Sargent Crabapple: *Malus sargentii*
Sargent's Weeping Hemlock: *Tsuga canadensis* 'Pendula'
Sasanqua Camellia: *Camellia sasanqua*
Sassafras: *Sassafras albidum*
Saucer Magnolia: *Magnolia soulangiana*
Scarlet Oak: *Quercus coccinea*
Scarlet Sage: *Salvia splendens*
Scented Geraniums: *Pelargonium* species
Schefflera: *Brassaia actinophylla*
Scotch Broom: *Cytisus scoparius*
Scotch Heather: *Calluna vulgaris*
Scotch Pine: *Pinus sylvestris*
Scotch Pink: *Dianthus plumarius*
Sea Pink: *Armeria maritima*
Sea Thrift: *Armeria maritima*
Sea Tomato: *Rosa rugosa*
Serbian Bellflower: *Campanula poscharskyana*
Serviceberry: *Amelanchier arborea*
Shadblow: *Amelanchier arborea*
Shadbush: *Amelanchier arborea*

Shasta Daisy: *Chrysanthemum × superbum*
She-oak: *Casuarina cunninghamia*
Shell Flower: *Tigridia pavonia*
Shining Sumac: *Rhus copallina*
Shiny Xylosma: *Xylosma congestum*
Shirley Poppy: *Papaver rhoeas*
Shore Juniper: *Juniperus conferta*
Showy Deutzia: *Deutzia × magnifica*
Showy Sedum: *Sedum spectabile*
Showy Stonecrop: *Sedum spectabile*
Shrub Althea: *Hibiscus syriacus*
Siberian Bugloss: *Brunnera macrophylla*
Siberian Crabapple: *Malus baccata*
Siberian Dogwood: *Cornus alba 'Sibirica'*
Siberian Elm: *Ulmus pumila*
Siberian Iris: *Iris sibirica*
Siberian Squill: *Scilla siberica*
Silk Tree: *Albizia julibrissin*
Silkworm Mulberry: *Morus alba*
Silver Dollar Eucalyptus: *Eucalyptus polyanthemos*
Silver Maple: *Acer saccharinum*
Silverberry: *Elaeagnus pungens*
Slender Deutzia: *Deutzia gracilis*
Small Himalayan Sarcococca: *Sarcococca hookeriana humilis*
Small-leaved Cotoneaster: *Cotoneaster microphyllus*
Smoke Tree: *Cotinus coggygria*
Smooth Arizona Cypress: *Cupressus glabra*
Smooth Sumac: *Rhus glabra*
Snake Plant: *Sansevieria trifasciata*
Snapdragon: *Antirrhinum majus*
Sneezeweed: *Helenium autumnale*
Snow-in-summer: *Cerastium tomentosum*
Snow-on-the-mountain: *Euphorbia marginata*
Snowball: *Viburnum opulus*
Snowdrop: *Galanthus*
Snowflake: *Leucojum*
Soft Maple: *Acer saccharinum*
Sour Gum: *Nyssa sylvatica*
Solomon's Seal: *Polygonatum commutatum*
Sourwood: *Oxydendrum arboreum*
Southern Bush Honeysuckle: *Diervilla sessilifolia*
Southern Catalpa: *Catalpa bignonioides*

Southern Indica Hybrid Azaleas: *Rhododendron*
Southern Live Oak: *Quercus virginiana*
Southern Magnolia: *Magnolia grandiflora*
Southernwood: *Artemisia abrotanum*
Spanish Broom: *Genista hispanica*
Spanish Gorse: *Genista hispanica*
Spathe Flower: *Spathiphyllum* species
Spearmint: *Mentha spicata*
Speedwell: *Veronica*
Spider Flower: *Cleome hasslerana*
Spider Plant: *Chlorophytum comosum*
Spider-lily: *Hymenocallis narcissiflora*
Spiderwort: *Tradescantia virginiana*
Spike Speedwell: *Veronica spicata*
Spike Winter Hazel: *Corylopsis spicata*
Split-leaf Philodendron: *Monstera deliciosa*
Sprenger Asparagus: *Asparagus densiflorus 'Sprengeri'*
Spring Cinquefoil: *Potentilla verna*
Spring Heath: *Erica carnea*
Spring Meadow Saffron: *Bulbocodium vernum*
Spring Snowflake: *Leucojum vernum*
Spruce: *Picea*
Spruce Pine: *Pinus glabra*
Spurge: *Euphorbia corollata*
Squill: *Scilla*
Squirrel's Foot Fern: *Davallia mariesii*
St. Augustine Grass: *Stenotaphrum secundatum*
St. John's Bread: *Ceratonia siliqua*
St. Johnswort: *Hypericum calycinum*
Staghorn Fern: *Platycerium bifurcatum*
Star Jasmine: *Trachelospermum jasminoides*
Star Magnolia: *Magnolia stellata*
Star-of-Bethlehem: *Ornithogalum umbellatum*
Star-of-Bethlehem: *Ornithogalum arabicum*
Statice: *Limonium sinuatum*
Stock: *Matthiola incana*
Stokes's Aster: *Stokesia laevis*
Stonecrop: *Sedum*
Strawberry Shrub: *Calycanthus floridus*
Strawberry Tree: *Arbutus unedo*
Strawflower: *Helichrysum bracteatum*

String-of-beads: *Senecio Rowleyanus*
String-of-hearts: *Ceropegia woodii*
Sugar Maple: *Acer saccharum*
Sumac: *Rhus*
Summer Phlox: *Phlox paniculata*
Summer Snowflake: *Leucojum aestivum*
Sun Rose: *Helianthemum nummularium*
Sunflower: *Helianthus annuus*
Swamp Azalea: *Rhododendron viscosum*
Swamp Maple: *Acer rubrum*
Swamp White Oak: *Quercus bicolor*
Swan River Daisy: *Brachycome iberidifolia*
Swedish Ivy: *Plectranthus australis*
Sweet Alyssum: *Lobularia maritima*
Sweet Azalea: *Rhododendron arborescens*
Sweet Basil: *Ocimum basilicum 'Dark Opal'*
Sweet Bay: *Laurus nobilis*
Sweet Gum: *Liquidambar styraciflua*
Sweet Marjoram: *Origanum majorana*
Sweet Mock Orange: *Philadelphus coronarius*
Sweet Orange: *Citrus sinensis*
Sweet Pea: *Lathyrus odoratus*
Sweet Violet: *Viola odorata*
Sweet William: *Dianthus barbatus*
Sweetbay Magnolia: *Magnolia virginiana*
Sword Fern: *Polystichum munitum*
Sweet Olive: *Osmanthus fragrans*

T
Tall Bearded Iris: *Iris × germanica*
Tall Fescue: *Festuca arundinacea*
Tamarisk: *Tamarix*
Tansy: *Tanacetum vulgare*
Tarragon: *Artemisia dracunculus*
Tartarian Honeysuckle: *Lonicera tatarica*
Tea Rose: *Rosa odorata*
Tea Tree: *Leptospermum laevigatum*
Teaberry: *Gaultheria procumbens*
Thornless Honeylocust: *Gleditsia triacanthos* var. *inermis*
Tiger Flower: *Tigridia pavonia*
Tobacco: *Nicotiana alata*
Tobira: *Pittosporum tobira*
Torch Lily: *Kniphofia uvaria*
Trailing African Daisy: *Osteospermum fruiticosum*

Trailing Lantana: *Lantana montevidensis*
Trailing Verbena: *Verbena peruviana*
Transvaal Daisy: *Gerbera jamesonii*
Treasure Flower: *Gazania rigens*
Tree Heath: *Erica arborea*
Tree Mallow: *Lavatera* hybrids
Tree Peony: *Paeonia suffruticosa*
Trident Maple: *Acer buergeranum*
Tuberose: *Polianthes tuberosa*
Tuberous Begonia: *Begonia* × *tuberhybrida*
Tufted Hair Grass: *Deschampsia caespitosa*
Tulip: *Tulipa*
Tulip Poplar: *Liriodendron tulipifera*
Tulip Tree: *Liriodendron tulipifera*
Turban Buttercup: *Ranunculus asiaticus*
Turf-type Perennial Ryegrass: *Lolium perenne*
Turkestan Onion: *Allium karataviense*
Twice-cut Philodendron: *Philodendron bipinnatifidum*

U, V

Umbrella Tree: *Brassaia actinophylla*
Urn Plant: *Aechmea fasciata*
Vanhoutte Spirea: *Spiraea* × *vanhouttei*
Variegated Bulbous Oatgrass: *Arrhenatherum elatius* 'Variegatum'
Varnish Tree: *Koelreuteria paniculata*
Velvet Plant: *Gynura aurantiaca*
Verbena: *Verbena* × *hybrida*
Vernal Witch Hazel: *Hamamelis vernalis*
Victorian Box: *Pittosporum undulatum*
Vine Hill Manzanita: *Arctosyaphylos densiflora*
Viola: *Viola* × *wittrockiana*
Violet: *Viola*
Virginia Bluebells: *Mertensia virginica*
Virginia Creeper: *Parthenocissus quinquefolia*
Virginia Pine: *Pinus virginiana*
Virginia Rose: *Rosa virginiana*
Virginia Sweetspire: *Itea virginica*
Virginia Willow: *Itea virginica*

W

Wall Rock Cress: *Arabis caucasica*
Wallflower: *Cheiranthus cheiri*
Walnut: *Juglans*
Wandering Jew: *Tradescantia* species
Warminster Broom: *Cytisus* × *praecox*
Washington Thorn: *Crataegus phaenopyrum*
Water Flag Iris: *Iris pseudacorus*
Water Oak: *Quercus nigra*
Waterlily Tulip: *Tulipa kaufmanniana*
Watermelon Pilea: *Pilea cadierei*
Wavy-leaf Plantain Lily: *Hosta undulata*
Wax Begonia: *Begonia* × *semperflorens-cultorum*
Wax Flower: *Hoya bella*
Weeping Fig: *Ficus benjamina*
Weeping Willow: *Salix babylonica*
Weigela: *Weigela florida*
Western Catalpa: *Catalpa speciosa*
Western Red Cedar: *Thuja plicata*
Western Sword Fern: *Polystichum munitum*
White Alder: *Alnus rhombifolia*
White Birch: *Betula pendula*
White Cedar: *Thuja occidentalis*
White Fir: *Abies concolor*
White Fringetree: *Chionanthus virginicus*
White Lilyturf: *Ophiopogon jaburan*
White Mulberry: *Morus alba*
White Oak: *Quercus alba*
White Pine: *Pinus strobus*
White Poplar: *Populus alba*
White Spruce: *Picea glauca*
Wild Ginger: *Asarum*
Wild Lilac: *Ceanothus* species
Wild Strawberry: *Fragaria chiloensis*
Willow Oak: *Quercus phellos*
Willowleaf Cotoneaster: *Cotoneaster salicifolius*
Winged Euonymus: *Euonymus alatas*
Winter Aconite: *Eranthis hyemalis*
Winter Daphne: *Daphne odora*
Winter Honeysuckle: *Lonicera fragrantissima*
Winter-blooming Bergenia: *Bergenia crassifolia*
Winterberry: *Ilex verticillata*
Wintercreeper Euonymus: *Euonymus fortunei*

Wintergreen: *Gaultheria procumbens*
Wintergreen Barberry: *Berberis julianae*
Wintersweet: *Chimonanthus praecox*
Wishbone Flower: *Torenia fournieri*
Witch Hazel: *Hamamelis*
Woadwaxen: *Genista tinctoria*
Wood Hyacinth: *Scilla nonscripta*
Woodbine: *Parthenocissus quinquefolia*
Woolly Speedwell: *Veronica incana*
Woolly Thyme: *Thymus pseudolanuginosus*
Wooly Betony: *Stachys byzantina*

Y

Yarrow: *Achillea millefolium*
Yaupon Holly: *Ilex vomitoria*
Yellow Loosestrife: *Lysimachia punctata*
Yellow Onion: *Allium flavum*
Yellow Poplar: *Liriodendron tulipifera*
Yellow Spider: *Lycoris aurea*
Yellowwood: *Cladrastis lutea*
Yew: *Taxus*
Yew Pine: *Podocarpus macrophyllus*

Z

Zebra Plant: *Cryptanthus zonatus*
Zebra Plant: *Aphelandra squarrosa*
Zebra Plant: *Calathea zebrina*
Zephyr-lily: *Zephyranthes candida*
Zinnia: *Zinnia elegans*
Zoysia Grass: *Zoysia* species

NAME	HABIT		FLOWERS		ADAPTATION	
	Type	Height	Color	Time	Zones	Light
Abelia × grandiflora Glossy Abelia	Evergreen shrub	4 to 8 ft	White	Early summer to first frost	6 to 10	Full sun to light shade
Abies concolor White Fir	Needled evergreen tree	80 to 100 ft			4 to 7	Full sun
Abies nordmanniana Nordmann Fir	Needled evergreen tree	55 to 65 ft			5 to 7	Full sun
Abies procera Noble Fir	Needled evergreen tree	100 to 150 ft			5 to 7	Full sun
Abutilon hybridum Chinese Lantern	Houseplant	to 5 ft	Pink, red, yellow, white	All year	10 or IN	Half-day sun
Abutilon pictum 'Thompsonii'	Houseplant	15 in	Orange	All year	10 or IN	Half-day sun
Acacia baileyana Bailey Acacia, Cootamundra Wattle	Evergreen tree	to 20 ft	Yellow	Winter	8 to 10	Full sun
Acacia melanoxylon Blackwood Acacia	Evergreen tree	to 40 ft	White	Spring	9 to 10	Full sun
Acanthus mollis Bear's-Breeches	Tender perennial	2 to 3 ft	White, lavender, pink	Spring	8 to 10	Light shade
Acer campestre Hedge Maple	Deciduous tree	25 to 40 ft			5 to 8	Full sun
Acer ginnala Amur Maple	Deciduous tree	to 20 ft	Yellow, cream-colored	Spring	4 to 8	Full sun
Acer palmatum dissectum Laceleaf Japanese Maple, Cutleaf Japanese Maple	Deciduous shrub	6 to 8 ft			6 to 9	Light shade
Acer palmatum Japanese Maple	Deciduous tree	15 to 25 ft			6 to 9	Full sun to light shade
Acer platanoides Norway Maple	Deciduous tree	40 to 50 ft	Yellow	Spring	4 to 7	Full sun
Acer rubrum Red Maple, Swamp Maple	Deciduous tree	50 to 60 ft	Red	Spring	3 to 9	Full sun
Acer saccharinum Silver Maple, Soft Maple	Deciduous tree	to 70 ft			3 to 8	Full sun

For a list of common names, see page 378.

| | CULTURE | | |
Soil	Water	Feeding	Special Characteristics
Good drainage	Medium water	Medium feeder	Effective specimen plant or informal hedge; sometimes deciduous; can be sheared, but doing so reduces flowering; graceful, rounded habit; foliage turns bronze in winter; showy white flowers have pink tinge.
Good drainage	Medium water	Medium feeder	Needles blue-green, 2″ long; upright cylindrical cones; protect from high winds.
Good drainage	Medium water	Medium feeder	Slow-moderate growing; shiny, dark green needles with silver undersides; dense foliage; can be grown in container for several years.
Good drainage	Medium water	Medium feeder	Fast-growing; narrow tree with stiff branching habit; needles blue-green with silver underside; best in cool climate.
Good drainage	Medium water	Medium feeder	Fast-growing; tropical, woody shrub; large, bell-shaped flowers; prune back in winter to keep 18–30″ high.
Good drainage	Medium water	Medium feeder	Fast-growing; tropical, viny shrub; prune back, in winter to 18–30″; variegated.
Good drainage	Let dry out between waterings	Medium feeder	Blue-gray, ferny foliage; massive spring blooms; fast-growing.
Good drainage	Let dry out between waterings	Light feeder	Fast-growing windbreak or screen; root system can break up pavement; not for confined situations.
Good drainage; rich soil	Medium water	Medium feeder	Grown for immense leaves and tall flower stalks; tolerates drought; tolerates full sun in cool climates.
Good drainage	Medium water	Medium feeder	Slow- to medium-growing; attractive fall foliage; tolerates dry, poor, or sandy soils; useful as small street tree or trained as hedge.
Good drainage	Medium water	Medium feeder	Fragrant flowers; attractive fall foliage; cold and wind tolerant; unless trained, grows as a multistemmed tree.
Good drainage; acid soil; organic matter	Medium water	Medium feeder	Tree used as shrub; open form; slow-growing; soft foliage in wide variety of shades and variegations; showy fall color; good as specimen, in containers or as bonsai subject; protect from cold, drying winds and late spring frosts.
Good drainage	Medium water	Medium feeder	Delicate tree; attractive all year long; good fall color; protect from hot, dry winds; attractive patio tree, bonsai, small lawn tree, or in container; prune to accentuate natural growth habit; many different cultivars available.
Good drainage	Medium water	Medium feeder	Dense shade; attractive fall color; tolerates many soils and climates; vigorous roots can be a problem.
Not particular	Medium water	Medium feeder	Attractive fall foliage; tolerates wet soil; fast-growing.
Good drainage	Medium water	Medium feeder	Fast-growing; quick shade; tolerates heat and dry winds; limb breakage a problem in storms.

NAME	HABIT		FLOWERS		ADAPTATION	
	Type	Height	Color	Time	Zones	Light
Acer saccharum Sugar Maple, Rock Maple	Deciduous tree	to 80 ft			3 to 7	Full sun
Achillea millefolium Yarrow	Hardy perennial herb	6 to 36 in	Pink, white, yellow	Late spring to fall	2 to 10	Full sun
Achimenes Magic Flower	Tender bulb	1 to 2 ft	Blue, pink, yellow, purple	Early spring to late fall	10 or IN	Light shade
Adiantum pedatum Five-finger Fern, Maidenhair Fern	Groundcover	2 ft			3 to 10	Full sun
Aeschynanthus speciosus Lipstick Plant	Houseplant	3 to 4 ft	Orange	All year	10 or IN	Light shade
Aesculus hippocastanum Horse Chestnut	Deciduous tree	50 to 75 ft	White	Late spring	3 to 9	Full sun
Aesculus parviflora Bottlebrush Buckeye	Deciduous shrub	8 to 12 ft	White	Summer	5 to 8	Full sun to deep shade
Aesculus pavia Red Buckeye	Deciduous shrub	8 to 15 ft	Red	Spring	5 to 8	Full sun to deep shade
Aesculus × carnea Red Horsechestnut	Deciduous tree	30 to 50 ft	Pink, red	Spring	4 to 8	Full sun
Agapanthus africanus Lily-of-the-Nile, African Lily	Tender bulb	10 to 20 in	Blue, white, purple	Early spring to late fall	9 to 10	Full sun to light shade
Agave americana Century Plant	Hardy perennial	to 10 ft	Yellow	Summer to fall	8 to 10	Full sun to half-day sun
Aglaonema modestum Chinese Evergreen	Houseplant	to 2 ft	White	Late summer to early fall	10 or IN	Light shade to deep shade
Agrostis palustris Creeping Bent Grass	Turfgrass	¾ in			3 to 6	Full sun to half-day sun
Ajuga reptans Carpet Bugle	Groundcover		Blue, pink, white	Spring	6 to 10	Light shade to half-day sun
Akebia quinata Five-leaf Akebia	Groundcover	Vine	Purple	Spring	4 to 10	Full sun to light shade

For a list of common names, see page 378.

	CULTURE		
Soil	**Water**	**Feeding**	**Special Characteristics**
Good drainage	Medium water	Medium feeder	Source of maple syrup and lumber for maple furniture; attractive fall foliage; less tolerant of hot, dry conditions and soil compaction than other maples.
Good drainage; grows in poor soil	Let dry out between waterings	Light feeder	Medicinal herb with gray-green, fernlike foliage; flowers in flat-headed umbels; fragrant foliage; tolerates very poor, dry soils; needs yearly division to be kept in place.
Good drainage; organic matter	Medium water	Heavy feeder	Good houseplant or greenhouse plant or in outside containers; prefers partial shade.
Organic matter		Medium feeder	Fine-textured fern; dark, wiry stems with 5 frondlets each; spreads by creeping rootstalks.
Good drainage	Medium water	Light feeder	Trailing stems; orange blossoms with rust-colored edges; needs warmth, humidity, and bright indirect light.
Good drainage	Medium water	Medium feeder	Dense foliage, provides heavy shade; palmately divided leaflets; flowers with pink markings, hang in plumes; heavy fruiting may be a nuisance; some mature trees have weak branches.
Good drainage; organic matter	Medium water	Medium feeder	Open, wide-spreading habit; suckers; attractive flowers; good specimen plant.
Good drainage; organic matter	Medium water	Medium feeder	Blooms in early spring; less hardy than *A. parviflora*; sometimes considered a small tree.
Good drainage	Medium water	Medium feeder	Slow-to-moderate growing; striking spring flowers; very manageable; good shade; best in areas of cool, moist summers; protect from winds.
Good drainage; organic matter	Medium water	Heavy feeder	Give shade in hot climates; divide every five years, or when flowering declines; good container plant.
Good drainage; sandy soil	Let dry out between waterings	Medium feeder	Rosette form; large, triangular leaves with sawtooth edges; blooms once after 15–30 years, then dies.
Good drainage	Medium water	Light feeder	Oblong, lance-shaped leaves, 6–9″ long; leaves marked with silver bars between pale lateral veins; yellowish red berries follow flowers; tolerates poor light and dry air; prefers moderate light and humidity.
Good drainage; organic matter	Wet; don't let dry out	Medium feeder to heavy feeder	Favorite grass for golf course putting greens; mow low; best in full sun; tolerates traffic fairly well.
Good drainage	Medium water	Medium feeder	Fast-growing; oval, waxy leaves borne in clusters; forms thick, low mat; spreads by creeping stems; protect from cold winter winds; mow lightly after blooming; a number of cultivars with variation in foliage color are available.
Good drainage	Medium water	Medium feeder	Usually semi-evergreen; evergreen in mild climates; deep green leaves divided into 5 leaflets; purple, fleshy pods; very adaptive; plant away from low-growing shrubs—aggressive habit will smother them.

NAME	HABIT		FLOWERS		ADAPTATION	
	Type	**Height**	**Color**	**Time**	**Zones**	**Light**
Albizia julibrissin Silk Tree, Mimosa	Deciduous tree	25 to 40 ft	Pink	Early summer to early fall	7 to 10	Full sun to light shade
Alcea rosea Hollyhock	Tender biennial	2 to 9 ft	Warm colors, pink, white	June–October	3 to 10	Full sun
Allium flavum Yellow Onion	Hardy bulb	12 to 18 in	Yellow	Summer	4 to 10	Full sun
Allium giganteum Giant Onion	Hardy bulb	to 5 ft	Violet	Summer	5 to 10	Full sun
Allium moly Golden Garlic	Hardy bulb	12 to 18 in	Yellow	Early summer	3 to 10	Full sun
Allium neapolitanum Naples Onion	Half-hardy bulb	to 12 in	White	Early summer	7 to 10	Full sun
Alnus cordata Italian Alder	Deciduous tree	40 to 70 ft			5 to 10	Full sun
Alnus glutinosa Common Alder, Black Alder, European Alder	Deciduous tree	40 to 60 ft			3 to 10	Full sun
Alnus rhombifolia White Alder	Deciduous tree	60 to 70 ft			4 to 10	Full sun
Alnus rubra Red Alder	Deciduous tree	40 to 70 ft			4 to 10	Full sun
Aloe barbadensis Aloe Vera	Houseplant	6 to 24 in	Red, yellow	All year	10 or IN	Full sun to light shade
Aloysia triphylla Lemon Verbena	Tender perennial	3 to 6 ft	White	Late summer	8 to 10	Full sun
Alstroemeria aurantiaca Alstroemeria	Half-hardy bulb	2½ to 4 ft	Orange	Summer	7 to 10	Full sun to light shade
Amaranthus tricolor Joseph's Coat	Tender annual	1 to 5 ft	Red	Summer		Full sun
Amaryllis belladonna Belladonna Lily, Naked Lady	Tender bulb	2 to 3 ft	Pink	Late summer	9 to 10	Full sun
Amelanchier arborea Serviceberry, Shadblow, Shadbush, Juneberry	Deciduous tree	20 to 40 ft	White	Early spring	4 to 8	Full sun
Anchusa azurea Italian Bugloss, Italian Alkanet	Hardy perennial	3 to 5 ft	Blue	Summer	3 to 10	Full sun to light shade

For a list of common names, see page 378.

	CULTURE		
Soil	**Water**	**Feeding**	**Special Characteristics**
Good drainage; slightly alkaline soil	Medium water	Medium feeder	Very showy tree; fernlike foliage folds at night; needs plenty of heat and alkaline soil; fast-growing; lawn, patio, container; prune widespreading branches; very susceptible to vascular wilt; some cultivars hardier and wilt-resistant.
Good drainage, organic matter	Wet; don't let dry out	Heavy feeder	Prone to rust disease; needs preventive spray.
Good drainage; rich soil	Medium water	Medium feeder	Bell-shaped flowers in loose umbels; gray-green foliage; may naturalize.
Good drainage; rich soil	Medium water	Heavy feeder	Huge flower balls; straplike leaves; good for dried arrangements; foliage dies in early summer.
Good drainage; rich soil	Medium water	Medium feeder	Starlike flowers in clusters; gray-green leaves; foliage dies in midsummer.
Good drainage; rich soil	Medium water	Medium feeder	Starlike flowers borne in loose umbels; fragrant; adapted to moist areas; in cold climates dig and store through winter.
Not particular	Medium water	Medium feeder	Fast-growing; upright growth; will tolerate wet soil; invasive roots; gray bark; tassellike catkins and small cones in late winter.
Not particular	Medium water	Medium feeder	Fast-growing; best as multistemmed tree; tolerates water and does well in poor soils; catkins in late winter.
Not particular	Medium water	Medium feeder	Fast-growing; quick screen; valuable in poorly drained soils; catkins in late winter.
Not particular	Wet; don't let dry out	Medium feeder	Fast-growing 'weed' tree; thrives in low, damp soil conditions; best as temporary shelter for more permanent trees and shrubs.
Good drainage	Let dry out between waterings	Light feeder	Thick, succulent leaves and spiny edges; older plants produce flower stalks; used in cosmetics and medicinally.
Good drainage	Medium water	Medium feeder	Container or indoor plant with pale green leaves in groups of three or four; usually deciduous; fragrant, lemon-scented foliage.
Good drainage; organic matter	Medium water	Heavy feeder	Difficult to divide; stake in windy areas; shade in hot climates; can be grown in colder climates if dug and protected in winter.
Tolerates clay soil	Let dry out between waterings	Light feeder	Brilliant leaf color; thrives in hot, dry location with poor soil.
Good drainage	Medium water	Heavy feeder	Fragrant flowers; straplike leaves; flowers borne on bare, reddish-brown stalks; good container plant; can be grown in colder climates if protected.
Good drainage	Medium water	Medium feeder	Moderate-growing; often multistemmed; attractive all year; showy spring flowers; purple fruit in summer; foliage yellow to red in fall; roots noninvasive; shade light; good tree to garden under.
Good drainage	Wet; don't let dry out	Light feeder	Striking flower color; cut back after first bloom to encourage second bloom; may need staking.

NAME	HABIT		FLOWERS		ADAPTATION	
	Type	Height	Color	Time	Zones	Light
Anchusa capensis Summer Forget-me-not, Cape Forget-me-not	Half-hardy annual	8 to 18 in	Blue	Early summer to first frost		Full sun to light shade
Anchusa officinalis Alkanet, Bugloss	Hardy biennial herb	to 2 ft	Blue, purple	Late spring to summer	5 to 10	Full sun to light shade
Anemone coronaria Poppy Anemone	Half-hardy bulb	6 to 18 in	Blue, red, violet	Spring	8 to 10	Full sun
Anemone × hybrida Japanese Anemone	Half-hardy perennial	2 to 5 ft	White, pink	Spring to fall	6 to 9	Light shade
Angelica *Angelica archangelica*	Hardy biennial herb	4 to 6 ft	White	Summer	3 to 10	Light shade
Anthemis tinctoria Golden Marguerite	Hardy perennial	2½ to 3 ft	Yellow	Summer to early fall	3 to 10	Full sun
Antirrhinum majus Snapdragon	Half-hardy annual	½ to 4 ft	Red, pink, white, orange, yellow	Late spring to first frost		Full sun
Aphelandra squarrosa Zebra Plant	Houseplant	1½ to 2 ft	Yellow	Fall	10 or IN	Light shade
Apple *Malus pumila*	Deciduous fruit tree	4 to 30 ft	White	Spring	4 to 9	Full sun
Apricot *Prunus armeniaca*	Deciduous fruit tree	15 to 25 ft	White	Early spring	6 to 9	Full sun
Aquilegia species and hybrids Columbine	Hardy perennial	1½ to 3 ft	Red, white, blue, purple, pink, orange, yellow	Late spring to early summer	3 to 10	Light shade
Arabis caucasica Rock Cress	Groundcover	to 12 in	White	Spring	6 to 10	Full sun
Araucaria bidwillii Bunya-bunya	Evergreen tree	30 to 50 ft			9 to 10	Full sun to light shade
Araucaria heterophylla Norfolk Island Pine	Evergreen tree	60 to 70 ft			9 to 10	Full sun to light shade

For a list of common names, see page 378.

| | CULTURE | | |
Soil	Water	Feeding	Special Characteristics
Good drainage	Medium water	Light feeder	Easy to grow; tolerates poor soil.
Good drainage; rich soil	Medium water	Heavy feeder	Herb with rough, hairy leaves 3–6″ long; flowers taste like cucumber; root yields red dye.
Good drainage	Medium water	Heavy feeder	Good cut flowers; dig bulbs and store over winter.
Good drainage; organic matter; rich soil	Medium water	Medium feeder	Good fall color; long-lived; resents disturbance once established; tolerates full sun in cool climates; avoid wet soil in winter.
Good drainage	Medium water	Medium feeder	Aromatic, celery-like herb with edible leaves; hollow stems; doesn't flower until second or third year.
Good drainage	Medium water	Medium feeder	Fernlike leaves, aromatic when bruised; short-lived flowers; avoid heavy, wet, clay soils.
Good drainage; organic matter	Medium water	Heavy feeder	Good spring color; rust is a serious problem on older cultivars; will bloom through winter in mild climates.
Good drainage	Medium water	Medium feeder	Shiny, nearly black elliptical leaves striped with ivory veins; conelike flowers emerge from golden bracts for 6 weeks in the fall; give indirect light or filtered sun; keep moist and humid; prune back in spring to keep bushy.
Good drainage; organic matter	Medium water	Medium feeder	Requires some cool winter temperatures; partially self-fertile, some require pollinators; pruning method depends on how you want to shape tree; water deeply; thin fruits 4–6 weeks after bloom; a wide selection of varieties available; early, mid and late season cultivars; variation in size, shape, and taste of fruit; variation in cultivar adaptation to different climates.
Good drainage; organic matter	Medium water	Medium feeder	Early bloom after last frost; thin fruit about 6 weeks after bloom to 3–4 inches apart; attractive, vigorous tree grows well in winter; avoid areas that are hot when fruit ripens (over 90 degrees F.) or select heat-tolerant varieties.
Good drainage; organic matter	Wet; don't let dry out	Medium feeder	Usually short-lived; tolerates full sun in cool summer climates; feed regularly with fertilizer applied half-strength; flowers are often bicolored.
Good drainage	Let dry out between waterings	Medium feeder	Fine, feltlike, whitish hairs give leaves grayish cast; profuse, fragrant flowers; drought-tolerant once established; cut back upright stems after flowering; not a large-scale groundcover.
Good drainage	Medium water	Medium feeder	Moderate-growing; overlapping needles are sharp and stiff; unusual branches; can be grown in container as small indoor tree.
Good drainage	Medium water	Medium feeder	Grows indoors to 10′; provide very bright, indirect light or a couple of hours of morning sun; watch for spider mites; soft, formal character; can be container grown for many years; good near coast.

NAME	HABIT		FLOWERS		ADAPTATION	
	Type	Height	Color	Time	Zones	Light
Arbutus menziesii Madrone, Madrona	Evergreen tree	20 to 40 ft	White, pink	Spring	7 to 9	Full sun
Arbutus unedo Strawberry Tree	Evergreen tree	10 to 25 ft	White	Fall to winter	7 to 9	Full sun to light shade
Arctostaphylos uva-vrsi Bearberry Manzanita, Kinnikinick	Groundcover	6 to 12 in	White	Late spring	2 to 8	Full sun to light shade
Arctosyaphylos densiflora Vine Hill Manzanita	Evergreen shrub	5 to 6 ft	White, pink	Spring	7 to 10	Full sun to light shade
Arctotis stoechadifolia African Daisy	Tender annual	10 to 20 in	Comes in all colors	Early summer to early fall		Full sun
Arenaria verna (A. caespitosa) Moss Sandwort	Groundcover	to 3 in	White	Summer	3 to 10	Light shade
Armeria maritima Sea Pink, Sea Thrift	Hardy perennial groundcover	6 to 10 in	White, pink	Late spring to early summer	3 to 10	Full sun
Aronia arbutifolia Red Chokeberry	Deciduous shrub	6 to 8 ft	White	Spring	5 to 9	Full sun
Artemisia abrotanum Southernwood	Hardy perennial	3 to 4 ft			4 to 10	Full sun
Artichoke *Cynara Scolymus*	Perennial vegetable	2 to 4 ft			8 to 10	Full sun to half-day sun
Asarum caudatum Wild ginger	Groundcover	7 to 10 in			5 to 9	Shade
Asparagus *Asparagus officinalis*	Hardy perennial vegetable	4 to 5 ft			5 to 10	Full sun to half-day sun
Asparagus densiflorus 'Sprengeri' Sprenger Asparagus, Asparagus Fern	Houseplant, groundcover	1 to 2 ft	White	Spring to early summer	10 or IN	Half-day sun to light shade
Aspidistra elatior Cast-iron Plant	Houseplant	1 to 2½ ft	Purple	Spring	10 or IN	Light shade to deep shade
Asplenium nidus Bird's-nest Fern	Houseplant	1 to 3 ft			10 or IN	Light shade

For a list of common names, see page 378.

	CULTURE		
Soil	**Water**	**Feeding**	**Special Characteristics**
Good drainage	Let dry out between waterings	Medium feeder	Slow-to-moderate growing; color all year; attractive red bark; leathery, copper to green foliage; red and orange berries in fall; deep, infrequent waterings.
Good drainage	Medium water	Medium feeder	Shrubby plant; slow-to-moderate growing; attractive red bark; flowers and red fruits appear in fall and winter; tolerates seacoast conditions.
Sandy soil	Let dry out between waterings	Light feeder	Low, mat-forming; tiny bell-shaped flowers followed by red berries; relatively slow growing; tolerates poor soil, seacoast conditions.
Needs good drainage	Let dry out between waterings	Light feeder	Smooth, red bark; crooked, spreading branches; 'Howard McMinn' variety is best for dense canopy.
Sandy soil; organic matter	Let dry out between waterings	Light feeder	Tolerates drought, poor soil; best in mild climates.
Good drainage	Medium water	Medium feeder	Mosslike, evergreen perennial; small, narrow, dark green leaves; dense, slow-spreading mat tolerates full sun and light foot traffic; give some winter protection in cold, exposed areas.
Good drainage; sandy soil	Let dry out between waterings	Light feeder	Tolerates seacoast conditions; blooms almost all year along coast; grasslike foliage.
Tolerates clay soil	Medium water	Medium feeder	Slow-growing; leggy, upright shrub; attractive fall foliage with profuse red berries; tolerates both drought and wet conditions and partial shade; best in masses and large groups; naturalized in wet areas.
Good drainage; sandy soil	Let dry out between waterings	Medium feeder	Lemon-scented herb grown mainly for feathery green foliage; woody stems; hardy and long-lived; rarely blooms; if grown as a shrub, prune to maintain shape.
Rich soil; organic matter	Wet; don't let dry out	Heavy feeder	Grown for edible flower buds; best in cool, humid, moderate climates; needs protection from frost and hot summer heat.
High organic matter	Wet, keep moist	Medium feeder	Heart-shaped leaves; inconspicuous flowers; gingerlike fragrance; protect from drying winds.
Good drainage; organic matter; sandy soil	Medium water	Medium feeder	Usually grown from 1-year-old crowns; plants produce for 10–15 years; thrives in most climates; plant crowns as early in spring as possible; don't harvest first two years.
Good drainage	Let dry out between waterings	Light feeder	Arching sprays of light green, needlelike leaves; inconspicuous flowers; small, bright red berries; trailing habit; drought-resistant; requires little care; restricted outdoors to warm-winter areas; several other ornamental asparagus available.
Good drainage	Medium water	Light feeder	Leathery, oblong, shiny dark green leaves; bell-shaped flowers; slow-growing, long-lasting; give indirect sun; tolerant of poor growing conditions.
Good drainage	Medium water	Medium feeder	Wavy, lance-shaped leaves with black rib uncurl from heart of plant; can reach 3' long; fronds dislike being touched; can be summered on shady patio; water accumulation in heart may cause crown rot.

NAME	HABIT		FLOWERS		ADAPTATION	
	Type	Height	Color	Time	Zones	Light
Aster species and hybrids Hardy Aster, Michaelmas Daisy	Hardy perennial	½ to 6 ft	Purple, blue, red, pink, white	Late summer to fall	4 to 10	Full sun to light shade
Astilbe species and hybrids False Spiraea, Astilbe	Hardy perennial	1 to 3 ft	White, pink, lavender, red	Summer	4 to 8	Light shade to deep shade
Aucuba japonica Japanese Aucuba	Evergreen shrub	6 to 10 ft	Purple	Early spring	7 to 10	Light shade to deep shade
Aurinia saxatilis Basket of Gold, Goldentuft	Hardy perennial	9 to 12 in	Yellow	Spring	3 to 10	Full sun
Baccharis pilularis Dwarf Coyote Bush	Groundcover	to 2 ft			7 to 10	Full sun to light shade
Basil Ocimum basilicum	Tender annual herb					Full sun
Bauhinia blakeana Hong Kong Orchid Tree	Deciduous tree	to 20 ft	Pink, purple	Fall to winter	9 to 10	Full sun
Bauhinia variegata Orchid Tree	Deciduous tree	20 to 25 ft	Lavender, pink, white	Winter to spring	7 to 10	Full sun
Beans, Lima Phaseolus lunatus	Tender annual vegetable	Climbing to 10 ft				Full sun
Beans, scarlet runner Phaesolus coccineus	Tender annual vegetable	Climbs to 8 ft	Red, white	Early summer		Full sun
Beans, snap or string Phaeseolus vulgaris	Tender annual vegetable	Climbs to 8 ft	White	Early summer		Full sun
Beaucarnea recurvata var. intermedia Elephant Foot Tree, Ponytail Palm	Houseplant	3 to 5 ft			10 or IN	Half-day sun
Beets Beta vulgaris	Hardy annual vegetable	6 to 12 in				Full sun to light shade
Begonia grandis Evans Begonia	Hardy bulb	to 24 in	Pink	Summer to late summer	6 to 10	Light shade
Begonia masoniana Iron-cross Begonia	Houseplant	to 18 in	Pink, not showy		10 or IN	Light shade to half-day sun

For a list of common names, see page 378.

Soil	Water	Feeding	Special Characteristics
Good drainage	Medium water	Light feeder	Good, late season color; give light shade in hot summer climates; pinch plants in late spring; stake varieties over 2' tall; divide plants every other year.
Rich soil; organic matter; good drainage	Wet; don't let dry out	Heavy feeder	Accepts full sun if watered deeply and often; divide every 3–4 years.
Organic matter	Medium water	Medium feeder	Leathery, large leaves; bright red berries in fall and winter; requires both male and female plant to set fruit; tolerates many soils; variegated varieties.
Sandy soil	Let dry out between waterings	Light feeder	Attractive gray-green foliage; profuse blooming; dwarf cultivars available.
Not particular	Medium water	Light feeder	Evergreen shrub; small, lightly toothed, dark green leaves; woody branches; very adaptable; tolerates drought and wet conditions; tolerates seacoast conditions; prune out deep wood and arching branches each spring; several good cultivars available.
Good drainage; organic matter	Medium water	Medium feeder	Fragrant, edible herb used medicinally and in cooking; thrives in heat; likes rich soil; dark-leaved cultivar available.
Good drainage	Medium water	Medium feeder	Large, striking flowers; moderate growing; good small shade tree; won't tolerate high heat and drought; umbrellalike canopy.
Good drainage	Medium water	Medium feeder	Moderate-growing; umbrellalike form; tends to get bushy and multitrunked; good street tree in areas of warm spring weather; mild, dry winter produces best bloom.
Good drainage; organic matter	Medium water	Medium feeder	Require higher temperature than snap beans to germinate well, and longer season to produce crop; pods may fail to set in extremely hot climates; several cultivars available of bush types and pole types.
Good drainage; organic matter	Medium water	Medium feeder	Closely related to common beans; more vigorous; larger seed pods and flowers; flowers are quite attractive.
Good drainage; organic matter	Medium water	Medium feeder	Plant seed when danger of frost is past; requires about 60 days of moderate temperatures to produce crop; beans are grouped as bush beans, bush wax beans, or pole beans; many cultivars are available in each group.
Good drainage; sandy soil	Let dry out between waterings	Medium feeder	Base of gray-brown trunk resembles onion when plant is young; long, thin green leaves arch out around apex of stem; likes warm environment; water thoroughly and let dry out between waterings.
Good drainage; organic matter	Medium water	Medium feeder	Prefers cool weather; sow seed as early as ground can be worked; add sand to soil for better root development; plant successively for continuous supply; many different cultivars are available.
Good drainage; organic matter	Medium water	Heavy feeder	Good container plant.
Good drainage	Medium water	Medium feeder	Green leaves, puckered surface, brown markings forming cross in center of leaves; give bright, indirect light and 4 hours direct sunlight during fall, winter.

NAME	HABIT		FLOWERS		ADAPTATION	
	Type	Height	Color	Time	Zones	Light
Begonia × rex-cultorum Rex Begonia	Houseplant	to 18 in			10 or IN	Light shade to half-day sun
Begonia × semperflorens-cultorum Wax Begonia, Fibrous-rooted Begonia	Half-hardy annual	6 to 12 in	Pink, red, white	Late spring to first frost		Half-day sun to light shade
Begonia × tuberhybrida Tuberous Begonia	Tender bulb	12 to 18 in	Red, orange, yellow, pink, white	Late spring to fall	10	Light shade
Berberis darwinii Darwin Barberry	Evergreen shrub	5 to 10 ft	Yellow	Early spring	8 to 10	Full sun
Berberis koreana Korean Barberry	Deciduous shrub	4 to 8 ft	Yellow	Late spring	4 to 7	Full sun
Berberis thunbergii Japanese Barberry	Deciduous shrub	3 to 6 ft			5 to 8	Full sun to light shade
Bergenia cordifolia Heart-leaf Bergenia	Hardy perennial	12 to 15 in	Pink, white	Spring	4 to 10	Full sun to light shade
Bergenia crassifolia Winter-blooming Bergenia	Hardy perennial groundcover	to 20 in	Pink, white, purple	Spring	3 to 10	Light shade
Betula maximowicziana Monarch Birch	Deciduous tree	80 to 100 ft			6 to 10	Full sun
Betula nigra River Birch	Deciduous tree	50 to 70 ft			5 to 9	Full sun
Betula papyrifera Paper Birch	Deciduous tree	40 to 60 ft			3 to 7	Full sun
Betula pendula European White Birch	Deciduous tree	to 60 ft			2 to 7	Full sun
Billbergia nutans Queen's Tears, Friendship Plant	Houseplant	1½ to 2 ft	Pink, green	Winter	10 or IN	Half-day sun
Blackberry *Rubus allegheniensis*	Deciduous vine	5 to 8 ft	White	Late spring to summer	3 to 10	Full sun to half-day sun
Blackeyed Pea—See Cowpea						
Blueberry *Vaccinium corymbosum*	Deciduous berry	6 to 12 ft	White	Late spring	3 to 7	Full sun to light shade

For a list of common names, see page 378.

	CULTURE		
Soil	**Water**	**Feeding**	**Special Characteristics**
Good drainage	Medium water	Medium feeder	Grown for large, hairy leaves patterned in green, red, silver, and white; give bright, indirect light and 4 hours direct sunlight in fall, winter.
Good drainage; organic matter	Medium water	Heavy feeder	Hard to start from seed; in hot climates keep well-watered and avoid full sun; will bloom through winter in mild climates.
Good drainage; organic matter	Medium water	Heavy feeder	Good container plant; dig in fall and store over winter.
Not particular	Medium water	Medium feeder	Fast-growing, loose, open form; profuse bloomer; dark blue berries; tolerates many soils; withstands drought well.
Not particular	Medium water	Medium feeder	Showy flowers and red fruit; dense, oval shape; thorny; suckers heavily; can prune as hedge.
Not particular	Medium water	Medium feeder	Attractive fall foliage; many variegated varieties; moderate-growing; tolerates drought; easy to transplant; thorny; best pruned as dense hedge or barrier plant.
Good drainage	Medium water	Medium feeder	Evergreen; cabbagelike leaves that turn reddish in winter; tolerates wide range of soils; give some shade in areas of hot summers.
Good drainage	Medium water	Medium feeder	6–8" leaves, finely toothed, wavy edges; flowers in winter in mild-climate areas; can take sun in cool, coastal areas; keep moist; protect from wind; divide clumps when crowded.
Good drainage	Medium water	Medium feeder	Fast-growing; largest leaves and catkins of all birches; young bark reddish brown, old bark white; tolerates cold, windy areas and dry sites; provide ample water and regular feedings.
Not particular	Wet; don't let dry out	Medium feeder	Young bark red, turns brown with age and peels off; leaves bright glossy green above, silver below; must have adequate moisture.
Good drainage	Medium water	Medium feeder	Papery, white bark; best grown in clumps; open and erect growth habit.
Good drainage	Medium water	Medium feeder	Attractive white bark with black markings; upright tree with weeping side branches; lends itself to planting in groves or clumps; many cultivars available.
Good drainage	Medium water	Medium feeder	Bromeliad with grasslike, gray-green leaves; rose bracts; blue edged green arching spray of flowers; keep water in center cup of plant.
Good drainage; organic matter	Medium water	Medium feeder	Stiff-caned, fairly hardy plant; roots are perennial, canes biennial; thorny; trailing.
Good drainage; organic matter; acid soil	Medium water	Medium feeder to heavy feeder	Needs a cool, moist, acid soil and good drainage; edible fruits borne in the summer months; shallow-rooted; avoid fertilizing the first year; don't prune for 2–3 seasons; choose two varieties for cross-pollination; many early, mid-season, and late varieties; some varieties adapted to warmer areas of the Southeast.

NAME	HABIT		FLOWERS		ADAPTATION	
	Type	Height	Color	Time	Zones	Light
Borage *Borago officinalis*	Half-hardy annual herb	1 to 3 ft	Blue	Early summer to early fall		Full sun to light shade
Brachychiton populneus Kurrajong	Evergreen tree	25 to 50 ft	White	Late spring to early summer	9 to 10	Full sun
Brachycome iberidifolia Swan River Daisy	Half-hardy annual	10 to 16 in	Blue, pink, violet, lavender, white	Summer		Full sun
Brassaia actinophylla Schefflera, Umbrella Tree	Houseplant	to 8 ft			10 or IN	Light shade
Brassica oleracea acephala Flowering Kale, Ornamental Cabbage	Hardy annual	10 to 15 in				Full sun
Broccoli *Brassica oleracea* var. *botrytis*	Hardy annual vegetable	1 to 2 ft				Full sun to half-day sun
Brodiaea coronaria (*B. grandiflora*) Harvest Brodiaea	Half-hardy bulb	to 18 in	Purple, violet	Summer	7 to 10	Full sun
Browallia speciosa Sapphire Flower	Tender annual	10 to 18 in	Blue, lavender, white	Late spring to first frost		Half-day sun to light shade
Brunnera macrophylla Siberian Bugloss	Hardy perennial	to 18 in	Blue	Spring	3 to 8	Light shade
Brussels sprouts *Brassica oleracea* var. *gemmifera*	Hardy biennial vegetable	to 3 ft				Full sun to half-day sun
Buddleia davidii Butterfly Bush	Deciduous shrub	6 to 10 ft	Blue, purple, lavender, white	Summer to first frost	5 to 10	Full sun
Bulbocodium vernum Spring Meadow Saffron	Hardy bulb	4 to 6 in	Lavender, pink	Spring	5 to 10	Full sun to light shade
Buxus microphylla* var. *japonica Japanese Boxwood	Evergreen shrub	3 to 4 ft			6 to 10	Full sun to light shade
Buxus sempervirens Common Boxwood	Evergreen shrub	10 to 20 ft			5 to 10	Full sun to light shade

For a list of common names, see page 378.

| | CULTURE | | |
Soil	Water	Feeding	Special Characteristics
Not particular	Medium water	Medium feeder	Herb with gray-green, hairy leaves; star-shaped, showy flowers; needs ample space; foliage and flowers have cucumberlike flavor; self-sows.
Good drainage	Medium water	Medium feeder	Slow- to moderate-growing; heavy, tapering trunk; dense, conical crown; leaves both lobed and unlobed; drought-resistant; effective as screen or windbreak.
Good drainage; organic matter	Medium water	Heavy feeder	Pleasant fragrance; short blooming season; prefers cool summers.
Good drainage	Medium water	Medium feeder	Fast-growing; glossy green leaflets spread out like an umbrella; give bright, indirect light.
Good drainage	Wet; don't let dry out	Light feeder	Vegetable used as an ornamental; color is best in fall; foliage composed of thick, blue-green outer leaves with white, pink, red, magenta, or purple inner leaves.
Good drainage; organic matter	Medium water	Heavy feeder	Member of cabbage family; cool-weather vegetable; best in temperatures between 65 and 80 degrees F; harvest flower buds while still tight; frost-hardy; requires high nitrogen; many cultivars varying in size and maturation time are available.
Good drainage; sandy soil	Medium water	Medium feeder	Needs adequate moisture while blooming, but must dry off following bloom; best in areas with dry summers.
Good drainage; organic matter	Medium water	Medium feeder	Easy to grow from seed; useful in hanging baskets; will bloom through winter in mild climates.
Grows in poor soil	Wet; don't let dry out	Medium feeder	Attractive leaves all season; adapts to full sun in coastal areas of the West; needs little attention.
Good drainage; organic matter	Medium water	Heavy feeder	Cool-weather vegetables, best where temperatures are between 65 and 80 degrees F; most cold-tolerant of cabbage family; exposure to frost improves flavor; pinch out growing tips when plants are 15–20" tall to promote uniform development of sprouts; several cultivars available.
Good drainage	Medium water	Medium feeder	Fragrant flowers; very fast-growing; wild, unruly growth habit; large, coarse leaves; best grown as herbaceous perennial in rear of border; prune to within a few inches of the ground after blooming; attracts butterflies.
Good drainage	Medium water	Medium feeder	Good in rock gardens; leaves appear after flowers.
Good drainage; organic matter	Medium water	Medium feeder	Light green leaves; may brown in cold-winter areas; slow-growing; compact; flowers are fragrant but not showy; tolerates dry heat and alkaline soil; can be left unpruned.
Good drainage; organic matter	Medium water	Medium feeder	Does not tolerate extremes of heat and cold; mulch heavily to keep roots cool; protect from drying winds; full sun in mild areas, shade in hotter climates; can be pruned as topiary, hedges, formed into many interesting shapes.

NAME	HABIT		FLOWERS		ADAPTATION	
	Type	**Height**	**Color**	**Time**	**Zones**	**Light**
Cabbage *Brassica oleracea* var. *capitata*	Hardy biennial vegetable	6 to 12 in				Full sun to light shade
Caladium × hortulanum Fancy-leaved Caladium	Tender bulb	to 12 in			10 or IN	Light shade
Calendula officinalis Pot Marigold	Hardy annual	10 to 24 in	White, orange, yellow	Spring to first frost		Full sun
Callistemon citrinus Lemon Bottlebrush	Evergreen tree	20 to 25 ft	Red	All year	8 to 10	Full sun
Callistephus chinensis China Aster	Tender annual	6 to 36 in	All colors	Early summer to late summer		Full sun to light shade
Calluna vulgaris Scotch Heather	Evergreen shrub groundcover	4 to 24 in	Pink, purple, white, red	Summer to early fall	5 to 8	Full sun to half-day sun
Calocedrus decurrens Incense Cedar	Needled evergreen tree	70 to 90 ft			5 to 9	Full sun
Caltha palustris Marsh Marigold	Hardy perennial	12 to 18 in	Yellow	Spring	3 to 10	Full sun to light shade
Calycanthus floridus Carolina Allspice, Strawberry Shrub	Deciduous shrub	6 to 9 ft	Bronze	Spring to summer	5 to 9	Light shade
Camassia cusickii Cussick Camass	Hardy bulb	3 to 4 ft	Blue	Early summer	3 to 10	Full sun to light shade
Camassia leichtlinii Leichtlin Camass	Hardy bulb	2 to 4 ft	Blue, white	Early summer	3 to 10	Full sun to light shade
Camellia japonica Common Camellia	Evergreen shrub	6 to 12 ft	White, pink, red	Fall to late spring	8 to 10	Light shade
Camellia sasanqua Sasanqua Camellia	Evergreen shrub	6 to 12 ft	Pink, red, white	Early fall to winter	8 to 10	Full sun to light shade
Campanula carpatica Carpathian Harebell	Hardy perennial	6 to 12 in	Blue, white, purple	Early summer to late summer	3 to 10	Full sun to light shade
Campanula elatines garganica Adriatic Bellflower	Groundcover	3 to 6 in	Blue	Late summer to early fall	3 to 10	Full sun to light shade

For a list of common names, see page 378.

	CULTURE		
Soil	**Water**	**Feeding**	**Special Characteristics**
Good drainage; organic matter	Medium water	Heavy feeder	Cool-weather vegetable; frost-hardy; requires high amounts of nitrogen; begin harvest when heads are firm, about the size of a softball; cut just beneath the head; wide choice of cultivars available.
Good drainage; organic matter	Medium water	Heavy feeder	Grown for colorful foliage; best in hot, humid climates; in colder climates plant as annuals, and dig up for winter protection.
Good drainage; organic matter	Medium water	Heavy feeder	Successive plantings guarantees color from late spring to fall; long blooming season; best in cool seasons; will bloom through winter in mild climates.
Good drainage	Medium water	Medium feeder	Fast-growing; tolerates both heat and cold; tolerates drought; screen, espaliered; can be trained as single-trunked tree; blooms periodically throughout year.
Sandy soil; organic matter	Medium water	Medium feeder	Never plant in same location two years in a row; rust is a serious problem, look for disease-resistant varieties; make successive plantings for color all summer.
Good drainage; organic matter	Medium water	Medium feeder	Low, restrained growth; needlelike leaves; needs soil that will retain moisture; tolerates light shade, but flowers less; mulch well and don't cultivate around shallow roots.
Good drainage	Medium water	Medium feeder	Slow-growing when young, but becomes fast growing; attractive reddish-brown bark; fragrant needles; deep, infrequent watering makes tree very drought-tolerant; good screen, windbreak.
Rich soil; organic matter	Wet; don't let dry out	Heavy feeder	Adapted to moist areas, edges of ponds, pools, etc.; will tolerate drier soil if well watered; foliage disappears by midsummer.
Rich soil	Medium water	Medium feeder	Slow-growing; neat, rounded shape; fragrant flowers; tolerates many soils; can grow in full sun, but won't grow as tall; can prune to shape when flowering is over.
Tolerates clay soil	Wet; don't let dry out	Medium feeder	Delicate flowers, grasslike leaves; prefers heavy soil.
Tolerates clay soil	Wet; don't let dry out	Medium feeder	Delicate flowers, grasslike leaves; prefers heavy soil.
Good drainage; organic matter	Medium water	Medium feeder	Dense, polished, dark green foliage; large flowers; bloom time varies according to cultivar; avoid cultivating around shallow roots; if necessary, prune immediately after flowering.
Good drainage	Medium water	Medium feeder	Blooms earlier than common camellia; range from low-growing, sprawling shrubs to hedge, or screen plants; can be pruned as bonsai or espalier.
Good drainage; organic matter	Medium water	Medium feeder	Neat, compact, and long-blooming.
Good drainage	Medium water	Light feeder	Loose, mat form; green, heart-shaped leaves; star-shaped flowers; shade in hot-summer areas, give sun elsewhere; divide when crowded, can become invasive.

NAME	HABIT		FLOWERS		ADAPTATION	
	Type	Height	Color	Time	Zones	Light
Campanula medium Canterbury Bells	Hardy annual	12 to 36 in	Blue, pink, lavender, white	Summer		Full sun to light shade
Campanula poscharskyana Serbian Bellflower	Groundcover	to 1 ft	Lavender	Late summer to fall	3 to 10	Full sun to light shade
Canna × generalis Old-fashioned Cannas	Tender bulb	2 to 6 ft	Pink, white, red, orange, yellow	Early summer to first frost	8 to 10	Full sun
Capsicum annuum Ornamental Pepper	Tender annual	10 to 12 in		Summer to first frost		Full sun to half-day sun
Carawat *Carum carvi*	Hardy biennial herb	to 2 ft	White	Late spring to early summer	4 to 10	Full sun
Cardoon *Cynara cardunculus*	Half-hardy perennial vegetable	to 6 ft		Summer	9 to 10	Full sun to half-day sun
Carissa grandiflora Natal Plum	Evergreen shrub	to 7 ft	White	All year	9 to 10	Full sun
Carpinus betulus European Hornbeam	Deciduous tree	30 to 40 ft			4 to 7	Full sun
Carpinus caroliniana American Hornbeam	Deciduous tree	20 to 40 ft			2 to 9	Light shade to deep shade
Carrot *Daucus carota* var. *sativa*	Hardy annual vegetable	to 3 ft				Full sun to light shade
Casuarina cunninghamiana Beefwood, River She-oak	Evergreen tree	to 70 ft			6 to 7	Full sun
Catalpa bignonioides Common Southern Catalpa, Indian Bean, Cigar Tree	Deciduous tree	30 to 40 ft	White	Late spring to early summer	5 to 9	Full sun
Catalpa speciosa Northern Catalpa, Western Catalpa	Deciduous tree	65 to 75 ft	White	Late spring to early summer	5 to 9	Full sun
Catharanthus roseus Vinca rosea, Madagascar Periwinkle	Tender annual	4 to 18 in	Pink, white, rose	Late spring to first frost		Full sun to half-day sun to light shade
Catnip *Nepeta cataria*	Hardy perennial herb	2 to 3 ft	Lavender, white	Early summer to early fall	4 to 10	Full sun to light shade
Cattleya orchids	Houseplant	12 to 20 in	All colors except blue		10 or IN	Light shade

For a list of common names, see page 378.

| | CULTURE | | |
Soil	Water	Feeding	Special Characteristics
Good drainage; organic matter	Medium water	Heavy feeder	Stake in windy areas; stems are flexible.
Good drainage	Medium water	Light feeder	Trailing growth habit; spreads by creeping runners; star-shaped flowers; shade in hot-summer climates, sun elsewhere; can become invasive.
	Medium water	Heavy feeder	Tropical-looking leaves 6–12″ long; flowers in showy spikes; dig in fall after frost kills foliage.
	Medium water	Light feeder	Vegetable used an an ornamental; attractive seed pods are red, yellow, orange, white, purple, or black; very heat-resistant.
Good drainage	Medium water	Medium feeder	Herb with carrotlike leaves; develops shoots and flowers during second year; edible foliage and seeds; flowers in umbels.
Rich soil; good drainage	Wet; don't let dry out	Heavy feeder	Cool-season plant; resembles artichoke; grown for young leafstalks; requires 120–150 days from seed to harvest; can become a weed where adapted.
Good drainage	Medium water	Light feeder	Shiny, deep green foliage; fragrant flowers bloom throughout the year; small, edible fruits; tolerates shade; many cultivars used as groundcovers.
Good drainage	Medium water	Medium feeder	Slow to moderate-growing; neat, manageable tree; attractive gray bark; fall color yellow; cultivar 'Fastigiata' best choice for screen or hedge.
Good drainage; rich soil	Medium water	Medium feeder	Moderate-growing; hardy; smooth, gray bark; dark green leaves with toothed edges; attractive fall color; good street tree; long-lived and well-behaved; thrives in moist conditions.
Good drainage; sandy soil	Medium water	Medium feeder	Prolonged heat produces shorter roots; slow to germinate; prefers deep, loose soil with high water-holding capacity; avoid raw manures and composts which cause knobby, branching carrots; many cultivars of all different lengths are available.
Sandy soil	Medium water	Medium feeder	Fast growing; pinelike appearance; tolerates dry or wet soil, heat, wind; very useful in desert areas.
Not particular	Medium water	Medium feeder	Fast growing; very adaptive to soils and climates; tolerates city smog; flowers followed by long bean pods which, can last into winter; best in large areas; messy.
Not particular	Medium water	Medium feeder	Similar to C. bigninioides; leaves larger, fewer flowers, slightly hardier; use only in areas with lots of space.
Good drainage; sandy soil	Medium water	Light feeder	Long blooming season; very heat-tolerant; slow-growing where summers are cool; will bloom through winter in mild climates.
Organic matter	Wet; don't let dry out	Medium feeder	Medicinal herb with heart-shaped leaves with toothed edges; becomes scraggly when in bloom; cats love this plant.
Good drainage	Medium water	Medium feeder	Vigorous plants; most popular orchid; straplike leaves and pseudobulbs; needs very bright, indirect light, protect from direct sun; ample humidity; avoid getting water on flowers.

NAME	HABIT		FLOWERS		ADAPTATION	
	Type	Height	Color	Time	Zones	Light
Cauliflower *Brassica oleracea*	Half hardy biennial vegetable	to 1 ft				Full sun to half-day sun
***Ceanothus* species** Wild Lilac	Evergreen shrub	8 to 30 in	Blue, white	Spring	8 to 10	Full sun
Cedrus atlantica Atlas Cedar	Needled evergreen tree	40 to 60 ft			7 to 9	Full sun
Cedrus deodara Deodar Cedar	Needled evergreen tree	40 to 75 ft			7 to 9	Full sun
Cedrus libani Cedar-of-Lebanon	Needled evergreen tree	40 to 70 ft			5 to 9	Full sun
Celeriac *Apium graveolens* var. *rapaceum*	Half-hardy biennial vegetable	to 3 ft				Half-day sun to light shade
Celery Cabbage—See Chinese Cabbage						
Celery *Apium graveolens dulce*	Half-hardy biennial vegetable	to 3 ft				Half-day sun to light shade
***Celosia cristata* (*C. plumosa*)** Cockscomb, Plume Celosia	Tender annual	½ to 3 ft	Red, orange, yellow, pink, purple	Early summer to fall		Full sun
Celtis australis European Hackberry	Deciduous tree	40 to 70 ft			7 to 9	Full sun
Celtis occidentalis Common Hackberry	Deciduous tree	35 to 45 ft			4 to 9	Full sun
Centaurea cyanus Bachelor's-Button	Hardy annual	1 to 3 ft	Blue, red, pink, white	Summer		Full sun
Cerastium tomentosum Snow-in-summer	Hardy perennial groundcover	4 to 6 in	White	Spring to summer	3 to 10	Full sun
Ceratonia siliqua Carob, St. John's Bread	Evergreen tree	25 to 40 ft			9 to 10	Full sun to light shade
Ceratostigma plumbaginoides Blue Plumbago	Half-hardy perennial	6 to 10 in	Blue	Late summer to first frost	6 to 10	Full sun to light shade

For a list of common names, see page 378.

Soil	Water	Feeding	Special Characteristics
Good drainage	Medium water	Heavy feeder	Member of cabbage family; the edible portion is the flower bud; not cold-tolerant; won't grow properly in very hot weather; best in cool, humid climate; several cultivars are available.
Sandy soil	Let dry out between waterings	Light feeder	Many varieties; attractive, fragrant flowers and glossy leaves; most useful in the West; intolerant of heavy soils; prune only during dry, summer months; best in large masses; does not grow well in the Southwest.
Good drainage	Medium water	Medium feeder	Slow- to moderate-growing; wide, pyramid shape when mature; fine-textured, bluish-green needles borne in stiff clusters; drought-tolerant; fine tree in large area; cultivar 'Glauca' has richest blue foliage.
Good drainage	Medium water	Medium feeder	Fast-growing; most refined, graceful cedar; lower branches sweep ground; needles green to bluish-green; tree top has nodding tip; good in parks and groves; needs ample space.
Good drainage	Medium water	Medium feeder	Slower growing and hardier than *C. atlantica*; needles bright green; give infrequent, deep watering; good skyline tree.
Rich soil; organic matter	Wet; don't let dry out	Heavy feeder	Grown like celery; harvest when roots reach 2–4" in diameter.
Rich soil; organic matter	Wet; don't let dry out	Heavy feeder	Demands constant attention; cool-weather plant; seed small, slow to germinate; requires constant moisture and temperature, blanching not usually necessary with modern varieties; several cultivars available.
Good drainage	Medium water	Light feeder	Will tolerate poor, dry soil.
Not particular	Medium water	Medium feeder	Moderate-growing; dark green leaves with toothed edges; deep rooted; once established, tolerates much heat, drought, winds, alkaline soil.
Not particular	Medium water	Medium feeder	Moderate-growing; leaves dull green with toothed edges; valuable shade tree in tough conditions; cultivar 'Prairie Pride' resists witch's broom.
Good drainage; rich soil	Medium water	Medium feeder	Good summer color; short blooming season; make successive plantings for prolonged bloom.
Good drainage	Medium water	Medium feeder	Evergreen; dense, matting growth habit; light gray foliage; profuse blooms; fast-spreading; drought-tolerant; mow lightly at end of blooming.
Good drainage	Let dry out between waterings	Medium feeder	Moderate-growing; dense, dark green foliage; flowers of male tree foul-smelling; tolerates heat, drought, city conditions; pods edible, used as chocolate substitute; naturally bushy, prune to tree shape.
Good drainage; organic matter	Medium water	Medium feeder	Tolerates drought; attractive fall foliage; long-lived; vigorous grower.

NAME	HABIT		FLOWERS		ADAPTATION	
	Type	Height	Color	Time	Zones	Light
Cercidiphyllum japonicum Katsura Tree	Deciduous tree	40 to 60 ft			4 to 9	Full sun to light shade
Cercis canadensis Eastern Redbud	Deciduous tree	20 to 30 ft	Pink	Spring	4 to 9	Full sun to light shade
Ceropegia woodii Rosary Vine, String-of-hearts	Houseplant	2 to 4 ft (trailing)			10 or IN	Light shade
Chaenomeles japonica Japanese Quince	Deciduous shrub	3 to 5 ft	Orange, red	Spring	5 to 9	Full sun
Chaenomeles speciosa Common Flowering Quince	Deciduous shrub	6 to 10 ft	Pink, red, white	Early spring	5 to 9	Full sun
Chamaecyparis lawsoniana Lawson Cypress, Port Orford Cedar	Needled evergreen tree	60 to 70 ft			6 to 8	Full sun
Chamaecyparis nootkatensis Alaska Cedar	Needled evergreen tree	70 to 100 ft			5 to 8	Full sun
Chamaecyparis obtusa Hinoki False Cypress	Evergreen tree	40 to 50 ft			5 to 8	Full sun
Chamaedorea elegans Parlor Palm	Houseplant	to 6 ft			10 or IN	Light shade
Chamomile *Chamaemelum nobile*	Hardy perennial herb	3 to 12 in	White	Late summer to first frost	4 to 10	Full sun to light shade
Chard, Swiss chard *Beta vulgaris cicla*	Hardy annual vegetable	to 3 ft				Full sun to light shade
Cheiranthus cheiri Wallflower	Hardy annual	1 to 2½ ft	Red, purple, orange, yellow	Spring to early summer		Full sun to light shade
Chenopodium bonus-henricus Good King Henry	Hardy perennial	to 2½ ft	Yellow	Summer	4 to 10	Light shade
Cherry, Sour or Pie *Prunus cerasus*	Deciduous fruit tree	15 to 25 ft	White	Spring	4 to 8	Full sun

For a list of common names, see page 378.

| | CULTURE | | |
Soil	Water	Feeding	Special Characteristics
Good drainage	Medium water	Medium feeder	Medium-growing; leaves purple in spring, dark green in summer, gold in fall; becomes vase-shaped with age; protect from hot sun and drying winds; some trees single-stemmed, others multistemmed.
Not particular	Medium water	Medium feeder	Moderate growing; attractive all year; blossoms appear early in spring; attractive leaves sometimes turn yellow in fall; interesting seed pods; grows in acid soil, alkaline soil, sun, shade.
Good drainage; sandy soil	Let dry out between waterings	Light feeder	Trailing stems of small, heart-shaped, dark green leaves, marbled with white; tiny flowers; give filtered sunlight; add extra humus to sandy potting soil.
Not particular	Medium water	Medium feeder	Lowest-growing species; wide-spreading branches; short spines; small fruit; tolerates light to heavy soil; prefers cool-winter climates.
Not particular	Medium water	Medium feeder	Usually rounded, dense shrub; thorns; tolerates drought; flowers best in full sun and when pruned heavily immediately after spring bloom; will not flower as prolifically in warm climates.
Good drainage	Medium water	Medium feeder	Fast-growing; pyramid shape with pendulous branches; bright green to blue-green needles; reddish-brown, fibrous bark; protect from hot, dry winds; prefers cool, coastal climate; screen, tall hedge, walk, and lawn specimen, container plant when young.
Good drainage	Medium water	Medium feeder	Moderate-growing; columnar shape; dark green needles fragrant when crushed; tolerates poor soil and low temperatures; thrives in moist, well-drained, acid soil.
Good drainage	Medium water	Medium feeder	Slow-growing; pyramid shape; deep, shiny green needles; good bonsai subject; can prune to shape; many dwarf varieties.
Good drainage; organic matter	Medium water	Medium feeder	Light green fronds; small yellow fruit near base of trunk; give bright, indirect light; water heavily; reduce water and fertilizer during winter; protect from dry air.
Good drainage; acid soil	Wet; don't let dry out	Medium feeder	Medicinal herb with soft, spreading, matting appearance; daisylike flowers; fragrant foliage.
Good drainage; organic matter	Medium water	Medium feeder	Both heat and drought resistant; tolerates light frost; grown for edible leaves and stalks; long-season harvest; several cultivars available.
Good drainage	Medium water	Medium feeder	Fragrant flowers; prefers coastal or mountainous regions with cool summers and high humidity.
Good drainage	Medium water	Medium feeder	Large, arrowhead leaves; edible foliage used as spinach substitute; early shoots eaten as asparagus substitute.
Good drainage	Medium water	Medium feeder	No fruit thinning needed; more tolerant of poor soil and growing conditions than sweet cherry.

NAME	HABIT		FLOWERS		ADAPTATION	
	Type	Height	Color	Time	Zones	Light
Cherry, Sweet *Prunus avium*	Deciduous fruit tree	15 to 40 ft	White	Spring	4 to 8	Full sun
Chervil *Anthriscus cerefolium*	Hardy annual herb	1½ to 2 ft				Light shade
Chick peas, Garbanzos *Cicer arietinum*	Tender annual vegetable	to 2 ft				Full sun
Chinese cabbage, Celery cabbage *Brassica chinensis*	Hardy annual vegetable	1 to 2 ft				Full sun to half-day sun
Chionodoxa luciliae Glory-of-the-snow	Hardy bulb	to 6 in	Blue	Spring	5 to 10	Full sun to light shade
Chives *Allium schoenoprasum*	Hardy perennial vegetable	to 2 ft	Lavender	Late summer	3 to 10	Full sun to light shade
Chlorophytum comosum Spider Plant, Airplane Plant	Houseplant	to 3 ft			10 or IN	Light shade
Choisya ternata Mexican Orange	Evergreen shrub	4 to 5 ft	White	Spring	8 to 10	Light shade
Chrysanthemum coccineum Pyrethrum, Painted Daisy	Hardy perennial	9 in to 3 ft	Pink, red, white	Early summer	2 to 10	Full sun to light shade
Chrysanthemum parthenium Feverfew, Matricaria	Hardy perennial	8 to 30 in	White	Summer	4 to 10	Full sun to light shade
***Chrysanthemum* hybrids** Hardy Chrysanthemum	Hardy perennial	1 to 4 ft	All colors except blue	Summer to late fall	4 to 10	Full sun to light shade
Chrysanthemum × superbum Shasta Daisy	Hardy perennial	2 to 4 ft	White	Early summer to first frost	4 to 10	Full sun to light shade
Cilantro—See Coriander						
Cimicifuga racemosa Black Snakeroot, Bugbane	Hardy perennial	2 to 3 ft	White	Early summer	3 to 8	Light shade
Cinnamomum camphora Camphor Tree	Evergreen tree	to 50 ft	Yellow	Late spring	6 to 10	Full sun
Cissus antarctica Kangaroo Vine	Houseplant	10 or 15 ft, (trailing)			10 or IN	Light shade

For a list of common names, see page 378.

| | CULTURE | | |
Soil	Water	Feeding	Special Characteristics
Good drainage	Medium water	Medium feeder	Require winter chilling; are damaged by intense cold in the fall and heavy rainfall; bear on long-lived spurs; needs little pruning after first two seasons of growth; all sweet cherries except 'Stella' need pollinators; birds are a major pest; many cultivars available; avoid areas of sand where bacterial canker is common; no fruit thinning needed; sweet cherry more upright in growth than sour cherry.
Rich soil	Wet; don't let dry out	Medium feeder	Culinary herb with fernlike green foliage and tiny flowers; self-sows freely.
Good drainage; organic matter	Medium water	Medium feeder	Requires 100 days growing season; produce s small pods with one or two seeds inside; harvested in green-shell stage, or as mature beans for drying.
Good drainage; organic matter	Medium water	Medium feeder	Cool-weather crop; bolts to seed in long days of late spring and summer; grow as fall and early winter vegetable; loose-leaf and heading cultivars available.
Good drainage	Medium water	Medium feeder	Star-shaped flowers; grasslike leaves; plant in early fall; blooms best in cold areas.
Good drainage; organic matter; rich soil	Medium water	Medium feeder	Culinary herb with grasslike, hollow leaves; grows in clumps; clip leaves to ground level when harvesting.
Good drainage	Medium water	Medium feeder	Wiry stems up to 5' long bear plantlets; grassy green, arching leaves usually striped with yellow or white; broad form; best in hanging pot; give bright, indirect light or partial shade; keep in moderate to cool location; water liberally during growing season.
Good drainage; organic matter	Medium water	Medium feeder	Fan-shaped foliage; very fragant flowers; tolerates full sun on the coast; place where delightful fragrance can be appreciated; very susceptible to spider mites.
Good drainage; organic matter; slightly alkaline soil	Medium water	Medium feeder	Tolerates moderate drought; long-lived; noninvasive.
Good drainage; sandy soil	Medium water	Medium water	Profuse bloomer; leaves have strong odor; self-sows freely; sometimes grown as annual.
Rich soil; good drainage; organic matter	Medium water	Heavy feeder	Tolerates mild drought; mulch in winter; tall varieties may need staking.
Good drainage; rich soil	Wet; don't let dry out	Medium feeder	Profuse bloomer; will not tolerate soggy soil in winter; provide good air circulation.
Good drainage; organic matter	Wet; don't let dry out	Medium feeder	Long-lived; excellent rear border; keep soil cool; will not flower well in deep shade.
Good drainage	Medium water	Medium feeder	Medium-growing; foliage aromatic; new growth reddish; small blackish fruits; good for street or lawn tree; competitive roots; thrives in summer heat.
Good drainage	Let dry out between waterings	Light feeder	Vigorous, trailing vine; grapelike tendrils; elongated, shiny green leaves; bright indirect light or partial shade; can stand neglect; leach plant frequently.

NAME	HABIT		FLOWERS		ADAPTATION	
	Type	Height	Color	Time	Zones	Light
Cissus rhombifolia Grape Ivy	Houseplant	3 to 6 ft, (trailing)			10 or IN	Light shade
Cistus species Rock Rose	Evergreen shrub	3 to 4 ft	Pink, red, white	Late spring to summer	8 to 10	Full sun
Cladrastis lutea Yellowwood	Deciduous tree	30 to 50 ft	White	Early summer	4 to 8	Full sun
Clarkia hybrids Godetia	Hardy annual	1½ to 2 ft	Pink, purple, red, white	Early summer to first frost		Full sun to light shade
Cleome hasslerana Spider Flower	Half-hardy annual	3 to 6 ft	White, pink, lavender	Early summer to early fall		Full sun
Clivia miniata Kaffir Lily	Tender bulb	to 1 ft	Orange, red	Late spring to summer	8 to 10	Light shade to deep shade
Codiaeum variegatum Croton	Houseplant	to 3 ft			10 or IN	Half-day sun
Colchicum luteum Autumn-Crocus	Half-hardy bulb	4 to 6 in	Yellow	Early spring	7 to 10	Full sun to light shade
Coleus × hybridus Coleus	Tender annual	1 to 3 ft				Half-day sun to light shade to deep shade
Collards *Brassica oleracea* var. *acephala*	Hardy biennial vegetable	1 to 2 ft			3 to 10	Full sun to half-day sun
Columnea gloriosa	Houseplant	1 to 3 ft (trailing)	Red	Winter to spring	10 or IN	Light shade
Comfrey *Symphytum officinale*	Hardy perennial herb	to 3 ft			3 to 10	Full sun to light shade
Consolida ambigua Rocket Larkspur, Annual Delphinium	Hardy annual	2 to 4 ft	White, pink, blue, purple	Early summer to early fall		Full sun to light shade
Convallaria majalis Lily-of-the-valley	Hardy bulb	6 to 8 in	White	Spring	3 to 7	Light shade
Convolvulus tricolor Dwarf Morning Glory	Hardy annual	to 1 ft	Blue, pink, white	Early summer to early fall		Full sun

For a list of common names, see page 378.

| | CULTURE | | |
Soil	Water	Feeding	Special Characteristics
Good drainage	Let dry out between waterings	Light feeder	Vigorous, trailing vine with grapelike tendrils; dark green leaves formed of 3 leaflets; give bright, indirect sunlight or partial shade; tolerates neglect; leach frequently.
Good drainage	Let dry out between waterings	Light feeder	Bushy, dense, rounded shape; fragrant foliage; tolerates drought, poor soil, seacoast conditions, and desert heat; good as large-scale bankcover and groundcover; doesn't transplant well after established.
Good drainage	Medium water	Medium feeder	Moderate growing; attractive bark and clean foliage that turns yellow in fall; fragrant flowers, profuse in alternate years; may not bloom until 10 years old; brown pods; good lawn, patio, park tree; when mature tolerates drought, heat, cold, alkaline soils.
Good drainage; sandy soil	Let dry out between waterings	Light feeder	Prefers cool nights.
Not particular	Medium water	Light feeder	Tolerates heat and drought; can be grown as temporary shrub if clustered; excellent as rear border; makes a good cut flower.
Rich soil; good drainage	Wet; don't let dry out	Heavy feeder	Green, straplike leaves; fragrant flowers; good in containers; blooms best when crowded.
Good drainage	Medium water	Medium feeder	Lance-shaped, leathery leaves up to 18" long; single trunk or stem; foliage color includes pink, red, orange, brown, and white; needs ample sun, warm location, and humidity; avoid dark location.
Good drainage	Medium water	Medium feeder	Foliage appears after blooming; plant in area where won't be disturbed.
Good drainage; organic matter	Wet; don't let dry out	Heavy feeder	Foliage has solid or multiple colors of pink, red, yellow, bronze, green, and chartreuse; pinch flowers to encourage foliage; makes a good houseplant.
Good drainage; organic matter	Medium water	Heavy feeder	Member of cabbage family; tolerates cold better than cabbage; exposure to frost improves flavor; withstands considerable heat; planting in spring and in fall produces almost year-round crop.
Good drainage	Medium water	Light feeder	Hairy leaves; give bright, indirect light; keep moist; reduce watering in winter; cut back after flowering ceases.
Rich soil; organic matter	Wet; don't let dry out	Medium feeder	Medicinal herb with large, hairy leaves up to 20" long; pinch off the star-shaped flowers to encourage leaf growth; foliage and roots edible.
Good drainage; organic matter	Medium water	Heavy feeder	Roots must be kept cool—mulch well; prefers cool climate.
Acid soil; organic matter	Wet; don't let dry out	Medium feeder	Very fragrant flowers; tiny, bell-shaped blossoms; keep quite moist during growing season.
Sandy soil; good drainage	Let dry out between waterings	Light feeder	Requires little water and fertilizer; needs summer heat.

NAME	HABIT		FLOWERS		ADAPTATION	
	Type	Height	Color	Time	Zones	Light
Coprosma rcpcns Mirror Plant	Evergreen shrub	8 to 10 ft			9 to 10	Full sun to light shade
Coprosma × kirkii Kirk's Coprosma	Evergreen groundcover	to 2 ft			9 to 10	Full sun to light shade
Cordyline stricta	Houseplant	6 to 12 ft	Lavender	Spring	10 or IN	Light shade
Coreopsis grandiflora	Hardy perennial	1 to 2 ft	Yellow	Summer	5 to 10	Full sun
Coreopsis tinctoria Calliopsis	Half-hardy annual	1 to 3 ft	Red, bicolored, orange, yellow	Late spring to early fall		Full sun
Coriander, Cilantro, Chinese Parsley *Coriandrum sativum*	Hardy annual herb	1 to 2½ ft				Full sun to light shade
Cornus alba 'Sibirica' Siberian Dogwood	Deciduous shrub	8 to 10 ft	White	Late spring to early summer	2 to 7	Full sun to light shade
Cornus alternifolia Pagoda Dogwood	Deciduous tree	15 to 25 ft	White	Late spring to early summer	3 to 7	Full sun to light shade
Cornus canadensis Bunchberry	Groundcover	to 9 in	White	Early spring	3 to 10	Half-day sun to light shade
Cornus florida Flowering Dogwood	Deciduous tree	20 to 30 ft	White	Late spring	5 to 9	Full sun to light shade
Cornus kousa Kousa Dogwood, Japanese Dogwood	Deciduous tree	15 to 20 ft	White	Summer	5 to 9	Full sun to light shade
Cornus sericea *(C. stolonifera)* *Red-osier Dogwood*	Deciduous shrub	8 to 10 ft	White	Late spring to early summer	2 to 8	Full sun to light shade
Corn *Zea mays rugosa*	Tender annual vegetable	5 to 8 ft				Full sun
Coronilla varia Crown Vetch	Groundcover	to 2 ft	Pink	Summer	3 to 10	Full sun to light shade
Cortaderia selloana Pampas Grass	Tender perennial	4 to 20 ft	White, pink	Late summer to winter	8 to 10	Full sun

For a list of common names, see page 378.

| | CULTURE | | |
Soil	Water	Feeding	Special Characteristics
Not particular	Let dry out between waterings	Light feeder	Round, very shiny leaves; prone to powdery mildew.
Not particular	Let dry out between waterings	Light feeder	Woody, upright, heavily branched stems; yellow-green, oblong leaves; drought-tolerant; can be used as small-scale groundcover; tolerates seacoast conditions.
Good drainage	Medium water	Light feeder	Leaves are swordlike, 2 feet long; dark green with a purplish tinge; easy to grow.
Good drainage	Let dry out between waterings	Light feeder	Weedy self-sower; short-lived perennial.
Good drainage; sandy soil	Medium water	Light feeder	Tolerant of poor soils; stems break in heavy wind or rain.
Good drainage; rich soil	Medium water	Medium feeder	Fast-growing culinary herb; oval leaves with serrated edges on main stems; fern-like side foliage; flowers in umbels; self-sows freely.
Not particular	Medium water	Medium feeder	Fast-growing; loose, open habit; attractive red, winter stems; best used in shrub border, massed on a large scale; prune hard each spring.
Rich soil	Medium water	Medium feeder	Fall color; less showy than other dogwoods, but hardier; shade from hot sun; slightly acid soil.
Good drainage; organic matter	Medium water	Medium feeder	Spreading habit; bright red fruits turn yellow to red in the fall; needs cool, moist climate, acid soil.
Rich soil	Medium water	Medium feeder	Moderate-growing; showy flowers; attractive red leaves in fall; red fruits; slightly acid soil; shade in hot-summer climates; many cultivars available.
Rich soil	Medium water	Medium feeder	Slow- to-moderate growing; yellow and scarlet fall color; berries in fall; tends to be multi-trunked; can prune to single stem.
Tolerates clay soil	Wet; don't let dry out	Medium feeder	Attractive dark red winter stem color; susceptible to canker.
Good drainage; organic matter	Wet; don't let dry out	Heavy feeder	Requires ample heat and water; wind-pollinated, best grown in block plantings; don't interplant different varieties of corn; for continuous supply, make successive plantings; wide variety of cultivars available, with different maturation dates, cob size, kernel color, taste, and disease resistance.
Not particular	Medium water	Light feeder	Dense growth; deep, soil-building roots; 1/2" leaflets; spreads by underground runners; can become invasive; tolerates drought; good for erosion control; dies back in winter; mass of brown stems may be a fire hazard in some areas.
Rich soil	Medium water	Medium water	Tolerates poor, dry soils; tolerates coastal conditions; fast-growing.

NAME	HABIT		FLOWERS		ADAPTATION	
	Type	Height	Color	Time	Zones	Light
Corylopsis spicata Spike Winter Hazel	Deciduous shrub	4 to 5 ft	Yellow	Early spring	6 to 8	Full sun to light shade
Corylus americana American Filbert	Deciduous shrub	9 to 10 ft	Brown	Early spring	5 to 9	Full sun to light shade
Corylus avellana 'Contorta' Harry Lauder's Walking Stick	Deciduous shrub	8 to 10 ft	Brown	Spring	5 to 8	Full sun to light shade
Cosmos bipinnatus Mexican Aster	Half-hardy annual	3 to 6 ft	Red, white, pink, lavender	Early summer to early fall		Full sun
Cotinus coggygria Common Smoke Tree	Deciduous shrub	15 to 25 ft	Lavender, purple	Early summer	5 to 10	Full sun
Cotoneaster apiculatus Cranberry Cotoneaster	Deciduous shrub, groundcover	3 to 4 ft	Pink	Late spring	4 to 10	Full sun to light shade
Cotoneaster conspicuus decorus Necklace Cotoneaster	Groundcover	1 to 1½ ft	White	Early summer	7 to 10	Full sun to half-day sun
Cotoneaster dammeri Bearberry Cotoneaster	Evergreen shrub, groundcover	1 to 1½ ft	White	Late spring to early summer	6 to 9	Full sun
Cotoneaster horizontalis Rock Cotoneaster	Deciduous shrub, groundcover	2 to 4 ft	Pink	Early summer	5 to 10	Full sun to half-day sun
Cotoneaster lucidus Hedge Cotoneaster	Deciduous shrub	10 to 15 ft	Pink	Spring	4 to 7	Full sun
Cotoneaster microphyllus Small-leaved Cotoneaster	Groundcover	2 to 3 ft	White	Early summer	6 to 10	Full sun to half-day sun
Cotoneaster salicifolius Willowleaf Cotoneaster	Evergreen shrub	to 15 ft	White	Spring	6 to 10	Full sun
Cowpea, Blackeye Pea *Vigna unguiculata*	Tender annual vegetable	to 2 ft			3 to 10	Full sun
Crassula argentea Jade Plant, Jade Tree	Houseplant	1 to 5 ft	White, pink		10 to IN	Full sun to half-day sun

For a list of common names, see page 378.

| | CULTURE | | |
Soil	Water	Feeding	Special Characteristics
Good drainage; organic matter	Medium water	Medium feeder	Fragrant flowers borne early in season; bright green, roundish leaves; slow-growing, open structure; very cold winters or late frosts often kill buds and blossoms; plant in sheltered location.
Not particular	Medium water	Medium feeder	Not as ornamental as *C. avellana*, although widely native on the East Coast; small, rounded nuts; male catkins; may reach 15' high; tends to sucker.
Not particular	Medium water	Medium feeder	Unique curled and twisting stems, twigs, and leaves; fast-growing; adaptable to many soils and easy to grow; use as accent or focal point; prune out suckers.
Good drainage	Let dry out between waterings	Light feeder	Do not fertilize or flowering will decrease; may need staking.
Good drainage	Let dry out between waterings	Light feeder	Moderate- to fast-growing; shrubby growth can be pruned to multistemmed tree; faded blooms give smokelike appearance all summer; leaves blue-green; good patio tree or planted in groups; adaptable, drought-tolerant, easy to grow.
Good drainage	Medium water	Medium feeder	Similar to *C. horizontalis* in growth habit; roundish leaves, bright green above and slightly hairy beneath; pinkish-white flowers; bright red fruits; occasionally prune out dead wood.
Tolerates clay soil	Medium water	Light feeder	Prostrate evergreen; 1/4-inch-long leaves, dark green on top, paler underneath; fairly large berries; best in containers or rock garden, not dense enough groundcover to shade out weeds.
Good drainage	Medium water	Medium feeder	Fast-growing; low, prostrate habit; glossy, dense leaves; red fruit in late summer; good choice for dry, rocky soil in exposed site; used as cover on banks or slopes, massed, or in shrub border.
Good drainage	Medium water	Light feeder	Grows 8–10' wide; semi-evergreen in mild climates, deciduous elsewhere; bright red berries; round leaves turn reddish before falling; heavily textured; good on banks and in low dividers; occasionally remove any dead wood; susceptible to fireblight.
Good drainage	Medium water	Medium feeder	Very dense growth; lustrous leaves; pinkish-white flowers; black fruit; may be pruned as hedge but more susceptible to fireblight and red spider mite in this shape; tolerates wind and poor, dry soils.
Tolerates clay soil	Medium water	Medium feeder	Evergreen; small leaves, shiny on top, hairy underneath; red berries in the fall; tangled, intermingling stems; well suited for banks or around rocks; benefits from soil amendments before planting; susceptible to fireblight; remove any dead wood.
Good drainage	Medium water	Medium feeder	Evergreen to semi-evergreen; vigorous, upright growth; arching branches; narrow, willowlike leaves; red fruits; use as screen, background plant or specimen plant.
Good drainage; organic matter	Medium water	Medium feeder	Grow like other beans; require warm days and warm nights to develop properly; Yardlong beans or Asparagus beans are a tall-growing variety of cowpea, grown as a climber; pods 1–2' long; very frost tender.
Good drainage; sandy soil	Let dry out between waterings	Light feeder	Compact, treelike form; stout, branching limbs with oblong, fleshy leaves 1–2" inches long; in direct sun, leaves become tinged with red; plants can be summered outdoors.

NAME	HABIT		FLOWERS		ADAPTATION	
	Type	Height	Color	Time	Zones	Light
Crataegus crus-galli Cockspur Thorn	Deciduous tree	20 to 30 ft	White	Late spring	4 to 9	Full sun
Crataegus laevigata English Hawthorn	Deciduous tree	15 to 25 ft	White, pink, red	Late spring	5 to 8	Full sun
Crataegus phaenopyrum Washington Thorn	Deciduous tree	20 to 30 ft	White	Late spring	5 to 8	Full sun
Crataegus viridis 'Winter King'	Deciduous tree	20 to 35 ft	White	Late spring	5 to 8	Full sun
Crataegus × lavallei Lavalle Hawthorn	Deciduous tree	20 ft	White	Late spring	5 to 9	Full sun
Crocus species Crocus	Hardy bulb	2 to 6 in	Lavender, purple, white, yellow	Spring	3 to 10	Full sun to light shade
Cryptomeria japonica Japanese Cedar	Needled evergreen tree	70 to 90 ft			6 to 9	Full sun
Cucumber *Cucumis sativus*	Tender annual vegetable	2 to 4 ft, (trailing)				Full sun
× *Cupressocyparis leylandii* Leyland cypress	Needled evergreen tree	40 to 50 ft			5 to 10	Full sun
Cupressus glabra Smooth Arizona Cypress	Needled evergreen tree	to 35 ft			7 to 10	Full sun
Cupressus macrocarpa Monterey Cypress	Needled evergreen tree	40 to 70 ft			8 to 10	Full sun to light shade
Cupressus sempervirens Italian Cypress	Needled evergreen tree	30 to 40 ft			8 to 10	Full sun
Currant *Ribes sativum*	Deciduous berry	3 to 5 ft			4 to 9	Full sun to light shade
Cyclamen hederifolium (*C. neapolitanum*) Neapolitan Cyclamen	Hardy bulb	4 to 5 in	Pink, white	Late summer to early fall	5 to 9	Light shade

For a list of common names, see page 378.

	CULTURE		
Soil	**Water**	**Feeding**	**Special Characteristics**
Good drainage; rich soil	Medium water	Medium feeder	Broad-crowned tree; thorny; leathery, toothed leaves; dull red fruit; fall color; give sunny location; prefers rich, loamy soil.
Not particular	Let dry out between waterings	Medium feeder	Moderate-growing, shrublike tree; does poorly in summer heat and humidity; many cultivars available—some with red fruit.
Not particular	Let dry out between waterings	Medium feeder	Broad, columnar tree; attractive fall foliage; red fruit; resistant to fireblight; grows well in city; one of the better hawthorns.
Not particular	Let dry out between waterings	Medium feeder	Glossy green leaves; dense, rounded head; long-lasting red fruits.
Not particular	Let dry out between waterings	Medium feeder	Moderate-growing; abundant flowers; dense foliage turns bronze-red in fall; thorns; orange to red fruits in fall and winter; tolerates seacoast conditions, highways, inner city conditions.
Good drainage	Medium water	Medium feeder	Plant in early fall; many varieties.
Good drainage	Medium water	Medium feeder	Moderate-growing; light green to bluish-green needles; reddish-brown bark; graceful appearance; good park tree—needs room to develop; deep soil.
Good drainage; organic matter	Medium water	Medium feeder	Warm-weather plant; water deeply; can be trained on trellis; keep all fruit picked to encourage setting of new fruits; major groups of cucumbers include slicing varieties, picking varieties, and dwarf plants; many cultivars available within each group.
Adaptive		Medium feeder	Fast-growing, columnar shape; good for tall hedges and screens; gray-green needles; tolerates wide range of soils and climates; may reach 100' high.
Sandy soil	Let dry out between waterings	Light feeder	Fast-growing; compact, narrow pyramid shape; reddish-brown bark; silver-gray to blue-green, scalelike foliage; good windbreak, screen, hedge; tolerates hot, dry climate, and poor, sandy soils.
Good drainage	Medium water	Medium feeder	Slow- to moderate-growing; windswept habit develops only in high winds along coast; best on West Coast; windbreak, or clipped hedge; subject to fatal canker disease.
Good drainage	Medium water	Medium feeder	Fast-growing; vertical column; scalelike, dark green foliage; tolerates wide range of soils and drought; stiff, formal appearance; needs large garden or driveway setting.
Good drainage; organic matter	Medium water	Medium feeder	Attractive shrub and fruit; productive and easy to care for; good fall color; keep moist; shade in hot-summer areas; prune to remove weak growth, old canes; maintain balance of 1, 2, and 3-year old wood; currants banned in areas of white pine because they carry diseases to these trees; check with your local Agricultural Extension before planting currants in your area.
Rich soil; organic matter	Medium water	Heavy feeder	Fragrant flowers appear before foliage; marbled leaves.

NAME	HABIT		FLOWERS		ADAPTATION	
	Type	Height	Color	Time	Zones	Light
Cyclamen persicum Florist's Cyclamen	Tender bulb	to 10 in	Lavender, pink, red, white	Late fall to spring	9 to 10 or IN	Light shade
Cynodon dactylon Bermuda Grass	Turfgrass	¾ to 1½ in			7 to 10	Full sun
Cynodon species Improved Bermuda Grass	Turfgrass	½ to 1 in			7 to 10	Full sun
Cynoglossum amabile Chinese Forget-me-not	Hardy biennial	1½ to 2 ft	Blue, pink, white	Late spring to late summer		Full sun to light shade
Cyrtomium falcatum Japanese Holly Fern	Groundcover, houseplant Houseplant	1 to 2 ft			10 or IN	Half-day sun to light shade
Cytisus scoparius Scotch Broom	Deciduous shrub	8 to 10 ft	Yellow	Late spring to early summer	6 to 10	Full sun
Cytisus × kewensis Kew Broom	Groundcover	6 to 10 in	Yellow	Late spring	7 to 10	Full sun
Cytisus × praecox Warminster Broom	Deciduous shrub	4 to 6 ft	Yellow	Late spring	6 to 9	Full sun
Dahlia hybrids Dahlia	Tender perennial	1 to 5 ft	All colors except blue	Summer to first frost	8 to 10	Full sun to light shade
Daphne cneorum Garland Flower, Rose Daphne	Evergreen groundcover	½ to 1 ft	Pink	Spring	5 to 7	Light shade
Daphne odora Winter Daphne	Evergreen shrub	3 to 4 ft	Pink	Winter to early spring	8 to 10	Light shade
Daphne × burkwoodii Burkwood Daphne	Deciduous shrub	3 to 4 ft	Pink, white	Late spring	5 to 8	Light shade
Davallia mariesii Squirrel's Foot Fern, Ball Fern	Houseplant	6 to 10 in			10 or IN	Light shade
Delphinium elatum Delphinium	Hardy perennial	4 to 8 ft	Blue, pink, white, red, violet	Summer	2 to 8	Full sun
Dendrobium orchids	Houseplant	1 to 2½ ft	Lavender, white, yellow	Varies among species	10 or IN	Light shade

For a list of common names, see page 378.

| | CULTURE | | |
Soil	Water	Feeding	Special Characteristics
Rich soil; good drainage	Wet; don't let dry out	Heavy feeder	Sold as potted plant; single, double, fringed, crested flowers; heart-shaped leaves; needs slightly acid soil; container or houseplant.
Good drainage; organic matter	Medium water	Medium to heavy feeder	Easy to grow in most soils; likes heat; tolerates drought; wears very well; invasive; won't tolerate shade; takes abuse, but makes attractive lawn when given extra care; often browns in fall until spring.
Good drainage; organic matter	Medium water	Heavy feeder	Softer, finer texture than common bermuda grass; shorter dormancy period; more water, fertilizer, and mowing needs than common bermuda grass; many cultivars available.
Good drainage; organic matter	Medium water	Medium feeder	Easy to grow and not particular about water or temperatures; usually grown as an annual.
Rich soil	Wet; don't let dry out	Heavy feeder	Dense groundcover in mild areas; common houseplant; shiny, leathery, light yellowish-green fronds; good in containers, under camellias, or similar shrubs.
Good drainage; grows in poor soil	Let dry out between waterings	Light feeder	Rampant, aggressive spreader; green stems provide winter interest.
Good drainage; acid soil	Let dry out between waterings	Light feeder	Trailing branches; very adaptable; best in dry, poor soils; tolerates drought and seacoast conditions, sandy soil; effective trailing over walls and down slopes; spreads 3' wide; prune if foliage becomes spindly.
Good drainage	Let dry out between waterings	Light feeder	Dense, vertical stems; foliage sparse, or nonexistent; showy flowers; prefers infertile, poor soil; good specimen in shrub border, rock garden; intolerant of pruning when mature.
Good drainage; organic matter	Medium water	Heavy feeder	Keep roots cool; lift roots in fall, store in sawdust; flowers vary from 1 inch wide to 7 or 8 inches; often grown as annual.
Good drainage	Medium water	Medium feeder	Spreading, loose mass; finely textured evergreen foliage; very fragrant flowers; neutral soil; protect from sun and drying winds; mulch to keep roots cool and moist.
Good drainage	Let dry out between waterings	Medium feeder	Lustrous, dark green leaves; fragrant flowers; unpredictable; plant high to avoid crown rot; water infrequently during summer to increase blooming.
Good drainage	Medium water	Medium feeder	Larger than *D. cneorum*; extremely fragrant flowers open pink and fade to white; easiest daphne to grow; semi-evergreen in some zones.
Good drainage	Medium water	Medium feeder	Wiry stems of small fronds with leaflets; brownish, furry, creeping rhizomes grow above ground; likes filtered light, high humidity, cool temperatures; good in hanging pot.
Rich soil; good drainage; slightly alkaline soil	Medium water	Medium feeder	Difficult to grow; requires staking; best in cool climates.
Good drainage	Medium water	Medium feeder	Both evergreen and deciduous orchids; large flowers bloom in clusters along stem; needs very bright, indirect light and humidity; avoid roots standing in water.

NAME	HABIT		FLOWERS		ADAPTATION	
	Type	Height	Color	Time	Zones	Light
Deutzia gracilis Slender Deutzia	Deciduous shrub	2 to 6 ft	White	Late spring	5 to 8	Full sun to light shade
Deutzia scabra	Deciduous shrub	6 to 10 ft	White	Late spring to early summer	5 to 8	Full sun to light shade
Deutzia × magnifica Showy Deutzia	Deciduous shrub	6 to 10 ft	White	Late spring to early summer	5 to 8	Full sun to light shade
Dianthus barbatus Sweet William	Half-hardy biennial	4 to 24 in	White, pink, red, purple	Summer to fall		Full sun to light shade
Dianthus caryophyllus Carnation	Half-hardy perennial	1 to 3 ft	Pink, red, white	Late spring to early summer	7 to 10	Full sun
Dianthus chinensis China Pink	Hardy annual	8 to 28 in	White, pink, purple, red, lavender	Summer to fall		Full sun to light shade
Dianthus deltoides Maiden Pink	Hardy perennial	8 to 12 in	Pink, purple, white	Early summer	3 to 10	Full sun
Dianthus plumarius Cottage Pink, Scotch Pink	Hardy perennial	to 12 in	Pink, red, white	Late spring to early summer	3 to 10	Full sun
Dicentra spectabilis Bleeding-heart	Hardy perennial	to 2½ ft	Pink, white	Late spring to early summer	2 to 8	Light shade
Dichondra micrantha (*D. repens*) Dichondra	Groundcover	to 3 in			9 to 10	Full sun to light shade
Dictamnus albus Gas Plant	Hardy perennial	to 3 ft	White	Late spring to early summer	2 to 10	Full sun to light shade
Dieffenbachia species Dumb Cane	Houseplant	to 6 ft			10 or IN	Light shade
Diervilla sessilifolia Southern Bush Honeysuckle	Deciduous shrub	3 to 5 ft	Yellow	Early summer	5 to 8	Full sun to light shade
Digitalis purpurea Foxglove	Hardy biennial	2 to 5 ft	Purple, pink, white, red, yellow	Summer	4 to 9	Light shade
Dill *Anethum graveolens*	Tender annual herb	2 to 4 ft	Yellow	Summer to early fall		Full sun
Dimorphotheca sinuata Cape Marigold	Half-hardy annual	6 to 15 in	White, orange, yellow, pink	Summer to early fall		Full sun

For a list of common names, see page 378.

	CULTURE		
Soil	**Water**	**Feeding**	**Special Characteristics**
Good drainage	Medium water	Medium feeder	Low, broad mounded shrub; graceful, upright branches; dull green foliage; flowers on old wood, so prune immediately after flowering; cut out any winter dieback; showy only when in bloom.
Good drainage	Medium water	Medium feeder	Dull green leaves with scallop-toothed edges; flowers white to pinkish; prune after flowering.
Good drainage	Medium water	Medium feeder	A double-flowering hybrid; prune after flowering.
Good drainage; slightly alkaline soil	Medium water	Light feeder	Grown as an annual; sweet, fragrant flowers; most flowers are bicolored.
Good drainage; sandy soil	Let dry out between waterings	Light feeder	Fragrant flowers; usually short-lived.
Good drainage; slightly alkaline soil	Medium water	Light feeder	Leaves are grasslike and blue-grey; flowers are often bicolored.
Good drainage; sandy soil	Let dry out between waterings	Light feeder	Low-growing and mat-forming.
Good drainage; organic matter; sandy soil	Let dry out between waterings	Light feeder	Best in cool areas; water during drought; long-lived; flowers are bicolored.
Rich soil; good drainage; organic matter	Medium water	Heavy feeder	Tends to die down after blooming; will tolerate deep shade; keep plants out of drying winds.
Good drainage	Wet; don't let dry out	Medium feeder	Masses of dark green, cupped, horseshoe-shaped leaves; lawn substitute; moderate spreader; rarely needs mowing; tolerates only light foot traffic; started from seed or plugs.
Rich soil; good drainage; organic matter	Medium water	Medium feeder	Fragrant, lemon-scented foliage; long-lived; large, bushy, showy perennial.
Good drainage	Medium water	Medium feeder	Arching, oblong, pointed leaves; single trunk when young, multiple trunks when mature; give bright, indirect light, many cultivars available; leaves and stem toxic if ingested.
Good drainage	Medium water	Medium feeder	Native to eastern United States; makes good groundcover for holding banks; spreads by underground stolons; good in rugged terrain where other plants will not survive; prune in early spring.
Good drainage; organic matter	Medium water	Medium feeder	Tolerates full sun; self-sows abundantly; good as rear border, grown as a perennial.
Good drainage; acid soil	Wet; don't let dry out	Medium feeder	Culinary herb with light green, feathery foliage; greenish-yellow flowers in umbels; self-sows readily; doesn't transplant well.
Good drainage; sandy soil	Let dry out between waterings	Light feeder	Best in dry areas.

NAME	HABIT		FLOWERS		ADAPTATION	
	Type	Height	Color	Time	Zones	Light
Dizygotheca elegantissima False Aralia	Houseplant	10 to 12 ft			10 or IN	Light shade
Dracaena deremensis 'Warneckii'	Houseplant	to 15 ft			10 or IN	Light shade
Dracaena fragrans Corn Plant	Houseplant	8 to 10 ft	White		10 or IN	Light shade
Dracaena godseffiana Gold Dust Dracaena, Spotted Dracaena	Houseplant	to 10 ft			10 or IN	Light shade
Dracaena marginata Red Margined Dracaena	Houseplant	8 to 10 ft			10 or IN	Light shade
Duchesnea indica Indian Strawberry, Mock Strawberry	Groundcover	to 2 in	Yellow	Spring	4 to 10	Light shade
Dyssodia tenuiloba Dahlberg Daisy, Golden Fleece	Hardy annual	4 to 8 in	Yellow	Spring to fall		Full sun
Echinacea purpurea Purple-coneflower	Hardy perennial	3 to 5 ft	Purple	Summer to early fall	3 to 9	Full sun to light shade
Echinops exaltatus Globe Thistle	Hardy perennial	3 to 6 ft	Blue	Summer	3 to 9	Full sun to light shade
Echinopsis species Sea Urchin Cactus	Houseplant	to 10 in	Pink, red, white, yellow	Summer	10 or IN	Half-day sun to full sun
Eggplant *Solanum melongena esculentum*	Tender annual vegetable	1½ to 3 ft				Full sun
Elaeagnus angustifolia Russian Olive	Deciduous tree	20 to 25 ft	Yellow	Early summer	2 to 9	Full sun
Elaeagnus pungens Silverberry	Evergreen shrub	6 to 15 ft	White	Fall	7 to 10	Full sun
Elaeagnus umbellata Autumn Elaeagnus	Deciduous shrub	12 to 18 ft	White	Late spring	4 to 8	Full sun
Endive *Cichorium endiva*	Hardy annual vegetable	to 3 ft				Full sun to light shade

For a list of common names, see page 378.

| | **CULTURE** | | |
Soil	**Water**	**Feeding**	**Special Characteristics**
Good drainage	Medium water	Medium feeder	Thin, dark green leaves with lighter veins; divided into 9 segments with saw-toothed edges; slow-growing; give bright, indirect light, older plants tolerate less light; very sensitive to water; avoid dry soil or wet soil; keep air moist.
Good drainage	Let dry out between waterings	Light feeder	Green leaves with white and gray streaks running lengthwise; leaves may reach 2' long, 2" wide; reliable foliage houseplant.
Good drainage	Let dry out between waterings	Light feeder	Single stem; tuft of arching, swordlike green leaves; variety D.f. 'Massangeana' is streaked with cream or yellow; occasionally yields sprays of fragrant white flowers; give bright, indirect light or filtered sun.
Good drainage	Medium water	Light feeder	Broad green leaves marbled with white and gold; keep soil moist, not soggy; give bright, indirect light or filtered sun.
Good drainage	Let dry out between waterings	Light feeder	Thin, red-edged leaves atop trunks that zig-zag and curve; very bright light is best.
Good drainage; sandy soil	Medium water	Medium feeder	Dense, low, mat-forming; spreads rapidly by runners; strawberrylike leaves and fruit.
Good drainage	Let dry out between waterings	Light feeder	Heat and drought tolerant; avoid overfertilizing; long blooming season; readily reseeds itself.
Good drainage; sandy soil	Medium water	Medium feeder	Drought and wind tolerant; shady conditions produce richer flower color.
Good drainage	Let dry out between waterings	Medium feeder	Flowers appear in balls; good for dried flower arrangements.
Good drainage; sandy soil	Let dry out between waterings	Medium feeder	Gray-green globular to oval stems; clusters of spines along ribbed stems; small-growing, free-flowering; keep moderately moist in the summer.
Good drainage; rich soil; organic matter	Medium water	Medium feeder to heavy feeder	Susceptible to low-temperature injury; likes heat; good in containers; pick fruits when young; good fruit has high gloss; plants heavy with fruit may need support; several cultivars available with differing color and size.
Good drainage	Medium water	Medium feeder	Fast-growing, shrubby tree; leaves willowlike, olive green above, silvery below; unusual, twisting trunk; attractive bark; thorny branches; yellow berries; tolerates cold and heat; fruits messy; can prune as hedge, screen, espalier.
Sandy soil	Medium water	Light feeder	Olive-colored foliage; thorny branches; edible red fruit; flowers inconspicuous but very fragrant; tolerates heat, drought, wind; prefers poor, infertile soil; good hedge plant; cultivars available with variegated foliage.
Good drainage	Medium water	Medium feeder	Fast-growing, spreading shrub; young foliage is silvery; fragrant flowers; silvery fruit matures to red.
Good drainage; organic matter	Medium water	Medium feeder	Grown in same way as lettuce; best if grown for fall or winter harvest; has nutlike flavor; several cultivars available.

NAME	HABIT		FLOWERS		ADAPTATION	
	Type	Height	Color	Time	Zones	Light
Epimedium grandiflorum Bishops-hat	Groundcover	to 1 ft	Red, violet, white	Late spring to early summer	3 to 10	Light shade
Epipremnum aureum Pothos, Devil's Ivy	Houseplant	3 to 5 ft (trailing)			10 or IN	Light shade
Episcia cupreata Flame Violet	Houseplant	to 6 in	Red	Summer	10 or IN	Light shade
Eranthis cilicica	Hardy bulb	2 to 8 in	Yellow	Early spring	4 to 9	Full sun to light shade
Eranthis hyemalis Winter Aconite	Hardy bulb	2 to 8 in	Yellow	Early spring	5 to 9	Full sun to light shade
Eremochloa ophiuroides Centipedegrass	Turfgrass	to 2 in			7 to 10	Full sun to light shade
Erica arborea Tree Heath	Evergreen shrub	10 to 20 ft	White	Spring	9 to 10	Full sun
Erica carnea Spring Heath	Evergreen shrub	6 to 16 in	Red	Winter to early summer	6 to 8	Full sun
Erica mediterranea Biscay Heath	Evergreen shrub	4 to 7 ft			8 to 10	Full sun
Erica vagans Cornish Heath	Evergreen shrub	2 to 3 ft	Pink	Summer to early fall	6 to 8	Full sun
Eriobotrya japonica Loquat	Evergreen tree	to 30 ft	White	Fall	8 to 10	Full sun
Erythronium species Fawn-lily	Hardy bulb	to 12 in	White, yellow, purple	Spring to early summer	3 to 10	Light shade
Escallonia rubra Red Escallonia	Evergreen shrub	6 to 15 ft	Red	Early summer to early fall	8 to 10	Light shade
Eschscholzia californica California Poppy	Hardy annual	12 to 15 in	Orange, yellow, red, white	Spring to early summer		Full sun to light shade
Eucalyptus cinerea Florist's Eucalyptus	Evergreen tree	30 to 40 ft	White	Winter to spring	9 to 10	Full sun to light shade

For a list of common names, see page 378.

	CULTURE		
Soil	**Water**	**Feeding**	**Special Characteristics**
Rich soil	Medium water	Heavy feeder	Long-lived; semi-evergreen; leathery, heart-shaped leaves turn reddish in fall; tolerates full sun if soil is rich, moist, and acidic; shallow, creeping roots; remove old leaves in spring.
Good drainage	Medium water	Light feeder	Climbing, trailing habit; heart-shaped green leaves splashed with white or cream; give bright, indirect light; keep warm and in humid location; pinch growth tips to encourage bushiness; avoid overfertilizing.
Good drainage; organic matter	Medium water	Medium feeder	Copper-colored leaves with silver veins; cascading stolons; good in hanging pot; small, tubular flowers; needs high humidity; keep moist; give bright light, no direct sun; pinch tips to encourage branching; leach plant with every watering.
Good drainage; organic matter	Medium water	Medium feeder	Green or bronze foliage; single, fragrant blossoms.
Good drainage; organic matter	Medium water	Medium feeder	Green or bronze foliage; single, fragrant flowers; good for naturalizing.
Good drainage; organic matter	Medium water	Light feeder	Adapts to poor soil; crowds out weeds; good, low-maintenance, general-purpose lawn; coarse-textured; shallow-rooted; tends to yellow from chlorosis; doesn't wear well.
Good drainage; sandy soil	Wet; don't let dry out	Light feeder	Awkward-looking shrub or small tree; fragrant flowers; needs infertile, acid soil; keep roots moist; shallow rooted.
Good drainage; sandy soil	Wet; don't let dry out	Light feeder	Dwarf, spreading form; infertile soil; keep roots moist; prefers acid soil; shallow roots.
Good drainage; sandy soil	Wet; don't let dry out	Light feeder	Flowers insignificant; use as background foliage; give infertile, moist soil; prefers acid soil.
Good drainage; sandy soil	Wet; don't let dry out	Light feeder	Bushy shrub; needs infertile soil; keep roots moist; prefers acid soil; shallow rooted; shear after blooming.
Good drainage	Medium water	Medium feeder	Moderate growing; large, dark-green, serrated leaves, rust-colored underside; fragrant flowers, not showy; abundant orange-to-yellow fruits ripen late winter or spring; takes pruning as groundcover, espalier, container; best in mild climate; tolerates alkaline soil.
Good drainage	Medium water	Medium feeder	Needs moisture all summer long; resents extreme heat; give sun in cool summer areas; mulch in fall.
Good drainage	Medium water	Medium feeder	Fast-growing; attractive, fragrant flowers produced year-round in mild climates; dense, rounded, upright habit; dark green foliage; tolerates coastal conditions, mild drought; full sun in cooler areas; screen, windbreak, shrub border; pruning lessens windbreak effect.
Sandy soil; good drainage	Let dry out between waterings	Light feeder	Tolerates drought and poor soils; does not transplant well—seed in place.
Not particular	Medium water	Medium feeder	Moderate- to fast-growing; blue-gray foliage; attractive bark; tends to have multiple trunks, can be pruned to one; branches decorative; withstands wind; best in dry site or with fast drainage; small seed cups.

NAME	HABIT		FLOWERS		ADAPTATION	
	Type	Height	Color	Time	Zones	Light
Eucalyptus ficifolia Flaming Gum, Red-Flowering Gum	Deciduous tree	25 ft	Orange, pink, red, white	All year	9 to 10	Full sun
Eucalyptus globulus Blue Gum	Evergreen tree	75 to 100 ft	White	Winter	9 to 10	Full sun
Eucalyptus gunnii Cider Gum	Evergreen tree	to 50 ft	White	Spring to early summer	9 to 10	Full sun
Eucalyptus polyanthemos Silver Dollar Eucalyptus	Evergreen tree	40 to 50 ft	White	Spring to summer	9 to 10	Full sun
Eucalyptus rudis Desert Gum	Evergreen tree	40 to 50 ft	White	Spring to summer	9 to 10	Full sun
Eucalyptus sideroxylon Red Ironbark	Evergreen tree	40 to 50 ft	Pink	Fall-spring	9 to 10	Full sun
Eucalyptus viminalis Manna Gum	Evergreen tree	to 100 ft	White	All year	9 to 10	Full sun
Eucharis grandiflora Amazon Lily	Tender bulb	to 1½ ft	White	Early spring	9 to 10	Light shade
Eugenia uniflora Surinam Cherry, Pitanga	Evergreen tree	13 to 25 ft	White	Late summer	10	Full sun
Euonymus alatas Burning Bush, Winged Euonymus	Deciduous shrub	15 to 20 ft			4 to 8	Full sun to deep shade
Euonymus fortunei Wintercreeper Euonymus	Groundcover	to 3 ft			5 to 8	Full sun to deep shade
Euonymus japonica Japanese Euonymus	Evergreen shrub	10 to 15 ft			7 to 10	
Euphorbia corollata Flowering Spurge	Hardy perennial	to 3 ft	White	Summer	4 to 9	Full sun
Euphorbia marginata Snow-on-the-mountain	Half-hardy annual	1½ to 2 ft	White	Summer to fall		Full sun to light shade
Euphorbia milii Crown of Thorns	Houseplant	3 to 4 ft	Warm colors, pink	All year	10 or IN	Light shade
Euphorbia myrsinites Myrtle Euphorbia	Hardy perennial	3 to 6 in	Yellow	Spring to early summer	4 to 9	Full sun

For a list of common names, see page 378.

	CULTURE		
Soil	**Water**	**Feeding**	**Special Characteristics**
Not particular	Medium water	Medium feeder	Fast-growing; dense foliage, leaves dark green, large, and heavy; striking blooms peak in July-August, most common color red; best on coast; frost tender; seed cups.
Not particular	Medium water	Medium feeder	Fast-growing; common in California; very messy; branches break easily.
Not particular	Medium water	Medium feeder	Fast-growing, upright; hardy; long, narrow, medium green leaves; good shade, windbreak, privacy screen; bell-shaped seed pods.
Good drainage	Medium water	Medium feeder	Fast-growing; silvery-gray foliage, attractive shape; good tree on seacoast or desert; cylindrical seed cups.
Not particular	Medium water	Light feeder	Fast-growing; gray-green foliage; rough, attractive bark; tolerates heat, wind, poor soil, coastal or desert conditions; seed capsules.
Good drainage	Medium water	Medium feeder	Moderate-growing; gray-green foliage; attractive flowers; strong tree; streets, parks, golf courses; goblet-shaped seed capsules.
Rich soil	Medium water	Medium feeder	Fast-growing; rich green, weeping foliage; trunk whitish; striking silhouette; needs lots of room; tolerates poor soil; small seed capsules; flowers insignificant.
Rich soil	Medium water	Heavy feeder	Evergreen; fragrant flowers; good container plant—blooms best when crowded; keep soil on dry side after blooming, until renewed growth is seen.
Good drainage	Medium water	Medium feeder	Moderate-growing; glossy green leaves that darken in cold weather; fragrant flowers; fruits green, turn crimson when ripe-edible; effective as tall hedge; can be sheared.
Good drainage	Medium water	Medium feeder	Neat, vase-shaped habit; brilliant scarlet fall foliage; best fall color if grown in full sun; tolerates most soils except very wet ones; pruning causes uneven growth.
Good drs-4ainage	Medium water	Medium feeder	Variable in habit and size; tolerates all but wet soils; transplants easily; susceptible to numerous diseases, insects; some cultivars produce berries; many cultivars used as groundcovers.
Good drainage	Medium water	Medium feeder	Low-maintenance, tough shrub or small tree; good for harsh conditions and poor soils; plant where air circulation is good and water doesn't stand; susceptible to mildew, insects.
Grows in poor soil	Let dry out between waterings	Light feeder	Attractive fall foliage; flowers form in sprays; extremely tough and adaptable.
Grows in poor soil	Let dry out between waterings	Light feeder	Grows in any soil; drought tolerant; if broken, the gray-green leaves with white margins exude juice that may irritate the skin.
Good drainage	Medium water	Medium feeder	Succulent, woody plant; long, sharp thorns; leaves only at or near end of branches; give bright light, no full sun; can tolerate some drought; may bloom all year.
Grows in poor soil	Let dry out between waterings	Light feeder	Evergreen; gray-green foliage; spreads invasively.

NAME	HABIT		FLOWERS		ADAPTATION	
	Type	Height	Color	Time	Zones	Light
Euphorbia pulcherrima Poinsettia	Houseplant	1 to 3 ft	Pink, red, white	Fall to winter	10 or IN	Half-day sun
Fagus sylvatica European Beech	Deciduous tree	70 to 80 ft			5 to 7	Full sun
Fatsia japonica Japanese Aralia	Tender perennial or houseplant	to 15 ft			9 to 10 or IN	Light shade to half-day sun
Festuca arundinacea Tall Fescue	Turfgrass	3 to 4 in			3 to 9	Full sun to light shade
Festuca ovina glauca Blue Fescue	Groundcover	10 in			3 to 10	Full sun
Festuca rubra commutata Chewing Fescue	Turfgrass	¾ to 1 in			4 to 8	Full sun to light shade
Festuca rubra Red Fescue, Creeping Red Fescue	Turfgrass	2 to 4 in			4 to 8	Full sun to light shade
Ficus benjamina Weeping Fig	Houseplant	2 to 18 ft			10 or IN	Light shade to half-day sun
Ficus elastica Rubber Plant	Houseplant	2 to 10 ft			10 or IN	Light shade
Ficus lyrata (F. pandurata) Fiddleleaf Fig	Houseplant	5 to 10 ft			10 or IN	Light shade
Ficus pumila Creeping Fig	Houseplant or vine	Climbs to 30 ft			9 to 10 or IN	Light shade to half-day sun
Fig *Ficus carica*	Deciduous fruit tree	12 to 30 ft			7 to 10	Full sun
Filbert *Corylus maxima*	Deciduous nut tree	15 to 25 ft			4 to 8	Full sun
Fittonia verschaffeltii var. argyroneura Nerve Plant, Mosaic Plant	Houseplant	6 to 8 in			10 or IN	Light shade

For a list of common names, see page 378.

Soil	Water	Feeding	Special Characteristics
Good drainage	Medium water	Medium feeder	Woody; shrublike; flowers are actually a group of bracts surrounding small, true flower; give plenty of sun while blooming, protect from hot afternoon exposure; prefers slightly acid soil; allow soil to dry somewhat between waterings; must give short days from Sept. 1–Oct. 30 to get flowers.
Good drainage	Medium water	Medium feeder	Slow growing; tall, wide tree with dense foliage, smooth gray bark; attractive fall color; demands lots of room.
Good drainage	Medium water	Heavy feeder	Bold, green, lobed leaves, some variegated; fast growing; cool location with bright, indirect light; feed every 2 weeks during growing season; decrease water during winter; prune back in spring.
Good drainage; organic matter	Medium water	Medium feeder	Good, tough play lawn; green all year; some disease and insect resistance; coarse textured; tends to clump; good drought tolerance; wears best in spring and fall; takes heat; best cool-season grass for transition areas.
Good drainage	Medium water	Medium feeder	Attractive ornamental grass; hairlike leaves; grows in rounded bluish-gray tufts; mounding habit; not practical lawn substitute; needs regular summer watering; clip back shaggy plants.
Good drainage; organic matter	Let dry out between waterings	Light feeder	Will tolerate close mowing in cool-climate areas; very susceptible to summer diseases in hot climates, especially in moist, fertile soils; wears poorly; best in cool-summer climates.
Good drainage; organic matter	Medium water	Light feeder	Fine texture; deep green color; grows well in shade or dry soils; tolerates acid soil; susceptible to summer diseases in hot climates, especially in moist, fertile soils; wears poorly; best in cool-summer areas.
Good drainage; rich soil	Medium water	Medium feeder	Arching, graceful branches; glossy, pointed leaves; give very bright, indirect light, frequent light feedings; keep evenly moist; avoid dry heat, sudden changes of environment; will tolerate direct sun if kept moist; prune out inner, shaded growth.
Good drainage; rich soil	Medium water	Medium feeder	Bold, dark green leaves; give bright light, frequent light feedings; avoid overfeeding; avoid dry heat, sudden changes of environment; keep evenly moist.
Good drainage; rich soil	Medium water	Medium feeder	Durable, deep green leaves shaped like a fiddle; give bright light, frequent light feedings; keep evenly moist; avoid dry heat, sudden changes in environment.
Good drainage; rich soil	Medium water	Medium feeder	Fast-growing, trailing or climbing plant; small leaves; likes more moisture, shade, and richer soil than other ficus.
Good drainage	Medium water	Light feeder	Low branched, spreading, large leafed, tropical-looking tree; bears two crops of fruit in a season; requires little attention; drought resistant once established; can be left unpruned or cut back to control size; pruning back usually eliminates first crop; will sprout again if killed by frost; several varieties available.
Good drainage	Medium water	Medium feeder	Produces fall crop of roundish to oblong nuts; two varieties needed for cross-pollination; remove suckers.
Good drainage	Let dry out between waterings	Medium feeder	Semiupright to trailing growth; mosaic pattern of white veins on oval, green leaves; place in warm spot; keep air moist; good in hanging pot.

NAME	HABIT		FLOWERS		ADAPTATION	
	Type	Height	Color	Time	Zones	Light
Forsythia × intermedia Border Forsythia	Deciduous shrub	8 to 10 ft	Yellow	Spring	5 to 9	Full sun
Fothergilla major Large Fothergilla	Deciduous shrub	6 to 10 ft	White	Spring	4 to 8	Full sun
Fragaria chiloensis Wild Strawberry, Sand Strawberry	Groundcover	to 6 in	White	Spring	6 to 10	Full sun
Franklinia alatamaha Franklinia	Deciduous tree	20 to 25 ft	White	Late summer to early fall	5 to 8	Light shade
Fraxinus excelsior European Ash	Deciduous tree	30 to 50 ft			4 to 7	Full sun
Fraxinus ornus Flowering Ash	Deciduous tree	to 35 ft	White	Late spring	6 to 8	Full sun
Fraxinus pennsylvanica Green Ash, Red Ash	Deciduous tree	30 to 50 ft			3 to 8	Full sun
Fraxinus velutina 'Modesto' Modesto Ash	Deciduous tree	to 50 ft			8 to 10	Full sun
Freesia refracta Common Freesia	Tender bulb	12 to 18 in	White, yellow, red, lavender	Late fall to early spring	9 to 10 or IN	Full sun
Fritillaria imperialis Crown Imperial	Hardy bulb	2½ to 4 ft	Yellow, orange, red,	Spring	5 to 8	Full sun
Fuchsia magellanica Hardy Fuchsia	Semi-evergreen shrub	3 to 8 ft	Red	Early summer to first frost	6 to 10	Light shade
Fuchsia × hybrida Common Fuchsia	Semi-evergreen shrub	2 to 6 ft	Comes in all colors	Early summer to first frost	9 to 10	Light shade
Gaillardia pulchella Blanket Flower	Half-hardy annual	10 to 18 in	Yellow, red	Early summer to first frost		Full sun
Gaillardia × grandiflora Blanket Flower	Hardy perennial	to 3 ft	Red, yellow	Early summer to early fall	2 to 10	Full sun
Galanthus nivalis Common Snowdrop	Hardy bulb	6 to 9 in	White	Winter to early spring	3 to 9	Full sun to light shade
Garbanzo—See Chick Pea						
Gardenia jasminoides Gardenia	Evergreen shrub	3 to 6 ft	White	Early summer to early fall	8 to 10	Light shade

For a list of common names, see page 378.

	CULTURE		
Soil	**Water**	**Feeding**	**Special Characteristics**
Not particular	Wet; don't let dry out	Medium feeder	Fast-growing; upright, vigorous, arching form; needs constant grooming; burst of early spring color; needs plenty of fertilizer; give lots of room to grow; remove one-third of canes annually right after flowering or cut to the ground.
Organic matter; good drainage	Medium water	Medium feeder	Neat, rounded habit; profuse, honey-scented blooms; attractive fall foliage; acid soil; tolerates light shade and dry, rocky soils.
Good drainage; sandy soil	Medium water	Medium feeder	Parent of all commercial strawberries; evergreen; dark green leaves turn reddish hue in winter; forms attractive, thick mat; strawberrylike leaves and fruit; tolerates seacoast conditions; mow lightly in spring; spreads by runners.
Rich soil	Medium water	Heavy feeder	Slow to moderate growing; open, upright shape; glossy green foliage turns orange-red in the fall; camellia-like flowers; acid soil; protect from wind; lawn or patio tree.
Good drainage	Medium water	Medium feeder	Glossy, dark green, leathery leaves; good shade tree; susceptible to scale and borers.
Not particular	Medium water	Medium feeder	Fragrant flowers; green leaves turn yellow in fall; best for cool areas; tolerates wet soil, poor drainage; lawn and shade tree.
Not particular	Medium water	Medium feeder	Moderate-growing; compact habit; easy to grow; tolerates drought, wet soil, severe cold.
Not particular	Medium water	Medium feeder	Upright branching habit; yellow fall color; weak wood; prone to anthracnose, mistletoe; good lawn and shade tree.
Good drainage	Medium water	Medium feeder	Very fragrant flowers; can be grown as a houseplant.
Good drainage organic matter	Medium water	Medium feeder	Musky-smelling flowers; flowers large, bell-like; good container plant.
Rich soil; good drainage	Wet; don't let dry out	Heavy feeder	Dies to the ground each winter in northern areas; can reach 8' high in deep South; profuse bloomer; flowers smaller than F. × hybrida.
Rich soil; organic matter	Wet; don't let dry out	Heavy feeder	Evergreen in frost-free areas; trailing to upright habit; best in areas with cool summers; mulch well; protect from hot winds; pinch or prune back to encourage dense growth.
Good drainage; sandy soil	Let dry out between waterings	Light feeder	Tolerates drought, heat and infertile soil.
Good drainage; sandy soil	Let dry out between waterings	Light feeder	Tolerates heat and drought; requires annual division; avoid rich, moist soils; short-lived; flowers are bicolored.
Good drainage	Medium water	Medium feeder	Bell-shaped flowers; blue-green foliage; may bloom earlier in mild climates.
Good drainage; organic matter	Medium water	Heavy feeder	Glossy leaves; very fragrant flowers; acid soil; needs hot summer to bloom well; good as specimen, in containers, hedges, low screen, espalier; provide full sun in foggy areas.

NAME	HABIT		FLOWERS		ADAPTATION	
	Type	Height	Color	Time	Zones	Light
Gardenia jasminoides 'Prostrata' (*G. radicans*) Creeping Gardenia	Groundcover	to 1 ft	White	Early summer	9 to 10	Half-day sun to light shade
Garlic Chives, Oriental Garlic *Allium tuberosum*	Hardy perennial herb	12 to 18 in	White	Summer	3 to 10	Full sun to light shade
Garlic *Allium sativum*	Hardy perennial vegetable	2 to 3 ft			3 to 10	Full sun to light shade
Gaultheria procumbens Wintergreen, Teaberry, Checkerberry	Groundcover	3 to 6 in	White	Late spring to early summer	3 to 8	Light shade
Gazania rigens Gazania Treasure Flower	Half-hardy annual	6 to 15 in	Warm colors (red, orange, yellow), pink, bicolored	Summer to first frost		Full sun
Gelsemium sempervirens Carolina Jasmine	Groundcover, evergreen vine	to 3 ft	Yellow	Early spring	9 to 10	Full sun to half-day sun
Genista hispanica Spanish Gorse, Spanish Broom	Deciduous shrub	1 to 2 ft	Yellow	Early summer	6 to 9	Full sun
Genista tinctoria Common Woadwaxen	Deciduous shrub	2 to 3 ft	Yellow	Early summer	4 to 7	Full sun
Geranium sanguineum Blood-red Geranium	Hardy perennial	to 1½ ft	Magenta, white	Late spring to late summer	3 to 10	Full sun to light shade
Gerbera jamesonii Transvaal Daisy	Tender perennial	12 to 18 in	Warm colors (red, orange, yellow), pink, white	Late spring to first frost		Full sun to light shade
Geum hybrids Avens	Half-hardy perennial	2 to 3½ ft	Warm colors (red, orange, yellow)	Late spring to late summer	5 to 10	Full sun
Ginkgo biloba Maidenhair Tree	Deciduous tree	60 to 100 ft			4 to 10	Full sun
Gladiolus hybridus Garden Gladiolus	Half-hardy bulb	to 6 ft	Comes in all colors, except blue	Late summer to fall	8 to 10	Full sun
Gleditsia triacanthos var. *inermis* Thornless Honeylocust	Deciduous tree	30 to 70 ft			4 to 9	Full sun
Gloriosa rothschildiana Glory Lily, Climbing Lily	Tender bulb	4 to 6 ft	Red	Summer to early fall	9 to 10	Full sun to light shade

For a list of common names, see page 378.

	CULTURE		
Soil	**Water**	**Feeding**	**Special Characteristics**
Good drainage; organic matter acid soil	Wet; don't let dry out	Medium feeder	Low, slow-growing, 2–3′ wide form of common gardenia; glossy, dark green leaves, often streaked with white; fragrant flowers; small-scale groundcover or container plant.
Good drainage; organic matter	Medium water	Medium feeder	Culinary herb with flat leaves, 1/4″ wide; starlike blossoms produced on umbels; when snipping leaves, cut to the ground.
Good drainage; rich soil	Medium water	Medium feeder	Grown for edible bulb; in all but coldest areas, plant in fall; in cold areas, plant in the spring; harvest garlic when tops fall over; 'Elephant garlic' is about 6 times larger than regular garlic, weighs up to a pound and has mild flavor.
Good drainage acid soil organic matter	Wet; don't let dry out	Light feeder	Spreads to form low mat of foliage; best used in naturalistic planting; produces bright red berries.
Good drainage; sandy soil	Let dry out between waterings	Light feeder	Drought and wind tolerant; prefers hot summers; avoid heavy soils; grown as a perennial in mild climates.
Good drainage; organic matter	Medium water	Medium feeder	Shiny green, finely textured leaves; deciduous in cold climates; fragrant flowers; prune frequently to keep low; best used to cover large area; can be trained up trellis or fence.
Good drainage	Let dry out between waterings	Light feeder	Prefers dry, infertile soil; tolerates drought and seacoast conditions; spiny growth.
Good drainage	Let dry out between waterings	Light feeder	Small, neat, round habit; vertical, almost leafless evergreen stems; prefers dry, infertile soils; tolerates drought and coastal conditions well.
Good drainage	Medium water	Light Feeder	Attractive fall foliage; mounded, spreading form; rich, moist soil promotes invasive growth; dwarf varieties available.
Good drainage; organic matter	Medium water	Heavy feeder	Acid soil; long, warm summers and high humidity; subject to crown rot; grown as an annual in all but the mildest climates.
Good drainage; organic matter	Medium water	Light feeder	Slow-growing; avoid wet soil in winter; reliable in low temperatures if soil is dry; profuse bloomer.
Good drainage	Medium water	Medium feeder	Slow-growing; bright green, fan-shaped leaves turn brilliant yellow in fall; very adaptable; tolerates smoke and air pollution; needs room; good park or large lawn tree.
Good drainage; organic matter	Medium water	Medium feeder	Will grow in colder zones if dug and stored in winter.
Not particular	Medium water	Medium feeder	Moderate-to-fast growing; lacy appearance; foliage leafs out late in spring; drops early in fall; light shade; tolerates air pollution, highway salting, winds; prune some new growth to maintain upright branching.
Good drainage; organic matter	Medium water	Heavy feeder	Climbing vine that can be grown as a houseplant, or container plant; provide trellis or support.

NAME	HABIT		FLOWERS		ADAPTATION	
	Type	Height	Color	Time	Zones	Light
Gomphrena globosa Globe Amaranth	Tender annual	9 to 30 in	Purple, lavender, white, pink, orange, yellow	Early summer to fall		Full sun
Gourds *Cucurbita* species	Tender annual vegetable	Climbs to 15 ft	Yellow	Summer		Full sun
Grapefruit *Citrus paradisi*	Evergreeen fruit tree	10 to 30 ft	White	Spring	9 to 10	Full sun to half-day sun
Grape *Vitis* species	Deciduous berry	Climbs to 30 ft			4 to 10	Full sun
Gynura aurantiaca Velvet Plant	Houseplant	to 9 ft (trailing)			10 or IN	Light shade
Gypsophila elegans Annual Baby's Breath	Hardy annual	8 to 24 in	White, pink, red, lavender	Early summer to fall		Full sun
Gypsophila paniculata Baby's Breath	Hardy perennial	to 3 ft	White, pink	Summer to early fall	3 to 10	Full sun
Halesia carolina Carolina Silverbell	Deciduous tree	30 to 40 ft	White	Late spring	5 to 10	Full sun to light shade
Hamamelis japonica Japanese Witch Hazel	Deciduous shrub	to 30 ft	Yellow	Winter to early spring	5 to 9	Full sun to light shade
Hamamelis mollis Chinese Witch Hazel	Deciduous shrub	to 30 ft	Yellow	Winter to early spring	5 to 8	Full sun to light shade
Hamamelis vernalis Vernal Witch Hazel	Deciduous shrub	6 to 10 ft	Yellow, orange	Winter	5 to 9	Full sun to light shade
Hamamelis virginiana Common Witch Hazel	Deciduous shrub	20 to 30 ft	Yellow	Late fall to winter	4 to 9	Full sun to light shade
Hamamelis × intermedia Hybrid Witch Hazel	Deciduous shrub	15 to 20 ft	Yellow	Winter to early spring	6 to 8	Full sun to light shade
Hedera canariensis Algerian Ivy	Groundcover	1 to 2½ ft			6 to 10	Full sun to light shade

For a list of common names, see page 378.

	CULTURE		
Soil	**Water**	**Feeding**	**Special Characteristics**
Sandy soil; good drainage	Medium water	Light feeder	Tolerates extreme heat, drought, wind and humidity; easy to grow; grown mainly for dried arrangements.
Good drainage; organic matter	Medium water	Medium feeder	Warm-season crop; require ample space to trail; can be trained on trellis; some bush varieties available; water deeply; much variation in size, shape, and color of cultivars.
Good drainage; organic matter	Medium water	Medium feeder	Best in hot areas, especially in the desert; in cool areas fruit is thick-skinned and pithy; plant trees high and avoid wetting the trunk and crown; self-fertile; fragrant flowers; prune only to remove dead or damaged branches and suckers.
Good drainage; organic matter	Medium water	Medium feeder	Ornamental and fruiting vine; divided into two main classes—European and American; European grapes are spur-pruned, American varieties need cane pruning; need only be fed nitrogen; provide a deep soil and good air circulation; subject to mildew; a large number of varieties available; many varieties adapted to specific parts of the country.
Good drainage	Medium water	Medium feeder	Dark green, toothed leaves covered with purple hairs; give bright light; keep moist; flowers have unpleasant odor—remove buds; prune plant to keep compact.
Good drainage	Medium water	Light feeder	Best in chalky, alkaline soil, low in fertility; make successive plantings two weeks apart throughout spring for continual summer bloom.
Good drainage; slightly alkaline soil	Let dry out between waterings	Light Feeder	Profuse bloomer; never invasive; long-lived; soggy soil fatal; resents transplanting.
Organic matter; rich soil	Medium water	Medium feeder	Slow to moderate growing; leaves turn yellow in fall; brown fruits in winter; attractive flowers; best in cool soil with ample water; open grower, several stems; good shelter plant for azaleas, rhododendrons; can prune to single stem.
Good drainage; organic matter	Medium water	Medium feeder	Shrub or small tree; flowers purplish near the base and slightly fragrant; red leaf color in the fall.
Good drainage; organic matter	Medium water	Medium feeder	Moderately slow-growing tree or shrub; very fragrant flowers; dark green leaves are slightly rough above, felted below; good fall color(yellow).
Rich soil	Wet; don't let dry out	Heavy feeder	Neater, smaller habit than *H. ×intermedia*; pungently fragrant flowers; good fall color.
Rich soil	Wet; don't let dry out	Heavy feeder	Hardiest but largest and rangiest witch hazel; yellow fall color; fragrant flowers.
Rich soil	Wet; don't let dry out	Heavy feeder	Fragrant flowers; good fall color; needs deep soil.
Good drainage	Medium water	Light feeder	Trailing vine; shiny green leaves with 3–5 lobes; roots itself as it spreads along the ground; tougher than English Ivy *(H. helix)*; requires more water and is more aggressive; mow every other year just prior to new growth.

NAME	HABIT		FLOWERS		ADAPTATION	
	Type	Height	Color	Time	Zones	Light
Hedera helix English Ivy	Groundcover, houseplant	6 to 18 in			5 to 10 or IN	Light shade to half-day sun
Helenium autumnale Sneezeweed	Hardy perennial	2½ to 6 ft	Warm colors, bicolored	Summer to first frost	3 to 10	Full sun
Helianthemum nummularium Sun Rose	Groundcover	6 to 8 in high, 3 ft wide	Pink, red, yellow	Summer	5 to 10	Full sun
Helianthus annuus Sunflower	Hardy annual	2 to 8 ft	Yellow	Summer		Full sun
Helichrysum bracteatum Strawflower, Everlasting	Half-hardy annual	1½ to 3 ft	Warm colors, white, pink, purple	Early summer to fall		Full sun
Heliotropium arborescens Heliotrope	Tender perennial	1 to 3 ft	Purple, pink, white	Late spring to early fall	7 to 10	Full sun
Helleborus lividus corsicus Corsican Hellebore	Half-hardy perennial	to 3 ft	Green	Spring	6 to 9	Light shade
Helleborus niger Christmas Rose	Hardy perennial	to 15 in	White	Late winter to spring	3 to 9	Light shade
Hemerocallis hybrids Daylily	Hardy perennial	1½ to 4 ft	Warm colors, white, pink, violet, bicolored	Late spring to early fall	3 to 10	Full sun to light shade
Heuchera sanguinea Coral-bells	Hardy perennial	1 to 2 ft	Pink, red, white	Summer	3 to 10	Full sun to light shade
Hibiscus rosa-sinensis Chinese Hibiscus	Evergreen shrub	5 to 15 ft	Pink, red, ellow, white	Late summer to first frost	9 to 10	Full sun
Hibiscus syriacus Shrub Althea, Rose of Sharon	Deciduous shrub	8 to 12 ft	Red, purple, violet, white	Late summer to first frost	6 to 9	Full sun
Hippeastrum species Amaryllis	Tender bulb	1 to 2 ft	Pink, red, white	Winter to late spring	9 to 10	Full sun to light shade
Horseradish *Armoracia rusticana*	Hardy perennial herb	1½ to 3 ft			4 to 10	Full sun
Hosta decorata Blunt-leaf Plantain Lily	Hardy perennial	to 2 ft	Violet	Summer	3 to 9	Light shade to deep shade

For a list of common names, see page 378.

	CULTURE		
Soil	**Water**	**Feeding**	**Special Characteristics**
Good drainage	Medium water	Medium feeder	Trailing or climbing habit; place in cool, bright spot; keep soil and air moist; prune back in spring to encourage bushy growth; use in hanging pot, large planter, groundcover, vine; indoors give 3–4 hours direct sun during summer; many cultivars available.
Organic matter; tolerates clay soil	Wet; don't let dry out	Medium Feeder	Profuse bloomer; tolerant of many soils; taller varieties need staking; divide annually or every other year to avoid overcrowding.
Good drainage	Let dry out between waterings	Light feeder	Hardy evergreen, adapted to dry summers; branches root as they spread to form thick mat; narrow, glossy or dull green leaves; flowers short-lived; tolerates infertile soils; shear in spring; fire-retardant.
Good drainage	Let dry out between waterings	Light feeder	Tolerant of heat and drought; tall varieties may need staking.
Good drainage; slightly alkaline soil	Medium water	Medium feeder	Best in areas of long, hot summers; plants may need support; popular for dried arrangements.
Good drainage; organic matter	Wet; don't let dry out	Heavy feeder	Some have a strong, sweet fragrance; dramatically dark foliage; will bloom through winter in mild climates. Container, greenhouse, or indoor plant; valued for vanilla-like fragrance of flowers; may grow 4–6' high.
Good drainage; organic matter	Wet; don't let dry out	Medium feeder	Takes more sun and drought than other hellebores once established; protect from cold, drying winds in winter.
Good drainage; organic matter; acid soil	Wet; don't let dry out	Medium feeder	Moderately difficult to grow; resents disturbance.
Good drainage; organic matter	Medium water	Light feeder	Long-lived, noninvasive; some varieties fragrant; requires light shade in hot areas.
Good drainage; organic matter	Medium water	Light feeder	Some varieties have attractive fall and winter foliage; adaptable; divide every three or four years.
Good drainage	Wet; don't let dry out	Medium feeder	Fast growing; needs sun and heat; protect from wind and frost; needs warm-hot summers for good blooms; prune out 1/3 of old wood each spring; feed monthly during growing season.
Good drainage	Medium water	Medium feeder	Medium-growing; large, erect, round-topped; tolerates coastal conditions; prefers hot summer; avoid wet weather; prune hard each spring to encourage blooming; best if grouped or massed in shrub border; leaves appear late in spring, drop early in fall.
Good drainage; organic matter	Medium water	Medium feeder	Grown mainly as a houseplant; can be planted outdoors in warm climates.
Good drainage; organic matter	Wet; don't let dry out	Medium feeder	Culinary herb with long, narrow leaves; can become invasive; grown for thick taproots; harvested in fall.
Good drainage; organic matter	Medium water	Medium feeder	6-inch leaves rimmed with silvery white; compact.

NAME	HABIT		FLOWERS		ADAPTATION	
	Type	**Height**	**Color**	**Time**	**Zones**	**Light**
Hosta lancifolia Narrow-Leaf Plantain Lily	Hardy perennial	2 ft	Lavender	Late summer	3 to 9	Light shade to deep shade
Hosta plantaginea Fragrant Plantain Lily	Hardy perennial	to 2 ft	White	Late summer to early fall	3 to 9	Light shade to deep shade
Hosta undulata Wavy-leaf Plantain Lily	Hardy perennial	1 to 2½ ft	Violet	Summer	3 to 9	Light shade to deep shade
Howea forsterana Kentia Palm	Houseplant	5 to 10 ft			10 or IN	Light shade
Hoya bella Wax Flower, Wax Plant	Houseplant	4 to 10 ft (trailing)	White	Summer	10 or IN	Half-day sun to light shade
Hyacinthus orientalis Common Hyacinth	Hardy bulb	12 to 15 in	Blue, white, purple	Spring	4 to 10	Full sun
Hydrangea macrophylla Bigleaf Hydrangea	Deciduous shrub	4 to 8 ft	Blue, pink, white	Summer	7 to 10	Light shade
Hydrangea quercifolia Oakleaf Hydrangea	Deciduous shrub	6 to 8 ft	White	Summer	6 to 9	Full sun to light shade
Hypericum calycinum Aaronsbeard, St. John's-wort	Semi-evergreen groundcover	to 12 in	Yellow	Summer	6 to 10	Full sun
Hypericum × moseranum Goldflower, St. John's-wort	Evergreen shrub	to 3 ft	Yellow	Summer	8 to 10	Full sun to light shade
Iberis amara Rocket Candytuft	Half-hardy annual	12 to 18 in	White	Early summer to first frost		Full sun
Iberis sempervirens Evergreen Candytuft	Hardy perennial groundcover	½ to 1 ft	White	Spring	5 to 9	Full sun to light shade
Ilex aquifolium English Holly	Evergreen tree	to 70 ft	White	Spring	7 to 9	Full sun to light shade
Ilex cornuta Chinese Holly	Evergreen tree	to 15 ft	White	Spring	7 to 9	Full sun to light shade
Ilex crenata Japanese Holly	Evergreen shrub	5 to 10 ft	White	Spring	6 to 9	Full sun to light shade
Ilex decidua Possum Haw Holly	Deciduous tree	to 20 ft	White	Spring	5 to 9	Full sun to light shade

For a list of common names, see page 378.

| | CULTURE | | |
Soil	Water	Feeding	Special Characteristics
Good drainage; organic matter	Medium water	Medium feeder	Large quantity of flower stalks with profuse blossoms.
Good drainage; organic matter	Medium water	Light feeder	Large, fragrant flowers; heart-shaped leaves up to 10" long; 'Honeybells' and 'Royal standard' commonly grown cultivars.
Good drainage; organic matter	Medium water	Medium feeder	Leaves striped with white and green, 6–8 inches long; more tolerant of full sun than other *Hostas*.
Good drainage; organic matter	Medium water	Medium feeder	Feather-shaped leaves arch outward from sturdy trunks; leaves scorch easily; water heavily and feed monthly during growing season, reduce in winter; protect from direct sun and dry air.
Good drainage	Medium water	Medium feeder	Shrubby plant, good for hanging baskets; waxy leaves; flowers tightly clustered, white with purple centers; allow soil to dry slightly between waterings; plants require less water and light during winter; best bloom if kept potbound.
Rich soil	Medium water	Medium feeder	Fragrant flowers; many hybrids are available.
Rich soil; organic matter	Medium water	Heavy feeder	Neat foliage, rounded shape; large flowers; accepts seacoast conditions; sun on coast, shade inland; acid soil produces blue flowers, alkaline soil produces pink flowers; prune just after flowering.
Rich soil; good drainage	Wet; don't let dry out	Heavy feeder	Slow-growing; upright, irregular shrub; coarse, clean foliage; lacy flowers; good fall color; needs slightly acid soil; tolerates heavy shade; mulch to keep roots cool; prune right after blooming; tends to sucker.
Good drainage	Medium water	Medium feeder	Semi-evergreen in colder climates; low-growing, spreading form; mow to ground every few years.
Good drainage	Medium water	Medium feeder	Low-growing shrub; one of few plants that will do well planted under eucalyptus trees.
Good drainage	Let dry out between waterings	Medium feeder	Tolerates drought, pollution and heat; flowers are fragrant.
Good drainage	Medium water	Medium feeder	Mat-forming shrub; showy in bloom; dark green, finely textured foliage; do not overfertilize or will become loose and rangy; prune hard each year after flowering.
Rich soil; good drainage	Medium water	Medium feeder	Moderate-growing; variable leaf shape, color and spininess; male plants will not have berries; protect from sun in hot, dry areas; many cultivars.
Rich soil; good drainage	Medium water	Medium feeder	Large, spiny, glossy, dark green leaves; large red berries on female form; needs long warm season to set fruit; grows as shrub or small tree.
Good drainage; acid soil	Medium water	Medium feeder	Neat, rounded shape; dark green, lustrous foliage; slow-growing; tolerates some shade, pollution; prunes easily into hedge or border.
Rich soil; good drainage	Medium water	Medium feeder	Moderate-growing; red berries retained well into winter; keep moist.

NAME	HABIT		FLOWERS		ADAPTATION	
	Type	**Height**	**Color**	**Time**	**Zones**	**Light**
Ilex glabra Inkberry	Evergreen shrub	6 to 8 ft	White	Spring	3 to 9	Full sun to light shade
Ilex opaca American Holly	Evergreen tree	45 to 50 ft	White	Spring	5 to 9	Full sun to light shade
Ilex verticillata Common Winterberry	Deciduous shrub	6 to 9 ft	White	Spring	4 to 9	Full sun to light shade
Ilex vomitoria Yaupon Holly	Evergreen tree	15 to 20 ft	White	Spring	7 to 10	Full sun to light shade
Impatiens balsamina Balsam	Hardy annual	1 to 3 ft	Red, purple, pink, white	Early summer to fall		Full sun to light shade
Impatiens wallerana Impatiens, Busy Lizzie	Half-hardy annual	6 to 18 in	Warm colors (red, orange, yellow), white, pink, bicolored	Early summer to first frost		Light shade to deep shade
Ipomoea alba Moonflower Vine	Half-hardy annual	to 15 ft (trailing)	White	Summer to first frost		Full sun
Ipomoea tricolor Morning-glory Vine	Half-hardy annual	8 to 10 ft (trailing)	Blue, purple, pink, red, white	Summer to first frost		Full sun
Iresine herbstii Beefsteak Plant, Bloodleaf	Houseplant	2 to 4 ft			10 or IN	Light shade to half-day sun
Iris cristata Crested Iris	Hardy bulb	3 to 4 in	Lavender	Early summer	5 to 10	Light shade
Iris danfordiae Danford Iris	Hardy bulb	to 1 ft	Yellow	Early spring	4 to 10	Full sun
Iris kaempferi Japanese Iris	Hardy bulb	3 to 4 ft	White, blue, purple, pink, lavender	Summer	4 to 10	Full sun to light shade
Iris pseudacorus Water Flag Iris	Hardy bulb	3 to 3½ ft	Yellow	Summer	4 to 10	Full sun to light shade
Iris reticulata Netted Iris	Hardy bulb	to 2 ft	Violet	Early spring	3 to 10	Full sun
Iris sibirica Siberian Iris	Hardy perennial	1½ to 3 ft	Cool colors	Early summer	2 to 10	Full sun to light shade
Iris **hybrids** Bearded Iris	Hardy bulb	½ to 4 ft	Comes in all colors	Spring to early summer	3 to 10	Full sun
Iris × germanica florentina Orris, German Iris	Hardy bulb	2 to 3 ft	White	Early spring to early summer	4 to 10	Full sun

For a list of common names, see page 378.

| | CULTURE | | |
Soil	Water	Feeding	Special Characteristics
Good drainage; acid soil	Wet; don't let dry out	Medium feeder	Very hardy; open spread, leggy; attractive dark green foliage; black fruits on female plants; heavy pruning.
Rich soil; good drainage	Medium water	Medium feeder	Slow-growing; pyramid shape; berries range in color from red, orange, yellow.
Good drainage; organic matter	Wet; don't let dry out	Medium feeder	Abundant red berries (need male and female plant to produce); tolerates dry soil, prefers slightly acid soil; best planted in masses in border.
Rich soil; good drainage	Medium water	Medium feeder	Narrow, inch-long, dark green leaves; profuse red berries; tolerates alkaline soil; small tree or large shrub; can be sheared into columnar form.
Organic matter; sandy soil	Medium water	Heavy feeder	Appreciates hot summers; young plants subject to damping off; in hottest areas give light shade.
Good drainage; sandy soil organic matter	Wet; don't let dry out	Medium feeder	One of the best of the flowering shade plants.
Sandy soil; good drainage	Medium water	Light feeder	Tolerates dry soil, infertile soils; blooms at night; fragrant flower.
Good drainage; sandy soil	Medium water	Light feeder	Tolerant of dry soil; grows almost anywhere; can be grown in a pot.
Good drainage	Medium water	Medium feeder	Heart-shaped leaves with light red veins; give bright light, keep moist; humid air; can summer outdoors in protected location; pinch back to encourage branching.
Good drainage	Medium water	Medium feeder	The rhizomes creep along soil surface and should not be covered with soil.
Good drainage	Medium water	Medium feeder	Water generously during active growth; short-lived; treat as an annual.
Organic matter; acid soil	Wet; don't let dry out	Medium feeder	Plant thrives in boggy, rich soil; lime and alkaline soil fatal; feed with acid fertilizer.
Rich soil; organic matter	Wet; don't let dry out	Medium feeder	Self-sows prolifically in boggy areas; needs acid soil.
Good drainage	Wet; don't let dry out	Medium feeder	Many hybrids available.
Rich soil; acid soil	Medium water	Medium feeder	Hardy, long-lived; tolerates wide range of soils.
Good drainage; organic matter	Medium water	Heavy feeder	Large and diverse group of plants; give light shade in hottest areas; never allow soil to remain soggy.
Good drainage	Medium water	Medium feeder	Swordlike leaves; large flowers with yellow beards, veined with blue; roots used in medicine and perfume.

NAME	HABIT		FLOWERS		ADAPTATION	
	Type	Height	Color	Time	Zones	Light
Jasminum mesnyi Primrose Jasmine, Japanese Jasmine	Evergreen shrub	to 10 ft	Yellow	Spring to summer	8 to 10	Full sun to light shade
Jasminum nudiflorum Winter Jasmine	Deciduous shrub	10 to 15 ft	Yellow	Spring	6 to 9	Full sun to light shade
Juglans nigra Black Walnut	Deciduous tree	50 to 150 ft			7 to 10	Full sun
Juniperus chinensis Chinese Juniper	Needled evergreen shrub or groundcover	to 50 ft			4 to 10	Full sun
Juniperus communis 'saxatilis'	Groundcover	to 1 ft			5 to 10	Full sun
Juniperus communis Common Juniper	Needled evergreen shrub	5 to 10 ft			2 to 7	Full sun
Juniperus conferta Shore Juniper	Needled evergreen shrub or groundcover	1 to 2 ft			6 to 10	Full sun
Juniperus horizontalis Creeping Juniper	Needled evergreen groundcover	to 1 ft			3 to 9	Full sun
Juniperus procumbens Japanese Garden Juniper	Needled evergreen groundcover	1 to 2 ft			5 to 10	Full sun
Juniperus scopulorum Rocky Mountain Juniper	Needled evergreen tree	35 to 45 ft			4 to 9	Full sun to light shade
Juniperus virginiana Eastern Red Cedar	Needled evergreen tree	35 to 45 ft			3 to 9	Full sun to light shade
Kalanchoe blossfeldiana Flaming Katy	Houseplant	to 15 in	Red, orange, pink, yellow	Winter to spring	10 or IN	Light shade
Kale *Brassica oleracea* var. *acephala*	Hardy biennial vegetable	2 to 3 ft				Full sun to light shade
Kalmia latifolia Mountain Laurel	Evergreen shrub	7 to 15 ft	Pink, white	Late spring to early summer	5 to 9	Full sun
Kerria japonica Japanese Kerria	Deciduous shrub	3 to 6 ft	Yellow	Spring	5 to 9	Light shade to half-day sun

For a list of common names, see page 378.

	CULTURE		
Soil	**Water**	**Feeding**	**Special Characteristics**
Good drainage	Medium water	Medium feeder	Vining or long, arching habit; dark green leaves; may flower during winter in mild climates; needs plenty of room; best if tied up at desired height.
Good drainage	Medium water	Medium feeder	Viny shrub; graceful, weeping branches; glossy green leaves; may bloom during winter in mild climates; train as *J. mesnyi* or use as a trailer; prune to control growth.
Adaptive	Medium water	Medium feeder	Large crowned shade tree; 1 to 1½ inch, edible nuts in hard, thick shells; tree inhibits growth of many vegetables and flowers.
Sandy soil; good drainage	Let dry out between waterings	Light feeder	Very diverse species; prefers alkaline soils; low maintenance.
Good drainage	Medium water	Light feeder	Prostrate form with upward-spreading branchlets; gray-green foliage; prickly clusters of tiny needle-leaves; tolerates some shade but becomes woody, loses color.
Good drainage; sandy soil	Let dry out between waterings	Light feeder	Spiny blue-green or gray needles that turn yellowish- or brownish-green in winter; adapts to poorest, driest soils; very susceptible to blight; spreads 8–12'.
Sandy soil; good drainage	Let dry out between waterings	Light feeder	Intense bluish-green foliage; procumbent growth; spreads slowly 6–8' wide; forms attractive, dense mat; tolerates seacoast conditions; good groundcover in coastal areas; will not tolerate wet, heavy soil.
Good drainage; sandy soil	Let dry out between waterings	Light feeder	Low, spreading groundcover; turns grayish-purple in winter; susceptible to blight.
Good drainage; sandy soil	Let dry out between waterings	Light feeder	Low, spreading form, slowly to 10–15' wide; susceptible to blight; *J. procumbens* 'Nana' is dwarf form that grows 6" high.
Good drainage	Medium water	Medium feeder	Slow-growing; broad, pyramid form; brownish-red bark; blue-gray foliage (needles); best juniper for areas of heat, drought; tall hedge, screen, windbreak; many different cultivars available.
Good drainage	Medium water	Medium feeder	Medium-growing; pyramid shape; bright green foliage (needles); foliage turns bronze in cold weather; attractive blue cones in winter; adaptive to soils and climates; avoid hot, dry winds; tall hedge; screen; windbreak.
Good drainage; sandy soil	Let dry out between waterings	Medium feeder	Shiny green, oval leaves tinged with red, smooth edged or scalloped; likes filtered sun or bright, indirect light, warm environment; after blooming, prune tops.
Good drainage; organic matter	Medium water	Heavy feeder	Member of cabbage family; doesn't tolerate heat as well as collards; grows best in cool of fall; flavor improved by frost; 'Dwarf Blue Curled' and 'Vates' are the most widely planted varieties; requires 55 days to maturity.
Good drainage; organic matter; acid soil	Medium water	Medium feeder	Slow-growing; dense, rounded and neat when young, becoming gnarled and picturesque in old age; shade in hot summer areas.
Good drainage; grows in poor soil	Medium water	Medium feeder	Slow-growing; tough, carefree shrub for shady places; too fertile soil decreases flowering, encourages rank, weedy growth; prune right after flowering.

NAME	HABIT		FLOWERS		ADAPTATION	
	Type	Height	Color	Time	Zones	Light
Kniphofia uvaria Torch Lily, Red-hot Poker	Hardy perennial	2 to 4 ft	Red	Late summer to early fall	7 to 10	Full sun
Koelreuteria paniculata Goldenrain Tree, Varnish Tree	Deciduous tree	25 to 35 ft	Yellow	Summer	5 to 9	Full sun
Kohlrabi *Brassica oleracea* var. *caulorapa*	Half-hardy biennial vegetable	2 to 3 ft				Full sun to half-day sun
Kolkwitzia amabilis Beautybush	Deciduous shrub	6 to 10 ft	Pink	Late spring	5 to 8	Full sun
Kumquat *Fortunella* species	Evergreen fruit tree	5 to 15 ft	White	Spring	9 to 10	Full sun to half-day sun
Laburnum × *watereri* 'Vossii' Golden-chain Tree	Deciduous tree	20 to 30 ft	Yellow	Late spring	5 to 7	Full sun to light shade
Lagerstroemia fauriei Japanese Crape Myrtle	Deciduous tree	12 to 20 ft	White	Summer to early fall	7 to 10	Full sun
Lagerstroemia indica Crape Myrtle	Deciduous tree	10 to 30 ft	Lavender, pink, red, white	Summer to early fall	7 to 10	Full sun
Lantana montevidensis Trailing Lantana	Tender perennial groundcover	1 to 2 ft	Lavender	All year	9 to 10	Full sun to half-day sun
Larix kaempferi Japanese Larch	Needled deciduous tree	50 to 60 ft			4 to 7	Full sun
Lathyrus odoratus Sweet Pea	Hardy annual	2 to 6 ft	Cool colors, purple, pink, red	Spring to early summer		Full sun to half-day sun
Laurus nobilis Sweet Bay, Laurel Bay, Grecian Laurel	Evergreen tree	12 to 30 ft	Yellow	Early summer	8 to 10	Full sun to light shade
Lavandula angustifolia English Lavender	Hardy perennial herb	1½ to 4 ft	Lavender, purple	Early summer to first frost	5 to 10	Full sun
Leek *Allium ampeloprasum*	Hardy perennial vegetable	to 3 ft			4 to 10	Full sun to half-day sun

For a list of common names, see page 378.

| | CULTURE | | |
Soil	Water	Feeding	Special Characteristics
Good drainage	Medium water	Light feeder	Foliage forms mounds 12–30″ high; leaves gray-green; plant long-lived; avoid windy spots.
Not particular	Medium water	Medium feeder	Moderate-growing; wide, spreading, open branches, flat top; soft, medium-green leaves; profuse summer bloomer; fruits in late summer, fall; deep-rooted; tolerates wind, drought, alkaline soil, cold winter temps.
Good drainage; organic matter	Medium water	Heavy feeder	Member of cabbage family; cool-weather vegetable; plant in early spring so most growth is complete before full heat of summer; harvest when 2–3″ in diameter, otherwise becomes tough; several cultivars available.
Good drainage	Medium water	Medium feeder	Fast-growing; upright, arching form; can become leggy; needs plenty of room; limited value when not in bloom; profuse bloomer; prune out older stems yearly after flowering; renew overgrown shrubs by cutting to ground.
Good drainage; organic matter	Medium water	Medium feeder	Related to citrus; tiny, round to oval orange fruit; sour flesh and sweet rind; foliage is attractive; fruit used in preserves or eaten fresh, skin and all.
Good drainage	Medium water	Medium feeder	Moderate-growing; dense, upright, vase-shaped crown; grown for flowers; leaves, fruit and flowers poisonous; protect from hot sun; best in mild climate.
Good drainage	Medium water	Medium feeder	Slow-growing; attractive bark; water infrequently but deeply; resists powdery mildew; prune to induce new growth, flowers.
Good drainage	Medium water	Medium feeder	Medium growing; vase-shaped when multitrunked, round-headed when trained to single stem; profuse blooms; attractive bark; best in hot, dry climate—subject to mildew; prune lightly to induce new growth and blooms.
Not particular	Let dry out between waterings	Light feeder	Fast-growing; vinelike stems, 3–4′ long, root as they spread; dark green, oval leaves; tolerates drought, poor soil; cut out dead patches in early spring; good for large-scale planting.
Not particular	Medium water	Medium feeder	Fast-growing; blue-green, feathery foliage; good yellow fall color; attractive cones hang on in winter; not for warm winter climates; can be dwarfed in container.
Organic matter; slightly alkaline soil	Wet; don't let dry out	Heavy feeder	Pleasant fragrance on some varieties; best in cool seasons; subject to powdery mildew fungus.
Good drainage	Medium water	Medium feeder	Slow-growing; compact, broad-based, often multi-stemmed; aromatic, dark green leaves used in cooking; small flowers; dark purple berries; little water once established; background shrub, small tree, container plant; easy to shape.
Good drainage; sandy soil	Medium water	Medium feeder	Bright green to gray foliage; woody stems; fragrant foliage and flowers; blooms on spikes.
Rich soil; good drainage	Wet; don't let dry out	Medium feeder to medium feeder	Culinary plant with long, flat leaves; used as a vegetable and sometimes as an herb; does not form bulbs; needs 140 days to grow from seed, 80 days from transplants; sow seeds in late winter; has round, thick stem. Harvested in fall of first year.

NAME	HABIT		FLOWERS		ADAPTATION	
	Type	Height	Color	Time	Zones	Light
Lemon Balm *Melissa officinalis*	Hardy perennial herb	2 to 3 ft			4 to 10	Full sun to light shade
Lemon *Citrus limon*	Evergreen fruit tree	4 to 25 ft	White	Spring	9 to 10	Full sun to half-day sun
Leptospermum laevigatum Tea Tree	Evergreen tree	15 to 30 ft	White, pink, red	Spring	9 to 10	Full sun
Lettuce *Lactuca sativa*	Hardy annual vegetable	to 2 ft				Full sun to light shade
Leucojum aestivum Summer Snowflake	Hardy bulb	to 1½ ft	White	Late spring	4 to 10	Full sun to light shade
Leucojum vernum Spring Snowflake	Hardy bulb	to 1 ft	White	Early spring to spring	4 to 10	Full sun to light shade
Leucothoe fontanesiana Drooping Leucothoe	Evergreen shrub	3 to 5 ft	White	Spring	5 to 7	Half-day sun
Ligustrum amurense Amur Privet	Deciduous shrub	12 to 15 ft	White	Early summer	4 to 7	Full sun to light shade
Ligustrum japonicum Japanese Privet	Evergreen shrub	6 to 12 ft	White	Early summer	7 to 10	Full sun to light shade
Ligustrum lucidum Glossy Privet	Evergreen tree	35 to 40 ft	White	Summer	8 to 10	Full sun to light shade
Ligustrum ovalifolium California Privet	Deciduous shrub	to 15 ft	White	Early summer	6 to 10	Full sun to light shade
Lilium candidum Madonna Lily	Hardy bulb	to 3½ ft	White	Early summer to summer	3 to 10	Full sun to light shade
Lilium speciosum Speciosum Lily	Hardy bulb	to 3 ft	Red, white	Late summer to early fall	3 to 10	Full sun to light shade
Lime *Citrus aurantifolia*	Evergreen fruit tree	7 to 15 ft	White	Spring	10	Full sun to half-day sun
Limonium sinuatum Statice, Notchleaf Sea Lavender	Half-hardy biennial	1 to 2½ ft	Cool colors, yellow, pink, red	Early summer to first frost		Full sun

For a list of common names, see page 378.

| | **CULTURE** | | |
Soil	**Water**	**Feeding**	**Special Characteristics**
Sandy soil	Medium water	Medium feeder	Culinary and medicinal herb has dark green, heart-shaped leaves with scalloped edges; inconspicuous flowers; lemon-scented foliage.
Good drainage; organic matter	Medium water	Medium feeder	Cannot tolerate excessive heat or cold; protect from frost; grow in southern coastal areas or mildest northern areas; fragrant flowers may appear again in summer; prune only dead or damaged wood and suckers; plant high; protect from hot, dry winds; several cultivars available.
Good drainage	Medium water	Medium feeder	Soft, casual branching habit; twisting to form good canopy; foliage gray-green; doesn't need much water; good as single specimen, or grouped to form thick screen.
Good drainage; organic matter	Wet; don't let dry out	Heavy feeder	Cool season vegetable, tolerates cold better than heat; keep moist; may be started in coldframe before outdoor sowing is possible; thin plants to avoid crowding; major lettuce groups include crisphead (iceberg-type), butterhead, leaf and bunching lettuces, and cos or romaine; much variation within each group.
Good drainage	Medium water	Medium feeder	Slightly larger than *L. vernum*; 4–8 bell-shaped flowers per stem.
Good drainage	Medium water	Medium feeder	Single, bell-shaped flowers; white with green tips.
Good drainage; organic matter	Medium water	Medium feeder	Graceful, fountainlike form; fragrant flowers; bright green to bronze foliage in spring turns purplish in winter; needs moist, acid soil; protect from drying winds, drought; good with azaleas, rhododendrons.
Good drainage	Medium water	Medium feeder	Hardy; clean, medium-to finely-textured foliage; good for hedge.
Good drainage	Wet; don't let dry out	Medium feeder	Dense, compact habit; lustrous leaves; fairly fast-growing; protect from hot sun; container, topiary, hedge, or screen plant.
Not particular	Medium water	Medium feeder	Fast-growing; dense, often multitrunked; glossy, deep green foliage; berry-like, blue-black fruit; tolerates salt winds and many soils; shade tree, street tree, container, sheared as hedge or screen.
Good drainage	Medium water	Medium feeder	Semi-evergreen, glossy leaves; popular hedge.
Good drainage	Medium water	Medium feeder	Adding lime to soil aids growth; sometimes difficult to establish.
Good drainage	Medium water	Medium feeder	One of the last lilies to bloom during season; fragrant flowers.
Good drainage; organic matter	Medium water	Medium feeder	Most tender of all citrus; needs mildest winters and high heat; bears fruit periodically all year with heaviest ripening in the summer and fall; very thorny and thick-headed, prune to remove dead/damaged wood, suckers and old fruiting wood; plant high; most common cultivars are 'Bearss' and 'Mexican'.
Good drainage; sandy soil	Let dry out between waterings	Light feeder	Tolerates seacoast conditions; tolerates heat and drought; irregular blooming habit; good for dried arrangement.

NAME	HABIT		FLOWERS		ADAPTATION	
	Type	Height	Color	Time	Zones	Light
Liquidambar formosana Chinese Sweet Gum	Deciduous tree	40 to 60 ft			6 to 9	Full sun
Liquidambar styraciflua American Sweet Gum	Deciduous tree	60 to 75 ft			6 to 9	Full sun
Liriodendron tulipifera Tulip Tree, Yellow Poplar, Tulip Poplar	Deciduous tree	60 to 70 ft	Yellow	Late spring to early summer	4 to 9	Full sun
Liriope muscari Big Leaf Lilyturf	Groundcover	to 2 ft	Violet	Summer to early fall	7 to 10	Light shade
Liriope spicata Creeping Lilyturf	Groundcover	to 1 ft	Lavender	Summer to early fall	5 to 10	Light shade
Lobelia cardinalis Cardinal Flower	Hardy perennial	3 to 4 ft	Red	Summer to early fall	2 to 9	Light shade
Lobelia erinus Edging Lobelia	Half-hardy annual	4 to 8 in	Cool colors, purple, violet	Late spring to early fall		Full sun to light shade
Lobularia maritima Sweet Alyssum	Hardy annual	4 to 8 in	Lavender, white, pink	Spring to first frost		Full sun to light shade
Lolium multiflorum Annual Ryegrass, Common Ryegrass, Italian Ryegrass	Turfgrass	1½ to 2 in			6 to 8	Full sun to light shade
Lolium perenne Turf-type Perennial Ryegrass	Turfgrass	1 to 2 in			4 to 9	Full sun to light shade
Lonicera fragrantissima Winter Honeysuckle	Deciduous shrub	6 to 10 ft	White	Spring	5 to 10	Full sun
Lonicera japonica 'Halliana' Hall's Japanese Honeysuckle	Groundcover	2 to 3 ft	White	Summer	5 to 10	Full sun to light shade
Lonicera maackii Amur Honeysuckle	Deciduous shrub	to 15 ft	White	Early summer	3 to 8	Full sun
Lonicera tatarica Tartarian Honeysuckle	Deciduous shrub	Climbs to 12 ft	Pink, red, white	Late spring	3 to 8	Full sun
Lotus berthelotii Parrot's-beak	Groundcover	3 to 4 in	Red	Late spring to summer	10	Full sun

For a list of common names, see page 378.

	CULTURE		
Soil	**Water**	**Feeding**	**Special Characteristics**
Good drainage; rich soil	Medium water	Medium feeder	Moderate-growing; maplelike leaves; very good fall color; flowers inconspicuous; prickly fruit in the fall; upright growth, spreading with age; good skyline, street, lawn or garden tree; effective tall screen; prune only to shape.
Rich soil	Medium water	Medium feeder	Slow- to moderate-growing; star-shaped leaves; rich, fall colors; prickly fruit in the fall; good skyline tree; home garden, street tree, tall screen, grove.
Rich soil; good drainage	Medium water	Heavy feeder	Fast-growing; bright green leaves, unusual shape, turn yellow in fall; tall, pyramid shape; needs lots of room—open areas, parks, golf courses, large lawn; good skyline tree; avoid drought areas.
Not particular	Let dry out between waterings	Light feeder	Coarse, clumping, dark green grasslike leaves; 4–8″ long spikelets of flowers; blue-black berries in the fall; clip off any yellowed leaves.
Not particular	Let dry out between waterings	Light feeder	Moderate-growing; coarse, clumping, dark green, grasslike leaves; spreads by underground stems; forms denser mat than *L. muscari*; cut out any yellowed leaves.
Rich soil; good drainage; organic matter	Wet; don't let dry out	Medium feeder	Short-lived; tolerant of full sun if kept moist; mulch well.
Sandy soil; organic matter	Wet; don't let dry out	Medium feeder	Doesn't withstand heat well; plant in partial shade in areas where summer is hot; good spring color.
Good drainage	Medium water	Light feeder	Tolerant of drought and heat; slightly fragrant flowers; self-sows freely.
Good drainage; organic matter	Wet; don't let dry out	Light to medium feeder	Aggressive; fast germinating, quick to establish; poor tolerance to heat and cold; doesn't mow clean.
Good drainage; organic matter	Medium water	Medium feeder	Fast germination and establishment; improved heat and cold resistance; tough play lawn; suffers from winterkill in coldest climates; cleaner mowing than annual ryegrass; impairs establishment of other grasses if more than 25% of a seed mix.
Good drainage	Medium water	Medium feeder	Arching, somewhat stiff growth; very fragrant flowers; red fruits; prune to shape; can be used as hedge or background plant.
Not particular	Medium water	Light feeder	Vine used as groundcover; evergreen in mild climates; twining, climbing growth habit to 15′ with support; soft, downy, green leaves; fragrant flowers; trumpet-shaped blooms turn yellow with age; drought tolerant; invasive.
Good drainage	Medium water	Medium feeder	One of the hardiest honeysuckles; tall and spreading growth; flowers white changing to yellowish color; red fruits follow.
Good drainage	Medium water	Medium feeder	Bluish-green, dense foliage; upright, arching form; fragrant flowers; showy red berries; can become leggy; prune after flowering; renew overgrown plants by pruning to the ground.
Good drainage	Medium water	Medium feeder	Low-growing, trailing, flat branches; clusters of soft, needlelike, silvery green leaves; vinelike, powder gray brown branches; profuse blooms, shaped like parrot's beak; good bank cover; give moderate to light waterings.

NAME	HABIT		FLOWERS		ADAPTATION	
	Type	**Height**	**Color**	**Time**	**Zones**	**Light**
Lupinus, **Russell hybrids** Russell Lupines	Hardy perennial	4 to 5 ft	Warm colors (red, orange, yel), blue, pink, purple, white	Early summer	3 to 9	Full sun to light shade
Lychnis chalcedonica Maltese Cross	Hardy perennial	2 to 3 ft	Red	Summer	3 to 10	Full sun
Lycoris aurea Yellow Spider	Half-hardy bulb	to 1½ ft	Yellow	Late summer	7 to 10	Full sun to light shade
Lysimachia nummularia Moneywort	Hardy perennial	1 to 2 ft	Yellow	Summer	3 to 10	Light shade to deep shade
Lythrum salicaria Purple Loosestrife	Hardy perennial	3 to 5 ft	Pink, purple	Summer to early fall	3 to 10	Full sun to light shade
Maclura pomifera Osage Orange	Deciduous tree	to 60 ft			4 to 10	Full sun
Magnolia acuminata Cucumber Tree	Deciduous tree	50 to 80 ft	Yellow	Late spring to summer	4 to 8	Full sun
Magnolia grandiflora Southern Magnolia	Evergreen tree	60 to 75 ft	White	Early summer to fall	6 to 9	Full sun
Magnolia quinquepeta Lily Magnolia	Deciduous shrub	8 to 12 ft	Purple	Spring	6 to 8	Full sun to light shade
Magnolia soulangiana Saucer Magnolia	Deciduous tree	20 to 30 ft	Pink, purple, white	Spring	5 to 9	Full sun to light shade
Magnolia stellata Star Magnolia	Deciduous tree	15 to 20 ft	White	Winter to early spring	4 to 9	Full sun to light shade
Magnolia virginiana Sweetbay Magnolia	Semi-evergreen tree	10 to 20 ft	White	Early summer to early fall	5 to 9	Full sun to light shade
Mahonia aquifolium Oregon Grape	Evergreen shrub	3 to 9 ft	Yellow	Spring	5 to 9	Light shade
Mahonia bealei Leatherleaf Mahonia	Evergreen shrub	10 to 12 ft	Yellow	Spring	6 to 10	Light shade
Mahonia repens Creeping Mahonia	Groundcover	1 to 2 ft	Yellow	Spring	6 to 10	Full sun to light shade

For a list of common names, see page 378.

	CULTURE		
Soil	**Water**	**Feeding**	**Special Characteristics**
Good drainage	Medium water	Light feeder	Adapted only to cool-summer, humid climates; mulch to keep roots cool; often short-lived.
Good drainage	Medium water	Light feeder	Can become invasive; generally short-lived.
Good drainage	Medium water	Medium feeder	Good in containers—best when crowded; leaves in spring only.
Rich soil; organic matter	Wet; don't let dry out	Medium feeder	Well adapted to boggy conditions; can be invasive.
Rich soil	Medium water	Light feeder	Reseeds heavily in wet areas; long-lived.
Not particular	Dry; let dry out between waterings	Light feeder	Fast-growing, thorny tree; usually 20–40' high under cultivation; open, spreading habit; medium green leaves; inedible, bumpy, yellow-green fruits on female plants if male plant also present; tolerates heat, cold, wind, drought, poor soil; can be used as a hedge or a tree; needs water until established.
Good drainage; rich soil; organic matter	Medium water	Heavy feeder	Fast-growing; glossy green leaves; dense shade; needs room; cold hardy; intolerant of hot, dry winds.
Good drainage; organic matter; rich soil	Medium water	Heavy feeder	Moderate-growing; lustrous, heavy-textured leaves; large, fragrant flowers; appreciates heat; avoid foot traffic around base; street, lawn, wall, large container, espalier; 'St. Mary's' stays smaller.
Good drainage; rich soil	Medium water	Heavy feeder	Slow-growing; showy, fragrant flowers purple on the outside, white inside; plant in protected location; specimen, in groups or in shrub border.
Good drainage; rich soil; organic matter	Medium water	Heavy feeder	Moderate growing; green foliage, rather coarse, not showy; lawn, garden specimen, corner.
Good drainage; rich soil; organic matter	Medium water	Heavy feeder	Moderate growing; fragrant, straplike petals; flowers can be damaged by frost; good specimen tree.
Good drainage; rich soil; organic matter	Medium water	Heavy feeder	Evergreen in the south, deciduous in colder areas; extremely fragrant flowers; leaves glossy above, whitish beneath; similar to *M. grandiflora*, except smaller tree may reach 60' high.
Organic matter; acid soil	Wet; don't let dry out	Medium feeder	Open, loose form; irregular, spreading habit; spiny, hollylike leaves, showy flowers; protect from hot sun and winds; best in shrub border; prune after flowering to maintain 3' height.
Rich soil	Wet; don't let dry out	Heavy feeder	Vertical form; good structural interest; showy flowers; blue, grapelike fruit; will not tolerate drought, hot sun or wind; difficult to prune.
Rich soil	Medium water	Medium feeder	Bluish green, spiny, hollylike leaves; flowers in clusters; dark purple, grapelike berries in the fall; spreads rapidly by underground stems; best in light shade.

NAME	HABIT		FLOWERS		ADAPTATION	
	Type	Height	Color	Time	Zones	Light
Malus species Crabapple	Deciduous tree	10 to 25 ft	Pink, red, white,	Spring	3 to 10	Full sun
Malus baccata Siberian Crabapple	Deciduous tree	15 to 30 ft	White	Spring	2 to 8	Full sun
Malus floribunda Japanese Flowering Crabapple	Deciduous tree	15 to 25 ft	White	Spring	4 to 8	Full sun
Malus sargentii Sargent crabapple	Deciduous fruit tree	to 8 ft	White	Late spring	4 to 8	Full sun
Mandarin Orange *Citrus reticulata*	Evergreen fruit tree	6 to 20 ft	White	Spring	9 to 10	Full sun to half-day sun
Maranta leuconeura Prayer Plant	Houseplant	to 8 in			10 or IN	Light shade
Matthiola incana Stock	Hardy biennial	12 to 30 in	White, pink, lavender, red, purple	Spring to early fall		Full sun to half-day sun
Maytenus boaria Mayten Tree	Evergreen tree	30 to 40 ft			8 to 10	Full sun to light shade
Melia azedarach Chinaberry	Deciduous tree	30 to 40 ft	Lavender	Early summer	7 to 10	Full sun
Mentha requienii Corsican Mint	Groundcover	1 to 3 in	Lavender	Summer	7 to 10	Full sun to light shade
Mertensia virginica Virginia Bluebells	Hardy perennial	12 to 24 in	Blue	Spring	3 to 8	Deep shade
Metasequoia glyptostroboides Dawn Redwood	Deciduous tree	80 to 100 ft			5 to 9	Full sun to light shade
Mimulus × hybridus 'Grandiflorus' Monkey Flower	Half-hardy annual	6 to 8 in	Yellow, red, bicolored	Early summer to early fall		Light shade

For a list of common names, see page 378.

Soil	Water	Feeding	Special Characteristics
Good drainage; organic matter	Medium water	Medium feeder	Very decorative fruit tree; many varieties available with variations in flower, fruit, and foliage size and color; much variation in zone tolerance; leaf color varies from green to bronze or red, some variegated; edible fruits used in jellies; self-fertile; produce abundant fruit on long-lived spurs; can be grafted; subject to same diseases as apples; scab often a problem; choose resistant varieties.
Good drainage	Medium water	Medium feeder	Vase-shaped; fragrant flowers; requires winter chilling; lawn, along fences, driveway, walk; prune only to establish framework.
Good drainage	Medium water	Medium feeder	Arching spread; buds red, turn pinkish-white when open; reddish-yellow fruit; profuse bloomer; requires winter chill; prune only to establish framework; lawn, driveway, fence, walkway.
Good drainage	Medium water	Medium feeder	Slow growing; dwarf, spreading; very disease resistant; fragrant flowers, red in bud; masses of dark red fruit; needs winter chill.
Good drainage; organic matter	Medium water	Medium feeder	Needs high heat or fruit will be sour; small, loose-skinned fruit sometimes called tangerine or satsuma; prune only to remove dead, diseased or sucker growth; plant high; protect from frosts; several cultivars available.
Organic matter	Medium water	Medium feeder	Green leaves marked with bronze; in daytime, foliage lies flat, at night it turns upward; give warm, humid environment; give bright, indirect light.
Good drainage; organic matter	Medium water	Heavy feeder	Pleasant fragrance; grows best in cool, moist weather; often grown as an annual; does not flower well in dry heat; will bloom through winter in mild climates.
Good drainage	Medium water	Medium feeder	Slow growing; graceful, weeping habit; tolerates heat, salinity, seaside conditions; lawn, patio, raised bed, driveway; remove any unwanted side growth.
Not particular	Let dry out between waterings	Light feeder	Fast-growing; spreading, umbrellalike crown; poisonous yellow berries; tolerates hot, dry climates; grows where most trees won't.
Good drainage; rich soil	Medium water	Medium feeder	Low-growing, vigorous spreader; forms soft, green carpet; fragrant foliage; self-sows; may die down in freezing temperatures, but will reappear in the spring; good groundcover for small spaces, between stepping stones.
Organic matter	Medium water	Medium feeder	Noninvasive; dies down in summer; prefers cool, moist soil; docs best in cool-summer climates.
Good drainage; organic matter	Medium water	Medium feeder	Fast growing; light green foliage; horizontal, pendulous branches; small cones; needles turn orange-brown to rust in fall; bark reddish-brown; avoid hot, dry winds or salt winds; keep moist; protect from hot sunlight in enclosed areas; best in groves; young tree, container.
Good drainage; organic matter	Wet; don't let dry out	Heavy feeder	Long bloom season; will adjust to boggy situations or occasional flooding.

NAME	HABIT		FLOWERS		ADAPTATION	
	Type	Height	Color	Time	Zones	Light
Mirabilis jalapa Four-o'clock, Beauty Of The Night, Marvel Of Peru	Tender perennial	1½ to 3 ft	White, yellow, red, pink, pink, bicolored	Early summer to early fall	8 to 10	Full sun to light shade
Moluccella laevis Bells-of-Ireland	Hardy annual	2 to 3 ft	Green	Early summer to first frost		Full sun to light shade
Monarda didyma Bergamot, Bee Balm, Oswego Tea	Hardy perennial herb	to 3 ft	Red	Summer	4 to 10	Full sun to light shade
Monstera deliciosa Monstera, Split-leaf Philodendron	Houseplant	to 6 ft			10 or IN	Light shade
Moraea iridoides *(Dietes vegeta)* Butterfly Iris, Fortnight Lily	Half-hardy bulb	to 4 ft	White	Late spring	8 to 10	Full sun
Morus alba White Mulberry, Fruitless Mulberry	Deciduous tree	30 to 50 ft			4 to 10	Full sun
Muscari botryoides Common Grape Hyacinth, Italian Grape Hyacinth	Hardy bulb	6 to 12 in	Blue	Spring to late spring	3 to 10	Full sun to light shade
Muskmelon *Cucumis melo*	Tender annual vegetable			Summer		Full sun
Mustard, Indian mustard, Mustard Greens *Brassica juncea*	Hardy annual vegetable	to 1½ ft				Full sun to light shade
Myosotis sylvatica Forget-me-not	Half-hardy biennial	6 to 12 in	Blue, pink, white	Early spring to summer		Light shade
Myrica pennsylvanica Northern Bayberry	Deciduous shrub	5 to 12 ft			2 to 7	Full sun to light shade
Myrtus communis Myrtle	Evergreen shrub	5 to 15 ft	White	Summer	9 to 10	Full sun to light shade
Nandina domestica Heavenly Bamboo	Evergreen shrub	6 to 8 ft	White	Early summer	7 to 10	Full sun to half-day sun

For a list of common names, see page 378.

Soil	CULTURE		
	Water	Feeding	Special Characteristics
Good drainage	Wet; don't let dry out	Heavy feeder	Fragrant; blooms afternoons and evenings; tolerates humidity, drought, heat, and air pollution; treated as an annual in colder climates; roots may be dug in fall and stored in winter for spring replanting.
Good drainage	Medium water	Heavy feeder	Needs staking; good for dried arrangements; appreciates long, mild summers.
Organic matter	Wet; don't let dry out	Medium feeder	Herb with oval, pointed leaves; aromatic foliage; flowers attract hummingbirds; prefers slightly acid soil; prune in the fall.
Good drainage	Let dry out between waterings	Medium feeder	Large, perforated and deeply cut leaves; climbing, vining habit; aerial roots; give bright, indirect light; tolerates shade; can cut top of plant back to limit growth.
Good drainage	Let dry out between waterings	Medium feeder	White flowers spotted with brownish yellow and purplish blue; can be planted outdoors in warm, practically frost-free areas.
Not particular	Medium water	Medium feeder	Bright green, irregularly lobed leaves; available as either a fruiting or fruitless tree; fruiting types produce white, pinkish or blackish-purple fruits; can be very messy; fruitless better as ornamental; fast-growing in hot climates; tolerates some drought; tolerates alkaline soils; good shade tree.
Good drainage	Medium water	Medium feeder	Fragrant flowers; good in containers; cultivar 'Album' has white flowers.
Good drainage; organic matter	Medium water	Medium feeder	Warm-season vegetable; requires ample space; requires plenty of water during vine stage but less during fruit ripening period; in short-season or cool-summer climates, grow extra-early varieties or start seeds indoors 3–4 weeks before outdoor planting; many cultivars available with variation in size, shape, flavor and maturation dates.
Rich soil	Medium water	Heavy feeder	Cool-weather, short-day crop; bolts to seed very early; plant as soon as soil can be worked.
Rich soil; good drainage	Wet; don't let dry out	Heavy feeder	Best in regions of long, cool springs; often grown as an annual; performs well in wet soil; self-sows freely; tolerates full sun in cool regions.
Sandy soil; tolerates clay soil	Medium water	Light feeder	Dense form; clean, lustrous green foliage; grayish-white, waxy berries on female plants; all plant parts aromatic; tolerates seacoast conditions, infertile, dry soils; good for large-scale massing; prune old, leggy plants to ground level.
Good drainage	Medium water	Medium feeder	Glossy, bright green foliage; round, bushy shrub; fragrant foliage; black berries; unpruned, can reach 15' tall; informal hedge, screen, mass, sheared as formal hedge; tolerates heat and drought.
Not particular	Medium water	Medium feeder	Vertical form; delicate, wispy foliage; bright red berries; good fall color; protect from hot sun; tolerates drought once established; semideciduous in colder climates; prune out old, leggy canes.

NAME	HABIT		FLOWERS		ADAPTATION	
	Type	**Height**	**Color**	**Time**	**Zones**	**Light**
Narcissus **hybrids** Daffodils	Half-hardy to hardy bulbs	4 to 18 in	yellow, orange, white	Early spring to late summer	4 to 10	Full sun to partial sha
Narcissus bulbocodium Petticoat Daffodil	Half-hardy bulb	to 15 in	Yellow	Early spring	7 to 10	Full sun to light shade
Narcissus jonquilla Jonquil	Hardy bulb	12 to 18 in	White, yellow	Early spring to late spring	5 to 10	Full sun to light shade
Narcissus tazetta Polyanthus Narcissus	Half-hardy bulb	12 to 18 in	White, yellow	Early spring to late spring	8 to 10	Full sun to light shade
Nectarine *Prunus persica* var. *nectarina*	Deciduous fruit tree	10 to 20 ft	Pink	Spring	5 to 9	Full sun
Nemophila menziesii Baby Blue Eyes	Half-hardy annual	6 to 12 in	Blue	Early summer to first frost		Full sun to half-day sun to light shade
Nephrolepis exaltata Sword Fern, Boston Fern	Houseplant	2 to 4 ft			10 or IN	Light shade
Nerium oleander Oleander	Evergreen shrub	8 to 12 ft	Pink, red, white, yellow	Late spring to fall	8 to 10	Full sun
Nicotiana alata Flowering Tobacco, Nicotiana	Tender annual	12 to 36 in	White, red, pink, green, yellow	Early summer to first frost		Full sun to light shade
Nierembergia hippomanica Cup Flower	Tender perennial	6 to 12 in	Purple, blue-violet	Early summer to early fall		Full sun to light shade
Nigella damascena Love-in-a-mist	Hardy annual	12 to 30 in	Blue, pink, white	Early summer to early fall		Full sun
Nyssa sylvatica Black Tupelo, Black Gum, Sour Gum, Pepperidge	Deciduous tree	30 to 50 ft			4 to 9	Full sun
Okra, Gumbo *Abelmoschus esculentus*	Tender annual vegetable		Yellow	Summer		Full sun
Olea europaea Olive	Evergreen tree	20 to 30 ft			9 to 10	Full sun
Onion *Allium cepa*	Hardy biennial vegetable					Full sun

For a list of common names, see page 378.

	CULTURE		
Soil	**Water**	**Feeding**	**Special Characteristics**
Good drainage	Medium water	Medium feeder	Colorful, fragrant flowers; available in hundreds of varieties.
Good drainage	Medium water	Medium feeder	Small flowers; good in containers; allow foliage to yellow before cutting back.
Good drainage	Medium water	Medium feeder	Flowers fragrant; good in containers; allow foliage to yellow before cutting back.
Good drainage	Medium water	Medium feeder	Fragrant flowers; often used for indoor forcing; good in containers; allow foliage to yellow before cutting back.
Good drainage; organic matter	Medium water	Medium feeder to heavy feeder	Nectarines differ from peaches only in having a smooth skin and a slightly different flavor; require same care as peaches but more susceptible to brown rot; many early, midseason, and late varieties available.
Sandy soil; good drainage	Medium water	Light feeder	Self-sows freely; easy to grow; water freely if grown in full sun.
Good drainage	Medium water	Medium feeder	Long, swordlike fronds; give bright light, no direct sun; provide some humidity, keep moist; common cultivars include 'Bostoniensis' (Boston fern), 'Fluffy Ruffles', and 'Whitmanii'.
Not particular	Let dry out between waterings	Light feeder	Broad, rounded, bulky form; coarse foliage; attractive flowers; tolerates heat, drought, salt; all parts poisonous; excellent in desert gardens.
Good drainage; organic matter	Wet; don't let dry out	Heavy feeder	Flowers open late in the day, release fragrance in the evening; daylight varieties available; flowers fade in full sun in dry climates.
Good drainage; organic matter; sandy soil	Medium water	Medium feeder	Provide shade in areas with hot summers; usually grown as an annual.
Good drainage; sandy soil	Let dry out between waterings	Heavy feeder	Attractive seed pods; short flower-season; may need staking; make successive plantings.
Not particular	Medium water	Medium feeder	Moderate growing; dense, glossy, dark green foliage; outstanding fall color (coppery-red); dramatic winter silhouette; tolerates poor drainage, any soil, occasional drought.
Good drainage; organic matter	Medium water	Medium feeder	Warm season vegetable grown for edible pods; several cultivars available.
Good drainage	Medium water	Medium feeder	Fast growing when young, slows down with age; gray-green, willowlike leaves; attractive, gnarled trunk; edible fruit; easy to transplant any age; tolerates shallow, alkaline, stony soil, little fertilizer; thrives in areas with hot, dry summers; withstands heavy pruning; 'Swan Hill' is fruitless.
Good drainage	Medium water	Heavy feeder	Culinary plant with bulbous root; long, green leaves; treated as biennial or long-season annual.

NAME	HABIT		FLOWERS		ADAPTATION	
	Type	Height	Color	Time	Zones	Light
Ophiopogon jaburan Jaburan Lilyturf, White Lilyturf	Groundcover	2 ft	White	Summer to early fall	7 to 10	Full sun to light shade
Ophiopogon japonicus Mondo Grass	Groundcover	8 to 10 in	Purple	Summer	7 to 10	Full sun to light shade
Orange *Citrus sinensis*	Evergreen fruit tree	10 to 30 ft	White	Spring	9 to 10	Full sun to half-day sun
Oregano *Origanum vulgare*	Hardy perennial herb	2½ ft			5 to 10	Full sun
Ornithogalum arabicum Arabian Star-of-Bethlehem	Half-hardy bulb	24 in	White	Late spring to early summer	8 to 10	Full sun
Ornithogalum umbellatum Star-of-Bethlehem	Hardy bulb	12 in	White	Spring to early summer	5 to 10	Full sun
Osmanthus americanus Devilwood Osmanthus, American Olive	Evergreen shrub	to 45 ft	White	Early spring	7 to 9	Full sun
Osmanthus fragrans Sweet Olive	Evergreen shrub	10 ft	White	Early spring to late fall	8 to 10	Light shade
Osmanthus heterophyllus Holly Olive	Evergreen shrub	4 to 8 ft	White	Fall	7 to 9	Light shade
Osteospermum fruiticosum African Daisy or Trailing African Daisy	Groundcover	6 to 12 in	Purple and red	Intermittently all year	8 to 10	Full sun
Ostrya virginiana American Hophornbeam	Deciduous tree	30 to 35 ft			4 to 9	Full sun
Oxalis bowiei Bowie Oxalis	Half-hardy bulb	6 to 12 in	Pink, purple	Summer to late summer	8 to 10	Full sun to light shade
Oxydendrum arboreum Sourwood	Deciduous tree	30 to 40 ft	White	Summer	6 to 9	Full sun
Pachysandra terminalis Japanese Spurge	Groundcover	6 to 8 in	White	Late spring	4 to 10	Light shade to deep shade
***Paeonia* hybrids** Herbaceous Peony	Hardy perennial	2 to 4 ft	Pink, red, white, yellow	Late spring to early summer	5 to 8	Full sun to light shade

For a list of common names, see page 378.

	CULTURE		
Soil	**Water**	**Feeding**	**Special Characteristics**
Good drainage	Medium water	Light feeder	Dense clumps of coarse, dark green leaves; green stems; give sun on coast, shade elsewhere; cultivar 'Variegatus' is low growing with white, striated flowers.
Good drainage	Medium water	Light feeder	Dense clumps of long, dark green leaves; coarse foliage; small flowers; pea-size blue fruit; spreads by means of fleshy, subsurface stems; slow-growing until established; give sun in coastal areas, shade elsewhere.
Good drainage; organic matter	Medium water	Medium feeder	Very attractive tree; fragrant blooms; popular fruit; prune only to remove dead, diseased, or sucker growth; plant high; some of the most popular varieties are 'Valencia', a juice orange, and 'Washington', a navel orange.
Good drainage	Medium water	Medium feeder	Culinary herb with oval leaves, dark green in color; shrubby growth; pale pinkish-white blossoms; aromatic foliage; good container plant.
Good drainage	Medium water	Medium feeder	Fragrant flowers; good in containers.
Good drainage	Medium water	Medium feeder	Blooms close at night; good in containers.
Good drainage	Medium water	Medium feeder	Shrub or small tree; fragrant flowers, olivelike fruit in the fall; slow to moderate growth; leaves are glossy green above, yellowish below; best planted in garden where watered and fertilized regularly.
Tolerates clay soil	Medium water	Light feeder	Compact, neat form; glossy foliage; fragrant flowers heaviest in spring and summer; very adaptable and easy to grow; prune any time of year.
Tolerates clay soil	Medium water	Light feeder	Lustrous, spiny, dark green leaves; fragrant flowers; very shade tolerant.
Good drainage	Medium water	Medium feeder	Rapidly spreading; good cover for banks and sunny areas; showy flowers with deep purple center, rays fading to white.
Not particular	Medium water	Medium feeder	Slow growing; small, graceful tree; attractive bark; medium green foliage turns yellow in fall; tolerates wide range of soil; somewhat difficult to transplant.
Good drainage	Medium water	Medium feeder	Cloverlike foliage.
Rich soil	Medium water	Medium water	Slow growing; pyramid form; light, feathery appearance; young leaves unfold amber red, turn green; brilliant scarlet fall color; large sprays of fragrant flowers; needs acid soil, no competition; terrace or patio tree.
Rich soil; acid soil	Wet; don't let dry out	Medium feeder	Veined, dark green, oval leaves toothed near the ends; spreads rapidly by underground runners; forms a dense cover of uniform height; evergreen; the cultivar 'Green Carpet' is darker green and has more flowers.
Rich soil; good drainage; organic matter	Medium water	Medium feeder	Long-lived; huge, often fragrant flowers; requires winter-chilling period to bloom well; needs good air circulation around plants; never allow fresh manure or fast-acting nitrogen to come in direct contact with roots.

NAME	HABIT		FLOWERS		ADAPTATION	
	Type	Height	Color	Time	Zones	Light
Paeonia suffruticosa Tree Peony	Deciduous shrub	4 ft	Red, purple, violet, orange, yellow	Late spring to early summer	5 to 7	Full sun to light shade
Papaver nudicaule Iceland Poppy	Tender perennial	2 to 3 ft	Red, purple, white, pink, orange	Spring to summer		Full sun
Papaver orientale Oriental Poppy	Hardy perennial	2 to 4 ft	Orange, pink, red, white	Early summer	2 to 9	Full sun to light shade
Papaver rhoeas Shirley Poppy, Field Poppy	Hardy annual	1 to 2 ft	Red, purple, white, pink, orange	Spring to summer		Full sun
Parsley *Petroselinum crispum*	Tender biennial herb	10 to 15 in			3 to 10	Full sun to light shade
Parsnip *Pastinaca sativa*	Half-hardy biennial vegetable	1½ ft				Full sun to light shade
Parthenocissus quinquefolia Virginia Creeper, Woodbine	Groundcover, vine	Climbs to 50 ft			4 to 10	Full sun to light shade
Paspalum notatum Bahia Grass	Turfgrass	2 to 3 in			8 to 10	Full sun to light shade
Paulownia tomentosa Empress Tree, Royal Paulownia	Deciduous tree	40 to 60 ft	Violet	Spring	5 to 9	Full sun
Paxistima myrsinites Oregon Boxwood	Groundcover	2 in	No flowers		6 to 10	Full sun
Pea, Garden Pea, English Pea *Pisum sativum*	Half-hardy annual vegetable	Climbs to 6 ft				Full sun to half-day sun
Peach *Prunus persica*	Deciduous fruit tree	10 to 20 ft	Pink	Spring	5 to 9	Full sun
Genetic Dwarf Peaches and Nectarines *Prunus persica*	Dwarf fruit trees	to 5 ft	Pink	Spring	6 to 9	Full sun

For a list of common names, see page 378.

| | CULTURE | | |
Soil	Water	Feeding	Special Characteristics
Rich soil; organic matter	Wet; don't let dry out	Heavy feeder	Open, leggy form; attractive, large flowers; blossoms short-lived; leaves are deeply lobed.
Sandy soil; good drainage; organic matter	Medium water	Heavy feeder	In mild climates, blooms in winter and early spring from plants set out in fall; short-lived perennial often grown as an annual.
Good drainage	Medium water	Light feeder	Foliage dies down in summer; best in regions of cool summers; short-lived in warm climates; mulch in summer to keep roots cool; brief flowering period.
Sandy soil; good drainage; organic matter	Medium water	Heavy feeder	Short bloom season; prefers cool-summer climates.
Rich soil	Wet; don't let dry out	Medium feeder	Tender herb, usually grown as annual; dark green, deeply curled leaves; slow to start; protect from frost; all parts edible.
Good drainage; organic matter	Medium water	Medium feeder	Grown as an annual; needs looses oil; requires 100–120 days from seed; roots can be left in ground all winter to develop sweet, nutlike flavor, or dig in the late fall and store in moist sand.
Rich soil	Wet; don't let dry out	Heavy feeder	Deciduous, rambling vine; fast-growing; leaves divided into heavily veined leaflets; blue fruits; foliage turns red in fall; covers large area quickly and densely.
Good drainage; organic matter	Medium water	Medium feeder	Fast-growing; needs frequent mowing; forms coarse, open lawn; drought tolerant; extensive root system valued for erosion control; tolerates infertile, sandy soils; wears well.
Rich soil; good drainage	Medium water	Medium feeder	Fast growing; dense foliage; wide, rounded head; vanilla-scented flowers; tolerates city pollution; needs mild climate to flower well; give plenty of space.
Good drainage; acid soil	Medium water	Medium feeder	Low-maintenance, evergreen; tolerates some shade; branches root as they spread.
Good drainage; organic matter	Medium water	Medium feeder	Cool-season crop; grown in early spring to midsummer in cooler areas; and in fall, winter and very early spring where warmer; available as low-growers or climbing vines.
Good drainage; organic matter	Medium water	Medium feeder to heavy feeder	Popular fruiting tree; cannot tolerate extreme winter cold or late frost; best if pruned heavily each year to maintain size and encourage new growth along branches; thin fruits to 6" apart when they are thumbnail size; most varieties self-fertile; require winter chill—pick varieties to suit climate; peach leaf curl can be a problem; many early, midseason and late varieties.
Good drainage; organic matter	Medium water	Medium feeder to heavy feeder	Form dense bushes with long leaves; showy, usually semidouble flowers; not winter hardy; normal-size fruit; can be kept in containers and pruned to 5' high; require minimal pruning, although fruit must be thinned; fruit not as good as standard varieties; more susceptible to mites; most require winter chill.

NAME	HABIT		FLOWERS		ADAPTATION	
	Type	Height	Color	Time	Zones	Light
Peanut *Arachis hypogaea*	Tender annual vegetable	12 to 18 in			7 to 10	Full sun to half-day sun
Pear *Pyrus communis*	Deciduous fruit tree	15 to 25 ft	White	Early spring	5 to 9	Full sun
Pecan *Carya illinoinensis*	Deciduous nut tree	to 75 ft			6 to 9	Full sun
Pelargonium × hortorum Geranium	Tender perennial	12 to 24 in	Red, pink, orange, white	Late spring to first frost		Full sun
Pelargonium domesticum Pelargonium, Martha Washington Geranium	Tender perennial	to 3 ft	White, pink, red, lavender, purple	Spring and summer		Full to light shade
Pelargonium peltatum Ivy Geranium	Tender perennial, groundcover	1 to 3 ft, (trailing)	White, pink, rose, red, lavender	Late winter to early fall		Full sun
***Pelargonium* species** Scented Geraniums	Tender perennial	2 to 4 ft	Pink, white	Summer	9 to 10	Full sun
Pellaea rotundifolia Button Fern	Houseplant	12 to 18 in			10 or IN	Light shade
Pennisetum alopecuroides Fountain Grass	Hardy perennial	2 to 3½ ft	Tan	Late summer to fall	6 to 10	Full sun
***Peperomia* species**	Houseplant	4 to 6 in	White		10 or IN	Light shade
Pepper grass, Garden cress *Lepidium Sativium*	Hardy annual vegetable	to 2 ft				Full sun to half-day sun
Peppermint *Mentha × piperita*	Hardy perennial herb	1 to 2 ft	Purple	Summer to early fall	4 to 10	Full sun to light shade
Peppers *Capsicum Species*	Tender perennial vegetable	2 to 4 ft			10	Full sun
Persimmon, American *Diospyros virginiana*	Deciduous fruit tree	30 to 50 ft			5 to 9	Full sun
Persimmon *Diospyros kaki*	Deciduous fruit tree	20 to 30 ft			7 to 10	Full sun

For a list of common names, see page 378.

	CULTURE		
Soil	**Water**	**Feeding**	**Special Characteristics**
Good drainage; sandy soil	Medium water	Medium feeder	Legume grown for underground pods; requires long, warm growing season; 110–120 days; needs generous supply of lime in top 3–4″ of soil where pods form; give adequate water up until 2 weeks before harvest, then cut back; Virginia peanuts—2 seeds per pod, Spanish peanuts—2 to 6 seeds per pod.
Good drainage; organic matter	Medium water	Medium feeder	Long-lived, pyramidal tree with strongly vertical branching habit; requires little pruning; tolerates damp, heavy soils better than most other fruit trees; bears fruit on long-lived spurs; requires pollinator; dwarf varieties available; easy to train, espalier; fireblight can be a problem; many varieties.
Good drainage	Medium water	Medium feeder	Moderate-growing; food tree; needs deep soil; susceptible to scab.
Acid soil; good drainage	Let dry out between waterings	Medium feeder	Long blooming season; attractive foliage; newer hybrids are more heat tolerant; often grown as an annual.
Good drainage	Medium water	Light feeder	Large showy flowers with brilliant blotches and markings of darker-colors; in warm weather, water deeply once a week; susceptible to aphids and whiteflies.
Good drainage	Medium water	Light feeder	Trailing plant with 2 upper petals blotch or striped; many varieties with profuse blooming.
Good drainage; sandy soil	Let dry out between waterings	Medium feeder	Shrubby form; wide variety of fragrances; foliage varies from small, delicate leaves to large, rounded leaves; variegated varieties.
Good drainage	Medium water	Medium feeder	Round, leathery leaflets; give filtered light.
Rich soil	Let dry out between waterings	Medium feeder	Yellow foliage in fall; tolerates drought; dormant in winter.
Good drainage	Let dry out between waterings	Medium feeder	Slow-growing; *P. argyreia* (Watermelon peperomia) and *P. caperata* (Emerald-ripple) are commonly grown species; wide variety of leaf shapes, textures and colors.
Good drainage; organic matter	Medium water	Medium feeder	Cool season plant; fast-growing; similar in appearance to parsley; best grown in short days of early spring or fall; seeds need light to germinate.
Rich soil	Wet; don't let dry out	Medium feeder	Fast-growing culinary and medicinal herb; aromatic leaves; can become invasive.
Good drainage; organic matter	Wet; don't let dry out	Medium feeder	Grown as an annual in colder zones; prefers hot-weather climates to set fruit properly; grow from seed or transplants; protect from any late frost; main groups are bell, hot, and pimento peppers.
Good drainage	Medium water	Medium feeder	Moderate growing; fruits ripen after frost; more widely adapted than D. kaki; tolerates wide range of soils and climates.
Good drainage; rich soil	Medium water	Medium feeder	Large, glossy foliage with good fall color; heavy crop of orange-red fruit in the fall, hangs on until winter; good fruit tree for ornamental use; prune only to remove dead wood or shape tree; will set fruit without pollination; several varieties available.

NAME	HABIT		FLOWERS		ADAPTATION	
	Type	Height	Color	Time	Zones	Light
Petunia × hybrida Petunia	Half-hardy perennial	10 to 18 in	Violet, pink, red, purple, yellow, white, bicolored	Late spring to first frost		Full sun
Phellodendron amurense Amur Corktree	Deciduous tree	30 to 50 ft			4 to 8	Light shade
Philadelphus coronarius Mock Orange	Deciduous shrub	10 to 12 ft	White	Late spring	5 to 8	Full sun to light shade
Philodendron bipinnatifidum Twice-cut Philodendron, Fiddle-leaf Philodendron	Houseplant	6 to 8 ft			10 or IN	Light shade
Philodendron scandens Heart-leaf Philodendron	Houseplant	2 to 5 ft			10 or IN	Light shade
Phlox drummondii Annual Phlox	Half-hardy annual	6 to 20 in	White, pink, red, bicolored	Late spring to first frost		Full sun
Phlox paniculata Summer Phlox, Garden Phlox	Hardy perennial	2 to 4 ft	Red, pink, purple, lavender, white	Summer to early fall	3 to 10	Full sun to half-day sun
Phlox subulata Moss Pink	Hardy perennial, groundcover	to 6 in	Lavender, pink, red, white	Spring	3 to 10	Full sun
Phoenix roebelenii Pygmy Date Palm	Houseplant	to 4 ft			9 to 10 or IN	Light shade
Photinia serrulata Chinese Photinia	Evergreen shrub	20 to 30 ft	White	Spring	7 to 10	Full sun
Photinia × fraseri Fraser Photinia	Evergreen shrub	10 to 15 ft	White	Spring	7 to 10	Full sun
Phyla nodiflora Lippia	Groundcover	2 to 6 in	Lavender	Spring to summer	9 to 10	Full sun to light shade
Picea abies Norway Spruce	Needled evergreen tree	40 to 60 ft			3 to 8	Full sun
Picea glauca White Spruce	Needled deciduous tree	40 to 60 ft			3 to 6	Full sun

For a list of common names, see page 378.

	CULTURE		
Soil	**Water**	**Feeding**	**Special Characteristics**
Good drainage; sandy soil	Medium water	Heavy feeder	Pinch young plants to promote blooming; dependable and versatile; young seedlings can withstand hot sun; grown as an annual in all but the mildest climates.
Rich soil; good drainage	Medium water	Heavy feeder	Moderate-growing; large, glossy, dark green leaves; attractive, corky bark, gray-black in color; shallow roots—avoid streets or lawns; good shade tree; black fruits; flowers inconspicuous; tolerates drought once established.
Not particular	Medium water	Medium feeder	Coarse, leggy, irregular form; very fragrant flowers; easy to grow; prune annually right after flowering.
Good drainage	Medium water	Medium feeder	Deeply cut, star-shaped, large leaves.
Good drainage	Medium water	Light feeder	Vigorous climbing habit; long, glossy, deep green leaves; give bright, indirect light; a subspecies, *P.s. oxycardium* is the commonly grown florist's philodendron.
Good drainage; sandy soil; organic matter	Medium water	Heavy feeder	Tolerates heat, but flowers will decline; avoid watering late in the day.
Rich soil; good drainage; organic matter	Wet; don't let dry out	Heavy feeder	Requires staking; provides massive color display; many cultivars available.
Sandy soil	Medium water	Medium water	Mat-forming; evergreen leaves; profuse bloomer.
Good drainage; organic matter	Medium water	Medium feeder	Delicate, dwarf form; straight, symmetrical shape; branching, narrow-leaf fronds with pendulous habit; give bright, indirect light; water heavily and feed monthly during growing season; reduce during winter; protect from dry air.
Good drainage	Medium water	Medium feeder	Large, coarsely textured leaves; profuse flowers; red berries; can prune as a screen.
Good drainage; organic matter	Medium water	Medium feeder	Moderate-growing, rounded form; foliage bronzy-red as new growth in spring; red berries easy to restrain; can prune as screen, hedge, espalier or train as single-stemmed small tree; susceptible to fireblight.
Good drainage	Medium water	Medium feeder	Perennial evergreen; green foliage forms dense mat; spreads by surface runners; good lawn substitute; flowers tiny, spotted with yellow; best in sun; mow flowers off for use as a lawn; drought and heat tolerant; in full sun, growth is more compact.
Not particular	Medium water	Medium feeder	Fast-growing; pyramidal form; branchlets become pendulous as tree ages; prefers cool, moist area; avoid low fertility; prune to shape only; good windbreak, tall screen, specimen; attractive cones; hot weather weakens tree.
Not particular	Medium water	Medium feeder	Moderate-growing; conical shape with drooping branchlets; blue-green foliage; tolerates very cold and very hot, dry conditions.

NAME	HABIT		FLOWERS		ADAPTATION	
	Type	Height	Color	Time	Zones	Light
Picea glauca 'Conica' Dwarf Alberta Spruce	Needled evergreen shrub	6 to 8 ft			2 to 7	Full sun
Picea pungens Colorado Spruce	Needled evergreen tree	80 to 100 ft			3 to 7	Full sun
Pieris forrestii Chinese Pieris	Evergreen shrub	6 to 10 ft	White	Spring	8 to 10	Light shade
Pieris japonica Japanese Pieris	Evergreen shrub	9 to 12 ft	Pink, white	Early spring	6 to 8	Light shade
Pilea cadierei Aluminum Plant	Houseplant	to 12 in			10 or IN	Light shade
Pilea nummulariifolia Creeping Charlie	Houseplant	3 to 5 ft			10 or IN	Light shade
Pinus canariensis Canary Island Pine	Needled evergreen tree	60 to 80 ft			8 to 10	Full sun
Pinus densiflora Japanese Red Pine	Needled evergreen tree	50 to 60 ft			4 to 7	Full sun
Pinus glabra Spruce Pine	Needled evergreen tree	to 100 ft			8 to 9	Full sun
Pinus mugo var. *mugo* Dwarf Mugo Pine	Needled evergreen shrub	2 to 4 ft			2 to 7	Full sun to light shade
Pinus nigra Austrian Pine	Needled evergreen tree	60 to 80 ft			4 to 8	Full sun
Pinus palustris Longleaf Pine	Needled evergreen tree	50 to 80 ft			8 to 9	Full sun
Pinus parviflora Japanese White Pine	Needled evergreen tree	25 to 50 ft			5 to 7	Full sun
Pinus radiata Monterey Pine	Needled evergreen tree	60 to 100 ft			8 to 10	Full sun
Pinus resinosa Red Pine, Norway Pine	Needled evergreen tree	50 to 80+ ft			2 to 7	Full sun

For a list of common names, see page 378.

Soil	Water	Feeding	Special Characteristics
Good drainage	Medium water	Medium feeder	Very slow-growing, stiff conical form; finely textured, light green needles.
Not particular	Medium water	Medium feeder	Growth slows as tree ages; stiff branches, forms narrow pyramidal shape; needles vary from dark green to blue green to steel blue; tends to lose its lower branches as it matures.
Good drainage	Medium water	Medium feeder	Denser, larger habit than *P. japonica*; new foliage is showy scarlet; fragrant flowers.
Good drainage; acid soil	Wet; don't let dry out	Medium feeder	Slow-growing; upright, irregular outline; attractive, dark green foliage; new spring growth is bronzy-red; needs protection from wind and winter sun.
Good drainage	Let dry out between waterings	Medium feeder	Fleshy stems, silver-splashed leaves; give bright, indirect light; avoid cold drafts.
Good drainage	Medium water	Heavy feeder	Fast-growing; small, round, slightly hairy leaves; creeping habit; give bright, indirect light; pinch back.
Good drainage	Medium water	Light feeder	Fast-growing; upright, pyramid; needles in bundles of 3, 9–12" long; cones 4–9"; foliage of young tree blue-green, darkens with age; drought tolerant; good shade tree.
Good drainage	Medium water	Light feeder	Fast-growing; open, loose habit; branches horizontal; usually two or more trunks; needles bright blue-green or yellow-green, bundles of 2, 2½–5" long; cones 2"; attractive reddish-orange bark; avoid cold winds.
Good drainage	Medium water	Light feeder	Low-branching tree; drooping branches; grows naturally in damp, coastal woods; when young use as screen; good specimen tree.
Rich soil	Let dry out between waterings	Medium feeder	May grow to 10' high; can be pruned annually by removing 2/3 of each young candle in spring; best in groupings or massed.
Good drainage	Medium water	Light feeder	Moderate-growing; dense growth; needles 2 in a bundle, sharp, stiff, 4–8" long; cones 3"; tolerates city conditions; withstands winter cold and wind.
Good drainage; sandy soil	Medium water	Light feeder	Needles in bundles of 3, 8–15" long; cones 6–12" long; sparse branches; tree "grasslike" when young; grows poorly in heavy soil.
Good drainage	Medium water	Light feeder	Slow-growing; hardy; needles in bundles of 5, 1½" long; cones 2–3", remain on tree 6–7 years; needs ample room; speciman tree; cultivar 'Glauca' has silver-blue needles.
Good drainage	Medium water	Light feeder	Fast-growing; needles bright-green, 2–3 in a bundle, 3–7" long; cones 3–5", stay on tree many years; develops roundish, flattish crown with age, often contorted by wind; thrives in cool, coastal climate; prune to maintain denseness; smog damage; windbreak, screen, large hedge.
Good drainage	Medium water	Light feeder	Medium-growing; very dense crown; slightly drooping branches; long, flexible, 4–6" dark green needles in bundles of 2; 4–7" long cones; reddish-brown bark tolerates cold; grows well in poor soils; can reach 125' high.

NAME	HABIT		FLOWERS		ADAPTATION	
	Type	Height	Color	Time	Zones	Light
Pinus strobus White Pine	Needled evergreen tree	50 to 80 ft			3 to 8	Full sun
Pinus sylvestris Scotch Pine, Scots Pine	Needled evergreen tree	30 to 60 ft			3 to 8	Full sun
Pinus taeda Loblolly Pine	Needled evergreen tree	60 to 80 ft			7 to 9	Full sun
Pinus thunbergiana Japanese Black Pine	Needled evergreen tree	20 to 40 ft			5 to 9	Full sun
Pistacia chinensis Chinese Pistache	Deciduous tree	50 to 60 ft			6 to 10	Full sun
Pittosporum tobira Tobira, Japanese Pittosporum	Evergreen shrub	6 to 15 ft	White	Spring	8 to 10	Full sun to light shade
Pittosporum undulatum Victorian Box	Evergreen tree	to 40 ft	White	Spring	9 to 10	Full sun to light shade
Platanus × acerifolia London Plane Tree	Deciduous tree	70 to 100 ft			5 to 9	Full sun
Platycerium bifurcatum Staghorn Fern	Houseplant	2 to 3 ft			10 or IN	Light shade
Platycodon grandiflorus Balloon Flower	Hardy perennial	2 to 3 ft	Blue, pink, white	Summer to early fall	3 to 10	Full sun to light shade
Plectranthus australis Swedish Ivy	Houseplant	3 to 10 ft	White		10 or IN	Light shade
Plum, European *Prunus domestica*	Deciduous fruit tree	15 to 20 ft	White	Late spring	5 to 8	Full sun
Plum, Japanese *Prunus salicina*	Deciduous fruit tree		White	Early spring	5 to 9	Full sun
Poa pratensis Common Kentucky Bluegrass	Turfgrass	2 to 3 in			3 to 7	Full sun to light shade

For a list of common names, see page 378.

	CULTURE		
Soil	**Water**	**Feeding**	**Special Characteristics**
Good drainage	Medium water	Light feeder	Slow-growing when young; needles in bundles of 5, 3–5″ long; best on sandy loam or silty soils; needs regular watering.
Good drainage	Medium water	Light feeder	Twisted, blue-green needles in bundles of 2, 1½–3″ long; cones 2″; bark of young tree reddish-brown, maturing to graying red-brown; drooping branches, picturesque when mature; popular Christmas and specimen tree.
Tolerates clay soil	Medium water	Light feeder	Needles in bundles of 3, 6–8″ long; grow in open area as shade tree; does poorly in sandy, well-drained soil.
Good drainage	Medium water	Light feeder	Fast-growing; needles bright green, stiff, in bundles of 2, 3–4″ long; cones 2–3″ long; large, white terminal buds; broad, spreading branches; good seacoast evergreen; can be sheared to Christmas-tree shape, bonsai, container, speciman.
Not particular	Medium water	Medium feeder	Moderate-growing; best in summer heat; bright green leaves up to 12″ long, brilliant shades of yellow, orange, red in fall; good lawn or street tree; female tree produces berries if male tree nearby; may need extra pruning when young to develop good shape.
Good drainage	Medium water	Medium feeder	Dark green, clean, leathery foliage; fragrant flowers; tolerates deep shade, mild drought; doesn't take heavy pruning; pinch back only.
Good drainage	Medium water	Medium feeder	Slow- to moderate-growing; fragrant flowers; leaves waxy, medium to dark green, wavy-edged; sticky fruit; lawn, street tree, container, pruned as screen; fruits can be messy.
Not particular	Medium water	Medium feeder	Fast-growing; open, spreading crown; maplelike, green leaves; brown, ball-shaped fruit; attractive green and white flaking bark; tolerates drought, poor soil, city conditions.
Organic matter	Medium water	Medium feeder	Broad, lancelike fronds divide in the middle, and ends look like stag antlers; best grown attached to bark or wood; air plant; keep moist; can summer outside on shaded patio.
Good drainage; sandy soil	Medium water	Medium feeder	Long-lived; tolerates many soils, but will not take wet soils in winter; will flower in hot, dry locations; tall plants may require staking.
Good drainage	Wet; don't let dry out	Heavy feeder	Waxy, leathery, bright green leaves; keep soil moist, not soggy; give bright, in direct light.
Good drainage; organic matter	Medium water	Medium feeder	Blooms later than Japanese plum, better adapted to areas of late frost, rainy spring weather; fruits range in color from green and yellow to almost black; requires moderately high chilling; trees need less pruning and thinning than Japanese varieties; most varieties are self-pollinating; makes good prunes when dried.
Good drainage; organic matter	Medium water	Medium feeder	Larger fruit than European varieties; range in colors from green through yellow
Good drainage; organic matter	Wet; don't let dry out	Heavy feeder	The most popular cool season lawn grass; not a good grass for the Southeast, but will grow in some warm areas of West Coast if given proper care; suffers in summer heat; poor wearability in summer, good in spring and fall; makes a dense, dark green, medium-textured lawn; many improved varieties available.

NAME	HABIT		FLOWERS		ADAPTATION	
	Type	**Height**	**Color**	**Time**	**Zones**	**Light**
Podocarpus macrophyllus Yew Pine	Evergreen tree	25 to 35 ft			8 to 10	Full sun to light shade
Polianthes tuberosa Tuberose	Tender bulb	to 3 ft	White	Late summer to early fall	9 to 10	Light shade
Polygonatum commutatum Great Solomon's-seal	Hardy perennial	3 to 5 ft	White	Late spring to early summer	4 to 10	Light shade to deep shade
Polygonum capitatum Pink Clover Blossom	Groundcover	5 to 8 in	Pink	All year	9 to 10	Full sun
Polypodium aureum Rabbit's-foot Fern, Golden Polypody Fern	Houseplant	to 3 ft			10 or IN	Light shade
Polystichum munitum Western Sword Fern	Groundcover	2 to 3½ ft			4 to 10	Deep shade
Pomegranate *Punica granatum*	Deciduous fruit tree	12 to 15 ft	Red, white, orange, yellow	Summer	7 to 10	Full sun
Populus alba White Poplar	Deciduous tree	40 to 70 ft			4 to 9	Full sun
Populus deltoides Eastern Poplar, Cottonwood	Deciduous tree	75 to 100 ft			2 to 10	Full sun
Populus nigra 'Italica' Lombardy Poplar	Deciduous tree	70 to 90 ft			2 to 9	Full sun
Portulaca grandiflora Rose Moss	Tender annual	4 to 8 in	Red, yellow, white, pink, purple	Late spring to first frost		Full sun
Potato *Solanum tuberosum*	Tender perennial vegetable	to 2 ft			9 to 10	Full sun
Potentilla cinerea Alpine Cinquefoil	Groundcover	to 4 in	Yellow	Spring to summer	3 to 10	Full sun to light shade
Potentilla fruticosa Bush Cinquefoil	Deciduous shrub, groundcover	1 to 4 ft	Red, orange, yellow	Early summer to first frost	2 to 7	Full sun to light shade

For a list of common names, see page 378.

	CULTURE		
Soil	**Water**	**Feeding**	**Special Characteristics**
Good drainage	Medium water	Medium feeder	Slow-growing; erect, columnar form; long, narrow, stiff leaves on lightly drooping branches; best in protected location; good container plant; easy to prune as espalier, hedge, topiary, screen, street, or lawn tree.
Good drainage	Medium water	Medium feeder	Strong, sweet fragrance; long growing season; often grown as annual because it may not bloom second year; needs warmth.
Organic matter	Medium water	Medium feeder	Attractive foliage; will tolerate dry soil, but best in cool, moist soil; long-lived; noninvasive.
Good drainage	Let dry out between waterings	Light feeder	Wiry, trailing, reddish stems; elliptical dark green to pinkish leaves; flowers bloom most of the year; mounding, spreading form.
Good drainage; organic matter	Medium water	Medium feeder	Low-growing; rusty brown, creeping rhizomes; wiry stems; straplike leaves; many deeply cut, ruffled leaflets; fronds grow 2–5' long, blue-green above and whitish below; good in hanging basket; give filtered light.
Organic matter	Wet; don't let dry out	Medium feeder	Hardy, evergreen fern; leathery, sword-shaped fronds.
Good drainage	Medium water	Medium feeder	Dense twiggy mass of arching foliage; showy flowers; edible fruits; yellow fall color; tolerates heat, drought, alkaline soils; water regularly and deeply for best fruit.
Not particular	Medium water	Medium feeder	Fast-growing; tall and wide-spreading, hardy; foliage dark green above and silvery-white below, shaped like small maple leaf; tolerates seacoast conditions, poor sandy soil; persistent sprouting from root system; the cultivar 'Pyramidalis' is a good screen, doesn't root-sprout and has a columnar form.
Not particular	Medium water	Medium feeder	Very fast-growing; soft, white wood; drooping catkins appear on leaves in spring; fruit is a small cap that produces "cottony" discharge; easy to cultivate; tolerates most soils; very invasive roots.
Not particular	Medium water	Medium feeder	Fast-growing; columnar with upward-reaching branches; foliage bright green, triangular, yellow in fall; suckers; roots invasive; good as tall screen, windbreak, accent; susceptible to stem canker; cultivar *P. nigra* 'Thevestina' has white bark, broader shape, and is more resistant to canker.
Good drainage; sandy soil	Let dry out between waterings	Light feeder	Heat and drought tolerant; flowers close late in day and in cloudy weather; reseeds readily.
Good drainage; organic matter	Medium water	Medium feeder	Grown as an annual; needs frost-free growing season; ideal climate has cool summer; needs loose, slightly acid soil, high in potash; mulch heavily; many early, midseason, and late varieties available.
Good drainage	Medium water	Medium feeder	Fast-growing; spreads by surface runners; grows in tufts; 5 wedge-shaped, bright green, coarsely toothed leaflets; popular in the Pacific Northwest.
Not particular	Medium water	Medium feeder	Dense, upright, rounded form; finely textured, bright green foliage; tolerates any soil, extreme cold and drought; flowers best in full sun; many cultivars in wide range of.

NAME	HABIT		FLOWERS		ADAPTATION	
	Type	Height	Color	Time	Zones	Light
Potentilla verna Spring Cinquefoil	Groundcover	3 to 6 in	Yellow	Spring to summer	6 to 10	Full sun to light shade
Primula japonica Japanese Primrose	Half-hardy perennial	to 30 in	Pink, purple, white	Late spring to early summer	5 to 10	Light shade
Primula vulgaris English Primrose	Half-hardy perennial	½ to 3 ft	All colors	Winter to late spring	5 to 10	Light shade
Primula × polyantha Polyantha Primrose	Hardy perennial	to 12 in	All colors	Winter to spring	5 to 10	Light shade
Prunus caroliniana Cherry Laurel	Evergreen tree	18 to 40 ft	White	Winter to spring	7 to 10	Full sun
Prunus cerasifera Cherry Plum	Deciduous tree	to 25 ft	White	Winter to early spring	4 to 8	Full sun
Prunus glandulosa Dwarf Flowering Almond	Deciduous shrub	4 to 5 ft	White, pink	Late spring	5 to 8	Full sun to light shade
Prunus ilicifolia Hollyleaf Cherry	Evergreen tree	12 to 35 ft	White	Early spring	9 to 10	Full sun to light shade
Prunus laurocerasus English Laurel	Evergreen shrub	25 to 30 ft	White	Spring	7 to 10	Light shade
Prunus sargentii Sargent Cherry	Deciduous tree	50 ft	Pink	Spring	5 to 8	Full sun
Prunus serrulata Japanese Flowering Cherry	Deciduous tree	20 to 25 ft	White	Spring	6 to 9	Full sun
Prunus tomentosa Nanking Cherry, Manchu Cherry	Deciduous shrub	6 to 10 ft	White	Spring	2 to 8	Full sun to light shade
Prunus triloba Flowering Almond	Deciduous shrub	12 to 15 ft	Pink	Spring	6 to 9	Full sun to light shade
Prunus virginiana Common Chokecherry	Deciduous tree	20 to 30 ft	White	Early spring to spring	2 to 7	Full sun
Prunus yedoensis Yoshino Cherry	Deciduous tree	to 40 ft	White, pink	Spring	6 to 8	Full sun
Pseudotsuga menziesii Douglas Fir	Needled evergreen tree	40 to 80 ft			5 to 7	Full sun to light shade

For a list of common names, see page 378.

| | CULTURE | | |
Soil	Water	Feeding	Special Characteristics
Good drainage	Medium water	Medium feeder	Fast-growing; spreads by surface runners; 5 wedge-shaped, bright green, coarsely toothed leaflets; 4-petaled flowers borne singly but in profusion.
Rich soil; organic matter; acid soil	Wet; don't let dry out	Heavy feeder	Boggy conditions are best.
Rich soil; good drainage; organic matter	Wet; don't let dry out	Heavy feeder	Best in mild, humid climates without extreme winter- or summer-temperature changes; protect from hot-afternoon sun.
Rich soil; good drainage; organic matter	Wet; don't let dry out	Medium feeder	Large, bold blooms; frequent division needed, otherwise plants are short-lived.
Good drainage	Medium water	Medium feeder	Large shrub or small tree; often forms dense thicket; dense foliage, glossy green leaves; black fruit; best in coastal areas; drought tolerant once mature.
Good drainage	Medium water	Medium feeder	Leaves dark green; fruit yellow or reddish, quite sweet; used as rootstock for various stone fruits; the cultivar 'Atropurpurea' has purple leaves.
Good drainage	Medium water	Medium feeder	Upright, awkward growth; unappealing when not in flower.
Good drainage	Medium water	Medium feeder	Moderate-growing; dark green, hollylike leaves; new growth lighter green; edible fruit; small tree, clipped hedge, or tall screen.
Good drainage	Medium water	Medium feeder	Fast-growing; large, dark green leaves; common as hedge, screen, or background plant; prune selectively—shearing mutilates large leaves; dwarf cultivars available.
Good drainage	Medium water	Medium feeder	Moderate-growing; hardy; attractive bark; good fall color.
Good drainage	Medium water	Medium feeder	Fragrant, double white flowers; over 120 cultivars— 'Amanogawa' is 20 ft. tall, narrow, upright, and has pink flowers; 'Kwanzan' is 12–18 ft. tall, hardy, and has double, deep pink flowers.
Good drainage	Medium water	Medium feeder	Picturesque, open form; attractive bark; fragrant flowers; edible fruit; can be sheared into an attractive, dense hedge although fruits are sacrificed.
Good drainage	Medium water	Medium feeder	Large, treelike shrub; profuse bloomer.
Good drainage	Medium water	Medium feeder	Dark purple fruits; the cultivar 'Shubert' has red leaves that last all summer.
Good drainage			Fast-growing; curving branches; open form; pinkish-white flowers; one of the best cherry varieties.
Good drainage	Medium water	Medium feeder	Fast-growing; pyramid shape; soft, flat, bluish-green needles arranged spirally on stems; fragrant foliage; reddish-brown cones hang down; takes some wind; can be grown as clipped hedge if topped and trimmed.

NAME	HABIT		FLOWERS		ADAPTATION	
	Type	Height	Color	Time	Zones	Light
Pumpkins *Cucurbita* species	Tender annual vegetable	8 to 12 ft	Summer			Full sun
Pyracantha coccinea Scarlet Firethorn	Evergreen shrub	6 to 18 ft	White	Spring	6 to 9	Full sun
***Pyracantha koidzumii* 'Santa Cruz Prostrate'** Firethorn	Groundcover	2 to 4 ft	White	Spring	8 to 10	Full sun
Pyrus calleryana Callery Pear	Deciduous tree	30 to 50 ft	White	Spring	5 to 9	Full sun
Pyrus kawakamii Evergreen Pear	Evergreen tree	to 30 ft	White	Winter to early spring	8 to 10	Full sun
Quercus agrifolia Coast Live Oak	Evergreen tree	20 to 70 ft			9 to 10	Full sun
Quercus alba White Oak	Deciduous tree	60 to 80 ft			4 to 9	Full sun
Quercus bicolor Swamp White Oak	Deciduous tree	60 to 70 ft			4 to 8	Full sun
Quercus coccinea Scarlet Oak	Deciduous tree	50 to 80 ft			3 to 8	Full sun
Quercus macrocarpa Bur Oak	Deciduous tree	60 to 80 ft			3 to 8	Full sun
Quercus nigra Water Oak, Possum Oak	Deciduous tree	50 to 80 ft			6 to 8	Full sun
Quercus palustris Pin Oak	Deciduous tree	60 to 80 ft			5 to 9	Full sun
Quercus phellos Willow Oak	Deciduous tree	50 to 80 ft			6 to 9	Full sun to light shade
Quercus robur English Oak	Deciduous tree	40 to 60 ft			5 to 8	Full sun
Quercus rubra Red Oak	Deciduous tree	60 to 80 ft			5 to 8	Full sun

For a list of common names, see page 378.

CULTURE			
Soil	**Water**	**Feeding**	**Special Characteristics**
Good drainage; organic matter	Medium water	Medium feeder	Warm-season crop; requires ample space to trail; can be trained on trellis; some bush varieties available; water deeply; many cultivars available.
Good drainage	Medium water	Light feeder	Variable forms; showy spring flowers; attractive red berries; thorns; evergreen to semi-evergreen in northern climates; hard to prune; give ample space; many cultivars available.
Not particular	Let dry out between waterings	Light feeder	Dark green, oval leaves serrated at the tips; masses of short-lived flowers; clusters of red berries in the fall; prostrate, rapidly spreading growth habit.
Good drainage	Medium water	Medium feeder	Moderate-growing; profuse bloomer; crimson-red fall color; shiny, dark green leaves with serrated edges; very adaptable; messy, inedible fruit; fireblight resistant; several important cultivars available; 'Bradford' is fruitless.
Not particular	Medium water	Medium feeder	Moderate-growing; grows naturally as spreading shrub, train as single or multitrunked tree; shiny green, wavy-edged leaves; good espalier, container, patio, street tree; aphids and fireblight a problem.
Rich soil	Medium water	Medium feeder	Rounded, wide-spreading head; smooth gray bark; shiny, hollylike leaves; good shade tree.
Good drainage	Medium water	Medium feeder	Slow-growing; pyramid shape when young, becomes dense and broad as it matures; keep moist; bright green, deeply lobed leaves turn red in fall; gray bark; rugged framework.
Rich soil	Medium water	Medium feeder	Slow-growing; broad, open crown; similar to *Q. alba*, but with coarser leaves; does well in moist to wet soils; native to eastern and central North America.
Rich soil	Medium water	Medium feeder	Fast-growing; high, light, open branching; bright green, deeply cut leaves; bright scarlet fall color; good street or lawn tree; roots grow deep.
Good drainage	Medium water	Medium feeder	Leaves glossy green above, whitish below; rugged appearance.
Rich soil	Wet; don't let dry out	Medium feeder	Conical to round top; mostly deciduous, but evergreen in some regions; small, lobed or entire leaves; easily transplanted; takes moist to wet conditions.
Good drainage	Medium water	Medium feeder	Moderate-to fast-growing; slender when young, more open and round-headed as matures; reddish-brown bark; lower branches droop; glossy, deep green leaves, deeply cut into lobes; leaves turn brown in fall and can hang on all winter; give ample water; stake young trees.
Good drainage	Medium water	Medium feeder	Fast-growing; pyramidal when young, opening with age; graceful appearance; bright green, willow-like leaves; yellowish fall color.
Good drainage	Medium water	Medium feeder	Wide head and fairly short trunk; fairly fast growth; leaves hold late in fall; little fall color.
Rich soil	Medium water	Medium feeder	Fast-growing; broad, round-topped crown; new leaves are red in spring, turning green; foliage sharp-pointed lobes; stake young plants; give ample water; deep roots; attractive fall color; big lawns, parks, broad avenues.

NAME	HABIT		FLOWERS		ADAPTATION	
	Type	Height	Color	Time	Zones	Light
Quercus virginiana Southern Live Oak, Live Oak	Evergreen tree	to 60 ft			8 to 10	Full sun
Radish *Raphanus sativus*	Half-hardy annual vegetable	4 to 12 in				Full sun to light shade
Ranunculus asiaticus Persian Buttercup, Turban Buttercup	Half-hardy bulb	18 to 24 in	Red, pink, white, orange, yellow	Late spring to early summer	8 to 10	Full sun
Raphiolepis indica India Hawthorn	Evergreen shrub	3 to 5 ft	White, pink	Winter to spring	8 to 10	Full sun
Raspberry (Red, Black, Purple) *Rubus* species	Cane berry	6 to 9 ft	White	Late spring to summer	3 to 9	Full sun
Rhamnus alaternus Italian Buckthorn	Evergreen tree	12 to 20 ft			7 to 9	Full sun to light shade
Rhamnus frangula Alder Buckthorn	Deciduous shrub	10 to 18 ft	White	Spring to summer	2 to 8	Full sun to light shade
Rhapis excelsa Bamboo Palm	Houseplant	5 to 10 ft			10 or IN	Light shade
Rhododendron arborescens Sweet Azalea	Deciduous shrub	8 to 20 ft	White	Summer	4 to 7	Light shade
Rhododendron impeditum Cloudland Rhododendron	Evergreen shrub	to 18 in	Lavender	Spring	5 to 7	Light shade
Rhododendron kaempferi	Deciduous shrub	4 to 8 ft	Red, pink, white, orange, yellow	Late spring to early summer	6 to 8	Light shade
Rhododendron vaseyi Pinkshell Azalea	Deciduous shrub	5 to 10 ft	Pink	Late spring	5 to 8	Light shade
Rhododendron viscosum Swamp Azalea	Deciduous shrub	3 to 8 ft	Pink, white	Summer	4 to 9	Light shade
Rhododendron Belgium Indica Hybrid Azaleas	Evergreen shrub	3 to 10 ft	Pink, red, violet, white	Fall to spring	9 to 10	Light shade
Rhododendron Gable Hybrid Azaleas	Evergreen shrub	2 to 4 ft	Pink, red, purple	Late spring	6 to 8	Light shade
Rhododendron Knaphill-Exbury Hybrid Azaleas	Deciduous shrub	4 to 8 ft	Red, pink, white, orange, yellow	Late spring to early summer	6 to 8	Light shade

For a list of common names, see page 378.

| | CULTURE | | |
Soil	Water	Feeding	Special Characteristics
Rich soil	Medium water	Medium feeder	Deciduous in northern limits of its habitat; moderate to fast-growing tree; broad, spreading habit; massive trunk and branches; smooth edged, shiny dark green leaves above, whitish below; thrives on ample water; very attractive oak.
Good drainage; organic matter	Medium water	Medium feeder	Very fast-growing; divided into 2 groups—summer and winter radishes.
Good drainage	Medium water	Medium feeder	Best in areas of cool nights and sunny, but not hot days; plant after danger of frost in the spring in zones colder than 8.
Good drainage	Medium water	Medium feeder	Neat, dense, restrained habit; leathery foliage; may repeat blooming in fall; tolerates partial shade, mild drought.
Good drainage; organic matter	Medium water	Medium feeder	Berries form on year-old canes; remove canes that have fruited; everbearing varieties bear on ends of new canes; remove ends after fruiting.
Not particular	Medium water	Medium feeder	Fast-growing; dense growth; tall shrub or multistem tree; can be pruned to single stem, sheared or shaped; bright green, oval, shiny leaves; flowers inconspicuous; tiny black fruits; tolerates drought, wind, heat; fast screen or clipped hedge.
Good drainage	Medium water	Medium feeder	Shrub or small tree; dense habit and rapid growth; lustrous, dark green leaves; fruits turn from green to red to black, appear while plant is still flowering; can be trained as hedge.
Good drainage; organic matter	Medium water	Medium feeder	6–12" wide fans composed of 4 to 10 thick, shiny leaves; hairy main trunk; thin, arching stems; give bright, indirect light; water heavily and feed monthly during growing season, reduce in winter; protect from dry air.
Good drainage; organic matter	Medium water	Medium feeder	Fragrant flowers; attractive fall foliage.
Good drainage; organic matter	Medium water	Medium feeder	Dense, tiny, gray-green foliage; attractive in sheltered spot of rock garden; more sensitive than most rhododendrons to hot, dry summers.
Good drainage; organic matter	Medium water	Medium feeder	Good fall foliage color; profuse bloomer; large flowers; relatively intolerant of hot summers.
Good drainage; organic matter	Medium water	Medium feeder	Graceful shape, irregular habit; attractive fall foliage color.
Organic matter	Wet; don't let dry out	Medium feeder	Loose, open habit; fragrant flowers; thrives in damp, soggy soils.
Good drainage; organic matter	Medium water	Medium feeder	More tender than Southern Indica Hybrids.
Good drainage; organic matter	Medium water	Medium feeder	Foliage tends to redden in northern climates and in the fall.
Good drainage; organic matter	Medium water	Medium feeder	Medium green foliage turns bright yellow, orange, or red in fall; profusion of large flowers; some cultivars hardy to zone 4.

NAME	HABIT		FLOWERS		ADAPTATION	
	Type	Height	Color	Time	Zones	Light
Rhododendron Southern Indica Hybrid Azaleas	Evergreen shrub	4 to 15 ft	Pink, red, violet, white	Spring	9 to 10	Light shade
Rhododendron × kosteranum Mollis Hybrid Azaleas	Deciduous shrub	3 to 8 ft	Red, white, orange, yellow	Late spring	5 to 7	Full sun to light shade
Rhoeo spathacea (R. discolor) Moses-in-the-cradle	Houseplant	12 to 18 in	White		10 or IN	Light shade
Rhoicissus capensis Oak Leaf Ivy	Houseplant	10 to 15 ft			10 or IN	Light shade
Rhubarb *Rheum rhabarbarum*	Hardy perennial vegetable	2 to 3 ft			3 to 10	Full sun to light shade
Rhus copallina Flame-leaf Sumac, Shining Sumac	Deciduous shrub	8 to 15 ft			5 to 9	Full sun
Rhus glabra Smooth Sumac	Deciduous shrub	10 to 20 ft	Green	Summer	3 to 7	Full sun to light shade
Rhus lancea African Sumac	Evergreen tree	to 25 ft			8 to 10	Full sun
Robinia pseudoacacia Black Locust	Deciduous tree	40 to 75 ft	White	Late spring to early summer	4 to 9	Full sun
Rosa banksiae Bank's Rose, Lady Bank's Rose	Semi-evergreen shrub	to 25 ft	White, yellow	Late spring to summer	7 to 10	Full sun to half-day sun
Rosa foetida Austrian Briar	Deciduous shrub	3 to 5 ft	Yellow	Late spring to early summer	4 to 10	Full sun to half-day sun
Rosa hugonis Father Hugo Rose	Deciduous shrub	to 8 ft	Yellow	Late spring	7 to 10	Full sun to half-day sun
Rosa multiflora Japanese Rose	Deciduous shrub	8 to 10 ft	White	Early summer	5 to 10	Full sun to half-day sun
Rosa odorata Tea Rose	Deciduous shrub	15 ft	Pink	Summer	7 to 10	Full sun to half-day sun

For a list of common names, see page 378.

CULTURE

Soil	Water	Feeding	Special Characteristics
Good drainage; organic matter	Medium water	Medium feeder	Tolerates more sun and grows more vigorously than Belgium Indica Hybrids.
Good drainage; organic matter	Medium water	Medium feeder	Restrained, rounded form; grows well in full sun.
Good drainage	Medium water	Medium feeder	Sword-shaped leaves, rather erect, dark green with purple undersides; small flowers held tightly in boat-shaped bracts down among the leaves; plant tolerates adverse conditions.
Good drainage	Let dry out between waterings	Light feeder	Vigorous trailing vine with grapelike tendrils; lobed leaves shaped like oak leaves; give bright, indirect light or partial shade; tolerates neglect; keep moist in heat; leach frequently.
Good drainage; organic matter	Medium water	Heavy feeder	Grown for edible leafstalks; leaves are poisonous; needs at least two months of temperatures near freezing and a long, cool spring; give ample space; begin harvesting in second year; start from root divisions.
Good drainage	Medium water	Medium feeder	Open, picturesque form; large, compound leaves; attractive fall color; can reach 30' high.
Good drainage	Medium water	Medium feeder	Large shrub or small tree; needs room; deep green leaves turn scarlet in fall; red fruits in fall and winter; berries used to make dye; common plant in eastern U.S.
Good drainage	Medium water	Light feeder	Slow-growing; open, spreading, graceful, weeping habit; small fruits on female tree; tolerates drought and high heat—good desert tree; dark red, rough bark; can prune as hedge, screen, single-trunked tree.
Not particular	Medium water	Light feeder	Fast-growing; sparse, open branches; often multistemmed; umbrellalike form; fragrant flowers; beanlike pods; thorny branches; deeply furrowed brown bark; tolerates heat, drought, neglect; invasive, suckering roots; train as young tree.
Good drainage	Medium water	Medium feeder	Trailing, climbing growth habit; good for covering arbors, fences; will trail along ground; *R.b.* 'Alba-plena' has double white, fragrant flowers; *R.b.* 'Lutea' produces double yellow scentless flowers; disease-resistant; semi-evergreen in warmer climate, deciduous in colder areas.
Good drainage; organic matter	Medium water	Medium feeder	Slender, erect, or branching stems; leaves smooth or slightly hairy; single flowers with strange odor; best in full sun, warm soil; the variety 'Bicolor' has coppery-red and yellow blooms; prune to remove weak and dead wood; semi-evergreen in warmer climate, deciduous in colder areas.
Good drainage; organic matter	Medium water	Medium feeder	Dense growth; arching stems; attractive foliage; profuse, faintly scented, single flowers; use in borders, screens, or trained on trellis; prune oldest wood to ground each year; water deeply; semi-evergreen in warmer climate; deciduous in colder areas.
Good drainage	Medium water	Medium feeder	Pink-flowered varieties also available; dense, arching growth habit; best for large areas; rapid and often invasive grower; semi-evergreen in warmer climate, deciduous in colder areas.
Good drainage	Medium water	Medium feeder	Pink flowers are double, very fragrant; semi-evergreen to evergreen in warmer climate, deciduous in colder areas.

NAME	HABIT		FLOWERS		ADAPTATION	
	Type	Height	Color	Time	Zones	Light
Rosa rugosa Ramanas Rose, Sea Tomato	Deciduous shrub	3 to 8 ft	Pink, red, white, yellow, purple	Summer	3 to 10	Full sun to half-day sun
Rosa virginiana Virginia Rose	Deciduous shrub	to 6 ft	Pink	Summer	4 to 10	Full sun to half-day sun
Rosa Climbing Roses	Deciduous shrub	6 to 20 ft	Red, yellow, orange, lavender, pink, white	Late spring to fall	3 to 10	Full sun to half-day sun
Rosa Floribunda Hybrids	Deciduous shrub	2 to 5 ft	Red, lavender, pink, white, orange, yellow	Early summer to first frost	4 to 10	Full sun to half-day sun
Rosa Grandiflora Hybrids	Deciduous shrub	8 to 10 ft	Warm colors (red, orange, yel), lavender, pink, white	Late spring to fall	4 to 10	Full sun
Rosa Hybrid Tea	Deciduous shrub	2 to 6 ft	Warm colors (red, orange, yel), lavender, pink, white	Spring to fall	3 to 10	Full sun to half-day sun
Rosa Miniature Roses	Semi-evergreen shrub	6 in to 3 ft	Pink, red, yellow, white	Late spring to fall	8 to 10	Full sun to light shade
Rosa Polyantha Roses	Deciduous shrub	18 to 24 in	Pink, yellow, white	Late spring to fall	3 to 10	Full sun to half-day sun
Rudbeckia fulgida Black-eyed Susan	Hardy perennial	1 to 2.5 ft	Yellow	Summer to early fall	4 to 10	Full sun
Rudbeckia hirta **var.** *pulcherrima* Gloriosa Daisy, Brown-eyed Susan	Half-hardy perennial	2 to 3 ft	Yellow, orange, bicolored	Early summer to fall		Full sun
Rutabaga *Brassica napa napobrassica*	Half-hardy biennial vegetable	1 to 2 ft				Full sun to light shade
Sage *Salvia officinalis*	Hardy perennial herb	to 2 ft	Blue, white, pink	Summer	4 to 10	Full sun
Sagina subulata Irish Moss	Groundcover	3 to 4 in	White	Summer	5 to 10	Full sun to light shade

For a list of common names, see page 378.

	CULTURE		
Soil	**Water**	**Feeding**	**Special Characteristics**
Good drainage; organic matter	Medium water	Medium feeder	Vigorous, extremely hardy shrub; single and double flowers; bright red hips; attractive foliage; tolerates hard freezes, wind, drought, seacoast conditions; water deeply; semi-evergreen in warmer climate, deciduous in colder areas.
Good drainage	Medium water	Medium feeder	Single, 2 to 3″ wide blooms; attractive fall color; bright red twigs in winter; easily kept to 3′ by pruning; semi-evergreen in warmer climate, deciduous in colder areas.
Good drainage; organic matter	Medium water	Medium feeder to heavy feeder	Long, pliable canes; produce blooms identical to parents; need good air circulation; tie to a support; after blooming, cut back flower clusters; protect in cold-winter areas.
Good drainage; organic matter	Medium water	Medium to heavy feeder	Semi-evergreen in warm climates to deciduous in colder ones; flowers borne in clusters; profuse bloomers; disease resistant, hardy, low-growing; best landscape roses—borders, informal hedges, containers; water deeply; provide winter protection in cold-winter areas.
Good drainage; organic matter	Medium water	Medium feeder to heavy feeder	Semi-evergreen in warm climates and deciduous in colder ones; roses developed between cross of floribundas and hybrid teas; flowers borne in clusters; blooms continuously; strong, hardy plants; protect in areas where winter temperatures consistently drop below 20 degrees Fahrenheit; water deeply.
Organic matter; good drainage	Medium water	Medium feeder to heavy feeder	Semi-evergreen in warm climates to deciduous in cold climates; flowers borne singly on long stems or in clusters; wide range of colors, many bicolored; most fragrant; continuous bloomers; water deeply; provide winter protection where winter temperatures persist below 20 degrees Fahrenheit.
Good drainage; organic matter	Medium water	Medium feeder	Can be grown indoors or outside, in containers or in the ground; hardier than hybrid teas; shallow-rooted; require constant watering; prune according to use; most are everblooming.
Good drainage; organic matter	Medium water	Medium feeder to heavy feeder	Small flowers borne in large clusters; low-growing; continuous blooming; use in bedding, low hedges, and front border plantings; good in containers; water deeply; semi-evergreen in warmer climate, deciduous in colder areas.
Good drainage	Dry, let dry out between waterings	Light feeder	Long-lived; profuse bloomer; restrained growth; water during dry periods.
Good drainage; organic matter	Medium water	Medium feeder	Tolerates poor, dry soil; appreciates hot summers; tall varieties may need staking; usually grown as an annual.
Good drainage; organic matter	Medium water	Medium feeder	Edible, yellow roots; matures late in year; stores well in the ground.
Good drainage; grows well in poor soil	Dry, let dry out between waterings	Light feeder	Culinary herb with long, oval, gray-green leaves; coarsely textured, fragrant leaves; cultivars with yellow or red leaf margins are available.
Good drainage; rich soil	Wet; don't let dry out	Heavy feeder	Evergreen; dense, rounded tufts of tiny, awl-shaped leaves; spread by creeping stems; deep green color.

NAME	HABIT		FLOWERS		ADAPTATION	
	Type	Height	Color	Time	Zones	Light
Saintpaulia species African Violets	Houseplant	3 to 6 in	Pink, red, violet, purple, white	All year	10 or IN	Light shade
Salix babylonica Weeping Willow	Deciduous tree	30 to 50 ft			5 to 9	Full sun
Salix discolor Pussy Willow	Deciduous shrub	to 20 ft	Gray	Early spring	4 to 8	Full sun to light shade
Salpiglossis sinuata Painted-tongue	Half-hardy annual	2 to 3 ft	Purple, red, yellow, blue, pink	Summer to first frost		Full sun
Salvia splendens Scarlet Sage	Tender annual	6 to 36 in	Red, pink, purple, white	Early summer to first frost		Full sun to light shade
Salvia × superba Perennial Salvia	Hardy perennial	2 to 3 ft	Purple	Summer	5 to 10	Full sun
Sansevieria trifasciata Sansevieria, Snake Plant, Mother-in-law's Tongue	Houseplant	1 to 4 ft			10 or IN	Light shade
Sarcococca hookeriana humilis Small Himalayan Sarcococca	Groundcover	2 ft	White	Spring	5 to 10	Light shade to deep shade
Sassafras albidum Common Sassafras	Deciduous tree	30 to 50 ft			5 to 8	Full sun
Scabiosa caucasica Pincushion Flower	Hardy perennial	to 2 1/2 ft	Blue, pink, purple, lavender, white	Early summer to early fall	2 to 10	Full sun
Schizanthus × wisetonensis Butterfly Flower, Poor Man's Orchid	Half-hardy annual	12 to 24 in	Pink, yellow, violet, red, bicolored	Late summer to first frost		Full sun to light shade
Schlumbergera bridgesii Christmas Cactus, Easter Cactus	Houseplant	to 18 in	Red	Winter	10 or IN	Light shade
Scilla siberica Siberian Squill	Hardy bulb	3 to 6 in	Blue	Early spring	3 to 8	Full sun to light shade
Sedum acre Mossy Stonecrop, Gold-moss Stonecrop	Groundcover	to 2 in	Yellow	Late spring to early summer	4 to 10	Full sun to half-day sun

For a list of common names, see page 378.

	CULTURE		
Soil	**Water**	**Feeding**	**Special Characteristics**
Organic matter	Medium water	Medium feeder	Rosettes of velvety leaves; clusters of flowers; needs plenty of bright, indirect light; protect from hot summer sun; heavy feeder during flowering; many cultivars available, including miniatures.
Not particular	Wet; don't let dry out	Heavy feeder	Fast-growing; heavy, rounded head; branchlets drooping to ground; long, medium olive-green leaves turn yellow in fall; needs room to grow; may need training to develop single trunk; aggressive roots; good screen, interesting winter silhouette.
Not particular	Wet; don't let dry out	Medium feeder	Attractive, fuzzy gray catkins; fast-growing; forms mass of upright stems; messy and unruly.
Good drainage; organic matter; sandy soil	Medium water	Medium feeder	Prefers cool summers; don't overfertilize—sensitive to nitrogen; may need staking.
Good drainage; organic matter; rich soil	Medium water	Heavy feeder	Tolerant of mild drought; tolerant of intense heat.
Good drainage; grows well in poor soil	Dry, let dry out between waterings	Light feeder	Flowers densely whorled on spikes; attractive gray-green foliage; leaves aromatic when crushed.
Good drainage	Dry, let dry out between waterings	Light feeder	Lance-shaped, dark green leaves with yellow-striped margins and horizontal bands of gray-green; rosette form; give bright, indirect light, warm location; tolerates poor growing conditions.
Organic matter; acid soil	Medium water	Medium feeder	Broadleaf, evergreen shrub; spreads by underground runners; glossy, dark green foliage; fragrant flowers; black berries; protect from wind; pinch tips to encourage horizontal branching.
Sandy soil; good drainage	Medium water	Medium feeder	Moderate-growing; various-shaped leaves, turn yellow to red in fall; flowers on female trees followed by dark blue berries on bright red stalks; needs acid soil; hard to transplant; won't take long, hot-summer drought; roots made into tea.
Good drainage; sandy soil; slightly alkaline soil	Medium water	Medium feeder	Long bloom season; avoid summer drought and winter sogginess; amend soil with organic matter.
Rich soil; good drainage; organic matter	Medium water	Medium feeder	Late bloomer; not adapted to intense heat; limited to cool-summer regions.
Rich soil	Medium water	Heavy feeder	Bright green arching branches; smooth, scalloped joints; drooping habit; multitrumpeted flowers; prefers bright, reflected light; can summer outdoors in partial shade; must have high light and cool nights to flower; short days in the fall; cut down on fertilizer during winter.
Good drainage; organic matter	Wet; don't let dry out	Medium feeder	Good for naturalizing; needs cold winters.
Not particular	Let dry out between waterings	Light feeder	Vigorous plant; tiny leaves less than ¼" long; stays green through coldest winters.

NAME	HABIT		FLOWERS		ADAPTATION	
	Type	Height	Color	Time	Zones	Light
Sedum morganianum Donkey's Tail, Burro's Tail	Houseplant	3 to 4 ft	Pink	Spring	10 or IN	Light shade
Sedum spectabile **& hybrids** Showy Stonecrop, Showy Sedum	Hardy perennial	to 2 ft	Pink, white	Late summer to early fall	3 to 10	Full sun to light shade
Sempervivum tectorum Hen and Chicks, Houseleek	Hardy perennial	6 to 12 in	Pink	Summer	4 to 10	Full sun
Senecio cineraria Dusty Miller	Tender perennial	8 to 16 in	Yellow	Early summer to early fall	10	Full sun to light shade
Senecio rowleyanus String-of-beads	Houseplant	2 to 6 ft			10 or IN	Light shade
Sequoia sempervirens Coast Redwood	Needled evergreen tree	50 to 90 ft			7 to 10	Full sun to light shade
Sequoiadendron giganteum Giant Redwood, Big Tree	Needled evergreen tree	to 350 ft			7 to 10	Full sun
Shallot *Allium cepa* var. *aggregatum*	Biennial vegetable	1 to 1½ ft	White	Late summer to early fall	3 to 10	Full sun to light shade
Sinningia speciosa Common Gloxinia	Tender bulb	6 to 10 in	Blue, red, white, purple	All year	10 or IN	Light shade
Skimmia japonica Japanese Skimmia	Evergreen shrub	4 to 5 ft	White	Spring	8 to 9	Light shade
Soleirolia soleirolii Baby's Tears	Houseplant	to 3 in			10 or IN	Light shade
Solidago **hybrids** Goldenrod	Hardy perennial	18 to 40 in	Yellow	Late summer to early fall	3 to 10	Full sun
Sophora japonica Japanese Pagoda Tree	Deciduous tree	50 to 75 ft	White	Summer to early fall	5 to 8	Full sun to light shade
Sorbus alnifolia Korean Mountain Ash	Deciduous tree	40 to 50 ft	White	Late spring	4 to 7	Full sun

For a list of common names, see page 378.

	CULTURE		
Soil	**Water**	**Feeding**	**Special Characteristics**
Good drainage; sandy soil	Let dry out between waterings	Medium feeder	Trailing habit; light gray to blue-green leaves ½–1" long, oval and plump; leaves cluster creating a braided or ropelike effect; ideally for hanging containers.
Grows in poor soil	Wet; don't let dry out	Light feeder	Blossoms of some cultivars turn bronze as they mature; leaves thick and fleshy; mounding growth; long-lived; noninvasive; will tolerate boggy soils; needs light shade in hot climates.
Good drainage	Let dry out between waterings	Light feeder	Succulent growth; thick leaves form rosette; mother plant dies when flowers appear, young plants take over.
Good drainage; organic matter	Let dry out between waterings	Light feeder	Grown for attractive silver-gray foliage; usually grown as an annual; tolerates drought and poor soil; remove flower buds.
Good drainage; sandy soil	Let dry out between waterings	Light feeder	Hanging stems bearing ½" spherical leaves with pointed tips and a single translucent band across them; look like green beads; flowers fragrant; give filtered sun or bright, indirect light.
Rich soil	Wet; don't let dry out	Medium feeder	Narrow, pyramid form; best adapted to fog belt of northern California and Oregon; fast-growing; reddish-brown bark; flat, pointed, narrow needles medium green on top, grayish underneath; small, round cones; near or on lawn, in grove; topped once a year as hedge.
Rich soil	Medium water	Medium feeder	Moderate-growing; pyramid form; dense, stiff foliage; gray-green needles; reddish-brown bark and cones; water deeply but infrequently; needs lots of room.
Good drainage; organic matter	Medium water	Medium feeder to light feeder	Grown as an annual; multiplier; type of onion, dividing into clump of smaller bulbs; most set no seeds; lift clusters of bulbs at end of each growing season and replant smaller ones in the fall; harvest when tops die down in summer.
Rich soil; good drainage	Medium water	Medium feeder	Houseplant, or greenhouse; all zones indoors; may bloom any time of year but requires 2–3 month rest period between flowerings; give bright light, but not direct sun.
Good drainage	Medium water	Medium feeder	Grown for fragrant flowers and attractive fruit; roundish growth habit; require both male and female plants to get the bright red berries; can be grown farther north in sheltered areas along the coast.
Good drainage	Medium water	Medium feeder	Compact, creeping form; tiny, delicate leaves on thin, trailing stems; give moist, greenhouse conditions, bright, indirect light; good in terrariums.
Good drainage	Medium water	Light feeder	Striking flower color; profuse blooms; long-lived; avoid either very wet or dry soil.
Not particular	Medium water	Medium feeder	Slow- to moderate-growing; blooms at 8–10 years old; dark green, divided leaves; yellow fall color; seed pods 2–3½" long; streets, gardens, parks, lawns.
Good drainage	Medium water	Medium feeder	Moderate-growing; dense, oval form; shiny green leaves; bright red berries in fall; brilliant, attractive fall foliage; the cultivar 'Redbird' has dark green leaves and is an abundant fruiter.

NAME	HABIT		FLOWERS		ADAPTATION	
	Type	Height	Color	Time	Zones	Light
Sorbus aucuparia European Mountain Ash	Deciduous tree	25 to 30 ft	White	Late spring	2 to 7	Full sun to light shade
Sorrel, French Sorrel *Rumex scutatus*	Hardy perennial herb	to 3 ft			3 to 10	Full sun
Spathiphyllum species Peace Lily, Spathe Flower	Houseplant	1 to 3 ft	White	Spring to fall	10 or IN	Light shade
Spearmint *Mentha spicata*	Hardy perennial herb	1 to 2 ft			4 to 10	Full sun to light shade
Spinach *Spinacia oleracea*	Half-hardy annual vegetable	to 2 ft				Full sun to half-day sun
Spiraea japonica Japanese Spirea	Deciduous shrub	4 to 5 ft	Pink	Summer	5 to 8	Full sun
Spiraea × vanhouttei Vanhoutte Spirea	Deciduous shrub	8 to 10 ft	White	Spring	5 to 9	Full sun
Squash *Cucurbita* species	Tender annual vegetable	4 to 12 ft		Summer		Full sun
Stachys byzantina Lamb's-ear, Wooly Betony	Hardy perennial	6 to 12 in	Purple	Summer to early fall	4 to 10	Full sun
Stenotaphrum secundatum St. Augustine Grass	Turfgrass	1½ to 2½ in			7 to 8	Full sun to light shade
Stokesia laevis Stokes's Aster	Hardy perennial	12 to 18 in	Blue	Summer	6 to 10	Full sun
Strawberry *Fragaria × ananassa*	Hardy perennial berry	½ to 1 ft	White	Spring to fall	3 to 10	Full sun
Streptocarpus species Cape Primrose	Houseplant	1 to 2 ft	Blue, red, pink, violet, white	Late winter to spring	10 or IN	Light shade
Styrax japonicus Japanese Snowbell	Deciduous tree	15 to 20 ft	White	Early summer	5 to 8	Full sun to light shade
Summer Savory *Satureja hortensis*	Hardy annual herb	to 18 in				Full sun

For a list of common names, see page 378.

| | CULTURE | | |
Soil	Water	Feeding	Special Characteristics
Good drainage	Medium water	Medium feeder	Moderate-growing; narrow, upright form, rounding with age; leaves divided, dull-green above, gray-green beneath; cluster of red berries late summer-early fall; fireblight.
Rich soil	Medium water	Medium feeder	Culinary herb with narrow, dark leaves; reddish green spikes of flowers; leaves slightly arrow-shaped.
Good drainage	Wet; don't let dry out	Medium feeder	White bract encloses true flowers; spoon-shaped leaves; can grow in dark location but will not flower; attractive foliage plant when not in bloom; heavy feeder in high summer heat.
Rich soil	Wet; don't let dry out	Medium feeder	Culinary and medicinal herb with crinkly, pointed leaves; reddish square stems; spreading invasive habit; aromatic leaves.
Good drainage; organic matter	Medium water	Medium feeder	Cool-weather crop; tends to bolt; use bolt-resistant varieties for spring planting; can be grown through winter in mild areas (tolerates temperatures into low 30s); many cultivars available.
Good drainage	Medium water	Medium feeder	Prune late winter–early spring; flowers range from pale to deep pink and sometimes white.
Good drainage	Medium water	Medium feeder	Fast-growing; arching, fountainlike form; needs lots of room; prune directly after bloom; borders, massing.
Good drainage; organic matter	Medium water	Medium feeder	Warm-season crop; requires ample space to trail and vine; can be trained on trellis; some bush varieties available; water deeply; major squash groups include summer and winter varieties; many cultivars of varying shapes, sizes, and colors are available.
Good drainage	Dry, let dry out between waterings	Light feeder	Silvery-white, wooly foliage; prone to rot in muggy, humid climates; divide regularly.
Good drainage; organic matter	Medium water	Medium feeder	Easy to grow; robust; good shade grass; tolerates a salty soil; needs frequent waterings; very susceptible to several diseases during prolonged rain; tends to thatch badly; wears poorly; likes neutral to lime soil.
Good drainage	Medium water	Light feeder	Most effective in mixed border; not particular about soil, but intolerant of wet soil in winter.
Good drainage; rich soil organic matter	Medium water	Medium feeder	Plant grown for its red berry; planting time varies among climates; may be grown in rows, hills or containers; plant with crown above soil; mulch well; water frequently; protect from hard winter frosts by mulching with straw; many varieties available adapted to different areas of the country.
Good drainage	Wet; don't let dry out	Medium feeder	Stemless, fleshy leaves; trumpetlike flowers; prefers cool environment, humidity; keep moist; provide very bright, indirect light.
Rich soil; good drainage	Medium water	Medium feeder	Slow- to moderate-growing; horizontal branching; spreading, flat-topped tree; attractive bark; neat, bushy form; profuse bloomer; train to control shrubbiness; lawn, patio tree.
Good drainage; rich soil	Medium water	Medium feeder	Culinary herb with small, narrow, dark green leaves; reddish stems; becomes slightly woody when plant flowers.

NAME	HABIT		FLOWERS		ADAPTATION	
	Type	**Height**	**Color**	**Time**	**Zones**	**Light**
Sweet Marjoram *Origanum majorana*	Tender perennial herb	1 to 2 ft			4 to 10	Full sun
Sweet Potato *Ipomoea batatas*	Tender perennial gegetable	to 2 ft				Full sun
Syngonium podophyllum Arrowhead Vine	Houseplant	2 to 5 ft, trailing			10 or IN	Light shade
Syringa × chinensis Chinese Lilac	Deciduous shrub	8 to 15 ft	Lavender, purple	Late spring	4 to 7	Full sun to light shade
Syringa oblata Korean Lilac	Deciduous shrub	to 12 ft	Lavender	Late spring	4 to 7	Full sun to light shade
Syringa × persica Persian Lilac	Deciduous shrub	4 to 8 ft	Lavender	Late spring	5 to 9	Full sun to light shade
Syringa reticulata Japanese Tree Lilac	Deciduous tree	20 to 35 ft	White	Early summer	4 to 8	Full sun to light shade
Syringa villosa Late Lilac	Deciduous shrub	9 to 10 ft	Lavender, pinkish-white	Early summer	3 to 7	Full sun to light shade
Syringa vulgaris Common Lilac	Deciduous shrub	8 to 15 ft	Lavender	Late spring	3 to 7	Full sun to light shade
Tagetes erecta African Marigold	Half-hardy annual	6 to 36 in	Yellow, orange	Early summer to first frost		Full sun
Tagetes erecta × patula Triploid Marigolds, 3-N Marigolds	Tender annual	12 to 20 in	Yellow, orange	Early summer to first frost		Full sun
Tagetes patula French Marigold	Half-hardy annual	6 to 18 in	Yellow, orange, bicolored	Early summer to first frost		Full sun
Tamarix hispida Kashgar Tamarisk	Deciduous shrub	4 to 6 ft	Pink	Late summer to early fall	5 to 8	Full sun
Tamarix ramosissima Five-stamen Tamarisk	Deciduous shrub	10 to 15 ft	Pink	Summer to early fall	2 to 8	Full sun
Tanacetum vulgare Tansy	Hardy perennial herb	to 3 ft	Yellow	Summer	4 to 10	Full sun

For a list of common names, see page 378.

| | CULTURE | | |
Soil	Water	Feeding	Special Characteristics
Good drainage slightly alkaline soil	Medium water	Medium feeder	Culinary herb with small, oval leaves light green on top, gray-green underneath; often grown as an annual.
Good drainage; organic matter	Medium water	Medium feeder	Grown as an annual; requires ample summer heat; feed with low-nitrogen fertilizer; start from slips; need long growing season; rarely flowers in U.S.; flavor improves with storage after harvesting; very frost-tender; trailing vine.
Good drainage	Medium water	Medium feeder	Climbing or trailing plant; young leaves 3" long, arrow-shaped, borne at end of erect stalks; dark green with silvery-white variegation; as plant matures, leaves become lobed, stems begin to climb, leaf fans into leaflets, turning solid green; give moist, warm environment; bright, indirect light.
Good drainage; slightly alkaline soil	Medium water	Medium feeder	Although can grow taller, usually reaches about 6' high; more graceful habit and finer-textured foliage than common lilac; blooms profusely; give light shade in hottest areas; fragrant flowers.
Good drainage; slightly alkaline soil	Medium water	Medium feeder	One of earliest-blooming lilacs; only lilac with fall color; fragrant flowers; heavy bloomer; give light shade in hottest areas.
Good drainage; slightly alkaline soil	Medium water	Medium feeder	Small leaves; heavy profusion of fragrant flowers; give light shade in hottest areas.
Good drainage; slightly alkaline soil	Medium water	Medium feeder	Moderate-growing; dense foliage; interesting bark; heavy-scented flowers; open, upright, spreading branches with round outline; very drought-resistant; small shade or street tree.
Good drainage; slightly alkaline soil	Medium water	Medium feeder	One of hardiest lilacs; dense, upright growth; profuse bloomer; fragrant flowers; give light shade in hottest areas.
Good drainage; slightly alkaline soil	Medium water	Medium feeder	Upright, irregular growth; gray to dark green or bluish-green leaves; fragrant flowers; long-lived; rejuvenate old plants by cutting to ground; very susceptible to mildew; light shade in hottest areas; many cultivars available.
Good drainage; rich soil	Medium water	Medium feeder	Self-sows profusely; tolerates moderately dry soil; don't overfertilize; taller varieties need staking.
Good drainage; rich soil	Medium water	Medium feeder	Tolerates moderately dry soil; don't overfertilize.
Good drainage; rich soil	Medium water	Medium feeder	Self-sows profusely; tolerates moderately dry soil; don't overfertilize.
Sandy soil	Medium water	Light feeder	Slender, wispy form; needlelike foliage; tolerates seacoast conditions, drought, harsh winds; periodic watering; leggy and rangy in fertile soil; prune early spring while dormant.
Sandy soil	Medium water	Light feeder	Large, leggy habit; hardy; invasive roots; tolerates seacoast conditions, drought, winds; prune hard in fall.
Not particular	Medium water	Medium feeder	Large, bright green medicinal herb; fernlike leaves; buttonlike flowers; fragrant foliage; easy to grow, can become invasive.

NAME	HABIT		FLOWERS		ADAPTATION	
	Type	**Height**	**Color**	**Time**	**Zones**	**Light**
Tangelo *Citrus reticulata × paradisi*	Evergreen fruit tree	10 to 30 ft	White	Spring	10	Full sun
Tarragon *Artemisia dracunculus*	Hardy perennial herb	2 to 3 ft			5 to 10	Full sun
Taxodium distichum Bald Cypress	Needled deciduous tree	70 to 80 ft			5 to 10	Full sun
Taxus baccata English Yew	Needled evergreen shrub	25 to 40 ft			6 to 7	Full sun
Taxus cuspidata Japanese Yew	Needled evergreen shrub	40 to 50 ft			5 to 7	Full sun
Taxus × media Anglojap Yew	Needled evergreen shrub	to 40 ft			5 to 7	Full sun
Thalictrum aquilegifolium Columbine Meadowrue	Hardy perennial	to 3 ft	Pink, white	Late spring to early summer	5 to 10	Light shade
Thuja occidentalis American Arborvitae, Northern White Cedar	Needled evergreen tree	40 to 50 ft			3 to 8	Full sun
Thuja plicata Western Red Cedar, Canoe Cedar, Giant Arborvitae	Needled evergreen tree	50 to 70 ft			5 to 7	Full sun
Thunbergeria alata Black-eyed Susan Vine, Clock Vine	Half-hardy annual	Climbs to 6 ft	Orange, yellow, white	Early summer to early fall		Full sun to light shade
Thyme *Thymus vulgaris*	Hardy perennial herb	to 12 in	Pink, white	Late spring to summer	4 to 10	Full sun
Thymus serpyllum Creeping Thyme	Hardy perennial groundcover	to 3 in	Pink	Late spring to early fall	4 to 10	Full sun
Tigridia pavonia Tiger Flower, Shell Flower	Half-hardy bulb	to 1½ ft	Red, orange, yellow, pink, white	Summer to late summer	7 to 10	Full sun
Tilia americana American Linden, Basswood	Deciduous tree	to 60+ ft	Yellow	Summer	2 to 9	Full sun
Tilia cordata Littleleaf Linden	Deciduous tree	60 to 70 ft	Yellow	Early summer to summer	4 to 7	Full sun
Tilia platyphyllos Big-leaf Linden	Deciduous tree	60 to 80+ ft	Yellow	Summer	4 to 9	Full sun

For a list of common names, see page 378.

	CULTURE		
Soil	**Water**	**Feeding**	**Special Characteristics**
Good drainage; organic matter	Medium water	Medium feeder	A cross between a mandarin and a grapefruit; loose skin; sugar content of a mandarin; requires cross-pollination from other citrus like the 'Valencia' orange; prune to remove only dead, diseased, or sucker growth; plant high.
Good drainage; sandy soil	Let dry out between waterings	Medium feeder	Culinary herb; does not produce seeds; propagate by division.
Not particular	Medium water	Medium feeder	Moderate- to fast-growing; deciduous conifer with tiny leaves; tolerates both drought and poor drainage; survives swampy conditions.
Good drainage	Medium water	Medium feeder	Dark green foliage; can be pruned into formal shapes, hedges.
Good drainage	Medium water	Medium feeder	Can prune into formal shapes, hedges.
Good drainage	Medium water	Medium feeder	Hybrid with wide variety of cultivars; can be pruned into formal shapes, hedges.
Rich soil; organic matter	Wet; don't let dry out	Medium feeder	Grayish-green foliage; leaves are smaller than columbine, but similar.
Good drainage	Medium water	Medium feeder	Slow- to moderate-growing; bright green to yellow-green foliage; flat sprays of needles on branches with upsweeping tips; effective hedge or tall screen; tolerates wet soil, but tends to yellow or brown in open, wet, windy areas.
Not particular	Medium water	Medium feeder	Slow-growing; pyramid form; bright green to dark green, lacy foliage; slender branches; tolerates wet soils; good skyline tree in large, open area; can be sheared as large hedge, or screen.
Good drainage; organic matter; rich soil	Wet; don't let dry out	Medium feeder	Best in cool-summer regions; grows rapidly; needs support for the vines.
Good drainage	Medium water	Medium feeder	Culinary herb with a shrubby form; opposite leaves, tiny woodlike stems; needs light soil; cultivar 'Argenteus' has small leaves with silver variegation.
Good drainage	Medium water	Medium feeder	Low-growing herb; delicate appearance; fragrant foliage; good groundcover.
Good drainage	Wet; don't let dry out	Medium feeder	Flowers last only one day but are quickly followed by others; dig up and store after foliage yellows in zones colder than 7.
Rich soil	Medium water	Medium feeder	Moderate-growing tree; straight trunk; dense crown; dull, dark green foliage; somewhat heart-shaped leaves; fragrant, yellowish flowers; keep moist; stake young trees; good street tree.
Rich soil	Medium water	Medium feeder	Moderate to fast-growing; symmetrical habit; dark green, heart-shaped leaves; very fragrant flowers; best in moist soils; tolerates heat, drought, city conditions; lawn or street tree.
Rich soil	Medium water	Medium feeder	Moderate-growing tree; largest leaves of any linden; fragrant yellow-white flowers; young trees need staking, shaping.

NAME	HABIT		FLOWERS		ADAPTATION	
	Type	**Height**	**Color**	**Time**	**Zones**	**Light**
Tilia × europaea European Linden	Deciduous tree	to 120 ft	Yellow	Summer	3 to 9	Full sun
Tithonia rotundifolia Mexican Sunflower	Half-hardy annual	4 to 6 ft	Red, orange	Summer to early fall		Full sun
Tolmiea menziesii Piggyback Plant, Mother-of-thousands	Houseplant	to 2 ft			10 or IN	Light shade
Tomato *Lycopersicon lycopersicum*	Tender perennial vegetable	to 6 ft			9 to 10	Full sun
Torenia fournieri Wishbone Flower	Tender annual	8 to 12 in	Bicolored	Early summer to early fall		Light shade to deep shade
Trachelospermum asiaticum Asiatic Jasmine	Groundcover	to 1 ft	Yellow	Early spring to summer	9 to 10	Light shade
Trachelospermum jasminoides Star Jasmine	Groundcover	to 1 ft	White	Early spring to summer	9 to 10	Light shade
***Tradescantia* species** Wandering Jew, Inch Plant	Houseplant	3 to 10 ft			10 or IN	Half-day sun to light shade
Tradescantia virginiana Spiderwort	Hardy perennial	18 to 36 in	Blue, pink, purple, red, white	Early summer to early fall	4 to 10	Full sun to deep shade
***Trollius europaeus* and hybrids** Common Globe Flower	Hardy perennial	1 to 3 ft	Yellow, orange	Spring	3 to 10	Light shade
Tropaeolum majus Nasturtium	Hardy annual	1 to 10 ft	Red, white, orange, yellow, bicolored	Early summer to early fall		Full sun
Tsuga canadensis Canadian or Eastern Hemlock	Needled evergreen tree	40 to 70 ft			4 to 8	Full sun to light shade
***Tsuga canadensis* 'Pendula'** Sargent's Weeping Hemlock	Needled evergreen shrub	5 to 10 ft			4 to 8	Light shade
Tsuga caroliniana Carolina Hemlock	Needled evergreen tree	50 to 70 ft			5 to 7	Full sun to light shade
***Tulipa* hybrids** Tulip Hybrids	Hardy bulbs	6 to 30 in	Variety of colors	Early spring to spring and fall	3 to 10	Full sun to light shade

For a list of common names, see page 378.

| | CULTURE | | |
Soil	Water	Feeding	Special Characteristics
Rich soil	Medium water	Medium feeder	Moderate-growing tree; somewhat heart-shaped leaves; fragrant flowers; suckers badly; linden most susceptible to aphids; stake and shape young trees.
Good drainage	Let dry out between waterings	Light feeder	Tolerates drought and heat; may require staking; use as background border; open, coarse habit.
Good drainage	Wet; don't let dry out	Medium feeder	Hairy, bright green leaves; plantlets form at junction of leaf and stem; give bright, indirect light, cool, well-ventilated spot; avoid hot, dry air; prune to shape.
Good drainage; organic matter	Medium water	Medium feeder	Grown as annual; requires warm weather; frost tender; sensitive to low night temperatures; give uniform moisture; grown from seed or transplant; many varieties available.
Good drainage; organic matter	Wet; don't let dry out	Heavy feeder	Appreciates high humidity; interesting flower shape.
Rich soil	Medium water	Medium feeder	Alternate leaves, somewhat broader than star jasmine; slow-growing, but sturdy once established; woody with age.
Rich soil	Medium water	Medium feeder	Twining rambler; long, woody stems; oval, deep-green leaves; small, fragrant, starlike flowers; slow-growing.
Good drainage	Medium water	Medium feeder	Trailing foliage; leaves alternate along thick, succulent stems; give bright light with some direct sun; fast-growing, easy to care for; many colorful cultivars available.
Rich soil	Wet; don't let dry out	Medium feeder	Foliage grasslike; long-lived; can become invasive.
Rich soil; organic matter	Wet; don't let dry out	Medium feeder	Excellent choice for moist, heavy soils or around a pool; grow in bushy, rounded masses; long-lived; restrained; tolerates full sun if kept moist; avoid boggy soil.
Good drainage; sandy soil	Medium water	Light feeder	Avoid high-nitrogen fertilizer; best in regions of dry, cool summers; tolerates drought; leaves and flowers edible; aphids may be a problem.
Rich soil	Medium water	Medium feeder	Moderate-growing; graceful pyramidal shape; horizontal branches; dense, flat, deep green sprays of needles; thrives in deep, moist loam; resents dry winds, drought, prolonged heat; can be sheared and trained as thick hedge.
Good drainage; acid soil	Wet; don't let dry out	Medium feeder	Graceful, pendulous habit; refined foliage; conifer; tolerates full sun; protect from wind, drought, waterlogged soil, hot summer temperatures; good in container, specimen plant.
Rich soil	Medium water	Medium feeder	Moderate-growing; pyramidal; not as hardy as *T. canadensis*; needs acid soil; more tolerant of city conditions; slightly pendulous branches give soft appearance.
Good drainage	Medium water	Medium feeder	Thousands of hybrids providing abundant choice of height, form, flower color, and blooming date; fall flowering possible from forced bulbs; do not naturalize well.

NAME	HABIT		FLOWERS		ADAPTATION	
	Type	**Height**	**Color**	**Time**	**Zones**	**Light**
Tulipa fosterana Foster Tulip	Hardy bulb	8 to 20 in	Red	Spring	5 to 10	Full sun to light shade
Tulipa greigii Greig Tulip	Hardy bulb	8 to 12 in	Red	Early spring to spring	5 to 10	Full sun to light shade
Tulipa kaufmanniana Waterlily Tulip	Hardy bulb	4 to 8 in	White, yellow	Early spring to spring	5 to 10	Full sun to light shade
Turnip *Brassica rapa*	Half-hardy biennial vegetable	1 to 2 ft				Full sun to light shade
Ulmus americana American Elm	Deciduous tree	60 to 80 ft			3 to 9	Full sun
Ulmus parvifolia Chinese Elm	Deciduous tree	40 to 60 ft			5 to 9	Full sun
Ulmus pumila Siberian Elm	Deciduous tree	30 to 50 ft			4 to 9	Full sun
Verbena × hybrida Garden Verbena	Half-hardy annual	6 to 8 in	Comes in all colors	Early summer to fall		Full sun
Verbena peruviana Peruvian Verbena, Trailing Verbena	Groundcover	4 to 6 in	Red	Spring to fall	10	Full sun
Veronica hybrids Speedwell	Hardy perennial	2 to 2 1/2 ft	Blue, pink, white, purple	Summer	4 to 10	Full sun
Veronica spicata Spike Speedwell	Hardy perennial	to 18 in	Blue	Summer	4 to 10	Full sun
Viburnum carlesii Korean-spice Viburnum	Deciduous shrub	4 to 8 ft	White	Spring	5 to 8	Full sun to light shade
Viburnum farreri (V. fragrans) Fragrant Viburnum	Deciduous shrub	8 to 12 ft	Pink, white	Winter to early spring	5 to 10	Full sun to light shade
Viburnum macrocephalum Chinese Snowball Virburnum	Deciduous shrub	6 to 15 ft	White	Late spring to early summer	7 to 10	Full sun to light shade
Viburnum opulus European Cranberry Bush	Deciduous shrub	8 to 12 ft	White	Late spring	4 to 8	Full sun to light shade
Viburnum × burkwoodii Burkwood Viburnum	Evergreen shrub	8 to 10 ft	White	Spring	4 to 8	Full sun to light shade
Vinca major Periwinkle	Groundcover	to 2 ft	Blue	Spring	6 to 10	Light shade

For a list of common names, see page 378.

| | CULTURE | | |
Soil	Water	Feeding	Special Characteristics
Good drainage	Medium water	Medium feeder	Early-flowering; 4-inch blossoms.
Good drainage	Medium water	Medium feeder	Long-lasting blooms.
Good drainage	Medium water	Medium feeder	Large, ornamental flowers.
Good drainage; organic matter	Medium water	Medium feeder	Grown as an annual; cool-weather vegetable; fast-maturing; grow in spring in northern areas; grow in fall and winter in warmer areas; different cultivars available.
Adaptive	Medium water	Medium feeder	Fast growing; stately, oval canopy; dark-green, toothed leaves; not recommended for planting due to Dutch elm disease.
Not particular	Medium water	Medium feeder	Fast growing; open canopy; subtle red fruit in fall; yellow to purple leaves in fall; loses outer bark with age, to reveal pale yellow inner bark; tolerates alkaline, poor, compact soil; tolerates heat, drought; may be semi-evergreen.
Adaptive	Medium water	Medium feeder	Hardy in extreme cold and heat; weak crotches; shallow roots; sometimes grown for shelterbelt; seldom useful as a single tree.
Good drainage; rich soil	Medium water	Heavy feeder	Heat-tolerant; prone to mildew in heavy, wet soil; will not flower well in shade; moderately tolerant of drought.
Good drainage	Medium water	Light feeder	Fast-growing; evergreen perennial; forms flat mat of green foliage; small leaves closely spaced along stems; good flower color, long bloom season; grown as annual in cold-winter areas; thrives in hot, sunny locations; drought-tolerant, once established; cut back severely in fall; tolerates seacoast conditions; many cultivars available.
Good drainage	Medium water	Medium feeder	Showy flower spikes; long-lived; tolerates light shade.
Good drainage	Medium water	Medium feeder	Many branches; densely produced flower spikes.
Not particular	Medium water	Medium feeder	Rounded, dense form; fragrant flowers; can prune to shape; tolerates both alkaline and acid soils.
Good drainage	Wet; don't let dry out	Medium feeder	Fragrant, very early flower clusters; tolerates both acid and alkaline soil and heavy soils; prune to shape.
Not particular	Medium water	Medium feeder	Dense, rounded shrub; large flower clusters; tolerates acid and alkaline soils.
Not particular	Medium water	Medium feeder	Large, spreading shrub; delicate flowers; bright red, berrylike fruits Sept.–Nov.; good fall color; susceptible to aphids; prune to shape; tolerates acid and alkaline soils.
Not particular	Medium water	Medium feeder	Upright habit; fragrant flowers; buds are pink; semi-evergreen or deciduous in cool climates in the North; can prune to shape.
Good drainage; organic matter	Medium water	Medium feeder	Evergreen trailer; spreads rapidly; rooting stems; glossy, dark green leaves; very invasive.

NAME	HABIT		FLOWERS		ADAPTATION	
	Type	Height	Color	Time	Zones	Light
Vinca minor Periwinkle	Groundcover	to 6 in	Blue	Spring	4 to 10	Light shade
Viola odorata Sweet Violet	Hardy perennial groundcover	to 8 in	Pink, violet, white	Spring	6 to 10	Light shade
Viola tricolor Johnny-jump-up	Hardy perennial	6 to 12 in	Purple, yellow, white	Spring to early fall	4 to 10	Full sun to light shade
Viola × wittrockiana Pansy, Viola	Tender perennial	4 to 9 in	White, purple, red, orange, yellow	Late spring to summer		Full sun to light shade
Walnut, English *Juglans regia*	Deciduous nut tree	40 to 60 ft			5 to 10	Full sun
Watermelon *Citrullus lanatus*	Tender annual vegetable					Full sun
Weigela florida Old-fashioned Weigela	Deciduous shrub	4 to 10 ft	Pink	Late spring to early summer	5 to 8	Full sun
Xylosma congestum Shiny Xylosma	Evergreen shrub	8 to 10 ft			8 to 10	Full sun to light shade
Zantedeschia aethiopica Common Calla Lily	Tender bulb	to 3 ft	White	Spring to summer	9 to 10	Light shade
Zantedeschia elliottiana Golden Calla	Tender bulb	18 to 24 in	Yellow	Early summer to summer	9 to 10	Light shade
Zelkova serrata Japanese Zelkova	Deciduous tree	50 to 60 ft			5 to 8	Full sun
Zephyranthes candida Autumn Zephyr-lily	Half-hardy bulb	to 8 in	White	Late summer to early fall	8 to 10 or IN	Full sun
Zinnia elegans Common Zinnia	Half-hardy annual	6 to 40 in	All colors except blue	Early summer to fall		Full sun
Zoysia species Zoysia Grass	Turfgrass	½ to 1½ in			8 to 10	Full sun to light shade
Zoysia tenuifolia Korean Grass, Mascarene Grass	Ornamental grass	3 to 5 in			9 to 10	Full sun to light shade

For a list of common names, see page 378.

| | CULTURE | | |
Soil	Water	Feeding	Special Characteristics
Good drainage; organic matter	Medium water	Medium feeder	Hardier than *V. major*; evergreen trailer; glossy green leaves; one of the best groundcovers; several cultivars available.
Rich soil	Wet; don't let dry out	Heavy feeder	Spreading, low-growing plant; heart-shaped leaves with crinkled edges; small, extremely fragrant flowers; cultivars have variations in flower color and shape.
Rich soil	Wet; don't let dry out	Medium feeder	Short-lived perennial, grown as annual; low, tufted growth; good bloomers; give partial shade in warmer areas; self-sows readily.
Good drainage; organic matter; rich soil	Wet; don't let dry out	Heavy feeder	Does not tolerate heat; best in cool-summer regions; highly cold-resistant; usually grown as an annual.
Good drainage	Medium water	Medium water	Silver-gray bark; dense foliage; fast-growing; bears nuts in summer; requires large area; can be very messy; tends to be out of leaf for long period of time; give deep irrigation; prune in summer or fall.
Good drainage; organic matter	Medium water	Medium feeder	Requires more summer heat than muskmelons; give ample water during vining period; needs lots of room.
Good drainage	Medium water	Medium feeder	Coarse, rangy form; profuse bloomer; adaptable to soil and shade; requires heavy pruning; best in borders, masses, groupings where awkward form is hidden when not in bloom; many cultivars available.
Not particular	Medium water	Medium feeder	Slow-growing, round, loose form; shiny, yellow-green foliage; tolerates any soil; responds well to pruning, can train as espalier; tolerates heat, drought.
Not particular	Wet; don't let dry out	Medium feeder	Blooms almost continuously in mild climates; can tolerate full sun on the coast; good houseplant; grows in boggy situations; nearly evergreen in mild areas.
Good drainage	Wet; don't let dry out	Medium feeder	Attractive leaves, spotted with silvery-white; needs plenty of moisture during growing season; good houseplant.
Good drainage	Medium water	Medium feeder	Moderate- to fast-growing; eventually vase-shaped; attractive fall foliage; gray bark, mottles with age; water deeply to encourage deep roots; head back and thin when young to promote strong framework.
Good drainage	Medium water	Medium feeder	Leaves evergreen in mild climates; rushlike foliage; flowers tinged with pink; good houseplant.
Good drainage; organic matter	Medium water	Medium feeder	Best in hot, dry climates with long summers; never water late in day; avoid cool locations and damp air; prone to powdery mildew at end of summer.
Good drainage; organic matter	Medium water	Medium feeder	Forms dense, fine-textured lawn; resistant to weeds; tolerates heat and drought; relatively free of diseases and insects; very slow to establish; won't thrive in cool or short summers; tough to mow if left too long; tends to build thatch; wears well.
Good drainage	Medium water	Medium feeder	A true grass; tufting, mounding habits; don't mow; velvety turf; fine, dense, dark green leaves; evergreen where temperatures above freezing; turns brown at first frost, but recovers; slow-spreading; drought-resistant; takes light traffic.